To John & Suza

Enjoy the read!

Best,
Lepie

Cardinal Sin

BY ALEXANDRA ARMITAGE

Published by Alexandra Armitage
Visit our Web site at www.cardinaltownsite.com

Printed in the United States of America.

For information, please write cardinalsin@rocketmail.com.

Cover and book design by Hilary Stojak

ISBN 9780615279558
Library of Congress Control Number: 2008903974

This book is dedicated to my family.

Names have been changed to protect the guilty.

Many thanks and much appreciation to Gary & Ivan Rosenberg, for putting this story between two covers; to Curt for loving me and making me laugh; my daughter, Sandi Betters and my Mom for keeping me moving forward with love and encouragement, Steve Betters, for giving me 23 years of love and support; Peter Betters for being true to himself; Larry Lewarton for reminding me to always have hope, John Hunt for naming the manuscript, Sean Redmond & Rita Golden Gelman for being my mentors; Hilary Stojak for book design, Jeff at Publication Printers; and to my editors Susan O'Donnell Dicken, Lacey Samuels, Doug Armitage, Dondi Barrowclough, Jeff Nussbaumer; and all the friends who read my manuscript and reacted for me.

Thank you to everyone who helped save the Cardinal Townsite and its Open Space; the Bergren Family, Chuck Miller, the Bakers, Emmy Patton, Carol Beam, Boulder County Commissioners Ron Stewart, Paul Danish and Jana Mendez, the Nederland Historic Society, Historic Boulder, Margaret Hansen, Tom Hendricks and Calais Mines, the State Historic Fund, the Ghost Town Group, State of Colorado WQCD, Paul Phillips, Mike Sawyer, Steve Black, Katie Fendel, Bjorn Courtney, Greg Ten Eyck, David Folkes, Angus Campbell, Loris and Associates, Nancy Miller, and all of the many Nederland Area subcontractors who provided the elbow grease.

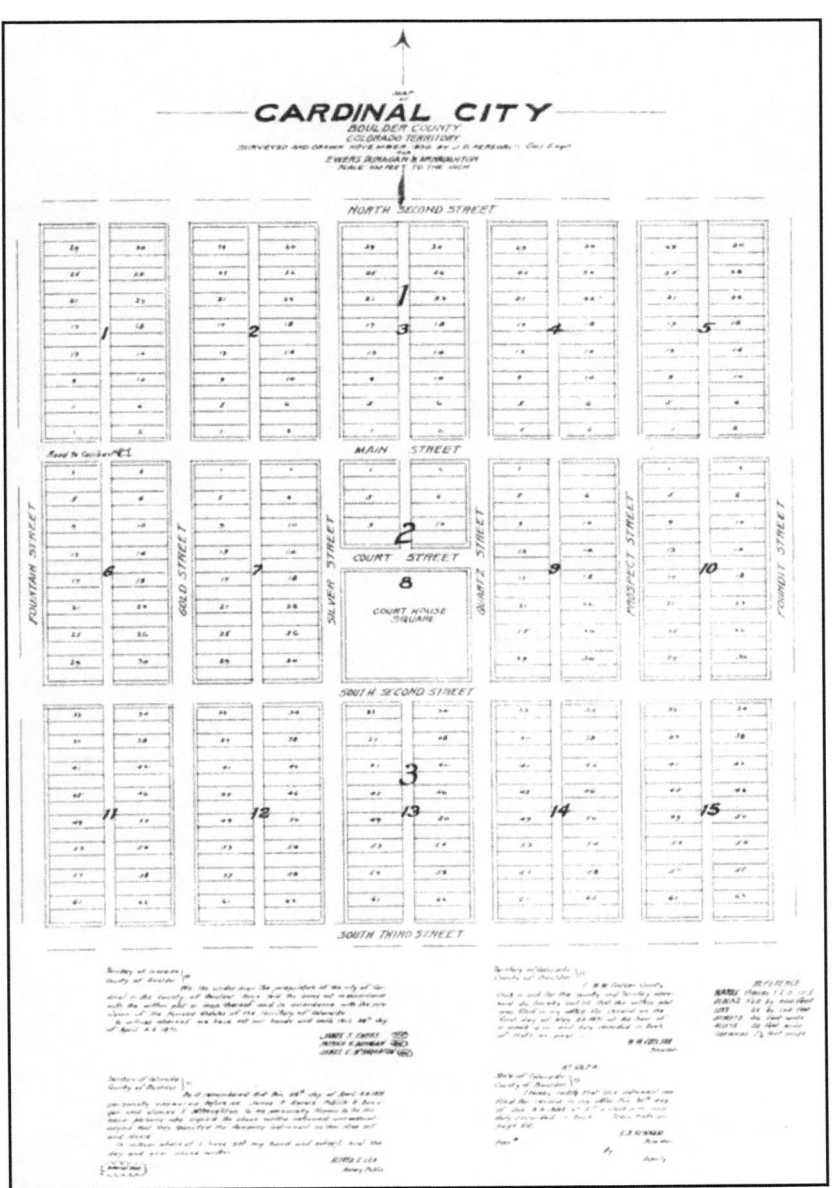

Cardinal City Plat 1870

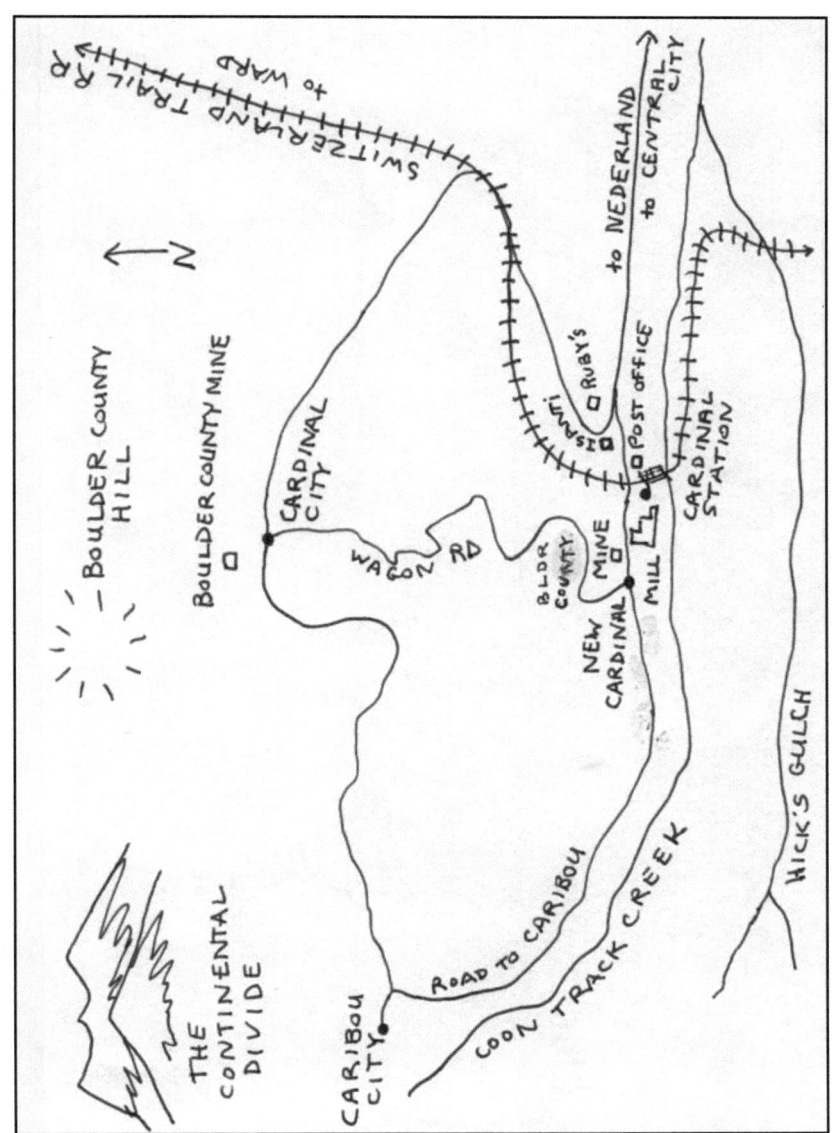

Caribou City, Cardinal City (Old Cardinal), New Cardinal

CARIBOU CITY, COLORADO
Denver Public Library, Western History Collection

CARIBOU SCHOOL HOUSE
Denver Public Library, Western History Collection

1881

CARIBOU, COLORADO

*M*iss Mabel Gurkin stomped last night's snow off her boots outside the doorstep of the Caribou schoolhouse. She opened the door to find the room icy cold. Mr. Lane had come by early, on his way to the silver mine, to light the fire for the children. In his haste, he had not stayed long enough to get a bed of coals going, and now the fire was out.

Mabel blew a couple of foggy breaths to confirm this. She crumpled a page of the "Caribou Post" to start the fire. Lighting paper would get the air drawing up the stovepipe. The children's fathers had split a winter's worth of kindling. Good and dry, the wood sparked and crackled as the fire came to life.

A page of the newspaper caught her eye, and Mabel stopped to read. It seemed that John Peregrine, the surveyor, was plotting a town. He had named the streets "Gold, Silver, Fountain, Quartz and Foundit". The town, Cardinal City, two miles below Caribou, had been growing daily. Mr. Peregrine even planned to put a courthouse in the middle of it. Unbelievable, thought the young school teacher, recalling just a year ago. She had first come up the steep "Coon Trail" road on a buckboard. Cardinal had been a cluster of shacks with saloons. She had been so relieved to keep going on up to Caribou. It was far more proper a place, with clapboard buildings, a post office, churches, and families.

Now the fire in the woodstove was holding its own. Mabel kept her coat and hat on, sat at her desk, and stared out the window. The sun was just rising up over the prairie to the east. It brought light streaming out toward the mountains, coloring them with pink alpenglow. She imagined the sun was springing up from St. Louis, such a long way out there. Leaving St. Louis had been her choice. Mabel thought wistfully about the restlessness in her spirit that had longed to see the West. And here she was, at ten thousand feet above sea level, with the wind whistling and thumping against the schoolhouse.

This day promised to be better than the last. Yesterday, Mabel had spent the whole day wondering if wooden planks, which the men had leaned against the leeward side of the building, would hold it against the tremendous winds. Today was clear. Once those down slope dawn breezes mellowed, it might shape up to be a lovely spring day.

The stove was beginning to warm the room, so Mabel took off her coat. She smoothed the long johns under her skirt. How about that John Peregrine! Plotting a town, him with his handsome smile. She blushed and chuckled to herself. After all, it was spring you know, even if there were ten-foot snow drifts on the east side of the schoolhouse.

Before noon, Mabel's students were getting quite restless, and the boys, in particular, were unable to attend to their lessons. Mabel decided there was no use fighting it, and let the children out to play in the yard. It had warmed up nicely, so she sat on the steps and watched everyone run. Up the hill, Mabel could see Roxy appear at the front of the hotel, and start down the street. She brought Mabel's lunch, provided by the town, from the hotel restaurant. Roxy was one of Ruby's girls in the evening, but she worked at the hotel restaurant during the day. It seemed unfortunate that the girl had decided on that line of work, but it was a living. If you weren't the church going type... and after all, Roxy had no parents left to disappoint. Mabel liked Roxy. She was always happy to chat, and Lord knows, Mabel often felt half starved for adult company.

Roxy waved when she saw the children outside. She had a springtime skip in her step. Roxy put down the lunch basket, and sat down with Mabel on the steps. Just as the two women began to talk, a ruckus broke out in the schoolyard. Two boys tangled with each other, thrashing on the ground. A small crowd was forming around them. Mabel got up quickly, and in an instant had them both by the scruffs of their necks.

"He's callin' my mother names!" blurted Lyle.

"She is so!" yelled Thomas.

"Is not!"

"Is so! I seen'er!"

Mabel sat the two culprits at the bottom of the stairs, on opposite ends. She went up to where Roxy sat with her nose in the air, looking far away, but obviously very aware of the subject at hand.

"There have been a lot of these kinds of problems, Roxy. Seems this town's getting too proper for itself."

"I know", said Roxy, "Mrs. Brand spit on Lucy at Beamer's store this mornin'. You know Mr. Beamer's been kicked out of his own house by his wife. The marrieds just can't keep their men out of Miss Ruby's." She giggled, and added, "There's a meetin' this afternoon at the hotel. The mayor and some of the businessmen are comin' in to talk about it. I'm worried they'll shut things down, and that ain't gonna work either. You know it ain't. There's just too many men around here, compared to women anyways."

"I guess there's no easy answer, Roxy. I hope it's handled respectfully. I hope nobody has to get hurt. These children deserve to be in school too. They don't deserve a licking for their mother every time they come here either. Let's have little Mister Rodgers write respect for others one hundred times on the blackboard."

At the end of the day, Ryan and Percy were the first boys out the schoolhouse door. They ran through the creek and climbed the fir tree as high as they could.

"I'm too starved!" yelled Percy.

"I know it, me too!" agreed Ryan. "Let's go to the hotel and ask Mr. Laughlin for a bite of something."

"We'd have to be quieter than mice, Ryan. Mama said no comin' around till that meetin's over. No comin' around!"

"Oh, let's go."

They slipped into the kitchen at the back door and slid along the back of the bar with their bread. Two hungry and curious boys can be quieter than church mice. Not a shhh, or a scuff, and they were settled unseen to listen to the meeting.

Mr. Randy had just finished speaking to the group, and all the men were grumbling among themselves. Caribou's mayor stood up and commanded the attention of all.

"Times in Caribou have changed, we know that. Used to be that all we had was workingmen... and of course there were the working women too. That was just the way of the west. The first stage that brought wives and children changed everything. It's just unfortunate that it didn't change overnight, and now we've got a problem. Churches, schools, wives and Miss Ruby's gals just don't mix, that's all."

"Kick out the wives!" yelled someone.

There was a good spell of laughter and the boys laughed too.

"It's more than just the girls that's causin' problems. The bettin' and card games too!"

"The boozin' just ain't civil!" hollered another man, "This town's gonna rot in Hell!"

Then Mr. Tate banged the table and began "You know we can't fold up Miss Ruby's operation without folding up the mines. There's not that much silver to keep a man up here through the winter."

He was interrupted by a fellow who spoke in a gravelly voice, "The silver's gonna play out, and this here's big business. Whatcha wanna do about that?"

Another yelled "There's more than Miss Ruby's girls too!"

The men bantered back and forth, pointing out all of the same, until John Peregrine stood up, and silently waited for quiet.

"I have a suggestion." He spoke softly and everyone listened. "I've got a few extra cabins in Cardinal City that could accommodate some girls. Quentin Blake is building the hotel as we speak, and now I don't know what kind of establishment Mr. Blake intends to keep, but as we've pointed out already...this is good business for a town. We've got everything going on down there to make a strong municipal base, and why, I say let's move those ladies on down the hill to Cardinal City."

With the suggestion came a stunned silence. Mayor Miller stood, and cleared his throat. It seemed like a good enough idea.

*All in favor show a hand."

It was as good as done. The boys were the first out, the kitchen door slamming hard behind them.

Mabel stood outside the schoolhouse for a moment, taking in the afternoon. The three o'clock stage had just rumbled up the hill, late again, probably due to the spring mud. Mabel waited for the dust to settle. The aspen trees were budding but wouldn't grow leaves until mid June. Between the huge remaining snowbanks lay last year's grass: flat, brown and matted. New shoots rose from between the old grass, and stood as single bright green blades. It was actually warm now. This weather instilled such hope.

As she descended the schoolhouse steps, Mabel caught a glimpse of a man coming down the road. Her breath ceased and her heart pounded, as she realized it was John Peregrine. She wished desperately that she was busy. But she obviously wasn't.

"Miss Gurkin", John smiled and bowed his head once. "I'd be honored to walk you down to your place on such a fine afternoon."

"Why thank you, Mr. Peregrine. That would be a pleasure." Now her knees were weak and she flushed with anger at herself for feeling this way.

"The robins are back, Miss Gurkin, I saw one just a minute ago."

"Yes. It's been a long time."

John Peregrine held his elbow out to assist the schoolteacher. He smiled broadly.

Mabel blushed again and struggled with what was really a very small armload of books. John took the books, and placed her hand on his arm. They started down the hill.

Why was she feeling this way! This wasn't at all what she had in mind. There wasn't a reason in the world to fall apart over this man. Mabel's knees threatened to buckle under her. She was glad to hold on.

"Miss Gurkin, there's some news today. It has been decided by the fathers of the Town of Caribou that all the boozers, gamblers and ladies of the night shall be moving to Cardinal as soon as possible."

Mabel drew a deep breath and felt her eyes widen. It shouldn't come as a surprise, but then, what a solution. She was stunned for a moment, and felt silly not coming up with a response, but John began again.

"Cardinal is a good place for them, I believe. It can be a place of their own. A sort of special place, you know, an entertainment place. Maybe there can be shows with the music. Perhaps it will be better. Easier on everyone, I'm sure."

Mabel stopped walking.

"Mr. Peregrine, I have six students whose mothers can't very well pack up and take them to Cardinal. There will be two more, if the Broken Arrow closes too!"

John had stopped and was looking her square in the eye. In fact, Mabel could see him working hard to keep his eyes from darting toward her waist. She kept him focused on the conversation, locking her eyes on his. She hoped this would keep his eyes in place, where they belonged.

"I'm sure there will be many who are happy with this decision." said Mabel. "But it will sure make Caribou a different sort of place."

"It will make Cardinal a different sort of place too. And there is plenty of room for a schoolhouse there too." He winked, smiled and opened the little iron-gate to Mabel's yard. He tipped his hat, and said, "Good day, Miss Gurkin."

Mabel smiled back, with a measure of self-control, and said "Thank you, Mr. Peregrine."

Inside the house, she threw her books on the sofa and spun around in tiny circles.

The next day, it was snowing again. This morning, Ryan, Mary, and Percy weren't at school. Things were changing already. At lunchtime, Roxy came in stomping snow across the room. She was fit to be tied. Mabel wondered who would bring her lunch tomorrow.

"Well, there you go! Didn't we know they was up to somethin'? We're packing up like there's gonna be a tornado. Doesn't anyone even ask us? No, siree. Nope, were off to Cardinal this afternoon. Miss Ruby's drinkin and doesn't want to go. Mr. Tate is shouting at the girls one min-

JOHN PEREGRINE
JUNE 12, 1880

ute and holdin'm and tellin'm it's gonna be alright the next. Your kids, all eight, are hidin' under their mama's skirts. They don't wanna go. And they're 'fraid to go to school'n git kilt by the bigger boys. It's not very nice right now up there, Mabel."

Mabel set the lunch box down and held Roxy in her arms.

"Oh Roxy, darling, it is going to be alright. It's going be a new chance down there for you. There will be everything you need. The stage comes through there before it even comes here. Mr. Peregrine will see that you all have everything to get you settled."

Roxy was crying into Mabel's dress. It felt like the world had judged these people and they were being sent away for the sins of everyone. It didn't feel fair. Mabel held Roxy close.

"There, there now Rox, things will be fine. Maybe even better."

By four o'clock more than half the town had gathered in front of the hotel. Men hung around with hats pulled low, leaning against hitching posts and clustering in small groups. Women made themselves look busier, passing in and out of the general store, the post office and grocery. But they were watching the crowd, and paying attention to who was there. Children darted in and out, leaping off porches and chasing each other. Three wagons loaded with furniture and chests stood waiting in front of the hotel. The first of two stages lurched forward and back in its spot, as the driver struggled to calm the team in the crowd. Three buckboards owned by good Christian families lined up to volunteer rides to the ladies.

When the first few ladies appeared at the door, catcalls went up from a group of young miners, drifters who had no name to protect in the community. Another cluster of girls were escorted down the street and were helped aboard the buckboards. A group of ladies from the church brought baskets of food, and handed them up onto the buckboards with best wishes that these souls may be saved.

Suddenly, the front doors of the hotel flew open and Miss Ruby, weeping and wailing, was half carried out to the waiting stage. Women looked on in disgust, righteously holding their heads high. Miss Ruby's special gals climbed in with her. They were looking their best for the occasion, feathered hats and gloves for traveling.

As the second stage pulled into place, Mabel saw her eight students being gently herded outside by Mr. Peregrine. Each held a large colorful round lollipop, along with personal treasures that were moving too. Ryan had his cat squeezed under his arm, tethered to his wrist by a string. Little Joe held two school reading books that his Grandma had given him. Roger Firth had his fishing pole and tried not to run it into anyone. Mr. Peregrine winked at Mabel as he passed. This group was then followed by a set of younger women, including Roxy. As they loaded into the stage, Mabel firmly made up her mind. She scooted out to join the group and was whisked aboard for Cardinal.

The departure of Caribou's riff-raff to Cardinal felt anticlimactic to those left standing in the street. Some wondered if the problems were over. Some felt like upstanding citizens who had followed through on what was only right and proper. Some, and there were many, thought about Friday night, and wished they could have a drink right now.

2008

CARIBOU, COLORADO

A ghost town is having its birthday. There will be cake, music and danc-ing. This Colorado mining town will be one hundred and thirty seven years old. It will be all dressed up for its birthday. The people who love this town and its history will be at the party.

We mark the birth date of the Town of Cardinal at the year 1871, when the Boulder County Tunnel was opened by Samuel Conger. Gold, silver and tungsten came from the mine.

Up the Coon Trail about one mile, nestled in a meadow, was the original townsite. "Old Cardinal" grew near the top of the Boulder County Mine. It blossomed when the town fathers of nearby Caribou kicked out all of the gam-blers, boozers and whores in 1881. They set up camp two miles down the road in Old Cardinal.

As I walk through the Cardinal Townsite, I feel its ghosts. This is a town that is celebrating its own history because it has just experienced a renaissance.

Mona Lisa, consulting with my spirit guides, told me that a great light comes from this spot. It is a light of resurrection. A light of not one entity but of a whole community of people. This energy, she told me, has something to do with why you are there. It has to do with your fate.

Cardinal almost died. It came very close several times. I sit on an old bench, letting the sun warm my face. I close my eyes, and think back through the series of events that brought Cardinal back from an untimely demise.

The first time was in the 1890's, when the United States stopped its purchase of silver and the great Caribou silver mines closed. Cardinal almost died again in 1919, when the Tungsten boom ended, and the railroad tracks for the Switzerland Trail were torn out. In 1942, for the War Effort, mining heavy metals precluded gold mining and the Cardinal Mill screeched to a halt. In 2000, the Town of Cardinal had all but died. Its structures stood quietly returning to the earth. This final time, the Townsite was saved by a team effort that was nothing short of a miracle.

It is my job to greet the birthday guests today. They will be the different individuals who contributed to this miracle, along with all of my dear friends, and my family.

I walk past the freshly painted white trim on the mine office, past the livery stable, and pause on the bridge that crosses Coon Track Creek. The leaves on the aspen trees are shimmering as they dance in the breeze. Small trout shoot away as they sense my presence near the clear stream. The water sparkles with light and life as it bubbles along. A very old twisted elder tree stands near the creek. This tree has seen it all. The elder tree will be an honored guest at the birthday party. It predates the town, and will probably stand for the next hundred years as well.

The Cardinal Townsite is not very big in the year 2008. The Cardinal Mill still stands, with all of its mining and milling machinery in place. The structure has been renovated by the State Historical Fund. The mine superintendent's house still sits perched high above the valley overlooking the road that comes into town. To enter the townsite, one must pass along this road, through a tight spot between the superintendent's house and the top of the Cardinal Mill.

As one walks west of that point, there is a view of the mining town sitting in its little valley where two creeks come together. Tiny railroad tracks connect the mining mill to the Boulder County Tunnel. Switch tracks allowed the train to return to the tramway house, or dump ore off the south end of the waste rock pile. Today, the train with its ore carts is perched cheerfully on its track, ready for the birthday party.

The portal to the Boulder County Tunnel is on the north side of the road. It goes into the mountain thirty two hundred feet, almost a mile. Then, up nine hundred feet, it emerges at what once was the townsite of Old Cardinal. The mouth of the tunnel has caved in just beyond the portal.

As you pass the mine, there is a blacksmith shop and tramway house on the left, and two ponds on the right. Just west of these buildings is the compressor house. An old mess hall and shower room overlook the ponds. It now functions as a community house. If it rains during the party today, we can go inside.

The Assay Office, which used to be a hub of activity, is where the ores were tested for value. A small building with a brick floor, it sits next to the creek.

The business office of the mine is now my home. This building sits in the sun with Coon Track Creek bubbling by, tucked out of the wind and nestled in trees. The craftsmanship that went into this structure included tall, narrow windows divided by mullions and white oak floors. The batten and board siding shows a century of weather. The office is the epitome of a Colorado mining camp cabin. But more than these physical features, this is a place permeated with history and its people.

Across the creek, and to the west, are two matching boarding houses. Time and deep winter snows have taken their toll on these twin buildings. The steep roof pitches date these buildings back to the beginning of the Cardinal Townsite.

When one follows the road up the valley to the last house, it feels like a hidden paradise. The valley has narrowed tightly by this point, and the sun only shines here in the summertime. In winter, the shadow of the mountain saves every snowflake that falls, and the snow pack stays several feet deep into May.

This spot feels like heaven on earth to those of us living in this century. It is the quietest place, locked in a timeless void. Coon Track Creek tumbles over a waterfall beside this cabin, and stops for a moment in a small clear pool. Across the creek, on the steep south facing side of the mountain, the sun beats down as hot as a desert, contrasting the cool of the valley.

Above the north side of the creek runs the old wagon road which goes two miles up to Caribou. Caribou City was a silver mining town of three thousand people in its heyday. It disappeared into the wind by the turn of the twentieth century.

The Town of Old Cardinal was bigger than New Cardinal is now. Some miners lived in canvas tents with portable woodstoves to warm them. Others lived in hastily built log cabins with no foundations. These were burned as firewood, when the mines went bust.

Up the hill at Old Cardinal, not a building remains. The State of Colorado capped the nine hundred foot shaft to the Boulder County Mine with a safety grate. You can throw rocks through the slots, down into the shaft, and never hear them land.

Today, the New Cardinal Townsite is alive and well. The stories and people have begun to emerge from the past. These stories are worth telling.

1881

CARIBOU, COLORADO

T wo miles down the hill from Caribou City, at the top of the Coon Track Road, was the wide meadow at Cardinal, which had recently been officially plotted into streets. New log cabins dotted the meadow, clustered more tightly around the place where the wagons unloaded after the trip from the prairies below. The hotel had taken shape and was already serving food and drinks. Sporting a United States Post Office, the hotel stood proudly waving an American flag. Several men worked on the roof and porches. Stables were ready at the back. The town boasted a blacksmith shop, a general store, mine offices, an Assay office and a bathhouse. The stage stop was a large platform, and this is where the ladies found themselves standing after the short ride.

John Peregrine slipped off his horse, and took stock of the situation. There were the ladies with their hat boxes and carpet bags. There were trunks and furniture still on wagons. There were the children. And it looked like they had brought their teacher as well.

Mabel was feeling more than a bit confused as she stood among this crowd, but she had a certain resolve about her.

When John Peregrine approached her, she blurted out "They couldn't go without school."

He was smiling and took her hand. "May I send for your things, Miss Gurkin?"

"That would be very helpful Mr. Peregrine, thank you."

As he smiled and turned away, Mabel wanted to crawl into the nearest hole. From behind she was hit in the back of the knees with a sudden force. It was little Mary, her youngest student, hugging her and holding on tightly. This made Mabel's heart soar, and she was glad she'd come.

In the next few days, the ladies and children settled in. Miss Ruby rented a room on the second floor of the hotel. She had an extra room from which to run her business, and would be expected to pay a small fee to the hotel for any girls working in rooms rented by men. Ruby would be happy as long as business was good.

The ladies themselves were living three to a cabin nearby. The women with children were paired up so they could share responsibilities. The hotel would serve meals for everyone, and Miss Ruby would pay the kitchen.

Mabel had been given a large two-room cabin for the school. She would live in the back room, where there was a small kitchen with a cook stove, and teach in the front. It was a very satisfactory arrangement. Much as Mabel had enjoyed the family that hosted her in Caribou, it would be incredible to have a home of her own.

As Mabel arranged benches in the schoolroom, Roxy knocked and poked her head in the door.

"Mabel? Can I come in?"

"Oh come see, Roxy, it's going to be really perfect. I'm so grateful to Mr. Peregrine."

"You haven't got a slate, Mabel. What will you do?"

"I suppose we'll be singing and chanting our lessons for a while, but we've been promised one!"

"Mabel, Miss Ruby has sent me over to ask you if you'd be interested in a job." Roxy burst into a huge grin. Mabel stared back in shock and disbelief.

Roxy held her breath as long as she could before she added, "As a show director, my dear. There is to be a show each night." Then she and Mabel laughed aloud together.

Mabel thought for a moment. Why... and why not? There wasn't much to do after school got out. She wasn't worried about what people would think. A show would take some real work, but it would be fun...and Mabel loved music.

"Please tell Miss Ruby that I'd be happy to be the show director. I'll come by the hotel for dinner tonight and talk to her then. Will you be one of the performers?" she asked Roxy.

"I will, I will! We will need everyone we can get!" Roxy pirouetted twice and said "Mabel, we will be the best in the west!"

It was Friday and the mine whistles were blowing all over the hills around town. People would be pouring into Cardinal tonight. This was the first weekend that all the nightlife had left Caribou. The gamblers, boozers and ladies of the night would show Caribou what a good time is! The air was electric with anticipation. The barroom in the hotel was already crowded at four- thirty when Mabel peeked in the room. Miners, trappers and teamsters lined the bar.

Miss Ruby sat at a table in the back corner with two of her gals and several men. Three tables were starting the card games. A fine looking man in a crisp white shirt and red armbands winked at Mabel. She smiled and averted her eyes. Mabel waved at Miss Ruby and pointed to the dining room. Miss Ruby, in her full glory, wore a frilly rose satin dress. She stood and waved back, then settled down again. Mabel turned quickly and went to the dining room.

As Mabel waited for Miss Ruby at her table, she assessed the situation in this town. She reflected on all those citizens of Caribou, who so righteously voiced their opinions. They could enjoy a quiet evening up there tonight, while Cardinal danced until sunrise. But weren't they missing out on a special part of life? Mabel thought about what she'd left behind in St. Louis. Nothing and no one. A bunch of stuffy hypocrites. Mabel had chosen a life of adventure. She wanted to have fun, to laugh and enjoy the Rocky Mountains. She had come west for freedom. So many things interested her that she'd never experienced. And Cardinal was pulsing with the same energy.

Mr. Peregrine put his hand on her shoulder, bringing her back to the reality of a schoolteacher.

"May I join you for dinner? Miss Gurkin?" he asked, seating himself right next to her.

"It would be my pleasure, Mr. Peregrine."

"I should be 'John' to you forevermore...please call me 'John'. Here we are in Cardinal now. I suppose we can be less formal."

"I was just reflecting on that myself. I left St. Louis because I was bored stiff. I'm here for something different, and John...I believe I've found it."

"Well, teacher, I was always naughty in school, so I guess Cardinal's the place for me too!"

"I don't believe for one minute that you were trouble. Why, you are the pillar of this community, such as it is."

They were both laughing heartily when Miss Ruby appeared and curt-sied grandly at John's side.

"Ah, Miss Ruby, I trust that you are settled in? How do you like it? Not bad, is it?"

"John Peregrine, I don't know what we'd do without you. We'd probably be on the stage to Denver, without a penny to pay for it."

"Miss Ruby is offering me a job, John!" Mabel grinned ear to ear.

There was a moment of silence before John, excused himself, stood, and abruptly left the room.

"There goes my dinner date." laughed Mabel.

Miss Ruby's half-bare chest heaved as she chuckled "I do believe he is smitten, and you've disappointed him, my dear."

"My guess is he'll be back for more, and we've certainly given him some-thing to think about!" Mabel was surprised by John's reaction, but it meant he must care.

Miss Ruby was pleased to have help with the show. Mabel promised to forego her afternoon walk for the next few weeks, and report to the barroom after school. Honky Tonk Joe would play piano for them. He played by ear, and there was nothing he didn't know. Miss Ruby had twelve girls to dance. Mr. Blake sent for a seamstress from Denver, and yards of satin for costumes. One of the gals could sing like a nightingale. She'd sung her way west, and could surely hold the show. Miss Ruby glowed with excitement, and Mabel was glad to be part of it.

After dinner, Mabel made her way back to the schoolhouse. She found John Peregrine sitting on the front steps.

"I have been hired as Director of the Honky Tonk Show. Starting next week, I will organize Miss Ruby's girls to dance. It shall be grand."

John buried his head between his knees, "You can imagine my relief." he said.

"I promise to remain an upstanding school teacher."

"You come from good roots, Mabel. I would expect that." John looked very serious.

"I'll walk you back to your dinner. You must be cold and hungry."

"Yes, cold, hungry and feeling a bit foolish."

"Don't worry. I'm flattered that you care. We were just having a little fun with you."

"I hope you will dine with me tomorrow night?"

"It would be my pleasure."

In one week's time, Miss Ruby's girls had come a long way. Mabel delighted in the fun and laughter she shared with these "wives of the multitudes". They were more fun than the stiff faced snobs Mabel had left behind at home. It seemed they had never been taught half the conventions of society, and they were truly wild and free in spirit. Mabel loved harnessing that energy into a performance. And she loved watching them hold their heads proudly with a sense of accomplishment as they grandly paraded about on stage.

As Honky Tonk Joe's fingers danced down the piano keyboard, twelve legs raised up and down in turn, making a motion that ran with the music. Twelve derrieres greeted the audience, turning quickly away to the left, to be replaced by twelve broad smiles. Mabel was pleased with the enthusiasm that the girls radiated from the stage.

The satin and the seamstress, Molly, had arrived in three days. Molly had sized up the situation, and used the mornings to put each dancer to work on her own costume. Things had come together enough for a dress rehearsal by Friday afternoon.

Mr. Blake, Miss Ruby, and Mabel sat in the middle of several rows of chairs. In front of them were six men who had been pulled from the streets of Cardinal, agreeing to spread the review of the show around Caribou that afternoon, in return for the preview.

As the house lights dimmed, the stage lights came up. The piano played a gay, spicy tune, as the dancers each made an individual appearance, twirling twice, before disappearing again. Then, the show began with Lady Lorna singing a solo,

"You are my flower, that's growing in the mountains so high
You are my flower, that's growing there for me."

With her brown hair piled high, and her tight satin dress, Lady Lorna held the attention of everyone. The audience was still clapping when the girls came out, surrounding Lady Lorna for "Honey, You Don't Know My Mind… I'm Lonesome All The Time."

The singing was fabulous, but as the dancing began, the men in the back at the bar started hooting and hollering. Whistles shrilled and the piano got louder. It was evident that this was exactly what Cardinal needed.

People could hear the excitement from down the street, and before the first dance number was over, the room began to fill. A fiddle player came out of the woodwork, and joined right in. A miner with a bandaged hand came up to the stage, and sang...

"Come listen you fellas so young and so fine
And seek not your fortune in the dark dreary mine
It will form as a habit and seep in your soul
Till the stream of your blood runs as black as the coal
Well it's dark as a dungeon, damp as the dew
Where the danger is double and the pleasures are few
Where the rain never falls and the sun never shines
It's dark as a dungeon, down in the mine.

There's many a man, I've known in my day
Who lived just to labor his whole life away
Like a fiend with his dope, or a drunkard his wine
A man will have lust for the lure of the mine
Well its dark as a dungeon, damp as the dew
Where the danger is double and the pleasures are few
Where the rain never falls and the sun never shines
It's dark as a dungeon, down in the mine."

By the time the finale was over, the room was packed with people cheering. Mabel looked proudly at Mr. Blake. Miss Ruby pulled Mabel up and squeezed her tightly.

Word spread quickly as the afternoon work shift poured out of the mines. Men lined up outside the bath houses in record numbers, and Miss Ruby hoped the dancers would still have something left for the men when the show ended later that night.

The full moon was rising, its first brightness reflecting upward from the horizon to the east. The tips of pine trees on the hills were silhouetted against the sky. Mabel had her arm threaded through John's as they weaved along the dirt road stepping in ruts and potholes the whole way.

They laughed together about the last part of the opening night show. It had ended with miners dancing on the stage with the girls. It certainly wasn't the plan, but had been started by a couple of drunken men. It turned out to be very funny. Then Miss Ruby had come up on stage and drew numbers out of a hat to choose the men who won girls for the night. The lottery probably saved a big fight. It was a wild crowd, and there was loud raucous cheering as each man took his prize. Mabel had never seen anything like it.

"Half the Town of Caribou made it down to Cardinal tonight." remarked John.

"Yes, and it looks like they will still be here when the moon sets this morning!"

Music and laughter poured out of the hotel, and was carried up the street on a breeze. Mabel couldn't remember a night that she had laughed so much. Her cheeks hurt from smiling and her spirit had lifted lighter than air.

"It's a far cry from St. Louis", she was saying, when she caught sight of someone standing in the east window of the schoolhouse. Then the person was gone.

"John, who's that?" she said, tightening her grip on his arm.

"Who's who?" he asked.

"There was someone in the window in the classroom."

"Ah, Miss Gurkin has had too much to drink", teased John lightly. "I'd better tuck her in carefully."

"No John, really. Someone's here, you'll see."

As they stepped up onto the front porch, the moon was half way at the horizon. It was so bright and white. The sight stopped the two for a moment. John reached to Mabel's waist and held her facing the moon.

"Look, how can it be so?" he said, "Magnificent."

The moon rose before their very eyes then shrank ever so slightly as it left the horizon. After a pause, Mabel turned to face John. His face was bright and he smiled gently at her. He took her hands and warmed them in his. Mabel felt his focus on her.

"Mabel", he whispered, "I'm very glad you are here."

John stepped closer, his eyes holding hers, "You are full of sweet surprises for me.", he said. He leaned down and softly, kissed her on the cheek.

Mabel lost her breath for a moment. She was caught off guard, surprised for an instant. Then it was quiet. Flustered, Mabel looked toward the schoolhouse door, noting that no one else was there.

"John, someone was here."

"My dear, please step in and we'll see what this is all about."

The schoolhouse was dark, except shafts of moonlight that shone through the tall windows and spilled onto the floor. Mabel held tight to John's hand, and led him toward the back room where she lit a lamp. No one. She was confused. She had clearly seen a figure in the window. She had been too far away to make it out. John seemed curious for a second then dismissed it as nothing. He suddenly felt awkward to be standing in Mabel's room.

"It has been a grand evening, Mabel. You are a talented director, and should be very proud. I'll see you tomorrow, so sleep well." John took a prompt and proper leave of the schoolhouse, shutting the front door behind him. Mabel stood there stunned. He certainly made her heart beat. She wished he could have stayed. Mabel paused to relish the evening. She felt the excitement of the crowd. She still felt the music. She felt John's presence still hanging in the air. Mabel wrapped her arms around herself and smiled.

As Mabel drifted off to sleep that night, she thought again of the person in the window. Perhaps she had imagined it. After all, Mabel had enjoyed a drink of scotch whiskey with Miss Ruby and the girls to celebrate opening night and fortify them for the show.

❧

Spring was winning out over winter. This day was warmer than the last, and it was still so early. Mabel walked up the mountainside behind the school, using a steep path worn by the miner's of the Happy Home claim. The path climbed up to the ridge top, then followed a dry grassy valley uphill to the west. Mabel walked through short aspen trees with spruce and pines warming in the morning sun.

These walks in the mountains made her feel so alive. Her legs had grown strong and there were some days that Mabel walked till dusk. Time just melted away, and pure contentment occupied her soul. Thoughts would come and go, like water in a stream. The breezes and sunshine powered her along.

As Mabel climbed higher, the snowcapped peaks began to dominate the west. They presented a wall of rock and snow, so clean and bright. Mabel eagerly recalled the flowers at tree line last summer. She would walk as high as the sky, drinking in the mountains. At the end of the day, her face would feel warm as she sat by the fire, and sleep would steal her away at darkness.

❧

School was going well in Cardinal. With a small class, Mabel was able to make such progress. She sensed that her students felt lucky to be there. They were a close little group, whose lives were similar. The friction that had existed in Caribou was gone. On cold days, this bunch would read aloud on a blanket near the fire, instead of sitting stiffly on the benches.

Mary, who was the youngest, at five years old, believed that a spirit named "Goodman" kept the fire burning. She spoke to him regularly, and when the fire would crack and pop, she could not contain her excitement. The older kids played along with her, and even teased Mary that she was in love with Goodman. Mabel said she had indeed seen him one night.

The children looked wide-eyed, and wanted to believe her. On May 30th, Mary brought small cakes for everyone and announced that it was Goodman's birthday. They each wrote a limerick for Goodman, and stood proudly in turn to recite them.

At night, when the kids were gone, Mabel often found herself talking to Goodman. She would chuckle to think of how she never felt lonesome living in a school. Thoughts of each day filled her dreams at night. It was amazing to Mabel how much she loved those children. She was a huge part of their lives, and they were hers. She loved her work and living in Cardinal.

On long summer evenings, John would come by after dinner, and Mabel would walk with him through the streets of Cardinal. He never showed interest in walking in the woods. He dressed quite properly, and preferred to take good care of his boots.

John and Mabel would hold hands, walking slowly, sharing the events of their respective days. John was always occupied with thoughts concerning Cardinal and its comings and goings. Mabel would listen and comment, while attending mostly to the way the sun was setting and the air was cooling as night came on. Her neck was often cranked toward the sky watching nighthawks flap and dive.

When John would travel to Boulder, Mabel would spend her evenings hiking up to the snow fields, arriving back just after dark, while her eyes could still see. Sometimes, as she walked, her thoughts would wander back to St. Louis, and she could smell fresh cut hay, and hear summertime crickets. These thoughts could be easily conjured, but mostly she didn't miss these things.

Mabel's heart was home high in these hills. But there were other memories from St. Louis that were not so easily forgotten. A memory burned in her of love that was deep and pure. There was a young man who was smooth and strong and full of life. She had met him when she was seventeen and he was eighteen. Tyler had been hired by Mabel's father to break four horses that summer. The horses were to be polished to perfection to pull a carriage in the city for Mr. Gurkin. Mabel and Tyler flirted over the fence rails each day, and spent the summer evenings talking on the Gurkin's front porch.

No love is as easy as a first true love, when two souls are young and unfettered with responsibility. There is plenty of time for dreams to come true. The sharing of ideas is as good as a promise, when one has hope that the dreams may come true. It seemed that this love had been in existence since before time began.

Mabel remembered the soft, quiet moments when the two had held each other, discovering what they had only fantasized before that. She held an image of a beam of moonlight coming through the slats of the barn, illuminating Tyler's shoulder and chest, and warm skin under blankets up in the sleeping loft. She recalled Tyler slowly turning in the center of a round pen with a Chesnut horse. Mabel measured the capacity of love she had always felt for Tyler. When Tyler left for Chicago to train horses to pull carts in the city, Mabel knew she would never stop loving him.

As beloved as those memories were, though, they felt far away from her mountain home. Up here it seemed that summertime would have just settled in; when Mabel would feel the first cold fall nip returning at night. John would come by for their walk a bit earlier each evening, and be preoccupied with getting wood cut and stored for winter. Mabel was grateful for this preoccupation, for John always took good care of her. She enjoyed that feeling, but wondered if there should be more, perhaps a spark which might grow into a fire.

Thomas Salter had been hired to be the new schoolmaster in Caribou. He had come from Denver, and before that, Kansas City. The few times Mabel had been back up to Caribou, she always paid a visit to the schoolhouse.

This fall, a huge bull elk had wandered into town. He scratched his back by rubbing his hide back and forth on the timbers that the men had put against the leeward side of the schoolhouse for support. Before the men could fix the fallen timbers, a horrific wind had blown in the night, and the schoolhouse had shifted on its foundation. Mabel was relieved not to have to worry about her building in Cardinal blowing away. She was counting on Goodman to protect her school.

One evening, in September, Mabel had walked high up toward the Continental Divide. The snow fields had shrunk to small dirty grey glaciers. The rocky mountain peaks were basking in a calm that betrayed the approaching winter. The wild flowers had passed, and the tundra had been nipped orange by frost. Mabel had a nagging feeling of impending doom.

As she came over the last ridge toward Cardinal, there was smoke and panicked shouting. Fire was racing up the east facing hillside. Men were running up the mountain with shovels and axes. Mabel ran down the hill into town, and went straight to the hotel.

The front porch was crowded with women and children. Everyone stood watching in horror as the fire raced toward the ridge top.

Many remembered the fire of 1879 that burned most of Caribou to the ground. Forest fires had been burning that summer and no one had put them out. That Sunday morning in September, the townspeople woke to see a glow to the west. Fire crowned the few trees left near town, and quickly burned cabins with cords of firewood stacked for winter.

It had sent people running helplessly down Coon Track Creek to Nederland carrying furniture and leading stock. In the end, sixty or more buildings had burned on the east end of Caribou. The water system had worked to save the main part of town,

Men would be cutting trees and clearing a swath to try to stop it. Luckily, there was only a light breeze and the fire was burning straight uphill. Long after dark, Mabel could still hear the men working. The fire was bedded down in the cool of the night, and the men worked hard to contain it. Mabel and the people of Cardinal slept restlessly that night.

When Mabel woke in the morning, two inches of snow had fallen during the night. The fire was out. It had burned a large swath up the mountainside and stopped at the top. All undergrowth was gone. It had burned hot and fast, leaving the tree trunks blackened but standing.

Every other day, during the workweek, the mail would come, up the Coon Track Road to Cardinal from Central City. By three o'clock, there would be a few people waiting in front of the hotel saloon for the stage. It was a steep climb for a mile up the hill from Coon Track Creek and the Boulder County Mine. The road took several tight switchbacks, and at a couple of corners the maneuvering was tight.

This particular day, the mail was late, as one of the mules in the team had bit the mule in front of it, causing the animals to panic and lurch wildly, just as the whole rig had been turning a tight corner. The stage had become wedged against trees and stuck. The whole team had to be unhitched, then two mules pulled the stage safely back onto the road. The driver and his boy worked under the supervision of the six passengers as each gave his opinion. By the time the mail arrived in Cardinal, the driver was fit to be tied. He called on Miss Ruby for the rest of the afternoon, and sent the boy to take the mail on up to Caribou.

Often, miners would come to the schoolhouse with a letter for Mabel to read aloud to them. She knew many by name and had heard most their life stories too. Today, a man had a letter from his cousin in St. Louis. This cousin would be moving to Caribou to open a new livery stable there. His name was Tyler Adam Stevens. As Mabel read the letter, her words came out in disbelief.

"I know your cousin!" said Mabel. The man broke into a toothless grin.

"It's a small world, Miss Gurkin, isn't it? You came from St. Louis did ya?"

"I sure did. Your cousin trained horses for my father. We were good friends."

"Well, I only knowed'm when we was kids, but he'd be younger than me. I'd forgot all about'm. Our mothers are sisters is what."

"When he comes to Caribou, please be sure to tell him that I am here. I would be quite tickled to see him again." Mabel's heart glowed.

"Yes Mam, and thank you ever so much for the readin.'"

One afternoon, before school was out, Roxy came peeking in the door of the schoolhouse. She had a mighty grin on her face.

"Mabel", she whispered, "Come down to the hotel after school. There is someone to see you." She winked, then turned and shook her bottom back and forth. Then she smiled at Mabel again, and disappeared. Mabel was glad the children were concentrating on a pack rat that Mabel had caught in a bucket.

As soon as school was out, Mabel went into her room to brush her hair and grab a coat. She added water to the potato soup on the cook stove, put another log in the fire box, damped the fire lower, and then she rushed out the front door.

At the hotel, Mabel found Roxy and Lila charming her friend Tyler at the bar. She stopped at the door, and just looked at him. He looked the very same. It was so splendid to see a familiar face, and of all faces... Tyler's!

Tyler recognized her right away. He ran over and swept her up and spun her around by the waist.

"Mabel! You really are here! My cousin told me. I have been in Caribou for a week, and he just mentioned it. I came right down. My, oh my... it's good to see you."

"It is splendid, Tyler." She squeezed his hands then pushed him back to take another good look at him. "I can't believe it!"

The girls at the bar giggled and blushed. They whispered to one another, and then slipped out the back door.

"Come with me, Tyler", said Mabel, "I've left soup on the stove. I want to show you my schoolhouse."

As they walked up the street, Tyler told Mabel about the new stable in Caribou. They were working to get it built before winter. He would be buying a few horses and mules, as well as boarding for overnighters. There would be a blacksmith shop and a full time blacksmith. Tyler was thrilled to have come west. He was excited to have made the trip, and now to get settled.

Mabel took him by the hand, and pulled him up the schoolhouse steps.

"Look, Tyler." Mabel was all fired up. "I live here in the back. I have a life of my own! I can come and go as I please. I even have a ghost. His name is "Goodman", he is friendly of course. Oh, Tyler, Cardinal is perfect for me."

Tyler walked through the classroom, nodding with approval. He could see that Mabel had found her niche. She had been a wild spirit in St Louis, too restless to be satisfied. This frontier life was just rugged enough to be challenging and interesting. And here was Mabel's home.

"And who is this in the bucket?" asked Tyler.

"Ah, yes, he will have his head chopped off when John Peregrine comes by tonight. But I was thinking I would walk him way up the mountain and let him go."

Tyler inspected Mabel's quarters at the back, "It's a far cry from your father's house in St Louis, Mabel. But I can see you are very happy here."

"It sure suits me, Tyler, I love the mountains. I love the wildness and the open spaces. The sky is so blue, and Tyler, the people are so real. They love Cardinal too. It has such promise. We are all so hopeful for the mines. Come on, I will take you up to see the view, and we will let this rascal go."

Tyler grinned broadly at Mabel, and said again, "It is so good to see you."

Mabel was beaming at Tyler as they walked up the hill. She peppered him with questions about St Louis, and the people they'd known. She wanted to know all about his plans at the livery stable, and how he had ended up coming to Caribou.

"There's more, Mabel, I have so much to tell you."

"Tyler", Mabel said, "Set down the bucket." She hopped up on a tree stump.

"Come here, Tyler, and hold me. I want to be in your arms."

Tyler set down the bucket, and wrapped his arms around Mabel. She felt so good. He buried his face in her hair at her neck, and thought of the times they had shared in the loft of the barn. He was lost in the moment, and held Mabel tight. He thought of kissing her, but fought the urge.

He released her and said, "Let's walk this critter up the hill. It will be dark before we know it."

Tyler could see that the town was growing by the day. Log cabins made from the fire blackened wood were going up in rows with only a few rocks for foundations. Beside the cabins stood canvas wall tents complete with their portable woodstoves wafting smoke.

Mabel chatted on about the honky tonk show, and her dancing girls. Tyler agreed that the girls looked very sweet, and were quite a commodity here in the mountains. She told him of her walks, high into the peaks. She bragged about her students. She sang him a few ditties.

They let the rat go near a spring that was tucked into a small gulch. It was against Tyler's best instincts to let a varmint go, but Mabel said he was a friend to the kids. They had loved him all afternoon. She had made a promise. This packrat had earned his freedom.

As Mabel and Tyler walked back down the hill, Tyler struggled to find words to break his news to Mabel. Mabel held Tyler's hand, and gazed at him with the utmost affection. Tyler was feeling the very same. It was so good to see Mabel again. She lit a spark in his heart like no other woman ever had.

"Mabel", he said finally, stopping and turning her to face him. "I must tell you that there have been a few developments since we have seen each other. It has been four years you know."

"I know, Tyler. I never stopped thinking of the times we shared. What has happened?"

"Well, for one thing, I have a wife in St. Louis. Then also, two small ones, Jake and Alice. I guess it all happened pretty fast. They will be coming to Caribou when I send that I am ready."

Mabel stood looking at Tyler, hardly able to imagine what he was saying. Had that much time passed so quickly? Did Tyler love another woman? Of course, there had been no commitment between Tyler and Mabel. What did she expect? Mabel was speechless.

"Mabel." Tyler said, as he watched her eyes well up with tears.

Mabel fought the urge to run down the hill to her cabin. Running wouldn't change anything. She knew now that what she had for Tyler was indeed love. She buried her head in his chest, and squeezed her eyes tightly to squelch her tears.

"Do you love her, Tyler?"

"I believe I do, Mabel...but being with you again, I do believe I love you too. I always have."

"Oh, Tyler, you have knocked the wind right out of me. I suppose I will have to get used to this, but right now, I feel I have lost something dear."

"We were so young, you and I. We never took it seriously, but what love we shared, aye Mabel? I have never forgotten it either."

"Tyler, I do love you. There's not much that can be done about that."

Tyler grabbed Mabel and held her tightly against his body. They stood together for a very long time. When they separated and looked at each other, both looked miserable, yet at the same time, happy to be in each other's company again.

"Please come down to the school to have some soup and bread." suggested Mabel, hoping to change the intensity of the moment.

After dinner, Mabel begged Tyler to walk to the top of South Arapahoe Peak with her on the next Sunday. Tyler agreed to go. He said he would skip church, for a change. On her part, Mabel would look so forward to the trip.

The two sat with their lower legs and feet entwined under Mabel's table. It seemed safe enough, respectful of Tyler's new situation. They talked until well after midnight, sharing the events of the years that had passed. Mabel told Tyler of the ruckus in Caribou that lead to the move to Cardinal. He heard about the school kids, the Honky Tonk Show, Mr. Goodman and Mabel's love for the mountain peaks.

Tyler told Mabel of his success in horse training, the births of his babies, and his incessant desire to come west. When Tyler walked the two miles up the road back to Caribou, Mabel tucked herself into bed. How incredible to have her friend back again. She fell asleep smiling and thinking of him.

The orange sunrise was spectacular. High clouds, to the east over the prairie, were lit up a bright pale orange color. Their tops were grey, giving way to a clear blue sky that would prevail all day in the mountains. The sun sat like a shining ball of fire in the notch between two hills, begging the eyes to stare right at it. Mabel knew that they had the right day to climb South Arapahoe Peak.

As planned, Tyler was at the schoolhouse by seven that morning. Mabel was finishing washing her clothes. Tyler sat on a bench in the classroom, and spoke to Mabel in the next room.

"Mabel, it's funny to me that men sneak to Cardinal to see Miss Ruby's girls, but I come here to see the school teacher. As innocently as I behave, I think I feel even guiltier than they do, because I am in love with the school-teacher. "

"You are a sinful man, Tyler." said Mabel. "The fact that you feel guilty is a credit to your character. When Lucinda arrives with the children, your visits to Cardinal shall cease, for I will not be seen with a married man, even in this town."

"Then I shall die of heartbreak."

"That may be so." Mabel squeezed the last frilly white undergarment and held it up for a look. She felt Tyler's eyes on her and spun around. He was standing in the doorway.

"Are you peeping at my underwear?" she asked modestly. He was!

"No, my dear, I am peeping at you."

"Then you had better get back in the classroom this instant, or I will put you in the corner chair." Mabel's face flushed. She simply could not help herself.

"Are you about done yet?"

"You are quite full of yourself today, are you not? Here, please heave this water out the back for me, and I am done."

"I cannot bear to watch you hang these lovely things on the line, so I shall walk down to the hotel for a coffee. Come meet me when you are ready to go."

"A good idea, I am sure." Mabel carried the basket out, as Tyler held the back door. As she passed, he leaned close to her, exaggerating his stretch to look like a deprived puppy dog. It seemed they had been taking turns struggling with their boundaries, but luckily, one or the other had kept their head at any given time.

Mabel lifted the first garment to the line.

"I'll see you down there soon." She glanced his way.

"On the other hand," he said, "Why would I miss the opportunity to watch you hang these lovely things on such a fine day?"

"It is a fine drying day indeed." She noticed he was not leaving.

Tyler came out to the line and stood with his nose sticking through the neck of a top. He smiled. Next, he moved to a skirt, and put his arms out each side. When he began sniffing her corset, Mabel giggled and whacked him with a wet pillowcase over the head. She hung the pillowcase, pretending he was not there, but beaming a tight controlled smile.

"It seems to me that you have not left yet." said Mabel.

"Maybe I changed my mind."

"Then you may as well help."

"I do not believe I should even be touching these. Oh, my..."

"That is it, young man; I believe you need a switching!"

Tyler jumped back, looking like a bad little boy with an impish grin. Then he took a lunge straight at Mabel, grabbed her at the waist and picked her up. He carried her over his shoulder toward the back door. Mabel fought back in vain.

Tyler set her down inside and said, "Get your coat and hat. If we don't get walking, I could be in trouble."

Mabel grabbed her things and looked him square in the eye. "You are right. Let's go."

They walked up the Boulder County Hill behind Cardinal using the mine path that led to the north. Mabel knew it was imperative that they walk the day away. With Lucinda and the children arriving soon, their time together was coming to an end. Mabel could hardly breathe when she thought about it.

They climbed the next hill, and stopped on a rock outcrop. The air was thin, and they both took a minute to rest looking out at the view. The mountains to the south were still shining with the winter's snow. High rock studded foothills towered to the southeast, standing as sentinels to the Rocky Mountains. The sky was a solid bright blue.

Mabel lead the way down the hillside to the west, looking out now over the Indian Peaks, where snowfields were shrinking each day. Below the hikers lay the wide flat valley. They crossed the creek by picking their way through dense willow brush at a point where the bushes were most sparse.

Tyler was quieter than Mabel had ever seen him. They walked up through the lodge pole pine, finally breaking out at tree line, where krumholz were the last of the evergreens to cling to the mountainside. Now rocks cloaked with lime green and orange lichens spotted the thick grassy tundra. The sky was bluer than the imagination could conjure.

As Mabel and Tyler climbed the ridge, the hillside gave way to a great slope to the north, and a chain of lakes was strung down the valley below. An eagle circled, fishing a lake. They were above, looking down on him. He took a fish and struggled to hold it. It was so heavy that he had a hard time gaining altitude with his catch.

Nearing eleven thousand feet above sea level, the air was colder and a stiff breeze blew steadily out of the west. They put on coats, gloves and hats. As they walked toward the southfacing side of the ridge, they came upon a place that was protected by large boulders. The sun warmed the thick grass, and the wind was quiet.

"Let's stop for a while." suggested Mabel. They had come such a long way up. They picked a spot sheltered by large rocks and warmed by the sun. The ground was covered with tiny flowers, tufts of grass and mosses. It grew thick, like a blossoming carpet. They sat against the rocks and looked at the craggy peaks against the sky. Tyler opened the knapsack he had carried, and offered Mabel salty jerked elk, a biscuit and some water. After the snack, Tyler lay down and stretched out on the grass. Mabel lay down next to him, and put her head on his shoulder. She wished she could stop time. Freeze the moment. She held this image in her mind, saving the memory for a lifetime. She bathed in Tyler's company and him in hers.

They lay in the grass at the top of the world for a long time. South Arapahoe Peak was just half a mile to the west and five hundred feet higher. Finally, Mabel said, "If we are to make it to the top, we must go now!", and they began to climb the mountain peak.

The rest of the way was over rocks and boulders. The air was so thin that they stopped to breathe every ten steps or so. By the top, they were almost on all fours. The view to the west astounded them. Neither Mabel nor Tyler had seen this sight before. It appeared that the snow capped mountains and forested valleys went on forever.

Vast grassy park lands stretched between ranges. They realized they had only touched the first of the Rocky Mountains.

It was cold up on top, and they were not able to linger. The scramble back down the rocks warmed them again. Going downhill was amazingly quick. It seemed too soon when they crossed the willowy creek, and headed south to the town of Caribou.

As Mabel walked with Tyler into town, she suddenly realized how very tired her legs had become. Tyler saddled two horses at his stable, and they rode the rest of the way, back to Cardinal.

Outside the schoolhouse, Tyler helped Mabel to the ground. He stood very close to her and gathered his words.

"Mabel", he said carefully, "This has been a most special time for us. I won't forget it, ever. You know how I feel about you...and I wanted to say it. Promise me we will find time for each other."

"I've thought about it too, Tyler. I've thought long and hard about times to come. I won't see you in the winter, unless you are riding through town. Would you stop at the school to say hello? But Tyler, when it's summer, and the moon is full, will you meet me at the top of the Boulder County Hill, just before the moon rises?"

"Of course I will. I must have a plan to see you again." The horses stood patiently waiting, as if they hung on each word. "Mabel, I will sure miss you."

"Good luck, Tyler, and I will get to see you soon. The moon is waxing and I know I will see you." She hugged him tightly for just a second. Then he jumped on his horse, and leading the other one, rode up toward Caribou.

More and more mining claims were being located, and men were settling into the Cardinal area. Many came just to work in the famous Boulder County Mine. Some brought canvas tents and pitched them on town lots. Others used the standing dead timbers from the fire swath to hastily build basic cabins. These were blackened by the fire and gave Cardinal a unique character. The town was growing so fast, you didn't know neighbors from strangers.

Three days a week the U.S Mail came to Cardinal through Central City, and Mabel would walk past the stage stop after school to read the letters for those who couldn't read. This saved everyone from having to come find her. As Mabel approached the platform, she could see that a small crowd was gathered, and the stage hadn't arrived yet. A huge thunderstorm had just past through and perhaps this had caused a delay. The sky was still grey at Cardinal and hail lay accumulated in ditches and on the west side of the buildings. It was cold enough that Mabel had grabbed her coat. To the east the storm had grown even larger. It was black as ink as it headed out over the prairies.

As Mabel stood wondering if she'd go over to the hotel, a rider came up the Coon Trail in an awful hurry. He was calling for help. It seemed that lightning had hit one of the horses on the team for the stage. It was killed dead on the spot, and sent the other horses into a panic. The stage had been saved by quick action on the part of the driver, who had unhitched it from the thrashing team, and unloaded his passengers. Everyone was okay. They were just a quarter mile down the trail.

Most of the men on the platform jumped off and headed down the hill. Mabel was curious to see such a sight, and headed on down herself.

The stage had slid backward and was half off the road, but it was safely braked in a tilted position. The dead horse lay in a heap where it had been struck. The other horses were being unhitched and calmed by the men who had arrived first. One was lead past Mabel. It was snorting and blowing with its eyes bulging from fear. Horses recognize death like anyone.

Up in the woods above the stage were the passengers. There were two women, two babies, and a very small man wearing glasses. They all looked panicked. Mabel cut above the scene through the woods toward the passengers.

As Mabel approached she could see that the people had been out in the rain, and were soaking wet and freezing cold. One of the women was just a teen. She was woefully underdressed. The other woman had the two children. She sat on the ground with the youngest one in her lap, and the toddler clinging to her side. A man in the glasses sat on the ground looking as if he would pass out if he stood. Mabel placed her coat to over the mother and baby.

"Good Lord! What a scare you have all had! It looks like you're alright though."

"Yes.", said the mother, "But we are very cold."

Indeed, they were shivering and practically blue. The man was speechless.

"Come on", urged Mabel, "Let's go up to town. It's not far. Walking will help warm you, and we will get you all some dry clothes. Come on little fellow."

Mabel picked up the boy. He seemed to be about two years old.

"Let me carry you." she said.

The travelers stiffly rose to their feet, and followed Mabel across the hillside to the wagon road.

"Where did you come from?" asked Mabel.

"St. Louis", said the young girl, "All of us, but we're not a family. Mr.

THE ONLY EXISTING PICTURE OF THE OLD CARDINAL CITY.
Denver Public Library, Western History Collection X-6789

Reed is an accountant, coming to Caribou to work for the mines. Mrs. Stevens and the children are here to meet her husband. He is at Caribou. And I am coming to live with my Aunt. My name is Sarah Murphy."

"I see." said Mabel, "Well, welcome to Cardinal City." She turned to the mother carrying the small baby, who, at this altitude, was struggling uphill with her load.

"Mrs. Stevens," said Mabel graciously, "My name is Mabel Gurkin. I am so pleased to meet you! I knew Mr. Stevens in St. Louis a few years back. He worked for my father. I'm sure he will be at the platform to greet you!"

"I'm pleased to meet you too." she replied, "Thank you so much for your help. It has been a difficult trip. This storm just took the last of it out of me. Thank you, again."

Mabel looked at her more closely this time. Tyler's wife was younger than Mabel. She had brown hair tucked up in a bun, pointy features, and was of slight build. She was dressed in St. Louis clothes, and Mabel thought she was a bit out of her element.

"I don't believe my husband is expecting us today." she said. "It's been hard to predict exactly when we'd arrive. How might I find him?"

"We will come to the hotel just up this hill, and we can send a rider up to Caribou to fetch him."

"And how far away might Caribou be?" she asked. Mrs. Stevens was on the verge of tears.

"It's only two miles. He will be down here in a jiffy, when he hears the news." Mabel hoisted her young passenger higher on her hip. He was shivering with cold, but not complaining one bit.

They came up to the open meadow at the beginning of town, and stopped to take it all in. As flatlanders, they were huffing and puffing in the thin air. Mr. Reed looked shocked at the sight of the rough, hastily built town site. He still said not a word.

The streets were thick with mud after the storm, and it stuck heavily on the boots of the travelers. They passed cabin after cabin constructed with the blackened logs from the forest fire. Mabel was sure they must be thinking that they had made an awful mistake in coming here. With the cold wind, grey sky, and mud, it looked quite depressing.

"We are very close now." she said, trying to cheer them up. "You can see the hotel up there on the right. We will make you comfortable."

As they climbed the front steps of the hotel, Mabel dispatched a rider to call on Tyler in Caribou. She ushered the group into the dining room, and called for hot tea and biscuits from the kitchen. Mabel sent upstairs for Roxy to bring dry clothes.

"You poor things." she crooned, "What a horrid introduction to the mountains. Don't you worry, you'll like it here when the sun comes back out. That will be very soon. This storm will blow out quickly, and we'll be back to blue sky."

She handed the boy a biscuit with jam, remembering that this would be little Jake. The baby would be Alice. Mabel decided she would not let on to how much she knew. She felt a bit stunned by the whole thing herself. Soon, Roxy came downstairs with dry clothes, and took the ladies away to change. Mabel held Jake wrapped in a blanket, with Alice propped on her other knee. Who would ever have thought this, she mused, as she stared across the table at the funny little man from the stage.

"Mr. Reed," she said finally, "What can I do to help you?"

By the time Tyler arrived with a buckboard, everyone had eaten. They were feeling much better. The sun was shining and the storm had moved east.

Tyler was so beholden to Mabel. He thanked her again and again for rescuing his little family. Mrs. Stevens was grateful too, and told Mabel to call her Lucinda. Mabel knew how precious this family was to Tyler. As she waved the buckboard off to Caribou, she felt happy to have had the opportunity to meet them. Sarah Murphy and Mr. Reed took a ride to Caribou in the back of the buckboard. Sarah smiled and waved heartily to Mabel as they headed uphill into the forest.

On Tuesdays and Wednesdays, Mabel went to the hotel after school to work with the show girls on a fresh number. They would practice until dinnertime then go to the dining room together for their meal. The practices were a lot of fun for Mabel because the girls had such a sense of humor. They would laugh so hard at themselves, they'd almost wet their pants. Honky Tonk Joe was patient with them. He'd roll his eyes, grin, and then take it over again. Mabel enjoyed the practices as much as the shows.

Each one of Miss Ruby's girls had told Mabel her story. They were from every walk of life, and each had ended up in Cardinal by some twist of fate. Mabel loved them all. After dinner, the girls would insist Mabel join them in the bar room for a drink and some fun. Sure enough, Mabel looked forward to these evenings. Mabel met people from all over the world right here in Cardinal. She often laughed imagining what her father would think of this group.

Mabel had acquired a taste for scotch. She had first tried it to celebrate the success of the show, but then decided she loved to sip it with water while relaxing with her friends. It gave her the giggles. It warmed her heart. Scotch was medicinal for female problems and anything else that ailed you.

This particular Wednesday night, Mabel had scotch and the good company of friends. There began a boisterous controversy among the women concerning men. The only men in the room at the time were all seated at the bar.

"What do you call a woman who knows where her husband is every night?" called out Sherrie.

The girls tittered and shrugged their shoulders.

"A widow." she answered, and they all roared with laughter.

Lorna stood up and put a coin in the middle of the table. "I'll bet you every man at that bar is married!" she challenged.

The girls all turned to the bar at once and started laughing. The men didn't even notice them. No one turned around.

"Come on, bet me. ", Lorna riled again.

"And who's going to find out?" asked Roxy.

"I know them all," said Ruby "and I'm not telling."

"Do you suppose there's a man out there somewhere who can love a woman and be true?" asked Anna May, "I want to believe it, really I do."

"Anna May" cried Holly, "You are not gonna find'm in here."

"He'd only be true because it's a long way to town" added Lizzie, "and he'd probably only have one leg."

"He'd be a trapper, pining away at the moon for a girl he met just once."

"What is it with men?" asked Rosie incredulously "When they're done with their thing, they always pass out and snore."

"I always wondered about that." mused Roxy. "Maybe it's not just me, huh?"

"Oh, baby, you're so young." said Lizzie. "Now, honey, you might as well know it, it's like a baby at a titty. They're all the same."

Shouts of laughter ran around the table.

"No offense to the women that came before us, but I think we should reinvent the role of women. This is the new West, and it'll be what we make it!" stated Lady Lorna, putting her boot up on the chair.

They ordered another round of whiskey and toasted to women. As the liquor slid down the hatch, the barroom doors swung in and there was John Peregrine back from a dusty trip to Central City.

Mabel beamed at John. And John beamed back at the schoolteacher.

"I am going to pretend I've just won a girl in the Friday Evening Drawing. I think I'll take this one." John held out his hand to Mabel. "Ladies, don't weep you'll get a turn one of these days. Good night Ladies and good luck to you."

Mabel giggled and blushed as John held her coat open for her, then escorted her out the door.

Outside the night was spectacular. The stars were so clear in the high mountain air that Mabel felt close to them, as if she could almost touch each one as she named them. The summer night temperature was cool, but warm compared to star gazing in the winter.

"Let's get a blanket and go to the meadow to look at the stars." suggested Mabel.

"The stars are beautiful tonight." said John.

"I'll get one at the schoolhouse. What do you say?"

"We could." offered John, without much enthusiasm. He was thinking he'd be just as happy looking at the stars sitting on a porch.

"Great!" said Mabel and she darted ahead to the school and emerged with the blanket. She carried the blanket, and lead John to the end of the road, where the meadow began.

The grass was very cold, but it was dry, and the blanket made a good spot. Mabel sat down and pulled John with her. As they lay on their backs, they were consumed by the heavens. For a few minutes they were silent. Nothing earthly seemed important on such a grand scale. Mabel had fleeting thoughts of St Louis far away, of high mountain peaks and meadows, of her student's eyes looking up eagerly at her. All of these things were just moments compared to what she could see. Looking up, she knew God was great.

"Mabel" John spoke in a serious tone, "to be just such a small part of this world, makes me value the everyday parts of my life." He held her hand between them and squeezed it gently. ""I think of you and how precious you are to me."

Mabel gave a squeeze back and said, "How lucky we are."

"Out here in the west, we must make our own families."

"Our friends are our families, aren't they? I have never had such good friends before, John. People I can laugh and be myself with. I feel like I have a place here, a reason to be here. Our friends are so dear."

"Our friends are dear, but Mabel, you and I ... we have something. We have a future together. The stars make me realize that our lives are quite short."

"We have a future together. A long and happy one, I'm sure." Mabel assured him.

"You fit my dream better than you think, Mabel. You and I are a stunning match. We've both come from good families. I'm sure I can give you everything you'll need, in time, of course. Cardinal has grown so fast. Why, it's on its way to becoming a respectable town."

"John, stop!" said Mabel firmly. "You must understand, I like my life just the way it is. I have my jobs and my friends, my freedom to come and go as I choose. I like Cardinal just as it is. Of course it's respectable. It is full of the most real people I've ever known. You are a very important part of my life here, John, and I cherish you dearly...but John, maybe I'm not the marrying type."

Mabel thought of her long walks. She relished her time alone in the forest. She thought of the absolute wildness of her new lady friends when they cut loose and had fun. Would a woman have to give these things up to live with a man? Certainly. And what of love? Mabel was sure she knew nothing about it. She had felt infatuation, more than once, but love would last forever. It would be love for Mabel before she would marry. Otherwise she would have stayed in St Louis, married to the man of her father's choice.

Mabel rolled to her side, facing John. She put her head on his shoulder. It was quiet for a long time. Finally, John said, "You might change your mind."

"I might." she said.

A pack of coyotes howled on the hillside above them. Pups yipped in higher voices than the others. It went on and on. The celebration of a rabbit perhaps. They sounded like a bunch of drunken Indians. In the end, the leader called the racket to a sudden halt, but the pups continued on until someone nipped their ears. The little yippers finally stopped with one last yip.

John and Mabel stayed in the meadow, looking up, until the cold had sunk into their bones.

Mabel peeked over the bank of the stream, looking for the deepest water. She slowly, carefully, drew back and maneuvered her fishing pole to drop the hook and worm just upstream of the pool. It settled against a log. She pulled it up and tried again. This time the worm floated downstream directly into the hole. Mabel felt a tingle of excitement and waited. Nothing. She got down on her hands and knees and drew closer. She peered into the pool. Nothing. With a "humpf", Mabel stood to her full height and stretched.

Minding the tip of her pole, and gathering her skirt, Mabel made her way quietly through the brush to the next pool upstream. It was shaded except for the ripples where the water came in. Mabel knelt down, keeping her body from sight of the pool. Reaching far, she dangled the worm out over the pool, and dropped it straight down. Immediately, she had a trout on the line. Her eyes wide with surprise, she gently lifted the fish from the stream and flipped it onto the grassy bank.

The trout had Mabel's favorite shade of green on its back, speckled with colorful highlights and spots down to its pale belly. It was decorated with red, black and white on its fins. A brookie, and what a beautiful dinner!

Mabel smacked the fish's head on a rock, and felt the life leave it. She slipped her knife beneath the tongue under the chin and cut forward. She slit the belly, stem to stern. With one move, pulled the guts and sent them flying into the bushes. Mabel rinsed the fish in the stream and hung it on a stick with her two other fish. That would do. Mabel gathered up her pole, and stood.

There on the hillside above the creek sat a man. He had been watching her! Mabel was startled and froze.

"Did your Daddy teach you that?'" he asked, as if it was any of his business.

"My Grand Daddy, thank you. Do you mind?'". Mabel was a bit afraid, and backed away from the stranger. As she did, she took note of a gentle but mischievous smile.

"Good day." she said, and marched right back down the creek the way she had come up.

When Mabel was far enough away to feel alone again, she stopped and wrapped the fish in some big leafy plants. She rolled them into a handkerchief and headed for home.

Little Mary had come by the schoolhouse to bring Mabel a message from Roxy. She asked that Mabel come down to her cabin as soon as possible. Roxy's cabin had one window, one door and one bedroom. Three women and one child lived there together. The floor was pine, which was better than the dirt floor in some of the other cabins. There was a small metal box made into a woodstove, which sufficed for warmth and the women took their meals at the hotel. Roxy was heating a flatiron on the stove and ironing handkerchiefs and curtains. She wept softly as she worked.

Mabel called to Roxy from the ditch by the road, "Hello, hello? Are you here?"

"In here, with the ironing, dear. Please come in!"

Mabel could see right away that something was terribly wrong.

Roxy set down the iron and tried to speak, but her voice came out in a squeak. "Mabel, I am with child. I am just sure of it."

Mabel was stunned. She had often wondered how such girls avoided this situation. She had heard of women putting a penny inside themselves.

"Roxy, it will be alright." The two women embraced and held on.

"When do you figure?" She smoothed Roxy's tears from her cheek.

"I suppose I 've known it for a while, but I... it might have just gone away, but it...oh, Mabel, I'm gonna carry this child full term. It is not what I'ad hoped for. This poor babe won't know a father. Mabel, I didn't want it to happen this way."

"Well, Roxy, it is happening this way. It's good that you are recognizing it. You need to be taking it easier now, honey. It will be alright."

"What will become of me? I can't work much longer in this condition. No one will want me, Mabel. Probably be thrown right out of here. I'm scared to death to tell Miss Ruby!"

Roxy started to sob again. She smoothed her dress over her belly and stood sideways to Mabel.

"Oh, honey, you've still got a long way to go, plenty of time to make plans and all." Mabel counted on her fingers from five months, just wagering a guess.

"Might be the sweetest Christmas present you have ever had!"

"I knew I could tell you, Mabel. I knew you'd look at the bright side, you always do...but oh, I'm in a pickle. I just can't tell her. I can't!" Roxy covered her face with a clean pressed hanky, wiping her eyes, then blowing her nose.

"Rox, you will be feeling much better when you do. You know Ruby understands these things. She'd see it as just a matter of time. Why, you know Ruby has helped all the girls when they need it. She loves you, honey. We'll just go on down to the hotel right now and get it over with." Mabel took Roxy by the hand and began to pull. Roxy leaned back for a moment, until Mabel gave her the same look she gave her students. Roxy hung her head, and started out of the cabin with Mabel.

It was only a couple of blocks to the hotel. Mabel explained to Roxy that she must go into Ruby's room with her head held high, and tell her the news with confidence. Roxy looked younger than ever, and winced at the thought. Mabel stopped her square in her tracks and held her firmly by the shoulders.

"You can do this Rox," she said.

Roxy shook her head, and swallowed a sob. "I will."

Mabel held her hand to the top of the mezzanine stairs, and then launched her in the direction of Miss Ruby's door as if it was important to keep Roxy's momentum up. Roxy knocked with a light tap, tap, tap and slowly entered the room. Mabel went downstairs and out onto the veranda.

The first thing Mabel heard was Miss Ruby shouting at the top of her lungs. "Lord, why me? Why me?"

This was followed by a bottle flying out the second story window and breaking in the street. Immediately, Roxy appeared at the front door of the hotel.

She has a sheepish grin on her face, and reported "I do feel better now that she's told." Mabel gave her a big hug and said "Good job, Roxy, I knew you could do it."

The two women walked back up the street to Roxy's cabin. They were planning on a bit of time to let Ruby simmer down. Roxy went back to her ironing. She was done with the tears for now.

Mabel put on a kettle for tea, and the two ladies chatted about regular things, like making meat pies, and sharing the well with the new folks two houses down. They wouldn't have much more to say about the baby until time went by.

Late in the afternoon on the next full moon, Mabel walked up to the top of the Boulder County Hill. By the time she settled on the tallest outcrop of rock, the sun was just setting behind the mountains. The last of the summer snowfields had shrunken small, and the shadow created by the ridge of the Divide cast the mountains grey and cold. The outcrop Mabel sat on gave her a panoramic view of the prairies. The moon was already projecting a glow from the east as it rose.

Mabel hoped that Tyler would climb the hill to visit with her. She had hardly been able to get him off her mind since they had said goodbye. She considered the possibility that he very well may not be able to get away. Perhaps he wouldn't have even thought of it. With his family commitments, why would he? He had told Mabel he loved Lucinda, right up front. Mabel struggled to keep it all in perspective. There was no future for the two of them. He had a family. They had promised each other to meet with the moon, but realistically, it would not be a practical idea. It was probably just the easiest way to say goodbye, but Mabel would have walked out to see the moon this evening anyway, so there was nothing to lose by going to the Boulder County Hill.

As Mabel looked over the prairie, convincing herself it might be best if Tyler did not show anyway, a voice came from behind her.

"Good evening, Lassie, I recognize you from the Coon Track Creek. Mind if I join you?"

Mabel turned to see the same fellow who had been watching her fish.

"I thought I would take in the sunset and the moonrise on this especially spectacular evening." he said, and then he sat on a knob of rock just twenty feet from Mabel. He settled down facing west to watch the last of the sun's glow set.

Mabel nodded, a bit too surprised and shy to speak. She kept her gaze to the east, wondering who this man was, and why he presumed that she might want his company. This speculation was followed by the thought that it would hardly be proper if Tyler was to arrive and find her in the company of a complete stranger.

Mabel grew more irritated by the minute. So many people were moving into the area that this rock was becoming a popular destination at sunset. When she could no longer sit still, she turned to the south, and climbed down off the rocks. When a meeting takes this much effort, and it does not fall into place, Mabel decided, it is simply not meant to be. She began to descend on the trail toward Cardinal.

On the south side of the Boulder County Hill, another trail led up the mountain from the Town of Caribou. Tyler climbed quickly as the dusk settled into a moonlit night. When he reached the rock pile at the top of the hill, he saw a figure sitting on the top. His heart beat a little faster as he climbed the last few yards up. He pulled himself over the top and found, to his surprise, a man watching the moonrise.

"Oh, excuse me." Tyler said, "I thought you were someone else. Fine evening though, is it not?"

"Yes, indeed it is fine." answered the man. "If your 'someone else' is an adventurous young lady, she has just headed down the hill toward Cardinal."

"As a matter of fact, that would be my dear cousin, I am sure. Thank you so much, I'll be off." And Tyler hopped off the rocks and followed the path toward town.

With a spring in his step, he made good time and caught site of Mabel on the path below. He cut out a switchback and hid behind a big ponderosa pine. As Mabel stepped past, he leapt out and grabbed her, giving her the fright of her life. Tyler held her tight, laughing at his cunning, as Mabel clutched her chest, gasping for air.

"You absolutely unscrupulous creep!" she howled. "I will remember this and you shall pay dearly!" Her heart was racing out of control. Mabel crumpled into a heap on the ground, and Tyler, still grinning had to help her to her feet.

"Are you proud?" she snapped, but Tyler could see she was happy he had found her.

"You had given up on me!" Tyler stuck out his bottom lip for sympathy.

"I wondered if it might be the wise thing to do." declared Mabel. Then her thoughts flashed for a moment on the man she had recognized from the creek. Mabel pondered that he had recognized her too.

"Mabel," Tyler said gently, "I have brought you something. Let's find a spot to sit down."

Mabel beamed like a child. Tyler had come after all, and she was thrilled. Her heart felt complete, as if their souls were two parts of a puzzle. He led her along the contour of the hillside to a spot where a promontory of rock faced east. The moon was just beginning to rise as they settled onto a bed of pine needles, backs against the rock.

The moon rose more quickly than the two of them could believe, illuminating the night into day again. Tyler unwrapped a paper package and presented Mabel with what he remembered was her favorite treat, ropes of red licorice. For a while, the rocks radiated heat from the day, and Tyler and Mabel enjoyed their perch above the town. They spoke of everything and nothing. They flirted like lovers and teased like siblings.

It was Mabel who asked about Tyler's little family. It seemed that they had adapted nicely to life in the mountains. Jake liked to visit his father's stables. Tiny Alice was growing quickly, and apparently was a good-natured baby with a sense of humor. Lucinda, who had been used to finer things about the home, was managing well, while she waited for more of her family belongings to be shipped across the prairie to Caribou. The Stevens home was bigger than many, boasting milled lumber framing, clapboard siding and two bedrooms.

Mabel took this in with curiosity. It all seemed more real to her after the day that the horse had been hit by lightning. Even though Mabel had to share Tyler, she had a comforting feeling that Tyler had been hers first, and no one could take away the times they had shared. What they had together would always be special.

When Tyler announced that he would be making his way home soon, Mabel was struck with the reality that their lives had changed. She was lucky to have had Tyler's company for even a little while.

As Mabel followed the moonlit trail back to Cardinal, she was happy that Tyler had promised to see her at the top of the Boulder County Hill again, with the next full moon. Mabel considered how inappropriate these visits were. She knew she should feel nothing but guilt and shame, but instead she was feeling a sweet warmth, and she relished it.

Mabel shook her head, in response to the complex situation. It was nothing she was at all familiar with. At the same time that she felt compassion for Tyler and his family, with a complete separateness, she felt her own love for him. Finally, decided Mabel, this was all something she would just have to live with. Intuition told her to leave it at that. Her life was enriched by her relationship with Tyler. Mabel felt very lucky to have him in Caribou.

As fall approached, the school children helped Mabel gather rosehips which had ripened on the hillsides and meadows at Cardinal. Their teacher stretched recess time and came up with excuses for the children to be outdoors, knowing that the warm days were numbered. The noonday sun was still hot, and Mabel savored it as the days grew shorter. Nights and mornings were cold enough for a fire in the woodstove.

Jim Brewster forgot his sweater at school each day, as it was so warm when the bell rang to go home. His mother sent him walking back up the hill a few minutes later, to fetch it, and he always cheerfully blamed Goodman for hiding it from him. Mabel would be sweeping out the classroom and smile as she told him, "I was just about to sweep it out the door." About the time he would learn to remember the sweater, the weather would turn to winter anyway.

Sarah Murphy won the jar of lollipops for guessing the date of the first snow in Caribou. September 6th brought eight inches of dry wintery snow. It filled every crevasse and drifted in the meadows. Everyone delighted in the clean white blanket that covered the hills. In three days, it was gone again.

Extra freight wagons had been arriving from Boulder and Central City for the past few weeks, as everyone filled their larders with food. Coal oil for lamps, flour by the ton, apples by the bushel, sugar from Colorado sugar beets and coffee enough to last. There were bolts of flannel, yards and yards of canvas, and skeins of wool. The big kids in each family handed their winter clothes down to the younger ones. Socks were darned, and trunks spilled out layers of woolens. Everyone had stacked wood on the windward side of their cabins.

Before school, one Tuesday morning, Mabel waved off a group of men as they departed for a few days of elk hunting. John Peregrine was among them. Happily perched on his horse, and outfitted with his Winchester, he tipped his hat toward Mabel and urged his horse forward.

Mabel sighed as she watched John Peregrine go. More and more the man cared for her and spoiled her, yet all of the reasons Mabel could muster still did not add up to John being a husband. Surely, it was only fair to continue to tell him that she had no intention of marrying, but it amazed her that he never gave up. His letters would come in the mail to her, inviting Mabel to join him for dinner at the hotel, upon his return from Central City. John's gentle voice, always eager to report the latest developments about the mountains, was stimulating company for Mabel. Mabel supposed that he might keep courting her forever, and perhaps that was an acceptable thing, as long as she was honest about her heartstrings.

As the men departed for the hunt, they were trailed by a string of pack-horses, hauling a kitchen, tents and supplies. They would return with an even heavier load. Then there would be a flurry of activity as the meat would be salted, smoked and jerked. Mabel always lent a hand, at the hotel kitchen, and with a few of her student's families as well. Upon the return of the hunting party, everyone would enjoy a "Harvest Square Dance".

When that day came, Mabel worked with the ladies, setting tubs of corn on the cob out on long tables. Two fiddlers, a banjo player, two guitarists and an upright bass player were setting up in the corner of the room. Children peeked in the door, anxious for the evening to begin.

As Mabel carried another tub of corn up the front steps, a young man relieved her of the load.

"We have never been properly introduced" he said, "but we have met a couple of times. I am happy to be of assistance."

Mabel just saw the backside of him as he whisked the tub into the room, "Thank you!" she said, and turned around to get the next load. In a jiffy, he was back. Mabel recognized him as the man who had been near the creek when she was fishing, and on the rocks at the top of the Boulder County Hill.

This time, he eagerly kept stride with Mabel, and began to talk as they walked.

"Can you imagine, that an occasion might happen to a man, who is in the highest sense a gentleman, wherein he sees a lady that he very greatly admires, however, he can in no way approach her without rendering himself impertinent and offensive?"

Full of curiosity now, Mabel turned his way, but continued out the door. Should she risk the indiscretion of a reply?

Outside, Mabel stopped, and gave a good long look at this man. He seemed to be a bit younger than she was. He was dressed in a clean, pressed shirt, but was otherwise a man of practical means. Mabel had to admit to herself that he was nothing short of dashing, but truly, who would be so presumptuous as to press an acquaintance in such a way?

"If such a gentleman would give his reasons for requesting the attention of this lady, perhaps the lady might see it fit to listen." she finally answered.

"My name is Alexander Buck. I am a trapper and a traveler. I have had the pleasure of seeing you in the most uncommon places, and I hoped that we could speak for a moment. Please tell me your name."

Mabel decided that perhaps acquaintance could be made, with a certain reserve. She moved out of the stream of people who were carrying food into the building.

"I am Miss Gurkin. I suppose you could bring me a root beer." Mabel smiled, wondering what in the world this fellow was getting at.

"Delighted." he said, and he slipped away, to return with two drinks and a beaming grin. They sat on a bench outside the hotel. Mabel immediately felt that this fellow had more energy than ten men. She was completely intrigued.

"May I ask you a personal question?" Mr. Buck inquired. Mabel nodded and blushed.

"The sphere of a woman's action and work is so widening that she can today, if she desires, handsomely and independently support herself. She need not marry for a home. How is it that you have not married, when you are as fresh as a spring flower waiting to be picked?"

Mabel delighted in Alexander Buck's language, in his straightforward manner, and again felt tickled by his gregarious nature.

"Mr. Buck", Mabel almost lost herself into his curious eyes. "My father would have had me married six times over had I been willing to accept a life without true love."

"It is a mark of judgment and rare good sense for a lady to go through life without wedlock if she cannot marry from love." Alexander offered.

"Miss Gurkin, it is quite unusual to find a lady that tends to be more in the forest than in town. Yet here you are, obviously very much a part of things here in Cardinal."

"Here in town, I am the school teacher. I have found that I have an insatiable desire to walk these mountains. I am so enjoying being here."

Mabel looked at the trapper. His eyes were riveted on hers. They were hazel, spotted with flecks of adventure. His hair was dark and thick. It curled about his neck in an unruly manner. His medium build was strong and she knew he was quick.

"It is wonderful that you love the mountains." Alexander offered, "They fill one's soul with joy and awe. My father, back in New York, had more ambitious plans for me. But alas, when I came west, it was immediately evident to me that I was born to roam this territory. I am bound for Mexico next." Alexander had had gleam in his eye, the gleam of a dreamer. Mabel wasn't so sure he would ever make it that far. It seemed to her that those who brag so readily about their dreams seldom accomplish them.

"You are full of spirit and exciting plans, Mr. Buck. I wish you good fortune all the way. If you make it back to these mountains, be sure to inquire as to my whereabouts. I shall be very interested to hear your tales."

Mabel liked the way he listened to her. It seemed his attention was on her only - such a dangerous focus for one who claimed to be a restless traveler. A conundrum, really.

"Do you walk about by yourself often? Twice I have seen you and you have been alone." Mr. Buck passed no judgment as he asked this question. He just sounded curious.

"Often, I suppose." responded Mabel, considering for herself. "It is difficult to find women who are compelled to walk. I could spend my life motivating them only to make no headway in the long run. I appreciate the solitude also time to think...with school. Also, I read the mail for many here in town. "

"Traveling with others has always been a dilemma for me. I'm not a solitary creature, yet I make better time alone and traveling light brings me good fortune. You know, even the best of friends has their own road to take."

The band was warming up sending notes floating out the door on a musical breeze. Mabel felt a stir of excitement as the notes strung together into melody. She began to consider what a fine dance partner she had found.

Mabel delighted in Alexander's tales of the places he'd been and the people he'd met. There was so much more she wanted to hear and ask, but the music drew them indoors to dance. Mabel danced every dance. With her students, with Ruby's girls, with Alexander and with John. The music brought light feet as the band played long into the night.

The hall filled, and people poured outside taking the highest and lowest sounds with them. They danced in the streets until they could dance no more, and then made their way home by moonlight.

In the end, it was John who walked Mabel back to the schoolhouse. As she closed her eyes to sleep, she giggled with giddiness. Yes, Mabel thought, I am drunk on friends.

It was Indian summer. Very early on Sunday morning, while the sun was beginning to glow red on the eastern horizon, there was a knock on the back door of the schoolhouse. Mabel was rousted from a dream of a runaway horse. She peeked out the windowpane to see Alexander hopping up and down, and immediately Mabel smiled and thought ' He is crazy!'

"I would be pleased if you would walk to the peaks with me." he offered, having opened the door just a crack. Mabel clutched her covers around her, and looked outside at the sky.

"I'm coming!" she assured him. Mabel's heart leaped with joy. She bounded from her bed. "But I will need a few minutes. Go around to the front, and I will meet you there."

Alexander sat on the schoolhouse steps watching the sun poke the first light into the sky. A few times, he felt the need to look over his shoulder. But there was no one there. He shrugged off an unconscious feeling that someone was scrutinizing him. When Mabel came around the corner of the building, he was startled, and asked again, "Will you come up the mountain with me today?"

Alexander noticed that Mabel had every manner of clothing heaped on her body to protect her from the morning chill, but she was beaming and said, "Here we go."

As daylight broke, the trees turned from silhouettes to forests. The walkers saw their breath in clouds as they drew hard for a second wind. The sun teased with its redness, promising heat, but delivering chill. Little was said between the two as they climbed the morning hillside. It felt like a sneak, with the town still quietly asleep. They walked until they found that the night had turned to daylight. It was then that Mabel and Alexander stopped to eat biscuits. They settled on a large rock, and let their talk emerge above an early morning whisper.

Alexander had been pondering the distinct presence he had felt at the schoolhouse. He wasn't sure what that was about.

"Mabel, that fellow John Peregrine, is this acceptable that you walk with me?"

Mabel laughed then tried to explain.

"John and I are friends of a peculiar type." she began. "He is quite interested in me but I am afraid I am not in love with him. I feel it is, to the highest degree, dishonorable to trifle with the affections of another, so I have let him know how I feel. We shall be friends forever..." and she found herself at a loss for words.

"It is not what I thought then." He paused trying to reckon with this. "This morning, I would swear your father was looking over my shoulder, trying to scare this suitor away!"

"Not my Father," clarified Mabel, "He is in St. Louis. You felt "Goodman", a spirit who has taken it upon himself to guard the children and their teacher. Don't mind him. He is not to meddle in these things."

When they stood to walk again, Mabel smiled to think that this man was sensitive enough to have felt Goodman. And he was neither skeptical nor scared away.

As the morning warmed, Alexander and Mabel stopped several times to take off layers of clothing. By the time they reached tree line, it had warmed enough to sit and rest in a hot patch of sunshine. The summer's flowers had been nipped away by frost and the thick blanket of tundra boasted colors of golden, orange and red. The wind blew hard overhead, but the hikers, nestled between the krumholtz, felt the last heat of summer on their faces. They talked of everything; people, parents, gold, love. They teased each other. They gave each other unsolicited advice. The morning passed with the chatter of two new friends.

But the fall weather was fickle. As they rested, hail began to spit on them through the sunshine. The clothes went back on, and it was time to walk to keep warm. Mabel and Alexander climbed above tree line. They hopped on rocks as they went, and felt the crush of parched tundra beneath their boots. The air was thin, causing a light- headedness equal to three ounces of whiskey. When the hail picked up its pace and the wind became a gale, they laughed at the contrast the sky had presented. As the hail turned to blowing snow, they shrieked with joy, for it made them feel so alive! This blizzard, forerunner of winter, charged Mabel and Alexander with anticipation.

Finally, after quite a while treading into the wind, they sat in the lee of a large rock. The two simply watched the weather as it played out over the mountains and onto the prairies. Time stood still. Only the wind was moving.

When they walked down the mountain, the wind carried them quickly. By the time they were back in the trees, it was a warm fall day. What a spot on this earth, where latitude and altitude combine into a climate that changes with the wind, from heaven to hell and back again.

They said goodbye on the edge of town, and Mabel walked with a skip in her step back to the schoolhouse. Her thoughts were on the good company that she had shared. Alexander was fascinating and funny. They had laughed, flirted, and talked so freely. It seemed she had known him forever. She hoped he liked her too.

The day had given Mabel a reminder of the wild weather to come. As she came in the backdoor, she filled her arms with firewood.

It was a cold afternoon in late October, when Roxy came to the schoolhouse, with a hopeful look in her eye. Mabel had just set a group of older kids reading to the young ones, so Roxy had one minute to talk to Mabel.

Roxy thought this would be the day the baby was coming. There were pains like never before, and a bloody show that had sent her walking to tell Mrs. Medoc, and now, Mabel. Roxy would go home now, to keep the fire stoked, and water on the stove.

After school, they agreed, Mabel would come down to check on her. Mrs. Medoc had delivered her share of babies, and she was not willing to come until things were really rolling. Especially, she had said, a first baby would take a long while.

"Roxy," Mabel promised, "all will go well. Stay calm and think about the baby. I will be down just as soon as school is over."

Roxy pulled generous layers of coats around her tummy, and disappeared back down the road toward her cabin.

Mabel's student, Ryan, was jumping with anticipation, for he and his mother shared their cabin with Roxy. He had waited long enough for the baby to come. Mabel told Ryan that after school he could walk with her to see if the baby had come yet. When the baby came, he would be staying at the neighbor's cabin for the night, and a few more days. Ryan was ready.

At three o'clock, the shift whistle at the Boulder County Mine blew once, signaling the end of the school day. The kids waited politely for Miss Gurkin to say "Good day" to each of them, youngest first, then they sped down the front steps to freedom.

Ryan said, "We best hurry, Miss Gurkin. There's a baby coming at my house today. This sure isn't everyday is it, Miss Gurkin? I am more excited than having kittens."

"Me too." grinned Mabel, and they grabbed their coats and hats in a hurry.

At the cabin, Ryan was thoroughly disappointed to find Roxy looking just like she had for the previous months. He was happy to pack a few clothes in a pillowcase and go on to Miss Carol's cabin next door.

When they were alone, the women took a peek and decided there was plenty of time for tea and biscuits. Between pains, Mabel and Roxy stitched pieces of a quilt. They carefully avoided any talk of what was to come. Then Roxy's water broke, and set off the flurry of activity that would continue until the following morning.

After much running back and forth on the part of Mabel, Mrs. Medoc came to the cabin about midnight. Mabel was glad the door could now stay closed against the cold night. The labor progressed slowly all night, with it stopping altogether a several times. But each time things paused; Mrs. Medoc had another trick to get labor moving again. She bathed Roxy's belly with warm washclothes. She switched her position more than once, despite the will of the laboring mother. At one point, she made Roxy drink a special tea that eventually made her throw up, and the labor move ahead in earnest.

Mabel was so glad Mrs. Medoc was there. She was comforted by her easy manner and experience. Mabel learned it was best to not empathize too much with each contraction, for it was a long night and one had to pace them self to see it through to the end. By now Roxy was so exhausted that she had given up fighting the labor and seemed to be progressing as a result. Mabel boiled water and boiled water. She had always wondered what the boiling water was for, and now it seemed she couldn't boil enough.

It was the blackest part of the night, and every other soul in the town of Cardinal was sound asleep, when the baby's head began to crown. First, there was a sleek black spot showing, which disappeared again for another few of contractions. When the spot showed again, Mabel could see that it was a hairy head, and both women smiled at each other, knowing this baby was presenting the right way.

Each time Roxy had another contraction, the head showed larger. Mrs. Medoc gently massaged the mother about the baby's crowning head to keep her supple as she stretched. Roxy pleaded with Mrs. Medoc to be able to push, but she told Roxy to wait. Mrs. Medoc puffed air dramatically with Roxy, so as not to let the babe come all at once.

Just when Mabel decided this couldn't go on much longer, Mrs. Medoc said, "Push steady now, dear". And the baby arrived. First the head, then one shoulder, then the rest all at once, completely. It was a boy. Roxy named him Christian.

As the sun rose over the prairie, Mabel left the new mother and babe sleeping, and walked slowly up to the schoolhouse to light a fire in the woodstove. She knew how tired she must be, but the thrill of seeing a baby born would sustain her through the day as she taught her lessons. She couldn't wait to tell Ryan about his new friend.

❧

The firewood for the schoolhouse had been neatly stacked against the west side of the schoolhouse by a group of miners. Mabel was quite sure that John Peregrine had bought them dinner at the hotel in exchange for their work. She hummed mining songs as she stacked the rest of the wood at the back near her own kitchen door. The days had grown cold, and from now on, there would always be a fire going.

Alexander appeared from around the corner, startling Mabel. She giggled with pleasure to see him. In the month since the Harvest Dance, Mabel had seen a lot of Alexander. Just when she would make up her mind that he probably wasn't thinking of her, he would call on her. They would walk and talk, or sit on the back step of the schoolhouse. Alexander loved to take Mabel to the hotel for ice cream.

This time, Alexander finished stacking the cordwood. He insisted she sit in the sun on the upside down washtub to keep him company. When he was done, Alexander and Mabel went into the schoolhouse for tea.

"Winter is just around the corner." said Alexander with a faraway look in his eyes. "I will close up my cabin, and be leaving for Mexico soon."

These words cut deep into Mabel's soul, but she was not surprised to hear of his plan. Alexander was a traveler. This was, in part, why he was such an interesting person. Mabel was quiet. Her emotions ran clearly. She would miss Alexander. She would miss the light he brought to her life, the spontaneity that he brought to her days.

"I thought I'd ride out in the morning. It looks like the weather will hold for the next few days, and I will need a good start across the prairies to get south of Pueblo."

Mabel smiled cheerfully at him, her heart feeling emptier by the minute. At once, she wanted to go with him. She wanted to see the places to the south. Mabel imagined herself riding up thinly forested slopes of pine, and across endless rolling grassy flats of high chaparral. She thought of bedrolls, cooking from one pot and of campfires. Her heart tugged at her to go. But she wasn't invited Mabel reminded herself.

Did he know she would like to go? Did he think she could do it, and enjoy it? But the reality of a woman on the trail was what brought Mabel back to the moment.

"Alexander," Mabel squeaked, "I will miss you very much." Her eyes welled up with tears. She opened them as wide as she could to stop the tears from showing. Crying was the last thing she wanted to do, but her eyes filled and one big tear rolled down each cheek.

"Come here" Alexander said as he pulled her to her feet and held her in his arms. "Spring will be here, and I'll be back to the high country to trap. The first girl I will look for will be you." He smiled.

Mabel giggled with relief. She stared into his hazel eyes and felt lucky to have him as a friend.

Alexander leaned toward her face. He looked at Mabel in a serious way. She felt her heart overwhelmed. Alexander came very close. He closed his eyes and kissed her long and softly on the lips. Mabel was surprised. Her spirit soared. When Alexander drew his lips away, he stepped back and looked at Mabel.

"There is peach ice cream waiting for you. Let's go."

Mabel was stunned. A smile warmed her face. He took her by the hand and helped her into her coat. They walked to the hotel.

Alexander chatted about the things he expected to see on his trip, places he had heard of, and stories of these faraway lands. There were rivers to follow, high dry mountain ranges, large fat lizards, cactus juice, javalinas and siestas.

She felt his excitement for travel growing, and as the evening passed, Mabel knew it was time for Alexander to go. When he walked her to the schoolhouse, Mabel protected her heart as he kissed her again. She enjoyed every second of this long lingering kiss knowing it could well be their last. Saying goodbye, she could already feel life without him, and she missed him.

Mabel met the mail on Saturdays, and sat in the parlor of the hotel reading for those who needed her service. This particular day, the snow blew sideways through town in big flakes. People came and went with business, bundled up against the shocking chill of the new season.

Today, the mail brought a postcard from Alexander. It had been sent from the "Taos of the Pueblo", and it showed square adobe buildings with ladders. There were mountains studded with juniper. Indians sat in sun busy with their hands. On the other side, neatly formed letters had guided the card to "Miss Mabel Gurkin, Cardinal City, Colorado".

Opposite the address, the card read, "Fond thoughts of you keep me. Yours Truly, Alexander"

Mabel read it and reread it several times. She closed her eyes and relished images of special moments she had shared with Alexander; his smiling face close to hers, the first time they had met on Coon Track Creek, and then later, huddling from the wind on the Great Divide. Mabel giggled to herself at the warm feelings she could conjure. She was grateful for these memories.

Roxy and a whirl of snowflakes blew through the door of the hotel carrying Christian all wrapped in blankets. He looked more like a load of laundry than a baby. Mabel handed Roxy the postcard, and took the bundle in exchange. She unwrapped two layers before finding a little face beaming up at her.

"Christian," Mabel cooed, "good morning, you precious fellow. Sweet baby, sweet baby. Smile for me, sweet boy."

"Oh, Mabel! So he's been to the Pueblo. And he wrote you! How romantic, Mabel. He misses you." Roxy had a dreamy look.

"Yes." said Mabel, "and I miss him too. But look at this boy!" Mabel pushed her sweet thoughts of Alexander far away, so she could live in the present.

"Christian, Christian, you light up my life." Christian kicked and smiled, his eyes riveted on Mabel's. Roxy stood and went over to peek in the door of the bar room. There was no one of interest to her so she came back and sat down with Mabel.

"I'm bored silly in the cabin with Christian." she said, sighing and slumping into a heap. "Was there any news come in with the mail today, Mabel?"

Now Mabel was holding Christian high over her head, making ga-ga noises, and shaking him gently. He stared at her with the utmost fascination.

"News is that investors are coming from New York to visit the mines in Caribou. Meantime, more miners are leaving the area to go to Leadville and the Black Hills.", said Mabel, not breaking her stare at Christian.

"I hope we see these men from the East." mused Roxy. "Does Ruby know they are coming?"

"Not yet."

"I'll go tell her now. I hope she'll let me work. Maybe she can charge extra for breast milk."

As preparations were being made for Christmas, the temperature dropped and the wind picked up. Drifts formed on the floor overnight as the snow blew through the cracks and under the doors.

Three big blizzards in a row caused the men at the New Jersey Mine to use a hemp rope tied in Caribou City to guide them to the portal of the mine. Sailors among the Cornish miners fashioned the ropes that brought the men home safely.

The people of Caribou and Cardinal were forced to spend their time indoors, so when the first influenza of the season began, it hit hard. At home, the children were given castor oil. If anyone mentioned a sore throat, the remedy was turpentine in a spoonful of sugar. Not a soul complained, as the remedy was worse than the suffering.

The school children were quick to pass the germs around. The classroom bucket of drinking water and its dipper, had been dubbed the "diphtheria dipper" in the winter of '79, when every family had lost someone. Now the name came back to haunt them. Mabel taught the children to tuck their lower lip inside the cup, so that no saliva would enter the dipper. Still, the children got sick and the school closed early for the holiday.

The week before Christmas was a sad one. Little Mary and Roger Firth both died, along with three children in Caribou, and two miners. Some graves had been dug in the Caribou Cemetery the summer before, and these received the bodies of the miners, who it seemed, had just a few acquaintances to mourn them.

Services were held for the children, and it seemed that the whole world wept as the small pine boxes were lowered into graves chiseled out of ground that was hard as stone. Mabel felt the loss particularly hard. So many hours had been shared with Little Mary and Roger. She pained for lives gone that had only just begun.

Mabel wondered about Goodman. The night Little Mary had died, the fire in the schoolhouse had been impossible to keep burning. As Mabel had struggled with a stove belching smoke, the smog formed a whirlwind that turned slowly in the open space of the classroom. Mabel stood up and watched until it blew itself out. She had never seen anything like it. The next morning, Mabel had learned about Little Mary.

Mabel tried to soften the loss experienced by the children's classmates, but there is a fine line between accepting a death and honoring a life.

As Christmas approached, people tried extra hard to spread good cheer with kind deeds. Each soul was softened by the reflection, that life is fragile and a very precious gift. People talked in hushed tones as they did their Christmas scurrying about the shops in Cardinal and Caribou.

When Christmas Eve came, the feasting and laughter were a welcome relief. John Peregrine came by the schoolhouse early in that evening to pick up Mabel. He spied the little ginger house made by Mabel and Ryan for Goodman.

John ate the peppermint off the top stating that he was sure it would otherwise go to waste.

John and Mabel joined the others at the Hotel for a service performed by an itinerant Minister of the Lord. A huge Christmas tree lit by candles and garlands hung around the walls of the dining room. A warn cinnamon smell drifted in the air.

In true Cardinal style, the service was followed by a Christmas Show, which included the Story of Bethlehem performed by Miss Ruby's girls and Cardinal's six remaining children. After the pageant, everyone joined to sing carols with accompaniment on the piano by Honky Tonk Joe.

The singing turned to dancing, which helped keep the drinking moderate. Parents would remember to be Santa Claus, and the rest of the folks could make it to the Christmas Day service looking respectable.

Outside, the snow piled up into drifts that crept up the first story windows. As John and Mabel walked back up the street to the schoolhouse, snow billowed under Mabel's skirts and soaked her to the knees. She let a blizzard in the front door. Mabel lit her lamp and saw that the ginger house was gone.

"Packrat", said John, as she stood considering the possibilities...

"Merry Christmas!" John said, and he kissed Mabel chastely on the cheek. Then he shuffled carefully down the steps and out into the snowy street. Mabel watched him go through a small melted spy hole she had cleared on the windowpane. She couldn't help wonder if he was feeling lonely.

In the morning, Mabel woke with a cold nose and feet. She put on several layers of extra clothes, and poked at the red hot glowing embers which Goodman had kept burning all night. Mabel had rekindled the fire in the woodstove and climbed back into bed, before she remembered it was Christmas morning.

Mabel kept the covers tight around her chin and stared out at the snow and sky. She wondered how it could be that one given morning could be so much more special than any other. She pondered Jesus. How could any one person have had such a profound influence on so many people for so long?

This special day is about love. All types of love. On a grand scale, the kind of love that one feels for all humanity, but it is also about the love one feels for each individual. It is about loving each person for who they are, despite their differences or their beliefs. And this day is a celebration of the personal loves in our lives–a day to remind us that we are here on earth to practice being more loving.

Mabel thought for a moment of John, then Tyler, and Alexander. All of these loves were very good things. Each man was different, and each enriched her life in his own way. Each filled a special need in her soul.

She thought of Ruby, Roxy and the girls. The love between women is perhaps one of the closest universal bonds ever to be. There are so many truths between women that are simply understood. There are commonalities shared that connect women. Intuition that is innate. Women have a certain unconditional love for each other.

Mabel smiled warmly as she considered the love that she had for the children...Ryan and his classmates, and now Baby Christian. And there was Tyler's family, she reflected, Mabel felt an intense love for them, as they were so important to him...and she loved him. Mabel closed her eyes and remembered Little Mary and Roger. She knew that the love she held for those children would be carried with her forever.

Even though Mabel hadn't darkened the door of a church since she left her father in St. Louis, she knew that she had taken this capacity to love from her upbringing, and it was serving her well. She grinned imagining the faces of the miners as they lit with excitement when Mabel read them their mail. Jesus' message was a lofty one, to love everyone, but Mabel saw it as the truth, and perfect. The more you loved, the more you were loved.

Life itself is worth loving. Everyone had been reminded of that in the past few weeks. How fragile, how precious and how beautiful. Mabel imagined the mountain peaks in the summer sunrise. She relished the feeling of the warmth of the wood fire on her face. Life was a delight to her. She tossed the blankets back and bounded out of bed to get on with Christmas with her friends.

Mabel carried a basket loaded with rosehip candles that she had made as presents. Tucked in with the candles, were cinnamon buns and a few very special presents. Snow had fallen in the night and there wasn't a breath of wind. That in itself was a Christmas gift. Mabel shuffled carefully along Foundit Street to the small cabin where Ryan and Christian lived with their mothers. Smoke curled from the stovepipe. The windows were half buried in snow and half hidden by icicles. Inside, Mabel could hear the bump and thump of Ryan's excitement.

Mabel knocked once then opened the door. She laughed when she saw every square inch of the floor covered with a Christmas morning mess. A small tree with popcorn strings and trinkets graced the cabin. Candles burned on the table, and holly hung around the door.

Ryan shouted, "Mabel! Look!" and jumped up from his new toys. His rough and tumble hug pulled her into the room. In two careful leaps, he was back in position, showing off a game of marbles set carefully in a cleared spot.

The ladies welcomed Mabel with "Merry Christmas" in ringing voices. Violet poured coffee. Roxy blew a kiss to Mabel from her place on the floor, where she sat under a blanket with Christian, who was happily taking this all in.

Mabel watched Ryan. He was totally immersed in his new game with a stream of explanation for Mabel's benefit. She would wait to give him his present. She set the basket by the door and began to dig for the cinnamon rolls. Such a sound naturally arouses the curiosity of a young boy, no matter what he is doing. Ryan leapt to the basket and politely offered to help.

"Mabel", he said eagerly, "I think there is something more in your basket."

Mabel smiled with a bit of a tease and responded "Yes, there is something for Christian in my basket."

She paused, her excitement giving her secret away.

"And for me too!" Ryan hopped up and down. "Me too!"

Mabel held out a small wrapped package. "This is for Christian. Youngest always goes first, but you will have to open it for him. He's too little."

Ryan brought the present to the floor and quickly tore away the paper.

"It's a soft wooly hat, Mabel!" he declared as he bounded over and crammed it on Christian's head. Christian began to howl.

"He doesn't like it! But he will when he's out in a blizzard, I bet."

Now Ryan stood straight and tall right next to the basket. A grin spread from ear to ear. He knew he didn't need to say a word.

Mabel handed him a box with a red ribbon.

"Don't forget to feed it," she said. Ryan's eyes opened wide.

"Thank you, Mabel. Thank you, thank you, thank you. One hundred times, thank you!"

"So open it up!" suggested Mabel impatiently.

With fingers as careful as a person could be, Ryan lifted a toy packrat from the box. His eyes were wide with wonder as he saw that it had a clay wheel underneath it. The wheel was a spool with a string wound around it. A twisted India rubber band was anchored inside to keep pressure on the wheel. Mabel showed Ryan how to set the packrat on the floor, gently lift the string, and stand up straight. Then she worked the string carefully to make the rat run hither and yon. Ryan shrieked with joy, and his feet danced as he anxiously waited his turn.

It was almost noon when they all bundled up and walked down the street to John Peregrine's house. The house was a two story whitewashed clapboard, a sign of the prosperity John hoped to see in the future for Cardinal. The front porch was shoveled clear, and a path led to the street. Pine boughs with large red bows festooned each side of the front door. Large candles lit the four front windows.

"Don't you sure love Christmas?" Ryan asked Mabel, and he squeezed her hand in his.

John greeted his guests with a flourish, and hugs all the way around. He took Christian from Roxy, so she could remove her coat. He planted a special kiss on Mabel's cheek.

The house smelled like every Christmas spice. A goose had been roasting all morning. In the kitchen, Lila, an old Cornish widow, had been cooking since dawn. She was dressed all in white, and wrapped in a white apron. She smiled like an angel when Mabel gave her a hug.

John's Christmas tree was grand, and Ryan ran to it immediately. Around the bottom was a beautifully handcrafted toy train on a track. Ryan lay on the floor to admire it.

"That, my friend, comes from the City of New York. Why, it came to Denver on a train itself. You will find it under my tree each year, and if you treat it respectfully, you are always welcome to play with it."

"It has wheels that really turn!" exclaimed Ryan.

"I have a present for each of you." said John, as he handed out small boxes wrapped in colored paper.

"But Mabel, your gift does not fit in a box, my dear. Stand right here with your eyes closed." He disappeared to the back room and made rustling noises for the longest time.

When he reappeared, he was carrying a lovely pair of skis.

"Oh my!" said Ryan.

"Open your eyes!" John commanded with glee.

Mabel was shocked and completely thrilled. She immediately knew that John understood who she was. These skis affirmed that he appreciated her spirit.

"John!" she gave him a huge hug, "They are the most precious gift I have ever received!"

Mabel ran her hand over the smooth hard ash and felt the polished grain. The skis widened at the middle for the foot, and a leather buckle tightened around the toe and heel.

"I will cut a green limb to steady you, Mabel. I am quite sure you will enjoy them."

"I must try them out this minute!" exclaimed Mabel. Ryan ran to the door with his coat.

Mabel put on everything she had brought, and shouldering the skis, she and Ryan walked up to the top of Foundit Street. The others watched from the safety of the porch. It was quite a while fumbling with the straps that first time, but finally, Mabel began to move. She slid slowly at first, then faster and faster. Ryan ran along beside her until she was too quick for him. He shouted after her as Mabel sailed down the hill. She put her hands on her knees and kept her feet apart. It seemed like the right thing to do. She passed the house at a very good clip, then ditched into the snow in the meadow beyond with a poof of powder for a grand finale. Everyone cheered when Mabel stood up and waved.

"It will take some practice." said Mabel, "But I can't wait! John, I have something for you too."

Mabel's gift to John came in a soft package wrapped in tissue paper and tied with a green ribbon. John sat in his favorite chair with everyone gathered around to watch. As he removed the ribbon, he hung it conveniently on Ryan's neck. Ryan thought it girlie, and pulled it off. John opened the package and held up a beautifully hand tailored white dress shirt made of the finest linen.

"I made it myself", said Mabel, "I almost thought you'd recognize it, you caught me working so many times! I'm quite sure it will fit, but please do try it on for me."

John was beaming as he descended the stairs to show off the shirt.

"May I eat my Christmas dinner in it, if I promise not to spill?" asked John.

As they took their places at the table, John asked Lila to join them for the blessing, which he followed with a very sincere thank you from all to Lila for cooking such a wonderful feast. Ryan peeked toward the kitchen, wondering what kind of a world it was, where the person who cooked the dinner, ate her dinner alone in the kitchen.

After the feast, and a feast it was, John poured a sweet coffee liquor into delicate little crystal glasses for the ladies. Mabel had never had anything like it, and decided it was like eating dessert. But apple pie with whipped cream came next, and everyone felt completely spoiled.

Just as they were getting up from the table, a knock came at the door. Ryan ran to open it, and there stood a cluster of carolers carefully arranged in position. They sang "O little Town of Bethlehem" and "We Three Kings". By then the house was like ice, and with many thanks, the door was closed.

It was dark when Mabel left Roxy, Christian, Violet and Ryan at their cabin, and walked back up the hill to the schoolhouse. She carried her new skis over her shoulder. The streets of town were emptier than Mabel ever remembered seeing them. It was peaceful.

When Mabel went to perk up the fire, it roared to life.

"Thank you, Goodman, and Merry Christmas." She took three hot round river stones off the top of the woodstove and put them into the foot of her bed. As Mabel climbed into bed she considered the wonderful day, her mind drifted everywhere, and eventually to thoughts of Alexander. Where might he be to-night? Dancing in a Mexican cantina? Perhaps, dining with the family of a great land baron, or sleeping under the stars in the desert. Mabel wondered if he ever thought of her. He felt very far away. Her last thoughts though, were of Goodman. She wondered if this special day was special to a ghost. For a few moments, Mabel was sure she smelled rum, and then she fell asleep.

The first five days of March brought endless snowfall in the high coun-try. By now, the schoolhouse, which sat higher than most cabins, was heaped with snow piles on each side of the front steps. The path that was shoveled from the street had walls of snow. Mabel could only reach the woodpile and the outhouse from her back door. She felt like a vole burrowing out along her little paths.

But the snow hadn't stopped the men from New York, who had come to seek investments in the Caribou mines. They had reached Denver by train, then Boulder, followed by stage to Brownsville, and now Caribou by sleigh.

The word was that they had left New York anticipating spring. Now, they had not left the hotel in Caribou for three days. They were speculating on mines that were a half-mile away, but had not the adventurous spirit to venture out to see them. Finally, on the fourth day, Saturday, the three men had taken the noon sleigh from Caribou down to Cardinal, and met, by prior arrangement, with some of Ruby's girls. They checked into rooms in the hotel, and hadn't been seen since. They were taking their meals upstairs.

Mabel had Christian all day at the schoolhouse. He had been an angel baby, but now it was wearing thin for both of them. Mabel guessed things were going well over at the hotel. She wondered why Roxy wasn't feeling the need for Christian because he was out of patience waiting. Mabel warmed more goat milk and soaked a cotton cloth with it for the baby to suck. They sat in the lamplight working in this fashion for quite some time. Mabel expected to hear footsteps at the door anytime.

Christian slowed his frantic pace after a while, and stared off toward the ceiling. He was watching something, but Mabel couldn't figure out what it was. His eyes tracked something that moved back and forth. At first, he would smile and giggle then he grew sleepier and sleepier, until he was sound asleep in Ma-bel's lap. Mabel waited for him to give a big sigh and carefully set him in her bed while she stoked the fire for the night. She blew out the light, and crawled under the covers next to Christian.

It was light outside when they awoke. Roxy had still not come. By now, Mabel knew she would take Christian to the hotel so she quickly dressed then bundled Christian up for the cold walk down the street. Mabel was mad, and Christian was hungry.

By the time they reached Ruby's room, Christian was crying nonstop. Ruby appeared in a disheveled state, glared at Mabel and Christian, then stomped past them to room six. She rapped loudly on the door three times, then stormed back past, disappearing into her room.

In just a minute, Roxy emerged. Her face showed not one particle of guilt. She looked drunk on love. Mabel thrust the baby into her arms, and went downstairs without a word. No words were needed, for Christian said it all.

In the lobby, a man stopped Mabel.

"Miss Gurkin, would you mind writing a letter for me this morning? I must get word to the east by U.S Mail."

Mabel had to unruffle herself. She gained enough composure to say it would be her pleasure.

"Excellent.", said the man, "I will get paper and ink."

The letter turned out to be a personal correspondence to this miner's dear mother, assuring her that her son was well and that his claim had been patented. He sent his love to a multitude of relatives and hoped to be sending money by spring. Mabel was glad to help, so when the miner asked what he could offer in return, Mabel had to think for a moment. She surprised herself by saying, "I am looking for an old pair of trousers."

"Pardon me, mam?" responded the miner.

"Yes, trousers, sir. Perhaps you have an old pair that you could pass down for a friend of mine." Now she felt very silly, but she was quite serious.

"I do have a pair of wool trousers. I can leave here at the hotel for you. I never use them anyhow. They'd be dress pants. Suppose they'll do, Miss Gurkin?"

Sizing him up, she replied, "I am sure that they will be just fine. I will look forward to receiving them, sir."

"Thank you so much for writing for me, mam. My mother thanks you too." The man bowed with a flourish, then beamed a toothless grin.

Mabel walked back to the schoolhouse with a smile. She would have a pair of trousers to wear under her skirt when she skied.

The month of March brought more snow than anyone could imagine. Mabel felt fortunate to have her skis, and not feel cooped up with the cabin fever that most people were experiencing. The men were faring better than the women, as they would venture out to the mines, chop wood out in the fresh air, and had more mobility to move between towns. But the women were showing signs of discontent. They spoke fondly of farms back east and fine things in the city. Ruby's girls were drinking more than was good for them. Mabel worried more than once that Roxy would leave Cardinal on an impulse and never return.

Mabel's policy was to hold school each weekday no matter what the weather. If she could keep the children busy until spring, everyone would make it through the winter without wringing each other's necks. The energy of a grade schooler could not be contained in a Cardinal cabin.

On Saturday morning, it was Mabel's turn to get outside. She stepped into her long underwear and pulled them up over her long thin legs. As she slid the miner's dress pants over her hips, she giggled thinking how different her life was than most. The trousers were perfect! Her anticipation of skis gliding over the fresh snow filled Mabel with an excitement that made her spirit soar.

Mabel tied the bottom of her pant legs snuggly around her boots using twine. She put a hot baked potato in her pocket, and headed out the door. The sun was beginning to warm the day, and it promised to be a beautiful one. Mabel scraped the snow from the bottom of her boots and carefully fit each boot into a metal toe piece on the skis. She had mastered the leather straps and arranged them tightly without a struggle. Off she went on the ski track that she had been using all winter.

The track followed the edge of the high mountain meadow, which cradled Cardinal above the world. It wound up hill toward Caribou, skirting along the edge of the north facing pine forest. The wind deposited huge amounts of snow at the base of the ridge, and Mabel's skis glided over the tops of the drifts. To Mabel's enjoyment, each night, the wind freshened the tracks with powder snow.

At one point, the trail crossed Coon Track Creek. The creek was deeply buried with only a sunken crease in the snow to trace its course. Mabel always paused here to listen to the gurgle of water from below. From this spot, it was a climb into the forest to the south. Mabel had learned to slow her pace just a bit, and breathe steadily as she went up the hill. She set each ski firmly, with determination, keeping her hands out in front.

When the trail leveled off, Mabel broke into long smooth strides again. She traversed the mountainside heading west through the trees. The wind would whistle overhead, blowing the early morning away. In the trees, it was calm. Mabel startled a baby vole. It ran across her path, so she stopped. It ran up over the first ski, skittering along the inside of the second one. Mabel watched with delight, as the tiny vole scampered over the tail of that ski and off into the safety of the forest.

By and by, the trail came to an overlook at the meadow at Caribou City. Homes and businesses filled the valley and its surrounding hills. Smoke rose from each chimney and disappeared to the east. Above her on the hillside, Mabel could hear clanking from the New Jersey Mine. Just below her, through a few trees, Mabel could see the round pen at Tyler's stable. It was built on a knoll that was licked clean by the wind.

The figures of a man and a horse were familiar to Mabel. She stood still for a long while, watching the timeless dance they performed with each other. The man held his hands in front and stepped smoothly as he rotated. The horse, ever vigilant, kept its head held high and its nose tipped a tad toward the man. She pranced in a circle about the man, holding herself just this side of control.

The two were silhouettes of form. As the man gave an imperceptible signal, the horse changed direction. She was light on her feet and moved effortlessly. Mabel watched, paralyzed by the grace of this relationship between man and horse.

When the man lowered his hands to his sides, the horse slowed, and trotted toward him. She approached the man, as if asking for more. She set her head on his shoulder. The man hung his arm affectionately about her neck. The two paused for a long moment, and then the man walked toward the gate with the horse following gently behind. At the gate, the horse stood to let the man pass first. She trailed him into the stable.

Mabel sprung her weight onto her skis and she glided down the hill toward the rough-hewn building.

"Tyler!" Mabel called from out on the snow.

In less than a minute, Tyler stood, eyes blinking, in the doorway of the stable, a big grin on his tanned face. He removed his hat, and his sandy blonde hair stood ruffled in peaks.

"I was watching you lunge her, she's looking good."

"What brings you up to Caribou today, my sweet?" he asked, adding a wink that made Mabel giggle.

"Just getting out. And how are you, and the children and Lucinda?"

"We are fine; the kid's noses are running. We're wintering over, we are." Tyler's words seemed detached from his mind, his eyes locked on Mabel with that look he always gave her when they were alone.

"Cardinal's got some cabin fever going. I'm lucky to be able to get out on my skis. It sure makes all the difference in the world. They are all drinking like fish down there. "

"To be honest, I'm not sure Lucinda's coping well herself. I know she misses her family, and it's an easier life back in St. Louis...but heck Mabel, she knew what she was signing up for."

"Maybe, Tyler." Mabel contemplated, "I don't know that anyone in St. Louis can really imagine Caribou. It's the place where the wind is born."

"Well, look at you. You love it here. You, with your skis!" he smiled.

"But I didn't follow someone here for love. And I'm not stuck in a cabin with two small children, day in and day out. I've got all kinds of people in my life, Tyler. Right now they just happen to be drunk," she added in jest, "but they're good company all the same."

"Did I tell you how beautiful you are today?" Tyler changed the subject.

Mabel shook her head, blushed and giggled. She loved this man and hoped that he would never change.

Just then, Tyler's stable boy came around the corner from the street. A hard breeze blew snow around in a whirlwind, dusting them all with wetness. Then it was gone again.

"I'm off!" said Mabel, giving herself a push with her long thin ski pole. Tyler waved and smiled, never taking his eyes off of her.

"It's all downhill from here", Mabel called out, for it was, all the way to the schoolhouse.

❧

The moon was full. It lit the snow, making the night as bright as daylight. Mabel plunged out of the hotel into the fresh air. The music and laughter dimmed as the door shut heavily. Mabel made her way home with the sounds of wild partying fading behind her.

The Honky Tonk Show had once again degenerated into dancing. A snip of liquor had loosened Mabel's legs. Oh, how she loved to dance. And how many schoolteachers were afforded such privilege? Mabel had lasted long into the night, until her legs reminded her that she had skied the day away. Maybe those legs deserved a rest.

Mabel's woodstove just needed a poke, and another log and then the fire danced alive with spirit. Mabel crawled happily into bed. The moon outside was so brilliant, Mabel could not close her eyes. She pulled the covers around her neck, and stared out the window at the brilliant white moonlit snow.

So many thoughts raced in her head. Mabel's body passed out, but her mind was filled with fascination and wonderment of the life that was hers. How could it be that there were so many other souls in this world? Could each be feeling that their life was as incredible as her experience? Mabel imagined people all over the world, and reminded herself that she was just one of so many. If she could hold awareness of that fact, how beautifully humbling.

Mabel thought for what seemed like a long while, about Roxy and the man from New York. She doubted that Roxy would ever be quite the same. She had had a taste of something that was rare in these parts, and now all she could want was more. How would Christian ever fit into this new fever? How would Roxy make it through the winter?

As the trees danced in the mountain wind, Mabel appreciated the shelter of the schoolhouse. She rose to stoke the fire with a big knotty log, and closed off the air to bank the coals. Mabel crawled back beneath the heavy covers, imagining wistfully what it would be like to take a man into bed with her.

Her thoughts fleeted directly to one man, and that was Alexander. It seemed to Mabel that she could imagine it exactly. Just how it would be. Not that she had a lot of experience in these matters, but it seemed she had recognized a progression that unfolded when two bodies came together in union. There would be attentiveness, prolonged and hungry; so sweet and so fine. Then there would be the period of sharing and pleasing, when the mind exists only in moment. With Alexander, she imagined, this could go on for eternity. And she would love that. The heat and passion would ebb and flow until both were quite done. This thought made Mabel draw a breath that sent her to another time and place. Afterwards, Alexander would fall into a deep slumber, but the Mabel would lay awake savoring love. Mabel's final thought, last before she slept, was the pondering of an age old mystery. Why did men always fall asleep afterwards? Surely it was the same kind of unexplainable mystery as why people make each other yawn.

Moonlight shone through the window of Tyler's house in Caribou, and lit Jake's pale little face into a white glow. The child had come down with a fever after dinner, and spent several hours burning up in delirium. Now Tyler held him in the rocking chair. Jake laid limp, sleeping, his lungs weakly drawing each breath. Tyler's head nodded to the side, he had drifted off long enough for the fire to get low. Lucinda had finally gone to sleep.

Tyler gently rose from the rocker, cradling Jake's small form in position. As he laid him on bunk bed, Jake opened his eyes and looked at Tyler. Tyler realized immediately that Jake could not draw a breath. Jake's gaze was fixed on Tyler. There was no panic in his son's expression. He just closed his eyes and left.

"Jake! Jake, no!" Tyler held him up quickly. His little son hung lifeless.

"Jake!" Tyler shouted. Lucinda sat up and cried out.

Tyler ran the boy outside into the cold night, as he had heard was done for the croup. But Jake was gone. Tyler shook him and pleaded with him. He begged God for mercy.

Lucinda hung on the door sobbing frantically. Time seemed to warp. Tyler knew that nothing would ever be the same. He hugged Jake tightly to his chest and came back inside. Tyler sat Lucinda on the bed and handed her their son. Jake seemed to be all arms and legs as there was no life force within him. Lucinda felt Jake's spirit in her chest. His essence held her heart firmly and the message came clearly to her. "It's alright, Mother. It is divine." But Lucinda cried out harder. Nothing would ever be the same again.

When the dawn finally came that morning, there was no warmth in it. Baby Alice woke to find that her brother had died in the night. She sat on her Mama's lap with her head cocked sideways and she didn't make a sound. Lucinda was holding her tightly. They sat silently, watching Jake as he lay prone beneath the covers in Mama's bed.

Tyler put on a coat, hat and gloves and went out find Doc Ritter, who was also the coroner. The world had stopped. He stood for a moment in the cold morning and hung his head. The first sunbeams of the day shone on the frozen snow making it sparkle at Tyler's feet. He felt he had been left behind. The memory of the night seemed surreal to Tyler, and somehow the veil to the heavens seemed thin.

Before school was to start that morning in Cardinal, Mr. Randy came to the schoolhouse from Caribou on horseback. As he hitched his mare to the post, Mabel watched from the front window. She knew someone had died in the night.

The children of Cardinal brought the energy of the coming spring into the classroom. Mabel had to jolt herself back to that reality. But the day wore on long, and her thoughts never left Tyler and Lucinda. Mabel's heart was saturated with pain. The children's voices seemed louder that day, as if to declare "We are still here and life goes on!" And indeed it does, whether we feel like it or not. Mabel swallowed the lump in her throat, and made it through the day.

After school, Mabel walked to the Lutheran Church, which sat just below the ridge at the top of Caribou. She sat for a long time in the wooden pew with her head bowed. It was a time when thoughts are prayer. In the end, Mabel did ask God specifically to wrap Lucinda and Tyler in a healing white light to protect them and guide them through the interminable grief they must be feeling. Mabel prayed that Tyler be comforted by the love that she held for him, and she sent out a strong ray of that love hoping he could feel it.

Mabel walked to the home of the Lutheran minister. He was gone to visit Tyler and Lucinda, but his wife was home. They spoke about the church ladies bringing meals to the family. Mabel offered her services and signed up to bring dinner the following Wednesday. By the time Mabel returned to Cardinal, the spring snow on the roads had turned to bumpy solid ice. She thought of calling on John Peregrine for company, but the treacherous roads had turned her instincts toward home. It had been a long day.

On Wednesday, Mabel borrowed John's horse and rode up to Caribou. She kept one hand safeguarding a pot of elk stew and oatmeal rolls were wrapped in a blanket tied to the horse's saddle. When no one answered her knock at the door, Mabel decided to leave the food inside. She was startled to find that Lucinda was home, wrapped in a quilt and lying in front of the fireplace.

"Lucinda", Mabel spoke quietly. Lucinda sat and turned toward Mabel. Her eyes were sunken in deep black rings and her eyebrows were knitted in pain. Lucinda leaned up on her arm, staying tethered to the floor, and tried to smile graciously before slumping back down into a heap. Her gaze was distant and she did not speak.

Mabel took off her boots and brought the dinner to stay warm by the fire. She sat on the floor behind Lucinda and put her hand on the woman's back.

"I was so sorry to hear." she said, and Lucinda began to sob.

"It's good to cry." said Mabel, feeling tears roll off her own cheeks. The two women sat together for a long time. There were no words that could bring hope. The sun was setting when Tyler came back from the stable with Alice. He smiled when he saw Mabel, but Mabel could see his heart was bleeding profusely. Lucinda sat up and Alice plopped into her lap.

"Mabel has been so kind to sit with me," offered Lucinda, her soul sounding empty.

"There is dinner here, Tyler." Mabel pointed to the pot over the fire. She rose and walked to the door where Tyler stood.

"I'm so sorry, Tyler. He was such a fine boy." Mabel reached for his hands and gave them a squeeze. She looked into Tyler's exhausted face and was instantly consumed by his sorrow. His firstborn son was gone.

"We will miss him, Mabel. Desperately. It was so quick. He was sick only a few days. Not even so sick really...until the end."

"It has been so sudden; it's hard to believe he's gone." Mabel affirmed.

Mabel could see that neither Lucinda nor Tyler had an appetite. She set the table for three. Mabel held out her arms to Alice, and Alice came to her without a fuss. Alice seemed to think Mabel was a rescue angel. Mabel pushed the baby's high chair into the table tightly and handed her a roll. Alice still had an appetite.

When the food was on the table, Mabel said, "I must get John's horse back before he worries. Please send for me if you need anything at all."

"Thank you, Mabel. You are very kind. We'll make it through this." Tyler's expression showed Mabel deep gratitude.

She squeezed his hands again, and nodded understanding. She knew it would be a long time before this little family would be okay. She hoped she had made this one day a little softer.

Mabel arrived at John's stable just as true darkness set in, and she was glad to see the warm light in John's kitchen.

The service for Jacob Tyler Stevens was held at noon. He was buried on a knoll that was blown free of snow in the graveyard at Caribou. The hard rock miners had chipped out a tiny grave. Over the winter, many had died of diphtheria and scarlet fever. On the warmer days, those bodies, now occupying a temporarily sacred spot in the wood shed behind the church, would be beginning to thaw. As soon as the ground softened at all, many new graves would have to be dug. Mabel knew this extra effort was made to comfort Tyler and Lucinda.

Mabel recalled the miner in early November, who was digging several graves at once. He himself was so sick, that he commented to his partner, "I'll dig one for me self. You'll be needing it by mornin'". Indeed, he died in the night. It had been a long winter and influenza had again taken its toll on Caribou.

Tyler and Lucinda stood with the Minister on the far side of the hole. Bagpipes crooned a single dirge as people assembled on the dried grass. Head stones from years past stuck up through the snowdrifts, as reminders of our impermanence on this earth. Tyler held Alice in his arms. Jake lay in a small pine box in the ground. One by one, people came forward to pay their respects, some dropping a trinket or treat onto the box. The minister spoke kind words praising God for sharing this life with the world, and reminding everyone that it is the most difficult thing for a child to pass before his parents.

A white stone marked Jake's resting place. The epitaph read, "This little bud was given to us to bud on earth and bloom in heaven".

As empty as Mabel's home felt when she returned, she knew Tyler's home felt emptier.

April was a difficult month. The sunny days teased of spring but the wind still blew cold and relentlessly. On the mountains above, it was truly winter with the depths of snow accumulated from the season. Down below, the Boulder Canyon road was almost impassable. The sleighs were retired, but the stages were quagmired in mud. Food supplies were down to the nub. Everyone was sick of dried meat and tack and pancakes with jam. The potatoes were almost gone. Most days in April, the mail arrived on horseback.

When the rider came up the Gulch from Coon Track Creek to Cardinal, he personally delivered a letter to his favorite gal, Roxy. The letter was from New York, and it was in an envelope made of linen paper with a red wax seal. Roxy rushed upstairs without taking a breath. Mr. Dalby had sent for her, and she knew she would go.

Roxy was to travel to Denver, where she would stay two nights at the Brown Palace Hotel. The letter included the address of a tailor who was at her service to fit her in traveling clothes. Mr. Dalby wrote that Roxy would have another tailor upon her arrival in New York. She was to rest up in Denver for the train ride east, and look forward to a reunion she would never forget.

When Roxy left her home the next morning, Christian was sitting in his high chair throwing breakfast at Ryan and laughing. She had kissed him on the cheek and received a pat with a handful of oatmeal in return. Ryan was to bring Christian to Mrs. Apple when the eight o'clock mine whistle blew, then get himself to school promptly. Mrs. Apple would find the note in the diaper bag.

As she looked back up the hill at the small log cabin, Roxy tried to picture the next time she would see Christian, but an image wouldn't come. She hustled down the road to catch the early stage. It would make good time to Boulder, passing over the frozen mud.

Before school was out for the day, John Peregrine came up the front steps and waited politely inside the door. Mabel knew there was good reason for such an interruption. She let the children outside to play.

"Mabel", John didn't know how to start. "I am finding myself in an extremely awkward situation. Roxy has gone to New York to be the mistress of Randolph Dalby. I don't expect we'll ever see her again."

Mabel cocked her head to one side, trying to fathom what was happening.

"Roxy has left Christian in my care." added John, and then he paused to let Mabel absorb this news.

"In your care?" asked Mabel completely confused. She struggled with an image of the big six-month-old baby crying in John's arms.

"What are you telling me, John?" Mabel was incredulous. "How could a mother leave her baby?"

"I am telling you that Mrs. Apple found a note stating that Roxy is gone. It said she trusts that John Peregrine will be sure Christian's needs will be cared for in the future."

"You are Christian's father?" Mabel asked in disbelief.

John laughed, and briefly held Mabel's hands in his.

"Absolutely not!" he declared, "I believe I am simply a safe choice, a man with resources and a kind heart. I am not sure what to do next."

"Certainly, we will send for her return." suggested Mabel.

"Certainly." John echoed hopelessly.

Two weeks had passed by with not a lead on Roxy. Ryan and Mabel sat in the fading sun on the large rock outcrop just south of John's house. They looked out over the deep valley of Coon Track Creek below them. The back door slammed behind John as he emerged from the house carrying Christian. He hoisted the boy to his shoulders and held the little hands tightly as he walked up the hill toward Ryan and Mabel.

"We'll take good care of him." said Ryan.

"Very good care." said Mabel.

"We'll take good care of him." said Ryan again louder and stronger this time.

"Very good care of him." added John smiling. He removed the baby from his shoulders and sat down to enjoy the sunset with the others.

Mabel felt her back giving out. She switched Christian to the other hip. She wondered if it was easier for mothers who had held their babies from infancy.

"Christian", she commented, "you are heavier than a sack of flour."

He looked about, as if he knew that they were waiting for the stagecoach. Mrs. Apple had gone shopping in Caribou, and was due back soon. Mabel finally set Christian on the platform at her feet.

"It's going to be a long while before you learn to walk, my friend. How will we ever manage?"

Just as the stage came around the corner, a whirlwind of dust blew through. The people on the platform blinked their eyes and turned. Mabel grabbed Christian and he began to howl.

Mrs. Apple was a short woman and large enough to require assistance getting down from the stage. A gentleman held out his hand to her. She stretched one foot down toward the little step on the coach, but couldn't reach. The other foot was no more successful. There was an embarrassing moment as the gentleman had to find additional assistance, and then the two men hoisted her by the upper arms to the platform. They held her a moment to be sure she stabilized.

"Oh dear", said Mrs. Apple to Mabel. "I bought too many packages. Wait till you see!"

"And this baby needs a mule of his own to get back up the hill." said Mabel.

A wiry little man climbed effortlessly to the top of the stage and handed down package after package. When the stage left for Boulder, and the crowd cleared away, Mabel stood helplessly looking at a particularly large box and sighed.

"Mrs. Apple", she finally said, "You hold Christian, while I go into the hotel and find us some help."

Mrs. Apple smiled graciously and extending her arms, welcomed Christian into her large bosom. He leaned over happily, throwing his full weight toward her. Mabel almost dropped him, and then she went into the hotel shaking her head and laughing to herself. What an interesting turn life had taken for all of them.

As Mabel rang the service bell at the counter, a door opened upstairs on the mezzanine. A cowboy backed from a room, replacing his hat. As he turned around, Mabel recognized him immediately. It was Alexander.

Mabel was frozen, realizing what Alexander had been up to. She didn't want to ring the bell again. And no one else was in sight. Alexander paused when he saw Mabel.

For an instant he looked sheepish, and then he straightened himself and headed for the stairs. Alexander didn't speak until he stood in front of Mabel.

"Mabel", he took her hand and kissed it. "You are the woman I have come back to Cardinal to see."

"I am obviously not the only one." Mabel responded. Her heart had stopped. Pain paralyzed her. Inside, she was devastated. Mabel drew a breath and held onto the counter. Still, no one had appeared to help.

Alexander's look softened from intensity into shame. He took her hand again, and she looked away, biting her lip.

"I have thought of you so often, Mabel. I was anxious to get back to Cardinal to see you. I didn't expect it to be like this. Forgive me, Mabel."

Alexander looked so wonderful, and made her so mad.

Mabel struggled with her conflicting perceptions until, overwhelmed, she stomped outside. Alexander stood gathering his sensibilities.

On the platform, Mrs. Apple had set Christian down and was sharing treats with him. Christian sat with one hand on the platform and the other in his mouth. A stream of candy colored drool ran down his chin to his belly, and he beamed at Mabel. Mabel looked at the two of them and fought the impulse to run.

"Did you find us a boy?" asked Mrs. Apple.

Before Mabel could muster an answer, Alexander appeared at her side. He stared hard at the baby, who smiled and squirmed then turned his head away from Alexander. Mabel had a child. The math didn't seem right. He composed himself.

"Please allow me to introduce myself." He shook Mrs. Apple's hand.

"My name is Alexander Buck. It appears that you ladies need a hand."

Alexander stacked himself up with more packages than a person should be able to hold, then offered, "Where to?"

Mabel smiled with delight despite herself. She picked up Christian and began to march up the hill toward John Peregrine's house.

Alexander, hiding behind the large stack of packages, struggled to count the months backwards in his head. He knew he hadn't been gone that long.

Just as Alexander was ready to set the load down and get his bearings, Mabel said, "I will get the gate. Be careful now."

As Alexander set the packages on the front porch, he remembered John Peregrine's house. He was confused all over again. Scratching his head, and straightening his back, he glanced back down the hill and saw the older woman slowly making her way up. He decided to take advantage of this moment alone with Mabel, who was setting the baby down on the parlor floor. He stepped inside.

"So it appears that you are Mrs. Peregrine."

"That would be presumptuous of you." was Mabel's retort. Alexander smiled curiously.

"Well, this is rather confusing. It seems that someone has taken up residence with John Peregrine, and started a nice little family as well." Alexander looked Mabel in the eyes and saw indignant hurt.

He approached her slowly and gently took her hands in his, never taking his eyes from hers.

"It seems that nothing is as it appears today." he said.

Mabel nodded. A tear welled up and ran down her cheek.

"Do you have time to walk and talk with me?" Alexander inquired, glancing toward Mrs. Apple.

Mabel nodded again, and bit her lip. She pulled her hands back and began to bring the packages inside.

Mrs. Apple came in the gate. Alexander helped carry the last of the load into the kitchen. Mabel put Christian in the high chair with a piece of bread, and kissed him on his sticky cheek.

"I'll be off now, Mrs. Apple. Mr. Buck has just returned from a long trip. He has much to tell me and has offered to buy me an ice cream." said Mabel, her voice sounding thin.

Alexander smiled at Mabel, and then kissed Mrs. Apple on the hand.

"It's been my pleasure." he told her. Mrs. Apple blushed and giggled.

"Mine too!" she simpered.

As Mabel and Alexander walked into the street, Mabel's mind flamed with jealousy. How could he have been with another woman? But then, he had been gone for six months. Of course he had been with other women. Mabel felt like a fool. How could he have the nerve to visit one of Ruby's girls in Cardinal? But then, half the married men in Caribou acted that way. Mabel knew that any man she could love would be true to her. That was it. Alexander simply was not who she had hoped he was.

Her face felt twisted and tight. Mabel hated the way she was feeling. She hated that she cared so much. She put her nose in the air and told herself that this too shall pass.

Alexander spoke first. "Slow down, Mabel, let me explain."

Mabel realized she was striding out ahead in an angry walk. Checking herself, Mabel squeezed her fists, closed her eyes and took a very deep breath. Why did she have to care so much? She turned toward Alexander and faced him. She knew why. He had been more fun and excitement than she had ever expected to find in her life.

"Mabel" Alexander took her hand and spoke to her eyes with conviction. "It had been a long time since I had been with a woman. It's all men or trouble between here and Mexico. You are the gal I thought of while I was gone. You are the girl I left behind. You are the girl I came back to see. You have been in my heart all these months. I am not in Carson City or Cripple Creek right now, am I? I am here in Cardinal because I wanted to see you."

Mabel could tell his words came from the heart, but sleeping with a hussy! It didn't add up! She couldn't think of a response before Alexander continued.

"Mabel, there are different kinds of women. You know that. You are the kind that a fellow would marry. I honor that about you. I couldn't just, well, let's say I think I'd be lucky to get a kiss this summer, wouldn't I? No disrespect to you. It's to your credit, it is who you are." Alexander realized that he had better stop talking before he backed himself into a corner.

"Alexander, you are a trapper and a traveler. You are not the marrying kind, so I think you've got eyes for the wrong girl."

"I'm not so sure about myself, so how can you be?" Alexander offered a gentle smile.

"I can see it in your spirit, Alexander. You wouldn't last a week of winter here in Cardinal and you'd be itching to go."

"Perhaps you're right about that. But I'm young enough and keeping an open mind. There's no a man on earth that doesn't think about settling down. Not that I am right now, of course. But Mabel, the point is I am here to see you."

"Me and who ever she was!"

Mabel was instantly embarrassed and turned, wanting to run away. Her heart crippling her legs, she began to cry.

Alexander turned Mabel around by the shoulders.

'Let's walk." he said.

"No ice cream." said Mabel. "I am a mess."

"Mabel," said Alexander, "I never meant to hurt you."

At that moment, Mabel knew this was true. Her heart softened, and Mabel realized that she would forgive Alexander.

They walked on the road toward Caribou, carefully talking of the winter past. The road wound around the side of the Boulder County Hill, through a thick forest of spruce and fir, until it overlooked the valley of Coon Track Creek. Below them, the new growth on the aspen trees was spring green. To Mabel, it seemed to be a color full of hope. Mabel reminded herself that she was lucky to have Alexander in her life.

It was the hours when Mabel was alone that she pondered Alexander's actions and his needs. How was it, that men could so easily separate sex from love? Apparently they were different than women, yet they seemed to desire a relationship of intimacy and emotional security. Mabel had watched countless men disappear behind doors with Ruby's girls, but it always seemed to her that their hearts must come out empty. Try as she might, Mabel couldn't shake the image of Alexander closing the door up on the mezzanine. All she knew was that her heart hurt.

Mabel poured wax into the candle moulds, thinking of Alexander riding endless trails through hot scrubby brush. She sewed shirtsleeves, thinking of his gentle eyes looking into hers. He sure seemed to care about her. Mabel washed the oil lamp chimneys, considering her plight of being "the kind a fellow would marry". Would she ever get the loving attention she craved? How could Alexander have taken that attention to someone else, and felt right about it? Mabel lost herself in kneading bread, feeling heartache, confusion, and love.

As Mabel placed the largest log she could fit into the woodstove, the fire snapped and burned furiously.

"Don't give me false hope, Goodman." she said, shrugging off the funny feeling of Goodman's presence. Mabel dampened the fire down for the night and crawled into her bed...

When spring came to Caribou City, it was very subtle. Tyler had first noticed it in the length of the days. As he left the white washed clapboard house that morning, green grass was daring to poke up along the south facing side. Later, he always wondered if he had pointed it out to Lucinda, if it would have made a difference.

But, from inside, the sprigs of green and the budding catkins on the aspen trees were not convincing. Nor was the temperature, indoors or out. Even in May the woodstove was not out long enough to remove the ashes. The snow that blew sideways off the Great Divide melted into the muddy ruts in the street. It stuck to huge drifts that still graced the north sides of everything.

Lucinda opened the steamer trunk. She had made the list in her mind so many times before, but now that she had decided to go, Lucinda realized she wouldn't take anything but their travelling clothes. The trunk was full of more linens than a person could use in a lifetime. Each white cotton edge stitched to perfection with flowers and lace. A testament to the fact that there was a reason she was losing her mind.

"I'm ridin' to St. Louis, Mudder. I pack up. I pack up.", repeated Alice. "Here dis. Here dis too, an dis, an dis too."

Alice heaved two cloth dolls and a small wooden horse into the trunk. Lucinda packed her largest handbag with diapers and Alice's clothes. She added crackers and raisins. From the top cupboard, she took the Western Union envelope which held just enough money to make it home. Then she sat down to write the note.

Of all the words she had rehearsed night after midnight as the wind shook the house, none seemed available now.

"I will be at Mother's in St. Louis." she wrote, and left it on the table in the kitchen.

"Carry these two dollies." Lucinda said to Alice. They both stood looking around the kitchen as if they were forgetting something.

"Bye-bye house. Bye-bye Jacob. Bye-bye Daddy." recited Lucinda for Alice.

"Bye-bye do-do. Bye-bye, Da Da. Bye-bye. Bye-bye. Bye-bye."

The ten o'clock stage took them from Caribou to Central City, with a brief stop in Cardinal to pick up the mail.

It was at suppertime that Tyler came home to find he had lost everything. He knew there was no point in chasing her. Lucinda was dying of a broken heart in Caribou. He knew she would never be back.

Tyler rode his mare bareback across the Caribou Flats, until daylight was waning, then he went home to the empty house. His heart felt as lonesome as a heart could be.

The sun was just peeking over the eastern horizon when John woke to the noise. He sat straight up in bed until he recognized the sound. It was a booming, cheerful voice, louder than anyone should be making at that hour of the day. It was little Christian, practically singing about something. Suddenly, John remembered, this was Sunday, and Mrs. Apple was gone to her sister's house. John lay back down and listened from his pillow. It was awfully early.

"Oh, oh, oh, oh...ga, gaaaa, ga, gaaaaa. Ab, ab, ab, ab...Da, Da, da, da. Da, Da, Da, Da!" It was getting even louder. But it was happy talk, so John just lay in his bed and listened.

He could hear big movement coming from Christian's crib, and John knew he was jumping and crashing. Christian would laugh at himself, and mutter as he got back up. John was amused. And he was amused at himself. Here he was almost forty years old, without a wife, and he had taken on charge of a child that wasn't even his. And he was enjoying this morning sound, this cheerful welcoming of the day.

"Dada...DA, DA, DAAA...DA...DA!", then there was a thump and a loud cry. This cry was not going to go away. So John got out of bed and staggered down the hall to Christian's room. Christian stood hanging onto the rungs of the crib with a tight grip. He had taken off his sleepers and was freezing in his wet diaper. His crib sheets were wet too. He looked at John, and started to cry harder.

John spoke softly to Christian as he lifted him from the crib. He told Christian that he was new at this, but not to be alarmed because in a little while, it would be breakfast time and Mabel would be coming to help him.

He carried the wet baby to the changing table. John thought this might be his biggest challenge. Christian lay flat on his back, very still and said something to John in baby talk. John answered, "Ah, yeah, yeah." and smiled at Christian. Christian laughed hard at this, so John did it again.

John slid the dry diaper under Christian's bottom, and over lapped the side cloths, just like Mrs. Apple had shown him. He managed the first pin beautifully.

"Look at that!" he bragged to Christian, "Nothing to it!"

But quick as a blink, Christian rolled over and was getting up.

"Oh, no.", said John, "We're not done yet." He laid Christian back down, but now the diaper was off and Christian was on his way back up. John realized he had never really gotten him back down.

John grabbed Christian under the armpits. Such a miniature person, he thought. With a mind of his own, he admitted, as he laid him more firmly on his back this time. But again Christian had rolled over and was getting away. The diaper fell to the floor.

John lowered Christian to the floor, and reached for the diaper. Christian shrieked with joy, looked at John, and then crawled away as fast as he could.

"You vixen!" cried John, as he gave chase. Christian was laughing as John grabbed him, but like a greased pig, Christian wriggled loose and was on the move again. This time, John was determined, but he himself was laughing too hard. He stopped for a moment and gathered his wits. When he tackled Christian, he was ready with the diaper, and pinned the baby down gently to the floor with one knee.

Victorious, John wrestled Christian into the wooly diaper cover and into a clean flannel baby suit. John released Christian onto the floor and sat down to take a rest. All this before breakfast, he thought. Christian was headed for the stairs.

In the kitchen, John stoked last night's fire in the cook stove. He handed Christian a piece of wood, which he began chewing on.

"Oh, wait fella!" John tried to take the wood. "We can do better than that."

Christian held on tightly and gave John a devilish smile. John traded him some raisins for the wood.

It was still hours before Mabel would arrive for Sunday breakfast. John knew he'd better feed the little tyke. Christian crawled over to the cupboard with the pots and pans, while John carefully measured out oatmeal for two. Pans began crashing out of the cupboard and onto the floor. A steady stream of excited talk came from Christian.

John looked on in amazement as Christian began to bang two pot lids together. Had someone taught him this, or was it an innate ability of all young boys? John could only tolerate a few minutes of this. He opened the back door and let the cat in. Christian threw the lids and crawled after the cat.

When the oatmeal was done, John sat Christian in the high chair. He tied a bib on the baby and sat down with the bowl of oatmeal and spoon.

"Here you go, Christian." said John offering a spoonful toward the mouth.

Christian reached out, and quickly as a snake, grabbed the oatmeal with his hand. He held the spoon tightly and made a squeezing face at John. When he released the spoon, he rubbed his hand in his hair. John made a face back at Christian.

"Okay, let's try again." offered John.

This time, John held the spoon back at a distance and taunted a little. He opened his mouth instinctively and Christian did too. Then John shoved the spoonful into Christian's mouth as quickly as possible. Christian took the bite and smiled. Then he squeezed the oatmeal back out the corners of that smile, and on down his front.

"Okay, little buddy, enough of this, I think it's time you learned to feed yourself."

He handed Christian the spoon. Christian beamed and shoved it completely into his own mouth and twisted it.

John found a small metal bowl. He transferred the oatmeal, and handed it to Christian. As he gathered the makings for coffee, he was afraid to look at Christian.

John sat with his coffee, in front of Christian. He tried to decide if the amount of oatmeal covering the boy was greater, or less than, what he had presented him with. In the end, John rubbed a wet washcloth over the sticky fellow, while Christian howled like an angry bear.

When Mabel arrived at nine o'clock for Sunday breakfast, John was lying on the parlor floor sleeping with Christian asleep on top of him.

It had been agreed upon. Alexander would care take the old miner's cabin for as long as he was in Cardinal, then lock it up tightly when he left for the winter. The Pipe Line claim would stay in the miner's name. One never knew, perhaps the mother lode was in there.

Alexander shook the old miner's hand one last time. He gave the mule a slap on the rear to get it moving. The miner waved without looking back as he set out ahead of the mule. Alexander stood watching them until they were out of sight. Illinois seemed an awful long way off for a guy that old, but he only had to do it once. Alexander imagined that old mule wouldn't see Illinois, but the miner would.

The little cabin had only one window and one door, and Alexander had to duck to get inside. He felt he should never fully stand up inside. It was dark in there alright, but with the door open, and once his eyes had adjusted, a fellow could find what he was looking for.

The cabin sat right next to Coon Track Creek facing southeast. It was just off the wagon road to Caribou City, not far from the junction where the road climbed the hill to Cardinal. Finest place you could conjure up for summer. It was winter's summer home.

This was the first place Alexander had hung his hat in more time than he could count. He tried to convince himself this had nothing to do with being sweet on a girl.

1894

❧

CARDINAL CITY, COLORADO

*A*s Mabel stood facing the chalkboard, writing as fast and neatly as she could, Christian looked out the window at the shimmering new aspen leaves and the dark clouds forming to the west. If school went on one more day, he thought he'd have to run away. Luckily, this was the last of it for the year, and Christian was waiting for the mine whistle to blow. He could tell from Mabel's focus, it would still be a while.

Christian hated being the only twelve year old in the school. Everyone else's parent's let their sons go to work by now, but not John Peregrine...oh, no. Christian was going to get an education and be a professional. So here he sat and it was torture.

All Christian could think about was a job in the mine. The Boulder County Mine. He had been to every mine within walking distance of Cardinal and Caribou. The Spencer Mine, Sovereign People, the Ready Cash, Eagle Bird, Pandora, The No Name, The Seven Thirty. He loved to hear the stories of how each got its name. Some were small mines with only one or two men working them. Others were bigger operations with a superintendent and crew. The mine, which he believed held the greatest fortune was the Boulder County Mine. It was going straight down into the mountain nine hundred feet deep. The men were digging in horizontally from a site on Coon Track Creek to meet the shaft and drain the water from above. When they joined, the tunnel would be almost a mile into the mountain from Coon Track. It would be a couple more years before the two would meet, and Christian wanted to be there that day more than anything he could imagine.

No one could work in the Boulder County Tunnel until they were fourteen. No boys allowed. No women either. The Cornish miners are such suspicious people, thought Christian. Women in a mine would cause disaster, so Mabel would never know what he loved about the mines. Rats in the mine were a lucky sign. A number of birds gathering outside the mine, that was unlucky.

Christian had sat for a whole afternoon last summer, listening to mining tales told in that impossibly thick Cornish brogue, when a flock of mountain jays had gathered outside the Jack Pot Mine, and the miners had given up working for the remainder of the day.

The "Cousin Jacks" had come from Cornwall, England. As Christian stared out of the schoolhouse window, he could see dozens of white canvas wall tents set across the meadow and up the side of the hill. These people were hard working miners. One of them was his good friend, Thomas. Thomas had let Christian see inside his tent. It was just like a cabin. Thomas had said, "There's no time to build a cabin, boy. This place dries up and I'll be packin' on to the next town."

"I'll miss you when you go, Thomas." Christian had replied.

"Aw, don't you worry. You folks'll be packin' it up too."

But Christian couldn't imagine John "packin' it up" or Mabel living anywhere but the schoolhouse. Cardinal City was their home, and when John Peregrine had surveyed the town he'd put the County Court House smack in the middle.

"Caribou silver will build that courthouse one of these days", John would say.

The Boulder County Mine had enough diggin' to go on forever. Christian had heard John say that a hundred times too.

A clap of thunder and flash of light brought Christian's attention back to the classroom. Three little ones ran squealing back to the kindergarten bench from the chalkboard. That chalkboard could give a person a nasty shock in an electrical storm. Mabel settled them back down and went to the piano. She always did this, thought Christian. Make us sing those same old songs, so no one will be scared of the storm outside.

Tomorrow morning, Christian would get up with the sun to be a miner. He had talked himself into a job at the Sweet Home Mine.

Mabel sat on the rocks outside John's house waiting for Christian to come home from the mine. The days were getting longer and the mine shifts were getting shorter, thanks to the success of the labor unions. New aspen leaves shimmered spring green in a light breeze that felt almost warm. The north sides of the hills still held a snowpack, but the grass in Cardinal's meadow was green, and the delicate fuzzy, purple pasque flowers were up.

Mabel saw him as he came down the road from Caribou. Christian was carrying his lunch pail and canvas jacket. He was wearing his helmet. He still looked like a boy from a distance. As he came closer, Mabel could make out the filthy over-alls, covered with hand-sewn patches, and his carbide lamp on the helmet.

"Eh, Mabel." he said, as he sat on the rock next to her.

"Christian," Mabel squinted up placing him between herself and the setting sun. "How is the life of a miner?'"

"Paid the doctor a dollar today. All of us guys did. He was headed back to St. Louis otherwise. Said he can't make a living pickin' bullets out of guys who don't own a nickel."

Christian picked at the wax from the candle drippings that covered him head to toe.

"Mabel, I just wish you could see it when we blast that rock!" he looked right at her shaking his head. "You'd love it, I know you would."

"Maybe I should dress like a young fella and sign on for the day." Mabel mused.

Christian jumped up with excitement.

"Would you, Mabel? Please?"

"You'd have to lend me those fine buckskin gloves."

Christian realized she was kidding, and he sat back down in a pout.

"Look what Jeremiah made me." he said, pulling a pair of glasses out of his jacket. "He said I'd go blind if I didn't take care when we come out of the mine. He made 'em himself! For me!"

Mabel took the glasses and admired the handiwork. They were made using an old pair. Leather filled the lenses and a hole was poked in front of each eye to let the light in slowly.

"We sit outside for a few minutes when we first come out. Blind alright, that's what you are when you emerge, and that's what you'd be, if you didn't have a pal like Jeremiah."

Mabel was watching a horse with a man slowly making its way up the road toward the house. Intuition touched a familiar place in her as she watched, and then suddenly, they both knew.

"Alexander!" Christian cried out, as he jumped up and ran toward him.

"I'll be darned.' muttered Mabel to herself. She rose to her feet, and stood stunned.

"I thought you might marry me this summer." Alexander said to Mabel from the back of the horse, and he followed it with a huge grin.

Mabel's eyes welled with tears and she broke into a laugh.

"I brought this for you, Christian."

Alexander reached into his coat and fished around for just long enough to make the boy hop with excitement. He pulled out a furry, spotted kitten and handed it down to Christian. It was big.

"Cougar." he said, "You can only keep it if it'll keep you."

Christian held it up to his face and looked it straight in the eyes.

"He'll keep me if John will." he said.

Mabel's heart was racing as Alexander dismounted and wrapped his arms all the way around her. He took the liberty of kissing each of her rosy cheeks.

"We'd wondered whatever became of you!" Mabel held him back to take a good look at him.

"Been away two summers, I guess." Alexander said shyly.

"They have invented the telegraph, you know! They send them up with the mail from Boulder." Mabel teased.

Alexander turned away, making to leave.

"That'd be just like a woman." he said, and then he spun around and grabbed her, hoisting her over his shoulder.

'I'll take ya anyway!" he said.

Mabel kicked, pounded and yelled until he set her down.

"Where'd this little fellow come from, Alexander?" asked Christian.

"They took her Ma down west of Pueblo. I put her in my pocket for a few days and when I set her back down, she followed me so long I took pity on her and decided she'd ride fine in my coat. She'll keep you warm."

"She's the sweetest thing I ever did see." Christian cooed, and he disappeared into the house with her.

"Eats meat. Only meat!" Alexander called after him.

"That's the natural thing...for cats." Alexander said as he stepped toward Mabel and held her closely again.

"I didn't know what had happened to you, Alexander." Mabel said again.

"Well," he said, as he guided her to sit beside him on the rocks. "I made my way to Mexico that first winter. Traded pretty good with the Indios down there. Lots of furs from the Arizona hills. Indios had dug gold...love metals. Anything shiny. I guess it's human nature. But they love those furs and I put gold in a bank in Tucson to keep me alive. There it sits. Who knows? Might get back and get it one day."

Mabel wrapped her arm around his.

"Why then, well, it's a very long way to Alaska, but that's where I went."

'Alaska!' Mabel marveled. The distances seemed impossible.

"I went to the coast. California had opportunities for sure, but I kept traveling north. Worked every kind of job and caught everything that moved. Before you knew it, I was workin' in a mine in Kennicott, Alaska. Copper. Thought I'd get out before winter. Hell, if I was gonna be under ground, I might as well be back here. But I didn't get out in time. The coastal ranges were heaped with snow. I didn't want to make my way over the glaciers to the interior, so I just kept working. Spring came eventually, and you've never seen water run like that. Wasn't any crossing those rivers except to climb up to where they're born and cross there. Sometimes, they'd get a cable across and people would come from miles around. A train ran down from the mine, and a guy could make passage on a steamer all the way back to Seattle, but not me. I made my way back through the Yukon, because I heard gold nuggets are lying around in the streambeds. No one tells you how big the bears are that are guarding it."

Alexander lifted his shirt and turned around. A claw had been drawn down his back, leaving a scar as long as a pick axe.

Mabel ran her fingers the length of it.

"I can't believe you are here!" was all she could think to say.

"Damn thing was gonna eat me for sure, till my buddy put a shot right there, between the ear and the temple. Only place to penetrate that thick skull. Saved me, he did. Course that bear lurched after him too. Damn near took his ear off. You know, that bear had fought a man before because hell if he wasn't missing an eye from a gunshot wound. Thing weighed about nine hundred pounds. Don't know why he's protecting that gold, do you?" Alexander grinned at Mabel and she laughed with relief.

"Come on. Get that kid, and we'll go on down to the hotel and spend some of the money that's been weighting me down."

"That kid will want to hear that bear story. I'm sure that kitten will be coming to dinner too."

When Alexander entered the bar room, everyone at the bar turned, and a cheer went up. Ruby's girls flocked around him. Mabel let him be seated and petted for a while. She smiled at him, and he winked at her. When the girls settled down and Alexander had worked his way down the bar shaking hands and pounding on backs, he sat down to dinner with Christian and Mabel. Christian had the cougar sleeping in his coat.

"The price of silver has been going down." Mabel said. "The Democrats and the Republicans won't support it. Colorado will elect a Populist for Governor, or that will be the end of these mines. Already, people are leaving for Central City and Cripple Creek. The demand will be for gold."

"And how about you, Mabel? And Christian, you're a miner now, will you leave Cardinal?"

"We choose to be optimistic at this time. The Western Federation of Miners has lobbying power. The mine owners are well connected financially in the East. The world relies on Colorado's resources. I hope to be living here the next time you breeze through." Mabel stated confidently.

"I'm going to strike it rich here; either the Sweet Home or the Boulder County Tunnel." Christian added. "John says politics will save silver and I think he's out to prove it. He's back in Denver tonight. Says it's getting pretty heated down there."

"Last stage is in!" someone yelled into the hotel from outside. A few minutes later, Tyler appeared, fresh in from St. Louis.

"Alexander, Sir." Tyler shook his hand, then gave him a hug and said, "I knew you'd be back." Tyler squeezed Mabel's hand and gave it a kiss accompanied by a long woeful look.

"You're back too!" said Mabel. "Tell us about St. Louis."

"I got off the stage here in Cardinal. I hoped I'd find company. It's going to be lonesome going home tonight." He sat down at the table.

Tyler hung his head and added, "They won't be coming back. My family won't be coming back to Caribou. I guess I might as well be honest about it. Lucinda's not well. She's not well in her mind. I'd hoped being back there a while might have helped, but she's gone mad with grief. Her family keeps her. She's really not able...not able anymore. I wanted to bring Alice back with me, but her Grandmother won't hear of it. They don't see how the west could be any place to raise a girl. And Lucinda needs Alice."

Hurt and pain hung on the silence that followed.

"Tyler," Christian said, "I am glad you came home."

Alexander nodded in agreement. "I'd like to buy you a shot of medicine, friend. I'm sorry to hear your news."

Mabel stood up and walked around the table and hugged Tyler's shoulders from behind. She stood there a long time resting her head on him.

The smell of dinner woke the sleeping kitten, and it emerged from Christian's coat to get all kinds of attention and a few scraps of meat.

After a frisky cat show, Tyler said, "Come on up to my place, Alexander. You've got to be as doggone tired as I am."

Each man pecked Mabel on the cheek, and they left her staring up the road after them.

"Christian," she finally said, "you'd better get off to sleep. Tomorrow's another day."

Mabel had never been to Central City. When she had come to Caribou so many years ago, Mabel had come up Boulder Canyon to Magnolia Townsite, then over to Brownsville and up to Caribou. She looked over at John and watched his head bump against the inside of the stagecoach. How could he sleep on such a rocky road? But John had done this so many times. His surveying business brought him to Central City regularly. Mabel wondered about the dreams of a man who never stopped thinking. John was passionate about silver. He was passionate about the politics that drove the economy and growth of the cities. And he is still passionate about me, thought Mabel. Will he ever lose his love for me? At times, it was wearisome to see that look upon his face. Mabel knew she would always temper her interactions with John so as not to misrepresent her feelings. He was dear to her. Maybe the best friend she'd ever had. And here they were going all the way to Denver to attend a political convention.

Mabel was thrilled to be going. On top of the stagecoach was her little traveler's trunk with two new dresses for the evenings, paid for by John, and one more that hadn't been worn since she lived in St. Louis. She hoped her hatboxes were securely tied above. How would they ever survive the trip? Mabel smoothed her green traveling dress and brushed the dust from her lap and shoulders. Even the visit to Central City would be such a treat! Then, they would take the train to Denver to stay in the new and already famous Brown Palace Hotel.

By the time the stage had rumbled over the bridge at South Boulder Creek, past the many gulches full of miners, and headed up the Apex Road, Mabel had had enough traveling for one day. A smithy who had joined them at Gamble Gulch, turned out to be stimulating company for John, and the whole way along, they had argued about the Sherman Silver Purchase Act. Mabel had her opinions, but kept them to herself.

The Federal government had been buying silver for several years. The Purchase Act had brought some stability to the boom and bust silver mining economy of Colorado, but it wasn't enough. Now, the threat loomed that the United States would stop coining silver and switch to a gold economy. It would mean the certain end of Caribou, which had already suffered greatly with the fluctuation of the prices in silver.

The debate raged on as the stage crested the rise above Central City and passed the graveyard sitting out on a cleared lonesome hill. Mabel thought the tombstones looked especially fancy compared to Caribou. As they descended Eureka Gulch into the city, beautiful homes began to line the street. People were everywhere.

The Colorado and Southern Railroad had reserved places in the executive car for John Peregrine and his guest to ride into Denver. As the train wound its way down from the mountains and out onto the prairie, a most delectable dinner was served.

The car clicked along into the city. Mabel feasted her eyes on every kind of sight imaginable. Suffering and misfortune sat awkwardly side by side with opulence.

The train passed neighborhoods of stately mansions with leaded glass windows, and elegant formal entries. Just blocks away were tenements with children sitting on stoops and skipping rope in the dust. There were yards of animals, vacant lots filled with weeds, even clusters of men sitting around open fires sharing coffee and no doubt, a snip off a bottle. Markets with fruits and vegetables, train yards eight tracks wide, and large industrial buildings blended into the mix. Mabel felt so privileged to be sitting with white tablecloths and fine china, rolling past this flashing potpourri that was the city.

John pointed to the Platte River, "Now we are entering the downtown. Look, trolley cars! See the Capitol with its big copper dome! Soon, we will be at Union Station."

Two large white horses drew them in a black carriage from Union Station toward the hotel. Mabel hadn't seen such fine looking horses in a long time. She thought of Tyler, and how his criteria for a good horse had changed since their St. Louis days. Tyler recognized a mountain horse as sturdy through the chest and nimble under foot, fearless, and with a spirit of conviction.

The downtown area was different than the surrounding city. The streets were cobbled and the carriage ride was dust free. Buildings loomed up several stories high. Looking up the sheer walls made Mabel dizzy and reminded her of the cliffs on the highest mountain peaks. The people strolling the promenades were of every kind. Women were dressed in long bustled skirts and linked arm in arm with each other as they browsed among the shops. Others flitted along hurriedly toward jobs as servants, or stood against buildings clutching sacks of belongings. Maybe it was the time of day, but Mabel decided that the "ladies of the night", so obvious in Cardinal and Central City, were nowhere to be seen on this street. Men in fine suits stood clustered in twos and threes, locked in discussion, in front of banks, brokerages, and business establishments. There were cowboys in clean shirts with satchels hung over their shoulders.

The Brown Palace was as grand a place as Mabel had ever seen. It was made of Colorado's famous pink granite and huge red sandstone blocks, rising nine stories above the prairie. Every room had tall glass windows so guests could enjoy the breathtaking views. Each of Colorado's wild animals was featured in a series of carvings set in circles that ringed the outside of the third story. The building was triangular in shape with a rounded ship's prow fronting on 17th Avenue and Broadway. The hotel was just one year old and talk of it had reached both coasts.

When the coach pulled up in front of the Brown Palace, liveried doormen attended the carriage. There was so much gracious activity that Mabel's senses were momentarily overwhelmed as she was offered a hand to step down. Her traveler's trunk caught her eye as it was loaded onto a rolling brass cart, and before she had missed them, her day bags were by her side, carried by an extra attendant.

John smiled haughtily for Mabel as he took her arm. He led her into the most splendid lobby, where the ceiling rose the entire height of the hotel, and was finished at the top with a huge colorful stained glass skylight which was more magnificent than Mabel's wildest imagination. Her senses were delighted as her eyes took in the rest. Mezzanines, stacked seven high, ringed the lobby with delicate lighted archways and copper filigreed railings. Marble floors and polished teak woodwork complemented this majesty. Mabel had never seen anything of such beauty made by the hands of men.

"Mr. John Peregrine and Miss Mabel Gurkin," John told the concierge.

"Welcome to the Brown Palace." the man said with a bow of the head and a bit of a flourish. "We are here to accommodate your every need, sir. Does the Lady prefer morning or afternoon sun in her room?"

Mabel thought for a moment. As much as she was an early riser, she longed to see the mountains from her window.

"Afternoon sun, please." she said.

"And for you, sir?"

"I will take the room next to Miss Gurkin, please"

"Of course, sir. It is done then. You will be on the sixth floor, rooms sixteen and eighteen. Our Gentlemen's Club is here on the street level, as well as our restaurant, offering fine dining, and tea is taken here in the lobby of the Brown Palace. If there is anything at all that you need, it is our pleasure to serve you."

"Thank you." John said. And they followed the bellhop to the elevator. Mabel had never ridden in an elevator before. She was familiar with the dumb waiter in her father's house, and smiled to think she was being carried upstairs like a tray of breakfast.

Electric lights, indoor plumbing, hot running water and a bedroom apparently set for royalty. That was the Brown Palace Hotel.

"John, thank you so much." Mabel said with sincerity, "The hotel is amazing. I think I shall be feeling like a queen for three days."

"That is the idea, my dear." John kissed her hand, and just for a second gave her a puppy dog look. "I will see you in an hour for dinner. For now, you'll be ready to draw a bath, I'm sure." And John went next door.

Mabel went to the window and gazed out across the prairie to see the mountains rising thirty miles to the west. The sun was setting and the Front Range was silhouetted against a glowing sky. Mabel thought of the schoolhouse, sitting empty, the fire in the woodstove long gone out by now.

It was the following day that Mabel intended to visit her old school chum from St. Louis at her home in downtown Denver. Mabel had called a laundry gal into her hotel room to help her do up her corset and the multitude of buttons down the back of her dress. Now, she stood, gusseted up, with a small handbag clutched in her hands, at the front of the Brown Palace. The directions she had received from the concierge sounded as if the house couldn't be more than a mile away, but Mabel stood in her dress boots knowing one couldn't expect to walk comfortably very far. She would have to hire a ride– funny place, the city.

Eliza was Mrs. Jerome Fitts now. Mabel didn't quite know what to expect, so she stayed open minded as the carriage drew up in front of one of Denver's finest mansions. Eliza had always cared that things were properly elegant, so Mabel assumed this would be suitable to Eliza. The house was of grand stature, made of beige stonework and black enameled trim with wrought iron fences, gates and porticos. Yellow roses, iris, pansies and foxglove lined the front walkway. In honor of the convention, American flags hung from the second floor windows, and the Colorado flag, from the front porch.

"Shall I wait?" asked the driver.

Mabel paused for a moment, and then remembering her footwear, said, "Yes, please."

A butler, dressed in all white, answered the bell.

"I'm calling on Mrs. Jerome Fitts.." Mabel offered.

"Yes, certainly. One moment please."

He returned with a small crystal tray bearing a calling card. Mabel took the card. It read, "Mrs. Jerome Fitts, Philanthropist and Contributor." Below was her address, "1550 Grant St., Denver , Colorado."

"Mrs. Fitts is not available at the moment," stated the butler. "May I tell her who has called?"

"Miss Mabel Gurkin of Cardinal, Colorado, formerly of St. Louis. I am a guest at the Brown Palace until Sunday."

Mabel was glad she had told her driver to wait.

Now that she was dressed to the nines, Mabel decided to roam about the shops, and then take some tea in the lobby of the hotel. John had plans to meet with various political lobbyists at the Gentleman's Club on the first floor of the hotel. John was working himself into a fever over the silver issue. Mabel could see it in his manner.

Mabel bought perfume for Miss Ruby, lace for the girls, a special candy stick for Tyler and a pair of Mexican Jumping Beans for Christian. The peculiar pinched feeling from being laced up into shoes and a presentable dress had tired her more than a day walking in the mountains. On the verge of being crabby, Mabel sat at a small table in the hotel lobby and looked up at the magnificent stained glass skylight.

"Miss Gurkin," a voice interrupted, "A telegram."

Mabel read the words in capital letters and was pleased.

PLSNT SURPRISE EXPECT YOUR PRESENCE AT TEA
TOMORROW 4PM 1550 GRANT -ELIZA

As Mabel thanked the messenger, she noticed a man standing by the piano, staring directly at her. Just as soon as the messenger had left, the man approached.

"May I be so bold as to introduce myself? I am Frederick James Robinson, an acquaintance of Mr. Peregrine, through his work here in Denver. And you are Miss Mabel Gurkin, also an acquaintance of Mr. Peregrine. May I join you?"

"Of course." Mabel regetted it immediately, suspicious from the start of Mr. Robinson's motivations.

"How does a mountain woman like you enjoy the big city, Miss Gurkin?" he asked leaning forward to look more closely into her eyes.

Mabel gazed off toward the pianist, who was beginning a piece by Bach. Her mind longed to lose itself in the notes as they rose to fill the air.

"It is quite different than the Rocky Mountains. However, I am originally from St. Louis, so the city is not entirely foreign to me."

"And what keeps you up there at Caribou? Certainly not the cruel winds we hear of. I don't expect there are any educated people, with the exception of John Peregrine, of course."

"You would be surprised at the variety of individuals who have found interest in the mines, Mr. Robinson. There is money to be made, you know. I am the school teacher."

"A Lady, such as you, must be a mite fearful up there. One must be on the lookout for wild animals, not to mention swindlers, hoodlums and opportunists. The people who choose to try their luck in the mountains usually have no legitimate roots to speak of. It must be tiresome for a cultured woman like you."

Mabel thought of her long walks in the forest, taken virtually without fear. She thought of the men lined up with their letters from the U.S. Mail, waiting patiently for Mabel to read them aloud. She thought of the camaraderie of the miners as they drank and sang the night away at the hotel in Cardinal.

"I find it all very stimulating, Mr. Robinson. The people there are resourceful and genuine. You might see it first hand for yourself someday."

"I can't imagine bothering, my dear. They can do the digging, and I shall be here to take their money. I am in investments and securities. I've got my hands quite full. It's like a game to me...handling people's money. Quite a responsibility, you know. Yes, I am toiling away with a ledger and a handshake, telegraphs and fine dining. Always watching the market, always staying a step ahead. Such is the life of a money man." He leaned even closer and grinned shamelessly.

"Well then, you must have your opinions in regard to the silver economy." Mabel regretted the statement as it came off her lips; an invitation for discussion.

"I am for gold, actually, and I'll have you to know that I am not in the minority. Silver, my dear, is a thing of the past. Mark my words. The year won't be out before we see the switch. If we are to become a world economy, it's gold."

Mabel put down her tea, and stood.

"Silver has served Colorado quite well, I believe. John Peregrine stands for silver. It has been a pleasure meeting you, Mr. Robinson. I shall be retiring to my room now."

Mr. Frederick Robinson rose.

"You are a catch of a woman, if I may say so. Until John Peregrine succeeds in marrying you, I shall be paying the utmost attention. Good afternoon, Miss Gurkin."

Trying her best to walk away with grace, Mabel fought the impulse to run. It helped that she had to concentrate on teetering along in her heeled dress boots. Shameless creep, she thought, he is an arrogant unpleasant individual. She turned to see him disappear into the Gentleman's Club.

The next day, dawned bright and clear for the convention rally in front of the Capitol Building. Mabel and John had breakfasted early in order to get to a place in the front of the crowd. As the carriage pulled up at the west end of the lawn, it was obvious there would be quite a crowd. To be in ear shot of the speakers, it would be standing room only. For the first time ever, the crowd was peppered with women, as they had just been granted the right to vote.

Mabel clung to John's arm, as he maneuvered them through the mob. She had never been in such a large group of people. She felt strangely that all eyes were upon her, yet at the same time, she felt lost in a sea of bodies. John settled them in a spot comfortably in front of the stage. Mabel knew it would be a long day on her feet, so eschewing fashion, had worn her mountain boots under her long green traveling dress. John, being as tall as he was, had removed his beaver top hat and held it carefully under his left arm.

A brass band struck up and played into the morning air. Excitement grew in the crowd, and when the rally began, it was minutes before the speaker could quiet the crowd. "Silver!" was the chant, and it was shouted with gusto by all.

Politicians, bankers, railroad men and big mine owners all took a turn at the podium, but it was Senator Wolcott, who impressed Mabel the most.

He had said. "The Sherman Act has saved us from infinitely greater disaster than we would have encountered. It has given us a currency backed by the credit of the government and by silver at its bullion value. If the Sherman Act is repealed, we hear, there will be increased confidentiality in Europe. Tell me all, how will it come, and from whom? It is for us to stand together on this great question, to save our common country from greater suffering and impoverishment."

John was pleased. Mabel could feel a tense anticipation in his arm as she clutched it tightly and he led her out of the thinning crowd.

"This was good." is all he said, when he had managed to commandeer a carriage, and they were seated among several other campaigners.

The day had flown by and the clock tower chimed four o'clock.

"I'm due at Eliza's!" Mabel cried out to John with horror. "I'll have to go to tea in my traveling clothes. I guess that will be alright, we're old friends."

John asked the driver to drop her at 1550 Grant on their way past.

Just a few minutes late, Mabel straightened herself up a bit before ringing the bell.

The same butler answered the door.

"I am calling on Mrs. Fitts." Mabel reported.

"Do come into the parlor, Madam. I'll let her know you have arrived."

He led the way through a grandly elegant foyer, and seated Mabel in the parlor.

As she sat waiting for Eliza, she took in the ambiance of the room. The straight-backed Victorian chairs were covered with silky steel grey brocade, with just a hint of golden pinstripe. The arms were ornately carved and polished with gold leaf. Mabel had thought twice about seating herself in her traveling dress.

The fireplace was white marble, and had been set with a large decorative painted fan for the summer season. Mabel mused as she knew she would still be burning wood for at least another month up in Cardinal.

"Mabel Gurkin, what a pleasant surprise!" Eliza whirled into the room dressed formally for tea.

She held Mabel's hands and stretched her arms out at a distance to look at her.

"Why look at the mountain girl you've become!" Eliza remarked entertained.

"I've just now come from the rally at the Capitol Building, so you must forgive my traveling dress. I hadn't time to go back to the hotel."

"And your boots! Oh, my!"

"Yes, it was a bit rough out there in the crowd...but the speeches, oh, Eliza, if the federal government doesn't back silver, this state will be in revolution!"

"Please, sit and tell me about this life you have chosen for yourself, Mabel." Eliza asked.

Mabel wondered if Eliza realized that the economy that supported her lifestyle was fed by the mines. Eliza rang a small silver bell for tea.

"I am the teacher in Cardinal. I live at the school house." said Mabel realizing that didn't describe it at all.

"And I understand you are here with John Peregrine. Perhaps you'll marry soon, and he certainly will have to move you down here to a proper life."

"Eliza, I am not in love with John. We are truly dear friends, and he has brought me to Denver to share the excitement of the Convention and see the city."

"There cannot be many other prospects in the mining district. Don't cut yourself short, my dear. We're not getting younger."

"I am not particularly focused on finding a husband. There are many men in my life every day, and it hasn't seemed obvious to me that any one man has all of the traits that I admire in so many of them."

Mabel thought of John, and how, for as kind as he was, she'd never felt the spark that she still felt with Tyler. Tyler was another woman's husband, and Mabel had accepted that from the time she'd found it out. But that spark showed her what must be there. And Alexander! She got a thrill just thinking of his spirit and resourcefulness. What would ever calm his wanderlust, and if he settled, who would he become?

"I am the Post Mistress at Cardinal too." said Mabel, hoping to change the subject.

"I meet the U.S. Mail as it comes in, and distribute the letters through the hotel. You wouldn't believe the number of people I read for. Everyone knows me. There is no end to the drama and action. It is a very stimulating life up there."

"Do you suppose you'll tire of it after a time? Mabel, it is not the way you were raised. Don't you miss the finer things in life, my dear?" Eliza nodded to dismiss the servant who had brought the teapot on a tray with cookies.

Mabel let the tea service steal the moment and didn't answer the questions. In truth, she thought, Ruby's girls had taught her that the finer things in life were laughs, camaraderie and freedom to express yourself.

"Tell me about yourself, Eliza. What are your pastimes in the city?" Mabel countered. "You seem quite content in your marriage and your home."

"My Darling, not a day goes by that I don't count my blessings. I am so fortunate to be married to one of the most prosperous men in Denver. I spend my days running his household, naturally. And what a job that is! We entertain constantly, you can imagine. I have a staff of nine, counting my driver and I must be a step ahead of them at all times. The book of "Who's Who" is just being written in Denver, you know. It's such a budding society. Quite an opportunity really, when you consider all that is coming our way; railroad money, mining wealth, the center of Colorado agriculture and ranching. Everyone comes to Denver to make their fortune, or spend it. Being a part of that is a delight to me."

"I hope your optimism serves you well, Eliza. The very reason John and I have come to Denver is that the mining industry on the brink of crisis."

"Mabel, it's not for you and me to worry ourselves over. Silver or gold, our state holds the resources the world needs. Colorado will undoubtedly prosper. So tell me, how do you pass the time up there? There can't be a soul of your breeding to start a bridge club. And what of doctors, and literature, or tailors..." Eliza's voice trailed on, while Mabel visualized the chorus line for Ruby's girls in the next show that they'd been working so hard on.

When Eliza was saying "...and your parents are worried sick that you'll become an old maid up there, with no options to turn to.." Mabel began to listen again.

Mabel closed her eyes and easily put herself on top of the Boulder County Hill at sunset. She put herself in the middle of the ladies all half dressed in their corsets and dance costumes, sharing laughs and a nip of whiskey just before the show. She pictured the schoolhouse in March with snowdrifts blocking the windows on the leeward side of the building.

"It's hard for me to describe life in the mountains to one who hasn't experienced it, Eliza. You will have to trust me when I say that the people are wonderful, life is full of exciting challenges, and I'm very happy in Cardinal. In fact, I am looking forward to my return tomorrow."

"Then Mabel, don't be a fool. Marry that man and consider yourself lucky."

"I am lucky, Eliza. My life is richer than you can imagine. And I won't marry for anything short of love."

Mabel stood up, feeling something like a caged animal. She walked to the window.

"Mabel, don't be so naive. If love played into it, there would be no Gentleman's Club. Men don't know what love is, Mabel."

"The Gentleman's Club?" Mabel inquired.

"Lord knows, there isn't a Gentleman in there. There is a tunnel at the Brown Palace that goes beneath the street and over to the brothel on the other side of Seventeenth Street. Men will always be looking in the wrong places. Always act so innocent. Marriage is the only hope for stability in our lives, Mabel.

And upward mobility. Don't cut yourself short!"

"Did you marry for love, Eliza?" asked Mabel.

"The definition of love is a broad one. Let us leave it at that. I have everything I need, Mabel, and then some." Eliza stood and examined herself in the mirror on the wall. She looked convincing enough to herself, at least upon first glance.

"I'll call for the carriage to take you to the Brown Palace. You are finding it grand, I'm sure. You know it is the talk coast to coast."

"So I've been told. Yes, it is delightful." Mabel confirmed, knowing it was best to give the answer Eliza wanted to hear, and end the visit on a positive note.

Then Mabel added, speaking as much to herself as to Eliza, "It is an amazing thing to see Henry Brown's vision manifested. The mind is a wonderful thing, and dreams can come true."

As the carriage drew up in front, Mabel hugged Eliza goodbye and looking her in the eye, wished her the best of health. For just an instant, she saw deeply into Eliza's troubled soul. Mabel knew they were each horses of a different color, and Mabel felt lucky to have her life instead.

MABEL AT THE FEDERATION BALL 1894
The Armitage Collection

Mabel wore her favorite of the dresses from John to the Federation Ball that evening. Dressing had been a ritual she knew from so long ago. She giggled to think of this dress in Cardinal. When would she ever have the opportunity to wear it again? It was indeed a beautiful dress. Only half teasing, she wondered if John would be offended if he saw it worn in a show at the hotel.

More than one person turned to watch as John entered the ballroom with Mabel on his arm, but Frederick James Robinson's eyes lingered longer than was appropriate. John locked his gaze on the man, backing him down. Mabel smiled and looked away. As she gazed out over the sea of people, she was amused to see how very perfect each man looked in his carefully tailored tuxedo. Mabel felt pleasantly entertained as she noticed each of the women's lovely dresses.

John brought Mabel a scotch, which raised a few eyebrows of the gentlemen they stood with.

"I'll say, Jefferson, if the Silver Act hadn't been paired with the McKinley Tariff Act, the legislation never would have passed to begin with."

"Mr. Peregrine, I suppose you are correct." Jefferson conceded, "It may be that silver has been supported by a false subsidy that had no real support from the get go, but certainly Washington can see that it has bolstered the economy for all."

"Cleveland sees the Sherman Act as socialism." remarked a fellow with southern drawl.

"Now, now, gentlemen, we all know Washington wants to support the railroads. That is big business, and the railroads won't be thriving without the silver mines."

"Quite right there." Peregrine added.

"The Easterners blame the Sherman Silver Act for their economic woes, but in actuality, it is their own over development that they cannot support."

"The Populist Party will be our saving grace."

"Colorado has vast natural resources. The East cannot ignore that!"

"Diversification is as important in mining as it is in anything else. The economy needs both gold and silver."

"The women have won the right to vote. What do you have to say about all this, Miss Gurkin?" There was a touch at her elbow.

Mabel turned to see that Fredrick Robinson was standing closely at her side.

"Despite the government's purchase of silver, the price of the metal has been steadily dropping, Mr. Robinson. My livelihood depends on silver, as does yours. Excuse me, gentlemen." Mabel smiled at John and made her way to the powder room.

"I don't suppose women will ever get a grip on this situation." Robinson spoke to her back.

"That's hardly the issue with this woman.'" John Peregrine pointed out. "It seems to me, and I know her well, that your company has driven Miss Gurkin away."

John took Mr. Robinson by the arm.

"Excuse us, men." he said, and he walked him from the circle.

"You can hardly think that she belongs to you, John." Robinson stated in his own defense.

"Miss Gurkin belongs to no one, Fredrick. And I doubt she ever will. But I know the look of a woman who wants nothing to do with a particular man, and this evening, it is you.'" John gave him a courteous but resolute stare.

"I suggest you visit the Gentleman's Club, Mr. Robinson, to find what you are looking for." And John walked back to join the discussion.

Mabel and John agreed that the dancing seemed cultured to the point of tame. John smiled warmly at Mabel as he led their steps.

"I miss the fiddle playing." said Mabel.

"I miss our smiling friends." said John.

"If only they could see us now!" Mabel mused.

"I don't suppose they'd even recognize us, would they?"

John walked Mabel to her room at the end of the night.

"John, thank you for everything. It has been truly wonderful. So grand to see it all, and feel the big city, the way of life here. Thank you for sharing it with me."

"You are quite welcome, Miss Belle of the Ball."

Mabel blushed and giggled.

"But you know", John added, "I'm quite ready to go home to Cardinal tomorrow."

"Me too." said Mabel, and she hugged him tightly and smiled.

The stage struggled up the last push to the Cardinal Townsite. Mabel could hardly wait to be let out. The sun was just set, and the sky held that familiar glow overhead. In the east, the moon rose, big and round and golden.

The platform at the hotel was full of people, and John and Mabel laughed to each other when they realized everyone had come out to greet them.

The afternoon thunderstorms had moved east from the mountains, forming huge thunderheads out over the prairies. By dark, a light show would ensue as the electricity bounced about the interior of the clouds, and sent thick bolts discharging into the earth. But for now, the sun shone brightly. Mabel relished the moisture which still hung in the air as the warm ground dried rapidly. She noticed every little alpine flower as she walked down from the high country toward Caribou City.

Caribou hardly qualified as a city anymore, she thought, as she passed through town. Silver prices had reached an all time low since cheap silver was making its way from India. Many houses were empty, long in need of a good coat of paint. There was only one market left. Most of all, Mabel missed the roller skating rink, now a collapsed building, with only fond memories remaining. She tromped on through town, trying not to let the decline make her feel that time was passing her by.

Mabel carried a basket creel with more trout than she could eat by herself, so she wondered who the lucky beneficiary would be. The road turned tightly in the gulch that ran off the south side of the Boulder County Hill. There, in the aspen trees, was a gypsy cart, perched at an odd angle. Clothes lines were strung hither and yon and a fire smoldered in a pit. A young girl in ruffled skirts ran out to Mabel and took her hand.

"I'll sing to you for a penny." she said.

"Haven't got a penny, sweetheart, but you can still sing to me. I'm only out fishing, see!"

Mabel lowered the creel and opened it to show off her catch. The trout were beautiful; every color of the rainbow.

"Change is coming." rang a voice from near the wagon.

"It's a lovely day now that the storm is passed." Mabel replied.

"Change is coming to you." the old woman crooned as she shuffled forward.

"Grandmother needs a fish." the gypsy girl begged. She manifested a hungry look herself, and twisted her bracelets in anticipation.

Mabel fought back her judgments about the gypsies. She did have extra fish. The woman was so old and the girl so young. There didn't seem to be anyone else around, so Mabel climbed the hill to the wagon.

The little girl pulled the strap off Mabel's shoulder and took the creel to her grandmother. This happened so fast, that again, Mabel had her suspicions about gypsies. She's only a child, Mabel reasoned.

"I take your fish, read your cards." stated the gypsy in broken English.

"You are very welcome to have a few fish for you and your granddaughter. I'll be needing some dinner myself when I get home.

The girl took the creel and disappeared into the cart, slamming the door as she went.

The grandmother turned to follow, so Mabel, determined to retrieve the creel and several of her fish, followed too. They climbed the short, steep steps that were set outside of the cart, and Mabel found herself uncomfortably in darkness. The child lit a candle and set it on a purple tablecloth.

Inside the gypsy cart, hung pots and pans, candles strung together by wicks, hand carved spoons, dolls, herbs, and ribbons, among a large variety of other trinkets. There were small moons and stars cut from aft and stern to let the fresh air in, and thick colorful blankets, draped as curtains, hung beside, for times of cold or travel.

"Sit." the old woman motioned with the back of her hand.

Mabel felt practically hunched over, so she sat.

The crone sat opposite her and shuffled a deck of well-worn Tarot cards. Mabel had never seen the cards, although she had been told of them since she was a child. She remembered the story of the origin of the Tarot. How the Christians had burned the great library in Alexandria, and then philosophers, mystics and savants had gathered together to encode the knowledge in the timeless set of cards. Mabel's curiosity was piqued further, when the woman sprinkled an unusual smelling ground herb powder over the candle flame.

Suddenly, the gypsy took a deep breath and made herself seem much larger. Mabel felt a power build in the woman's presence. She looked aside to see that the young girl had settled silently into the corner bed, and was watching wide-eyed.

The gypsy gave a long, slow exhale, and began to lay out the cards.

"The Empress." muttered the gypsy, looking up at Mabel acknowledging her with a nod. "You alone are the keeper of the flame."

She dealt more cards, reading left to right.

"You are a lioness. Strong." She solidly held a fist to her heart to show Mabel.

"Those who love you..." she closed her eyes and paused. "Three men, a boy; I see four. Those who love you will vanish into the wind."

Mabel fought an emotion deep inside her. She momentarily struggled with the unknown. She recognized a card that was the Fool. The duality of foolishness and wisdom.

"There will be a shift in the physical realm. You go with the shift, but you are held by the mountain...by the rock...bound by the rock...by the gold."

Mabel felt there was already more information than she could digest. It all rang too familiar. She listened on, almost amused.

"In time, your loves will return, only to pass, one by one into the other world."

"What shall I do?" Mabel asked feebly.

The woman pointed to an upside down man jumping off of a cliff.

"Stay." was all the gypsy said. Then she closed her eyes and sat in a meditative way for several minutes. Wondering what that meant, and if there was more, Mabel sat quietly. The gypsy girl didn't move or blink.

At last, the Grandmother opened her eyes and sighed. She removed all of the fish from the creel but two. She handed Mabel the creel, opened the wagon door, and trundled down the steps.

Mabel took one last look around the gypsy cart. The young girl blew out the candle, and left too. Mabel followed her outside, only to find herself momentarily blinded by light.

As she rounded the corner of the wagon, the old woman approached her from an outdoor makeshift kitchen. She handed Mabel a fiddle and bow.

"This was for you." she said.

Completely confused, Mabel offered it back.

"I couldn't possibly take it." she said.

The gypsy turned and waved her hand in dismissal.

"You need it." was all she said and she went to work cooking the fish.

Mabel stood watching. She felt one foot still in a mystical world. Her head swirled as if in a crystal ball.

The granddaughter squatted on a stump watching Mabel. Just as Mabel decided to leave, the girl jumped down, and led her away with the hand that held the fiddle bow.

"Thank you." Mabel called back to the gypsy, who waved back without turning around.

The gypsy girl skipped along beside Mabel for a quarter of a mile, singing her a song, and then she shyly turned around and ran back toward the wagon. Twilight turned the sky into a glow that warmed the quivering aspens and made the greens greener. Everything seemed surreal.

Considering what she had been told, Mabel felt oddly comforted. It was as if these things might well be true, but were a path she could walk. She felt for the first time in her life, that she was not alone. It was as if others sat on her shoulders, coaching and cheering her on. It was a funny feeling. It was bigger than she. It was full of love and a sense of humor. The only spooky part of the whole experience was that it had happened at all.

When Mabel reached the schoolhouse, she took the fiddle to her bedroom and leaned it against the wall on a shelf. She stood back and looked at the musical instrument. It was a very beautiful thing.

"Even with Lucinda gone, we still sit on these rocks every full moon." Tyler pointed out.

"I guess it always was the right thing to do." mused Mabel.

The moon was rising into a light sky as the summer days were long. Behind them, the sun had disappeared just moments before, leaving the mountains in shadow. The two sat closely, leaning backs against the highest rocks, looking east.

"Tyler," Mabel had been wondering, "What if the Sherman Act is repealed? What will it mean for you? What will you do if Caribou goes bust?"

"I don't rightfully know." he answered.

There was a long quiet spell between them and they watched the nighthawks perform their bug catching ritual in the air above them. The birds flew high, and then flapped just enough to keep their altitude. It was human nature to want to keep an eye on a single bird. The intermittent flapping seemed absurd. The birds appeared injured, but weren't. How could so few flaps keep them in the air? Then suddenly, a night hawk would drop like a stone, a thousand feet down, presumably to snatch a bug into its beak in mid-air, only to fly back up to the heights and start again. The ritual was only performed at dusk, which Mabel thought, made it very special.

"I guess," Tyler had been thinking, "I have not been focused on the possibility of Caribou going bust. I have been saddled by other problems, so to speak. Leaving Lucinda in St.Louis..."

Tyler rubbed his blond hair in every direction, and then looked up at Mabel. "It is highly unnatural to surrender one's wife and child; yet, it feels completely right to be back here in the mountains of Colorado. Back with the horses...and you, Mabel."

Mabel smiled at Tyler, acknowledging what he had just said. She did love him still. Theirs was a rare relationship. To go back in time as young lovers, and to have shared the trials of their lives over the years and to still be keeping each other's company, was indeed rare and precious.

"A gold economy will change everything if you think about it." said Mabel returning to the subject. She was unable to shake what the gypsy had told her.

"I suppose we'd survive it." Tyler said. "There's gold around here somewhere."

"Certainly."

Mabel wanted to share the story of the gypsies, but each time she tried to start, the words wouldn't come. She gazed out at the huge moonrise.

Tyler stood. He took Mabel's hand and pulled her to her feet so he could look her in the eyes.

"Mabel, I love you." he said.

Mabel had always known it was true. She closed the space between them, and wrapped her arms around Tyler. She closed her eyes and held him tightly. Her mind struggled. She remembered leaving her impractical love for him in St. Louis so long ago. She felt the love she had squelched when she learned Tyler had married. Mabel knew he still made her blush like no other. And Mabel thought of her independence...how she had worked hard to keep it."

Tyler held her too long. Mabel felt she should speak.

"Tyler," she said stepping out of his grasp, "we do love each other, but it is a different kind of love. You are married, my friend. Married. We have each other to rely on, though, don't we? We can enjoy each other."

Tyler let their hands drop to show his disappointment.

"You are right, Mabel. I am married; married to a dream that didn't come true."

Mabel took his hand and sat him back down against the rocks.

They sat holding hands in silence as darkness fell, and the nighthawks went home.

The morning of the day that everything changed had started out like most others. Mabel stumbled out of bed early to rekindle coals in the wood-stove from the night before. She remembered last night's thunderstorm. It had been violent. Truly cold air had come across the mountains from the northwest, colliding with the hot summer prairie air. The result was small piles of hail slammed up against trees and buildings, still lingering this morning after the cold night. The hail would melt just as soon as the sun got high enough.

Mabel opened the door to the woodstove and smiled to see that coals had made it through the night, even though it had been a small fire, just enough to take the chill off.

"Goodman," Mabel spoke to the spirit aloud, "what would I do without you? I'd be lonelier, that's for sure. Who says I don't have a man around the house?"

Mabel climbed back into bed for a while, listening to the roar and crackle of the fire and letting it warm the schoolhouse. And that is how it was that summer morning. It was the last morning that was quite like all the others had been in Cardinal.

It was when Mabel had gone to meet the mail, that John reminded her that the decision on whether or not to repeal the Sherman Silver Act, would be made in Congress this day. Nervously, he paced the hotel lobby, until he decided to take the U.S. Mail stage down to Boulder. When it rumbled back through, after its trip up to Caribou, John left. He had to know the verdict today.

Of all people that Mabel worried about, it was John. He had hung so many hopes and dreams on silver. He had taken such pride in being part of the building of the great mines and cities. His surveying was only part of it. It was the lobbying and politicking that he embraced so fully. He had helped build this grand economy and his identity stood precariously on that fact.

John promised to send word to Caribou and Cardinal with a messenger on horseback, just as soon as the news came in. Mabel hugged him tightly before he stepped onto the stage, and then squeezed his hand through the open window until the carriage rolled away. She felt relief to see him go, and take his pacing elsewhere. He could sweat it out with other fellow pacers in Boulder.

Mabel realized that her way of thinking was different. A person didn't have consumption until they were diagnosed with consumption. A woman wasn't pregnant until she was pregnant. And the price of silver hadn't crashed until it had crashed. It was this thinking, perhaps, that made the news so devastating.

In the late afternoon, a small crowd had gathered on the platform. The people waited for the news to come by horseback, special delivery from the telegraph office in Boulder, all the way from Washington, D.C.

When the horseman rode up, he slowed for the last stretch. It was not a good sign.

"Repealed." was all he said. Then he held his hat over his heart and bowed his head.

The crowd was silent. After a minute, mumbling began amongst the parties. Slowly, some drifted away. Alexander put his arm around Mabel's waist, and they walked to the barroom to discuss the news with the others.

Ryan, Christian and some other young miners had knocked off early to come down to the hotel. They filled three tables. The men sat fairly quietly, getting used to the news. Christian stood and leaned his head on top of Mabel's.

"Guess I'm a gold miner now." he said, and managed a smile for Mabel.

The older fellows, some of whom had mined in Caribou for twenty five years, lined the bar. They looked tired and finished. The barkeep was pouring them whiskey, right down the line.

Mr. Blake waved his hand in the air, with his head hung in defeat, and said out loud to the crowd, "Drinks are on the house for everyone in the room. Might as well take some medicine to dull the pain. All I've got in the world is right here, boys."

Mabel and Alexander sat with Miss Ruby. She dabbed at her eyes with a handkerchief, and the corners of her mouth drooped like someone she loved had passed away.

"I don't know." she'd worry, "I just don't know." A minute later, she'd sob, and then say it again.

Ruby's girls tried weakly to work the crowd, but the men were too stunned to be ready for comfort. The girls wore looks of disappointment, with underlying fear.

"I suppose these men will be gone before long.", was all Alexander could muster. He himself was always moving on anyway, but he had to admit to himself, that Cardinal had felt most like home to him.

All Mabel knew was that she was not going back to St. Louis.

After a while, two fiddlers and a guitarist took to the stage, and played music as if nothing was different. It seemed to Mabel that men had a way of making things seem normal, even when the air of reality was profoundly strange. Oddly, she felt comforted by the behavior.

Just two days later, the price of silver had dropped to twenty-three cents an ounce. Half of the canvas wall tents were already down and gone, leaving Cardinal looking like a party that was over.

Mabel rode a neighbor's pony up to see Tyler in Caribou. The whole way along the road, she was moving against the flow of people leaving town. The exodus seemed surreal to Mabel. Some rode in wagons, some were on horseback, mule or on foot. A couple of times, she thought she recognized people, but they moved on without a farewell or even a wave of the hand. There was nothing to say, Mabel guessed, when none would probably cross paths again.

At the curve in the road, the gypsies were still parked up the hill in the aspen grove. Mabel thought of the old woman's words. She had said that Mabel's men would vanish, only to return again. Even with the silver crash, that seemed impossible. Mabel thought of the fiddle, propped against the wall in the schoolhouse. Why had the woman said the fiddle was for her? Mabel turned her head away from the gypsy cart, hoping she wouldn't be recognized.

At Tyler's stable, there was a line of people waiting to inquire about hiring horse and mule teams. Tyler appeared at the door, and waving his hand, announced that the last of the teams had just been rented. He offered a waiting list to those who might return tomorrow.

"My business is booming at the moment, Mabel. I can't do enough, but once the last of them goes, it's gonna be mighty quiet around here."

Mabel watched the crowd disperse.

"I've sold off every animal that wasn't part of a team. Did you know you can't get a ticket on the stage for over a week? There are teamsters from Denver running folks outta here by the wagonload, along with everything from beds and chairs to cook stoves."

"I passed them on the way up here. The dust is unbelievable."

"When the last team returns, when the last of the folks are gone, I'll drive'm down to Boulder. There's a chap with a stable, says his business growing no matter what. I'll join him for now. He's got a place I can hang my hat."

"Well, I suppose a man's got to work. Maybe there'll be enough people left up here. Time will tell."

"Boulder's not so far away. You and I will still see each other. Who knows, you might be down there looking for pupils to teach yourself!"

"I'll be staying up here." Mabel said resolutely. "I can always make my way."

"Hop back on that pony, and I'll ride with you back to Cardinal and grab some supper at the hotel. Let's take the trail and avoid that dust."

In the meadow below the gypsy cart, Mabel and Tyler found Christian teaching his kitten to hunt rabbits. The cat had grown to a gangly size, and was rather good at walking on a lead. John said it would never be able to hunt for itself, but Christian was determined to teach him.

"That cat's gonna eat you one day." said Tyler in jest.

"If he can't catch a rabbit, he'll never catch me!" responded Christian with a wink. "I sure do enjoy him. Never thought I'd fall in love with a cat, but he's made a real soft spot in my heart."

"Got a few soft spots for animals myself." said Tyler.

"We'll see you in Cardinal." said Mabel, as they rode away.

"John is taking Christian to visit the Colorado School of Mines next week. He determined to get that young man educated, and of course I'm all for it. He will be interviewed by the Dean. I'm quite sure the school will accept him. He's a good student, if I may say so myself."

'Well-spoken, too." added Tyler.

"I'll miss him terribly." said Mabel. "But I know this is a good opportunity for Christian."

"How about John?" Tyler paused. "What will he do now?"

"John is considering several ideas. He'll continue to survey, of course. The gold mines near Central City can keep him plenty busy, but he is still interested in politics. I wouldn't be surprised if he ends up in Denver, maybe Golden with Christian."

"How do you fit into his plans?" asked Tyler. The question had been begging to be asked.

Mabel stared straight ahead up the path, with Tyler's horse trotting along behind to keep up with the pony. Tyler waited patiently for an answer.

Mabel finally spoke, "I have told John that I am staying here in Cardinal."

"You might be the only one!" Tyler pointed out.

"We'll see." said Mabel. "There's still gold in the Boulder County Tunnel."

Christian slowly got up from his sunny spot in the meadow. The cougar was fifty yards away. For a moment, Christian had thought the cat was finally going to get its own meal, but now it had given up its crouch, and plopped down in the grass.

Christian moved closer slowly to see what was over there. The cat was still attending to something. There must be something under the blue spruce tree. The cat stood and moved a little closer, then plopped down again, this time, playfully with a slight exaggeration. He cocked his head all the way to the side with a funny look.

Now, the cat rolled belly up, and Christian knew this was no longer a hunt. Christian stood to his full height and walked to the animal. He bent down and looked under the tree out of curiosity.

There sat a young girl. She was dressed in layers of colorful clothing and span dangled with bracelets and ribbons. She was a gypsy girl. The little girl was silent and wide-eyed. Of course, she must be scared out of her wits, thought Christian.

"It's okay." said Christian, "he's a pet. He's tame."

Spooked like a deer, the girl dashed across the meadow, and disappeared into the aspens on the other side. The cougar sat up quickly, and watched her go.

Christian spoke aloud to the cat.

"For once, I'm glad you didn't catch something, you beast."

The cat stood and sauntered over to Christian. He dropped himself at Christian's feet and lay blinking in the afternoon sun.

It was in the fall, after Alexander had left, that Mr. Blake closed the hotel. The next week, a crew of a dozen men came up to raze it and haul the lumber down the hill to Nederland. The sound of nails being wrenched, with great pounding and crashing, drove Mabel out of the schoolhouse and over the Boulder County Hill. She walked north at an elevation that was full of bright yellow aspen trees and golden meadows.

When she returned to Cardinal all that was left of the hotel was the floor, and piles of lumber. Mabel watched the last wagon of the day pull away. She sat on a rock overlooking the town. With the hotel gone now, Mabel was suddenly aware of how very many buildings had already been left and hauled off to be burned as someone's firewood. Emptiness spread through her heart.

A big tear welled up and fell from Mabel's eyes, then another, then a whole flood of them. Sadness so overwhelming struggled with an anger, which could be focused on no one in particular. How could a town die? How could the people just give up and walk away?

Mabel cried and cried. She cried for Mr. Blake, Honky Tonk Joe and Miss Ruby. She cried for all the times the mail had been delivered to the hotel, and the music that had drifted off into the night. When Mabel remembered that John and Christian would be leaving soon to spend the winter in Golden, she began to sob out loud.

When she was done, Mabel mopped her face with her skirt, took a few deep breaths and walked miserably down the hill to the schoolhouse.

Christian was waiting for her on the steps out front.

"Dusty Cougar is gone." he said.

"What? Where did he go?" Mabel asked.

"He's never left before." Christian added with his head hung low and his mouth in a pout. "Strange thing is, he was tied under the tree, and his cable is gone too. I think someone took him. He's gone."

To Mabel, this news came as a final blow, and she started to cry all over again.

Christian stood and held her. He was so much taller than her now. He wrapped his strong arms around her and cooed her like she used to do to him.

"Don't cry, Mabe. Come on, sweetie, don't cry. He's off on his next adventure. It's okay, Mabe."

Mabel was at a loss for words. There was just too much loss. It engulfed from all around.

"Mabel, I couldn't have taken him to school with me. You know that. You know I was trying to figure where he was goin' anyway. You know I really wanted him to be with you. But Mabe, I don't even know what you're gonna do."

Mabel looked up at Christian. He'd never seen her like this and found it most unsettling.

"The hotel's gone too." she said.

"I know it.", said Christian. "I know it."

With Mabel's insistence upon staying in Cardinal, John had insisted she move into his house. At least, there was a sunny kitchen with the big cook stove, and the bedroom, directly upstairs stayed warm. He had tried to get her to move to Golden with them, but there was no way Mabel would leave her Rocky Mountains.

Now, old cabins were cut up and stacked into cordwood on the west side of John's house. Each time a weather front blew through, it brought new snow. Winter came in earnest. The population of Caribou had dwindled from six thousand, in its heyday, to three hundred and forty two. Cardinal, formerly a town of twenty five hundred, had only sixteen people left. Most of the people who remained were, like Mabel, folks clinging to the past.

Mabel had only three students that winter. In November, they stopped heating the schoolhouse and Mabel taught in John's kitchen, by the stove. By December, they stopped school altogether, agreeing to resume between blizzards in April.

The mail came only every other day. It was received at John's house by Mabel, as the mail rider came through on his way to Caribou.

Mabel passed her time reading books, which trickled in a steady stream via John, through the U.S. Mail, from the Golden Library. Mabel was careful to ration the words, so as not to find herself out of a book.

Everyday, Mabel picked up the gypsy fiddle. It had begun to fit quite naturally under her chin. She had developed an ear for all of her school songs, and the ones her father had sung to her as a young girl. Each time she played, a stray cat who had been left by miners, would come up and sit on the parlor windowsill. He never let Mabel pet him and was gone in a flash each time she tried. Mabel couldn't decide whether his company made her feel comfort or more loneliness. The fiddle was often the only noise Mabel would hear in a day.

She loved the sound of the notes when they rang clearly. The fiddle became an old friend. Mabel caught herself talking to it more than once.

When Mabel went out on her skis each day, she stayed on the more travelled and level paths, her sense of adventure stymied by no one to miss her if she didn't make it home. Mabel's meals were usually simple and taken alone.

On Wednesday evenings, Mabel joined Mrs. Medoc, whose husband had passed. They were stitching a quilt together. Mrs. Medoc had seen a lot in her years, but had to be prompted for her stories. Mostly, Mabel loved the accounts of the many babies Mrs. Medoc had brought into the world.

On Saturdays, there was usually a gathering at one house or another for the few who remained in town. Even the most reclusive souls sought the company of others by Saturday. Mabel brought the fiddle to join up with a guitar, a mandolin and whatever someone tapped on to keep a steady beat. They'd often gamble with cards or dice, and drink a bit. Privately, the pious would ask forgiveness in their Sunday prayers.

Mabel spent the long quiet hours thinking about her friends. Alexander would be far to the south by now. Perhaps he had taken up with the Apaches or gone further into Mexico to fish the Yucatan Peninsula. Ruby sent regular letters from Denver, where her new business was booming on Wazee Street. The word from Christian was that school was hard work, but he was slowly and surely becoming a mining engineer.

John and Tyler came to visit a few times that winter. John always slept on the trundle bed in the parlor, insisting Mabel keep his old bedroom.

Tyler, on the other hand, crept into Mabel's bed after the lamps were out. He spooned his body with hers, and purred like a kitten. Mabel reminded him each time that he was only welcome on his best behavior and that he had a wife in St. Louis. In the morning, she would push him out of bed to rekindle the fire before daylight.

Oddly enough, it seemed Goodman had made the move with Mabel, for the fires at John's House blazed with the least bit of encouragement. Tyler found it highly unnatural that a fire would spring to life so easily, and other times burn when it should have long gone out. Mabel wondered about the spirit. Where had he come from? And how did he follow her across town when the schoolhouse closed? She was absolutely sure he was there.

Amazingly, no one got sick that winter. Thankfully, no one had to be buried.

At Christmastime, Mabel went by sleigh through Central City, and on down Clear Creek Canyon to Golden. She was glad to see that Christian had already found friends who monopolized his spare time. John talked incessantly about politics, and barely set his work down for the holiday. Before the week was up, she was antsy to be back up in Cardinal for city life dulled her senses.

The period of time between Christmas and spring's arrival was indeed longer than any Mabel could remember. The snows were relentless, and the famous Caribou winds howled the nights away. Mabel picked up the fiddle each day, coaxing new sounds out of it. She wondered if she had traded a cougar for a fiddle. As the winds stacked snow against the windows, she thought it was probably a very good trade. The fiddle brought her great joy.

When spring finally came, those who had stuck out the winter in Cardinal made their way down the mountain, resettling along Coon Track Creek or in Nederland three miles downhill.

In June, Alexander returned to Cardinal to find Mabel living as the last resident of the townsite.

"I can't say I'm the least bit surprised to find you as the last remaining resident of Cardinal." he said as he flopped his packsaddle on the west end of the summer porch to serve as his chest of drawers.

Mabel looked out across the meadow, which once had been Cardinal. She gazed at Alexander's two horses grazing untethered.

"It has been pretty lonesome the last few weeks. Everyone has moved down to Coon Track Creek near the portal of the Boulder County Mine."

"All seven of them?" Alexander smiled.

"It was eight actually. But this weekend, Christian's classes will be ended, and he will return to work in the Boulder County Mine for the summer. The population of Old Cardinal shall swell to three, counting you, Alexander."

"The price of gold is rewarding enough. I could stay for a while and see what comes of it."

That summer, the shaft at Old Cardinal went from five hundred and ninety-six feet deep to six hundred and ninety two. Down on Coon Track Creek, the Boulder County Tunnel pushed deeper into the mountain, slowly heading for its planned intersection with the shaft.

Mabel relished the company of her two men. She cooked for them, did their laundry, and enjoyed lively evenings, which often turned into wrestling matches between wisdom and youth.

When the Colorado School of Mines resumed in the fall, Alexander began to get restless. Mabel weighed her options. In the end, Tyler brought them a third horse. They boarded up John's house, packed a parfleche with hot coals from the fire, and Mabel left Cardinal to travel south with Alexander and Goodman.

1905

NEW CARDINAL, COLORADO

*T*he first snow had fallen on gold aspen leaves. It wasn't the first time that Mabel had been given a dusting of snow for her birthday. When the sun came out, this harbinger of winter would melt, and there would be Indian summer for a couple of weeks. Mabel recalled her year in Kennecott, Alaska, where she had landed a job managing the office of the copper mine. The days had been too long in the summer and too short in the winter. She was glad to be back to Cardinal, to forty degrees of latitude, where the sun still had warmth even in January.

Cardinal had seen many changes in the few years Mabel had been gone. The Boulder County Mine had kept Cardinal from disappearing altogether. In 1903, C.F.Lake had patented the Cardinal Millsite Claim. Gold was in demand, and the Boulder County Mine's tunnel down on Coon Track Creek was a grand producer. The Cardinal Townsite had moved a mile down the gulch to the creek to be near the huge new Cardinal Mill. The nature of the town had changed from a honky tonk to a real company mining town.

Old Cardinal had just two inhabitants left. They were old time miners who had nowhere else to go, and took advantage of the abandoned structures as firewood. One lived in a cabin near the top of the Boulder County Mine, and the other had squatted in John's house as "caretaker" so long that John gave up thoughts of having the old man ever leave. The wind had taken its toll on the clapboard building and John imagined that one day, the place would just blow away.

The news of the railroad coming had brought excitement beyond imagination in New Cardinal. The Switzerland Trail of America was its name, a tourist train. People rode up to see the snow capped peaks and pick wildflowers. Cardinal's train station sat just north of the tall trestle which spanned Coon Track Creek as the train crossed on its way south to the gold mining camp of Eldora.

The train coming through Cardinal Station brought supplies to the townsite and surrounding communities. Cardinal turned into a bee hive of activity when the train arrived. In the winter, the great rotary snow plow cleared the tracks, keeping Cardinal in touch with the outside world far more than it ever had been before. Winter was a constant struggle for the train crews. Sometimes, it was weeks at a time before the train could make it through. Spring was Mabel's favorite time to travel along the Switzerland Trail. Some drift cuts were as much as forty-feet high.

No. 32 CROSSING THE TRESTLE AT CARDINAL
The Kindig Collection

The one thing that hadn't changed was that Cardinal still received the U.S. Mail, only now the mail came by train from Boulder, and Mabel was a U.S. Postmistress.

Mabel bolted the front door of the Boulder County Mine Office, and flipped the sign over to read "closed". She set a heavy knotted log in the huge woodstove, and the coals kicked up a shower of sparks from the cast iron belly.

Goodman had traveled from Cardinal to Taos to the Yucatan to Placerville to Vancouver then Juneau, lived in Kennecott, where Mabel spent two winters as office manager for the copper mill, then returned to Cardinal by way of the Yukon.

Mabel's eyes grew wide at the maelstrom in the woodstove. It cracked and popped, threatening to jump out onto the floor.

"Happy Birthday to me, Goodman! Thank you!"

"It's done, Mabel!"

There came a thump, followed by groaning in the pipes, then the beautiful sound of water running from a tap.

Mabel ran through the meeting room, and into the caretaker's quarters, where Tyler stood beaming, wrench in hand.

"Happy Birthday to the only woman in Cardinal to have running water!"

"Tyler, you are truly amazing! Thank you!"

Mabel wrapped her arms around him and squeezed tightly.

"Well now, don't get too excited. We'll have to drain the pipes in a couple of weeks so they won't freeze in winter."

"It's still the best present a gal could get!"

Mabel released Tyler and turned the faucet on and off giggling with delight.

"I'll go wash up, and be right back for the party. When John arrives, send him directly over to the bunkhouse to claim a bed. They're hard to come by this week."

"You are my hero, Tyler. I shall think of you every time I turn on the water!"

Mabel picked up the fiddle and began to play a hero's tune. Tyler laughed, waved goodbye and modestly shook his head as he walked away. Still love that girl, he thought, always will. He was elated that Mabel had returned to Cardinal to run the office of the mine.

Mabel took a moment to change into more comfortable clothes. Many months of traveling disguised as a young man had spoiled her into appreciating the relaxed mode of dress granted to men. She put on her well worn traveling shirt, Indian moccasins and her favorite "house skirt". She brushed her long brown hair out and fastened it loosely at the nap of her neck.

Christian and John knocked on the solid wooden door, and Mabel peeked through the glass window and smiled. It was great to be back among friends.

"A bottle of the best scotch money can buy!" sang Christian.

"Happy Birthday, old girl!" offered John.

"Come on in, fellas!" Mabel opened the door and let the party begin.

"When did you get here, John?" she asked.

"Came up on the train this afternoon and busied myself inspecting goings on in the Mill, 'til Christian knocked off work. He runs a tight crew on his shift. Those boys are getting over half an ounce of gold to a ton, and a few ounces of silver to boot."

Mabel smiled proudly at Christian, and put her arm around John.

"He's a good foreman, and they say he's fair too."

"I'm as fair as a non-union guy can be, but I'm wondering how long they'll be callin' me that. Cardinal Mill's not the only place with labor issues." added Christian.

"This mill is one of the only ones left that'll keep guys going twelve hours a day." pointed out Mabel. "You'd better believe I hear about that!"

"We work till we get to a stopping point. Bet they don't mind the extra pay."

"Your men looked like they were making out okay there today." John acknowledged.

"Well, that's cause I told'm I'm off early to get cleaned up for a very special birthday party."

"And did you put them up to all coming up here to sing to me?" Mabel blushed.

"No, I believe they'll find any reason to come see you, Mabe!"

Tyler knocked once and came right in. He had a smile bursting on his face.

"There's another little something for you, Mabel, and she's tied right out here on your hitching post."

All three jumped for the door, but Mabel made it out first.

There stood a mare, just half a hand bigger than a pony. She was a dappled grey with black socks and muzzle. Her reins lay loosely across the log rail, and she turned her head toward the commotion with steadfast confidence. There was a sweet gentle look in her eyes.

"She's a gift from all three of us!" stated Tyler.

Mabel hugged each one of her guys, and then approached the mare with her hand turned upward.

"She goes by Smokey, but on paper her name is Princess Gracie Faye."

"She's absolutely perfect!" said Mabel, and she leaned in close to the horse's head.

The three men were smiling at the looks of it all, when suddenly a rider came flying down the road behind the office from Caribou. He pulled his frothing horse tightly around the corner and drew up in front of the little group.

"Don't ya know!" he yelled, "Caribou's on fire!"

The horse danced in place and the rider didn't dismount.

Smokey braced her legs under herself, but stood alert and still as could be.

"Started in the store, a defective flue. The men set off dynamite to stop it before it got to Billy Donald's. Ya'll are needed up there. It ain't good." And then he was gone to the east.

Tyler and John ran next door to the livery to hitch up Tyler's buckboard, while Christian saddled his horse. Mabel ran back inside to the office and telegraphed down to Nederland, "CARIBOU ON FIRE-M.G-CARDINAL"

Slipping long johns under her skirt, she ran outside and jumped on

Smokey bareback.

Christian and Mabel headed up the Coon Trail with the buckboard banging along behind. As they broke out of the valley below Caribou City, they saw the plume of smoke. Just before town, they ran into the first of a stream of people heading downhill. They were the old men, women and children. Some carried satchels and furniture. Some led frightened stock. Others pulled hand carts loaded to the brim. All of them were running with fear.

On the edge of the fire, men ran this way and that, working away.

Tyler parked the buckboard well upwind of the fire, on the flat where his stables used to be. Mabel held Christian's horse. She stood next to a small crowd of less able characters.

"It started in the store." offered a fellow, who looked as if he could have been helping.

"The water works are not functioning." added an old man on Mabel's left.

Mabel was speechless as she watched the blaze. She could see the charred remains where the fire had started, and two dozen structures stood as skeletons collapsing into flames. Stacks of cordwood, piled high for the coming winter, burned hot on the west side of each building. This was everyone's worst nightmare.

"They set off dynamite to stop the fire before it got to the old Sherman House." stated the old man. "Name's Wesley Tisick, Mam. I heard that dynamite all the way in Old Cardinal, I did. Came right up here to see about the bang, 'course then I seen the smoke. Oh, Lord."

Mabel shook her head in his direction, and felt big tears roll off her cheeks.

"Caribou taxes built the Boulder County Courthouse, you know" the old miner continued. "Guess this'll pretty well finish this old place off."

The snow was piled high around the Mine Office. The windows along the back, which faced the hill, no longer let in any natural light. One could only see snow and ice in the cavernous space beneath the deep snow drifts. Mabel could no longer see the window of the livery stable to the west of her living quarters. When Mabel went out to shovel the deck in front of the office, the snow cascaded off the roof in an avalanche, landing at her feet, dusting down the back of Mabel's neck, and causing her to have to start the job all over again. It seemed there was nowhere else to pile the snow, yet it kept coming. Mabel could only persevere and dream of the warmer days and spectacular summer evenings.

It was still dark, the early morning hours, when the thumping, whipping winds woke Mabel. She went back to sleep, all too aware of the problems this wind would create, for the train, the miners and even herself. The drifts by the train trestle would be horrendous.

By dawn, the winds had even accelerated more. It was evident that few would venture up from the Mill to the Office. It would be a quiet day of keeping the fire burning, balancing the books for the company, and preparing Payroll for the miners for the following day. There was no point in shoveling until the wind stopped. The drifts that formed half way up the doors would only be back in an hour's time if they were shoveled away.

Snow blew sideways past the front windows. It blew in the cracks of the window sashes and built drifts at the bottoms of the doors. The wind howled down the street toward the Mill, accelerating as it went.

Along about noon, a figure could be seen working its way against the gale toward the Mine Office. Mabel watched the man lean into the wind, sometimes stopping just to hold his ground. When he was almost to the Office, Mabel stood to open the door and greet him. He stepped in from the snow drift, and down onto the Office floor, bringing a pile of snow with him.

When the face was unwrapped, Mabel was delighted to find that it was Alexander, who had made his way to bring her company. He uncharacteristically held a bottle of whiskey in his coat.

"I can't take it anymore. I don't like the job on a good day. Milling's not for me. Those men have been in that building for too long. Tempers are worsening with the wind. Christian just caught a fella taking ore into his pocket off the shaker table. He was too easy on the man. The others aren't happy with that. The air is thick enough to cut with a knife."

"So you just up and left?" asked Mabel.

Well, Christian knows my heart's not in it. I told him I was cutting out. Decided I would get this bottle and sip the afternoon away, try to forget the fact that there's no where left for a trapper like me." Alexander sighed, took a swig and set the bottle on the desk.

"No, I won't join you, so don't even ask. I've got work to do, and I thought I might get something done if you boys would stay in that Mill on account of this wind."

"Well, having come out on this hellatious day, I might as well have a drink while I'm here."

"It's not like you to be drinking during the day, Alexander."

"Don't I know it, but this weather drives me to it. It'll help me decide what the hell I'm doing here at 8800 feet in February, and what I will do about that. Maybe next year it'll be the canyons of Utah, at least they're dry. Maybe I'll go back on down to those Apaches. We do alright together." Alexander took an especially long pull on the bottle, and then looked far away to somewhere he had been.

"You are forty six years old. Maybe sleeping in a bed's not such a bad thing." Mabel suggested.

Tyler came through the door just in time to hear Alexander say "Wouldn't mind if it was your bed, Mabel."

He took one look at the bottle and knew he didn't like what he'd heard. He saw Mabel turn away and carry a stack of papers to the back of the office.

"Tyler!" Mabel called from the back, "You are just in time to save me!"

Tyler took her all too seriously.

"What the hell are you doing drinking in here, and disrespecting a woman?" Tyler threw the words in Alexander's face.

"Certainly that comment was made with total respect." Alexander said sharply. "I'm drinking in here because this hellacious wind and six feet of snow has got the better of me, that's what. And watch out, cause this weather makes me wanna fight." With that, he slugged down enough whiskey to burn a line down his throat.

"Well, I ain't fightin' a drunken man." said Tyler.

"Not unless you're drunk too." suggested Alexander with a grin.

Tyler took a firm grasp on the bottle and poured a goodly amount down to his gut.

"What is with you two?" asked Mabel looking up from the books.

"I am here to defend your honor, Missy, and it looks like just in the nick of time." Tyler stood tall and proud. He took another belt.

"Catchin' up is what he's doing." Alexander slapped Tyler on the back and took the bottle from him. "And tryin' to pick a fight." he added.

"You son of a bitch!" Tyler took the bottle back and drank some more.

"Watch what you say about my dog." Alexander was clearly drunk.

"About your Mother!"

"That's it! Damn, I been wanting to hit somebody." Alexander stood, swaggered, and opened the door as an invitation. The wind blew all around the room, lifting papers and rearranging things.

"Close the door!" yelled Mabel.

"Ooo, I love that girl!" Alexander shut the door and leaned against it.

"She's mine, and you know it!" Tyler exclaimed, winking over at Mabel. "An' I never fight a man who's drunker than I am." He polished off what was left in the bottle.

"This girl's in love with me!" Alexander challenged.

"You bastard, she loves me!" Tyler stood right in Alexander's face.

"Oh, for crying out loud. You two deserve each other!" Mabel laughed at the two of them. She looked up just in time to see the door open again, and both men fly out onto the snow. As they jumped to their feet, they were squaring off for a fight.

Mabel couldn't believe her eyes. Immediately, the thought crossed her mind that men are certainly a different animal. What in the world were they thinking? They wanted to fight!

Tyler cast his coat aside just as Alexander hit him from the left. Tyler went down, but staggering to his feet in the snow, he stood for a moment and managed a broad smile.

Alexander approached again, but Tyler's arm took a fast shot from the right. Alexander caught the arm and held it down. The pair were locked together like rutting bulls.

Mabel stood in the doorway feeling every kind of emotion. She suddenly realized that if she didn't do something, this would end badly. She ran to the side of the woodstove, where a bucket of water sat ready for warming. Mabel came close to the tangled men and heaved the bucket load of water on top of them as evenly as she could. They didn't feel a thing.

She ran all the way back to her room and grabbed a bottle of perfume from the dresser top. A present from John Peregrine, another attempt to bring culture into Mabel's life. As Mabel rushed out onto the porch, the two crashed into each other heads down, one pulled back and threw a punch, but the other ducked and came back strong. Mabel got as close as possible and began to squirt the atomizer at the men.

"Argh."

"Jesus." The two were choking, and separated immediately. It was then that Mabel realized she was crying.

"What the hell, Mabel?"

"You didn't have to do that!"

They looked up at her, then each wiped a hand across his lips and saw blood. How could they look surprised, and a little pleased! Mabel went inside and slammed the office door hard.

"What's with her?" Alexander asked Tyler.

"Beats me?"

Inside, Mabel paced the length of the building several times before she looked out the east window to see the two of them walking off together toward the Mill with the wind pushing them down the street.

It had been several weeks since the train had been able to make it through the snow drifts from Sunset to Cardinal. Word had come that they'd break through today. Supplies had been getting scarce and everyone realized how dependent Cardinal had become upon the railroad. Mabel had been receiving the mail by sleigh from Boulder Canyon for the last two weeks, and she expected the rest of the delayed mail to arrive by train at last.

This was a particularly balmy spring morning. The winds had vanished and the sun was so bright on the snow that Mabel wore her sunglasses. A fine gift from John, the sunglasses had mica lenses and were lined with fur so they sat pleasantly on the face.

Expecting a goodly load of mail, Mabel tugged at the wooden box on runners that she used to haul loads up from the train. She tipped it upside down and rubbed candle wax along the runners until she was sure the sled would slide across the snow and ice.

Mabel left the Postmaster's horn inside, as the arrival of the train would suffice to announce the mail.

As Mabel approached the Superintendent's house on the east end of town, she could hear the engines ram at full speed to plow through the drifted snow. This train would have Locomotives #30 and #32 coupled to a plow and just one freight car, as it fought the perilous battle with the last of winter. Mabel left the sled, and took the wagon road up behind the Superintendent's to watch the ordeal. It might still be a while before the train would finally pull up to the Depot at the Cardinal Trestle.

From her perch above the railroad, Mabel could see the engineers back the train far enough up the hill to get a good run at the huge drifts that had settled in the gulch where the tracks curved above Cardinal. As they started forward, they quickly gave the engines full throttle, picking up enough speed to slam the snow pile. When the locomotives struck, the drive wheels spun crazily until the engineers could regain their senses after the impact and pull back on

Snow shovelers with rotary plow at Cardinal clear the spur switch by hand
Carnegie Branch Library for Local History, Boulder Historical Society Collection

Three engines pushing the rotary at Cardinal
Carnegie Branch Library for Local History, Boulder Historical Society Collection

the throttles. Exhaust poured out the smokestacks, and the sounds travelled like thunder through the surrounding hillsides.

Relay crews of snow shovelers worked the tracks in between rammings. Mabel watched the procedure for six more times, until at last the plow burst all the way through the worst of it and the train appeared out on the trestle. With that, the whistle blew loudly up at the Cardinal Mill, and the workers moving in small bunches, came down to see the train.

Mabel ran back along the wagon road to her sled, and hustled it down to the Depot.

"Bring me a letter!"

"Is this my lucky day?" the men shouted to her as she went past.

"I'll see you up at the Office!" Mabel called back. "The mail will be ready by five." she reminded them.

Mabel pulled her little sled alongside the Colorado and Northwestern Engine # 30, where Engineer Robert Cook tossed out three bags of mail. Mabel greeted him with a smile and a wave. He jumped to the ground and cheerfully loaded the sacks onto Mabel's sled. He gave Mabel the latest news, enjoying the company of a woman for just a few minutes, then tipped his hat and was back to business. It would be that two years later, Mr. Cook would be the fifth railroad worker to lose his life to the snows along the Switzerland Trail, when a derailed tender would slip from the rails, taking his locomotive four hundred feet down the mountain.

Before Mabel could even give the rig a tug, a miner had picked up the rope, and the sled lurched forward. His companion tagged along to help get the load up the steep hill to town.

"Number 30 will be back up tomorrow, if that wind doesn't howl all night!" Cook called out to the crowd. "She'll bring you all kinds of things! A load of hay..." his voice trailed off as he thought... and twenty four hundred pounds of dynamite for the Boulder County Mine.

The railroad crew climbed back up into the engines and when the pressure built up sufficiently, the train proceeded across the trestle toward Eldora. There would be two more big drifts to contend with as the train passed through the deep rock cuts at Hick's Gulch, and a steady snow pack of four feet deep the rest of the way along.

Everyone stopped and watched the train until it turned to the south about a mile past the trestle and snuck out of sight. It was an awesome creation of man, and had certainly brought great hope to the mining district.

The men pulling the sled were almost to the top of the hill when Mabel caught up with them. She was breathing hard, taking her responsibility to escort the U.S. Mail very seriously.

"Thank you, fellas. It's a bigger load than usual today!"

"Our pleasure, Miss Gurkin. What's the news?" asked the miner walking along side the sled.

"Mr. Cook said that the C & N Railroad is cutting ice from Glacier Lake this spring and running it down to Boulder and Denver. Nice blue blocks of ice. It's going to be a big seller! Why they'll have ice through mid June!"

"The railroad's good for Boulder County. Did you know that starting June, you'll be able to ride clear to Union Station in Denver? We'll be hitched up to the rest of the world!"

"And they're gonna run ore down the hill for a buck fifty a ton, if it's not worth more than twenty dollars a ton. Of course, if you've got ore worth more than that, it's gonna get special treatment and cost you more too."

"Fair enough." the pulling man spoke up. "You get ore worth that, and everybody's gonna take their cut all the way along!"

"Sure enough, and don't you know the guy digging it out, gets the least of it." added the miner by his side.

"The owner's are the greediest sons of bitches!"

"Watch your language, Red. There's a lady present."

"Yes, and one who is directly employed by the greedy owners!" Mabel smiled up at them both. It wasn't the first time she'd heard the miners grumble about wages, but doing the books for the company, Mabel knew it took more than just digging to turn a profit.

"Seems like the owners just collect profits, but the truth is they've sunk a lot into this operation from the start. If it wasn't for the owners, you'd be standing in the creek, talking to a donkey, and probably wouldn't have much to show for it." Mabel added in the absentee owners' defense.

"I came west thinkin' of gettin' rich on ore, and I've already spent last week's pay. Four bucks a ton for coal! A dollar fer a hundred pounds of potatoes. I've gotta save up for new shoes." the miner whined.

"Well, for fifty cents, you get a ride on outta here on that train! You got a better idea?" his partner asked.

"Hell, no!" the miner grinned back.

"Thank you, fellas!" Mabel offered as the sled crowned the hill by the Mill. "I can get it from here. I appreciate the help."

'You have a great afternoon, mam, and we'll see you later for the mail."

The other miner tipped his hat graciously and bowed. "Miss Gurkin," he said.

Mabel spent the afternoon sorting mail into the fifty mail boxes on the office wall. Many of the letters went into "General Delivery".

At one point in the afternoon, the sunshine begged Mabel to come outside. She stood out front of the Mine Office listening to sleigh bells as a rig descended behind the office on the Coon Trail from Caribou. The sleigh gathered speed as the horses broke out of the trees and onto the street in Cardinal. It was then Mabel could see that the sleigh carried four coffins toward the train. She said a prayer for those who had not "wintered over".

In the old days, people's coffins were stacked like cordwood in the shed on the north side of the church until spring, and then buried hastily at the first thaw in the Caribou Cemetery. Now days, folks could be shipped to their home state by train in the wintertime. It surely was a changing world.

Mid - afternoon she heard the train blow it's whistle as it crossed Cardinal's high trestle on its way back to Boulder.

Excursionists rode the train up from the prairies, from Boulder or Denver, to take the sightseeing "Trip to Cloudland". The wildflower tours were advertised widely, and tourists from all over the country, paid a dollar to ride round-trip to the Pavilion at Glacier Lake for the famous "Wildflower Picnic". From the lake, the snow covered Indian Peaks formed a backdrop that rivaled the Swiss Alps.

Mabel and Alexander decided they would have to enjoy the journey from the top down. It seemed to be the perfect afternoon, when they paid what the engineer called the "locals rate", and climbed with their knapsacks aboard the passenger coach as it headed down from Eldora. Hitched behind them were four observation cars which had brought excursionists to picnic at Mt. Alto and Glacier Lake.

As the train rolled north from Cardinal toward the Bluebird Mine, Alexander took Mabel's hand, and led her out the door of the passenger coach toward the first observation car. Having dropped its picnic passengers on its way past the lake that morning, the observation car was now empty.

"You are crazy!" Mabel yelled to Alexander, as he stepped across the metal grates with the couplers rattling loudly beneath them. The cars jerked and swayed uncomfortably for Mabel. The noise was almost more than she could bear. Gathering her wits, she clung to the metal hand holds, and watching her boots carefully, she mustered the bravery to step across the moving platform to the observation car. Alexander stood proudly with a hand out to receive her on the other side.

The cars seemed to roll smoothly along the track once one was safely seated. From the open air car, the pine forests whizzed by. Mabel was impressed by the speed of the train.

To the east, the sweltering prairies baked in the summer sun. To the west, storm clouds had gathered as the afternoon progressed, and were beginning to spit large drops of rain on Mabel and Alexander. As the train curved around the wide open meadows of Delonde Gulch, the droplets at once turned to hail stones, and the passengers had to make their way back across the scary platform to escape the weather.

"A benefit of riding the "Wildflower Tour" in reverse!" yelled Alexander, as they made their way back across. "Usually, the picnickers are herded like cattle onto the observation car, and do not have the option of escaping to the coach!"

"Usually, the picnickers are already picnicking by the time the afternoon storms hit!" Mabel pointed out as they shook the water and hailstones onto the wooden floor of the coach.

"Good point!" acknowledged Alexander.

Now the train stopped at the Bluebird Depot, where two gentlemen dressed in suits climbed aboard the coach. They shook half an inch of accumulated hail off their shoulders and hats.

The locomotive built up a head of steam, and with a pull on the whistle, began to roll out once again. The train switched back and forth to climb to Glacier Lake and all the while it poured rain and hail outside. Mabel sat happily watching out the windows of the coach, feeling especially lucky to be dry.

By the time the brakes brought the train to a halt at Glacier Lake, the weather had moved east, forming huge thunderheads higher than castles over the prairies. The station platform was crowded with people of all ages waiting to ride back to Boulder. They held armloads of wildflowers which were already beginning to wilt in the sun.

Women dressed in long dark skirts and white blouses had taken on too much sun despite their broad brimmed hats. The men carried picnic baskets, no doubt much lighter than when they had arrived. Most appeared to have enjoyed a bit of beer on the lake, and held satisfied looks of leisure well taken. Children were the first to jump on board, running the length of the car, and then settling in beside their mothers to fall asleep with hot red faces.

Alexander and Mabel traded places with this crowd, and hauled their knapsacks to their backs as the train began to roll out. When the train pulled away and out of sight, it all seemed strangely quiet at first.

The travelers smiled at each other. It had been a long time since they had been on an adventure, and this, right in their own backyard, was an adventure of great luxury!

The Pavilion was quiet at this time of day. They shucked their packs there, and walked excitedly to the lakeshore where rowboats sat lined up, ready for launching. Alexander carried two beers, and a festive mood. The two rowed gently around the lake enjoying the calm of the evening and the alpenglow as the sun set behind the Indian Peaks.

When the temperature dropped rapidly, they rowed to shore, put on wool coats and hats, and cooked dinner over an open fire. Staring up at the stars and remembering the nights they had spent travelling together, Alexander and Mabel talked themselves off to sleep by the fire.

"These are the memories I love. These are my treasures." was the last thing Mabel heard Alexander say. She smiled broadly to herself in the dark and rolled up closely to Alexander's warmth.

Mabel woke to the familiar sound and smell of Alexander making cowboy coffee. The morning sun warmed her sleeping bag and the whole world seemed very still, except for the birds busying themselves quietly. To hold this moment, thought Mabel. She giggled as she thought of the contrast of this, with the intensity of the winter, which had ended not so long ago, and would be back in no time at all.

The novelty of floating about in boats drew them back onto the lake that morning. Trout surfaced as the day warmed, then swam deep as the breezes picked up, and the day got underway.

By noon, the train arrived with its load of hundreds of passengers. The excursionists went in every direction, hiking, climbing, and sitting on the rocks, fishing from boats and the shores. The pavilion was crowded with those less disposed to activity, and that is where Mabel, observing out of curiosity, met her old friend, Miss Ruby!

"I'm retiring." stated Ruby, when they settled down to talk. "I'm old, and I'm retiring."

"Ruby, you're not old enough to be old." said Mabel.

"Well, Lord knows I'm old enough to be retiring."

"So what does that mean?" Mabel inquired, thinking one couldn't last forever in Ruby's profession.

"It means the few old Fellas that were mine, if you know what I mean, they've either lost interest, if you know what I mean, or up and died. I still got the girls, you know, for now. But I'm tired. I'm tired of it all. Tired of keepin' tabs on those girls. Tired of keepin' them outta trouble. Tired of stayin' up half the night...and wringin' money outta those boys before they get started."

"You know, it's been good. I can't complain." Ruby continued. "It's been real good down there on account of there bein' so many people. But, I'm tired."

"So you're retiring..." Mabel restated. "That's wonderful. How do you do that?"

"Well", Ruby said in a low gravelly voice, "I don't exactly know yet. I'm finding a way."

"Will you go live with relatives? Back in Missouri?"

"Ain't got none, never did, you know."

"Well, surely you've got a fine home in Denver?"

"Wasn't a home, honey. It was a business."

"Right."

There was a long pause before Ruby said it.

"I was thinkin' ah coming back up here. Back to Cardinal."

Mabel was speechless. In her panic, her eyes searched for Alexander out on the lake. The very idea of Ruby coming back seemed preposterous! Everything about Cardinal was different now.

"Y'all are all I really ever had for friends, you know." Ruby looked a little sad when she said that. "Like, how about John? How is he doing?"

"John is well, Ruby. He's well."

"He was always a kind and generous man."

"He still is, Ruby. He doesn't live in Cardinal anymore though. He's down in Golden. Still being a surveyor too. Working real hard. Gets all over these hills. Still politicking some too."

"And how about the boy?"

"Christian is fine. A fine young man. Hard working too. He is a foreman at the New Cardinal Mill. Graduated from the School of Mines!"

"You're lucky to have'm aren't ya?"

"You bet, Ruby. You bet."

"So you never settled down with a fella, did ya? No ring, honey? Why not? A gal like you!" Ruby shook her head, like it was a big waste.

"Ruby, you know me! I've been too independent from the day I was born. Men are afraid of a woman like me. "

Mabel looked out over the lake, wondering why that was so true. The sun was shimmering off the water, and for a moment she wished she'd been wearing her sunglasses, until she realized how silly they'd look.

"Guess it's the same for me, sweetheart. And that's why we got to stick together."

"Maybe that's right." Mabel said, a little absentmindedly on purpose.

Mabel jumped up.

"There's Alexander! He would love to see you!" She ran out into the sun and grabbed Alexander by the hand and led him in to see Ruby.

Alexander was blinded in the shade of the pavilion and blinked until his eyes adjusted. Suddenly, he could see that the place was filled with mostly women, who had come to the mountains and found themselves quite out of their element. They shied from the high altitude sun. And there, right in front of him was Miss Ruby.

"Miss Ruby!" he exclaimed, "It's been a very long time...since Old Cardinal went by the way."

"Alexander." heaved Ruby, as she buried his face in her neck and bosom as only Miss Ruby could do. Mabel laughed to see that nothing about her had changed.

"I've been in Denver eleven years now." she noted. "Been running a lovely establishment across the street from the Brown Palace. Things have gone well."

"Ruby is thinking of retirement!" added Mabel.

Miss Ruby blushed and swayed, and looked coyly up at the ceiling. Alexander glanced at Mabel with a wink.

"Miss Ruby, it seems you've done well for yourself! You have brought more pleasure to men than there are stars in the sky."

"And now I intend to rest." she said.

"Well, you deserve it. You must have a fine home in the City of Denver."

"Miss Ruby is considering her retirement in New Cardinal!" Mabel said, with a smug smile.

Alexander stared at the aging woman, remembering her dressed in gay nineties rose satin evening wear. The move seemed highly unlikely, but he decided to humor her.

"What a delight it would be to have you back up here in the hills with us. The night life definitely took a downturn when you and the ladies left town. Why, there are two shifts of twenty men each working the Cardinal Mill these days. Most of them live in the east end of the Mill, and they haven't had a lick of fun since time began. We don't have a church goer in town."

Mabel listened in disbelief. What had happened to the proper gentleman who had first approached her at the Harvest Feast years ago? He had lost all of the gentrification he was raised with. He had spent too many nights sleeping by a fire under the sky. He had become relaxed and familiar with his dear friends, and perhaps a bit nostalgic for the good times at the hotel in Old Cardinal. He wasn't alone at that.

"Oh, Alexander" Ruby cooed, "It is good to see you! Such a handsome boy still."

"Watch it, Miss Ruby" Alexander challenged, "I've been a man since the day I met you!"

"I am dead serious about coming back to Cardinal. I was telling Mabel, my heart lies there. I've never felt so at home, such a part of a place, as my days with ya'll. I'd like to build me a little clapboard house, and settle back in. I'm tired of big business. I been at it a long, long time."

MABEL RODE #32 ALONG THE SWITZERLAND TRAIL
Carnegie Branch Library for Local History, Boulder Historical Society Collection

MABEL & RUBY AT GLACIER LAKE; ENGINE #33, SWITZERLAND TRAIL, C &N RAILWAY
Carnegie Branch Library for Local History, Boulder Historical Society Collection

"Miss Ruby, you wouldn't be there a day before you had some sweet young things living with you. The men would be prowling around like tomcats. I believe your retirement would be premature."

"You might be right about that. I'd need a gal or two just to shovel snow and stoke the fire anyways, wouldn't I?"

"I'm telling you, Ruby. There'll always be a market for your business, as long as there's a mine in operation. And the Boulder County Mine, it's a producer!"

The train whistle blew from somewhere to the south. The pavilion began to empty.

"Let's walk you out to the train, dear." offered Mabel, taking Miss Ruby by the arm. Mabel couldn't imagine why a woman this age, who never set foot out in the snow in all her years in Cardinal, would ever consider coming back. She kissed Ruby goodbye as if she'd probably never see her again. It was a kiss of love and affection, a kiss to send her off with all the luck in the world.

When the train had disappeared from sight, heading back to the prairies, Alexander and Mabel took their fishing poles out in a boat to watch one more glorious sunset over Glacier Lake.

Mabel rose especially early on this particularly spectacular fall morning. The first serious breezes of autumn blew in the dark hours before dawn, awakening her. Squirrels ran up the outside of the building as they gathered seeds for the coming winter. She had remembered that this was payday; also the mail would arrive in time for the miners to collect both at the same time. Ernestine, her office girl, was gone to Central City to see her sister's new baby boy. It would be a very busy day. Mabel made a quick breakfast and stoked the fire in the huge office woodstove. Before she left for her morning walk, she placed a cast iron frying pan full of water on the stove to bring some humidity into the office.

The town was quiet as she slipped out into the cool morning air. The yellow aspen quivered and rustled in the wind. The sky was an azure blue that could only be seen at this very time of year. There was nothing quite like an early fall morning on the Rocky Mountains. When Mabel climbed the hill toward Old Cardinal, she startled a bull elk. He went off crashing through the woods with complete abandon. Mabel walked on until she crested the hill and found the meadow that had not long ago been the Town of Cardinal.

"Old Cardinal." she said aloud. "Old Cardinal."

She felt too young for this place to be old. Too young for a town to have grown and disappeared again. Mabel reminded herself, that she was probably half way through her lifetime. She expected to live to be an old crone. Mabel wondered for just a moment, what she would do with her time and her mind when she was truly old. She had no idea what it would be like. When her thoughts progressed to leaving this world, she decided to take it all a day at a time, and returned her focus to the brilliant colors of red and orange grasses that filled the Cardinal meadow. She gathered ripe rose hips from around the old rock foundations, which were already crumbling. They had never been built with mortar to begin with. They had been built with the same haste that they were disappearing with. As Mabel sucked on a rose hip, she mused that a lifetime, with some luck, was probably long enough by the end.

As Mabel came down the Coon Trail behind the Office, she saw a man turn the corner of the Office building on the west side, near her living quarters. Strange that anyone would be there. By the time she rounded the front, there was no one to be seen. She went next door to the stable and threw a few flakes of hay to Smokey.

Mabel checked her room. She opened the door that faced south, and looked around the corner to the west. No one in sight. Mabel changed her clothes with an eye to the window, and headed into the Office at the east end of the building to get to work.

The first shift of miners would be in by two o'clock. The second shift would collect their pay just before that, when they went to work. Mabel would arrange an envelope, stamped with the company name, for each miner. The more permanent fellows got company checks, and cashed them at the new bank in Nederland. The temporaries would collect cash, and sometimes take a percentage of ore as well; in which case, they would bring her a paper note from the Assay Office to show the value of their ore. Ernestine had written out the checks before she left, and Mabel would sit down to sign them. Everything would be recorded in ledgers.

Mabel sat at her desk near the woodstove. She signed the checks. She would get his accomplished before the mail would arrive on the train about ten o'clock, then hustle back to sort the letters.

The door to the Office opened. A man let himself in.

"The Office is closed." Mabel stated, as she took in the fact that she didn't recognize this particular man.

He smiled a small smile and walked up to the brown fence that separated the miners from the office ladies. He was wearing travelling clothes. Rough ones, like a trail rider.

"The sign still says closed." Mabel pointed out. The man removed his hat.

The man opened the gate and stepped past Ernestine's desk. Mabel stood, and stepped to the side of her desk toward the woodstove. Time seemed to stand still.

"I reckon you've got some money for me, being payday and all." the man said.

"I don't believe I know you, Sir." Mabel was absolutely sure this man was not employed at the mine or mill. She kept her breathing steady, but felt herself rapidly losing her normal presence. Her blood seemed to drain from her heart and she felt weak.

"I'm asking you to put what payday cash you have into this sack, mam, without any trouble." The man glared black eyes at her. He was scared too.

A squirrel jumped onto the side of the building outside the window, and the man turned to check the noise. Mabel grabbed the frying pan from the top of the woodstove, and bringing it down like an axe, hit him hard on top of the head. He fell to the floor, and didn't move.

Mabel ran through the swinging gate and out onto the front deck. There was no one in the street. She ran toward the Mill. As Mabel passed the Blacksmith Shop, she caught a glimpse of the smithy and two more men. They had already dropped their business when they saw Mabel running like the house was on fire.

Breathlessly, she cried, "The Office has been robbed!"

The men, armed with a hot poker and horse whips, ran together down the street toward the Office. For just a minute, Mabel almost went with them, but she gathered her wits and crossed to the Compressor House for more support.

Three more fellows raced toward the Office, and Mabel sat down on a bench to cry.

The men searched the building. One stood on guard at the front. There was nothing they could do when a horse burst from the livery stable next door, and flew past them at a gallop. The man headed the horse east and was past the Mill in just seconds.

Mabel looked up through her tears, and felt her fear turn to anger when the horse bolted by. This man had stolen Smokey! And he was on the getaway and riding her too hard.

Mabel ran toward the Superintendent's House and looked over the valley to the east just in time to see the train set its brakes at the Depot. The man on the Smokey was trapped. The train was well onto the trestle out in front, and was long into the railroad cut through the rock as far as the eye could see. The road to Nederland was blocked by the train.

Smokey danced and bucked in confusion, and the man kicked her uselessly in the sides. Finally, he rode the horse down the steep embankment and

Cardinal on D. B. and W. Railroad

CARDINAL ON THE D. B. & W. RAILROAD *Carnegie Branch Library for Local History, Boulder Historical Society Collection*

under the train trestle. He sped off down the dirt road faster than Mabel would ever push her horse.

The men came in pursuit. Four on horseback did the same dance in front of the train, but one of the men had taken the railroad spur that ran along the south, and he made good time as he raced alongside the tracks heading east.

Tyler rounded the tight curve just east of the Alton Mill and Tunnel, one half mile from Cardinal. He stopped his horses and considered for a moment, whether or not to water them at the creek or push on. He recognized Smokey immediately as she rounded the curve full tilt, so he dropped his string, and stepped his mare into the path of the moving horse. The horses recognized each other and Smokey came to an abrupt halt. For one surreal moment, she and the mare sniffed each other's noses, and with a start the man kicked Smokey and pulled hard to the right.

"Whoa, Smoke!" shouted Tyler in a loud but familiar tone.

The horse struggled against the man. The rider from Cardinal barreled down Hick's Gulch Road and across the creek, intersecting the two at the curve. His rope swung around the man's neck, just as Tyler's rope caught Smokey's head and shoulder. Tyler jumped to the ground and steadied the frightened horses, as the lariat tightened, trapping the thief.

When news of the capture made it back to the Office, Mabel was sitting at her desk with Christian, who had come at once from the Mill. He had shown the good sense to pour her a whiskey.

The man was taken to the Marshal's Office in Nederland, where they most likely made him quite miserable, before he was escorted to Boulder and placed on a train to be met by the law in his home town of Kansas City. Mabel kept an eye for that man for the rest of her days. Christian insisted she keep a shotgun by her bed, just out of principal, but Mabel was glad she didn't have a gun the day the office was almost robbed.

THE CARDINAL MILL IN ITS HEYDAY CIRCA 1920
Carnegie Branch Library for Local History,
Boulder Historical Society Collection

1917

❧

CARDINAL, COLORADO

*A*s Mabel rounded the corner just east of the Cardinal Mill, she paused on the road to take in the view. Mabel gazed to the east, imagining the far off land across the ocean where the great World War was being fought. It seemed impossibly far away, and Mabel felt safe from it here on these mountain tops. Yet it was the need for the black tungsten ore that was driving nearby Nederland's economy. The heavy metal was used to harden the steel for armaments in the war effort. News of the war seemed unreal to Mabel, as she looked out toward the sea of prairies where the sun was rising. Out there, across the

THE ROD MILL IN 2000
Photo by Ed Raines

Atlantic the day at war was well under way and Americans were dying.

Below her, the Cardinal Mill had three new sections added to provide living quarters and a new mess hall for the miners. Now, the gold mill ran two eight hour shifts a day, and Mabel could hear the first shift banging and clanging relentlessly in the main part of the mill. New electric lines now ran up from the hydro plant at Tungsten from the dam at Nederland's Barker Meadow replacing the old coal fired boiler, which now sat languishing on its brick stand near the blacksmith shop. The new power allowed for a rod mill for crushing the ore. Mabel had watched men unload the huge cylindrical monster and its four-ton motor from the train. She was always amazed at what men could do when they teamed up and put their minds to a job.

The sounds that emanated from the mill could be separated out like instruments in a band. From the top section, Mabel could hear men yelling above the general din as they pulled the tram into the top of the mill to dump ore onto the first grizzly. The clang of a sledgehammer rang out signaling the first cart had been dumped, and the ore was being broken up by hand to fit through the slats on the grizzly, and fall into the shaft below.

In the mid-section, Mabel could hear the whine of the motor, which drove the big thumping belts, which in turn lifted the ore with a bucket elevator to dump it. Rhythmic crashes kept a beat, as each bucket crested the top of the belt elevator and dumped its load to fall two stories down into the hopper.

Deep within it all, came the loud screech and deafening tumble of the giant motor and the rotating mill itself. It was the heart of the operation.

The Addit Cut, Boulder County Mine circa 1915
Carnegie Branch Library for Local History, Boulder Historical Society Collection

Machinery chugged away agitating flotation mixture in cells, and the metals rose to the top in a foam. Mabel remembered the men hauling the buckets toward the tables.

From the base of the mill, came the low rumble of the shaker tables. Each had its own small motor. The slightly inclined tables shook the high-grade ore, as men washed it over slats which caught the heavy metals.

Shouts of men rose here and there, all over the mill, forming the melody. The machinery was the rhythm, and together, it all made a song of men at work.

Mabel smiled on her good fortune to have been born a female, and to be standing outside in the warm morning sunshine. Of course, being female had its curses, but overall, she was glad of her lot in life. She smoothed her long skirts, patted her tightly pinned hair, and sat down on a large rock looking over the valley.

Changes had come to this place, and Mabel had been witness to them all. The train, the Cardinal Mill, the forest coming down one tree at a time until a fellow had to bring firewood by wagon to his home. The valley was spotted with cabins, even clapboard homes, like Ruby's. At the moment, each trailed a wisp of smoke from the chimney as the morning fires were dampened down after breakfast.

And what of the changes in the world? The new inventions of the day spurred the imagination to wonder. Mabel had heard that mail was now being flown by aeroplane! Last year, the telephone had connected San Francisco to New York. Only a decade ago, Molly Brown had mesmerized Denver with her Fritchie Electric car, which could travel one hundred miles on a single electric charge. Now, the electric car was to be replaced with a gasoline engine! And Mabel herself had a phonograph, presented to her by none other than John Peregrine. It was the only one for miles around. It was a good thing Mabel lived at the Mine Office, where it could bring joy to many.

There were changes in the business of mining and milling. Used to be that miner's came out west looking for glory, staking a claim and working it. But nowadays, most places had been staked and the miner's worked for owners in the places, which had stood the test of time. The owners controlled the districts. Now, the miners had labor concerns instead of gold fever. It made for a different sort entirely, thought Mabel. She wistfully remembered the days when men full of hope would ride into town, clutching a small sack of ore, and be content to sell it at the Assay Office and enjoy the fruits of their labors. She thought for a moment of the honky tonk shows, and piano music and she felt time slipping away.

Changes had come for Mabel personally as well. The hardest thing she'd ever experienced was the broken heart that would never go away. Alexander had left three summers ago to pan gold in the Yukon. The only place left, he'd said. When he didn't return the first winter, Mabel waited patiently at first, as the mail came in with no word from Alexander.

She made it through that first winter by choosing to believe that Alexander had been snowed in up north. She imagined him sharing a cabin by a river with a few other men. Trappers, perhaps. But when the ice went out and the boats travelled the big rivers north again, Alexander did not reappear. Possibly, his luck had been good and he had struck out into the wilderness once more with the coming of spring.

Mabel had spent that summer looking over her shoulder, walking down to wait for the train, and eagerly sorting Cardinal's U.S. Mail. All to no avail. As Mabel's hopeless depression had set in with the fall, John went on a campaign to locate Alexander. In November, when the north once again closed for the season, the final word came in the form of a letter from Whitehorse. No one had seen Alexander from the time he had originally left Yellowknife.

Mabel nursed her ache and emptiness, lost in the finality of it all. She carried her grief everywhere, trying to keep some hope alive that Alexander would yet return. When Mabel took sick that winter, Ruby sat by her bedside, pointing out that this grief would kill her if she didn't start to let it go. Ruby said this is not what Alexander would have wanted, and Mabel knew in her heart that Ruby was right. Mabel made a choice to live, and slowly recovered.

Mabel thought of Alexander's life of itinerant trapping, trading and panning, and how in recent years his ways had been pinched by changing times. She wondered if that had anything to do with his leaving this world. The thought was just comforting nonsense, she decided, a man could still live that way up north.

The community built a U.S. Post Office across the tracks from the Cardinal Train Depot, and hired a postmistress. Mabel decided to forego the position, and became New Cardinal's schoolteacher instead. It was Christian's five year old twin sons, along with three other students, who daily reminded Mabel that life must go on among the living.

One of those students was six-year-old Margaret. Margaret lived in the Post Office with her mother, Catherine, the new postmistress. Each morning, such as it was this day, Mabel would walk down to the Post Office and have a coffee with Catherine. She would braid Margaret's long blonde hair while the two women chatted. When Margaret could no longer stand the waiting, she would take Mabel by the hand and they would walk back up the hill to have school with the others in the old Mess Hall.

This day, when Mabel reached the Post Office, Margaret sat up on the rooftop and announced that she was not coming down until it was time to go to school. She was dressed in her play clothes and her hair was unbrushed.

"And why is that, Margaret?"

"I'm very cross." she said, and folded her arms in front of her.

"When you come down, you will have to tell me about that." Mabel suggested and she went in to join Catherine in the kitchen.

"There is trouble brewing, Mabel, and I'm not talking about what's up on the roof." Catherine warned.

"Yes, there's talk been going 'round" said Mabel.

"They want to shut the Mill down." finished Catherine, "if the man don't come and change things pretty quick."

"I'm afraid, Catherine, because the only ones that can change anything are in New York. They don't know what it's like to be working here for this pay, and trying to make a living."

"The men outside this morning, real early... there was some real talk. Serious talk. Low voices and all." Catherine put her hand to her head and scrunched her face. "I'm afraid too, Mabel, and I don't like it one bit."

"I'm ready to go." came a small voice in the doorway.

Catherine smiled and nodded as Mabel and Margaret departed.

"So what's eating you, Margaret? Why are you cross?" Mabel asked as they crossed the tracks and headed up the road.

"It's those miners, Miss Gurkin. I've had about enough of them."

Mabel bit her lip to control her smile and appear sympathetic, which she genuinely was.

MARGARET 1917 *The Baker Collection*

'Free'

Margaret 'free' *The Baker Collection*

MARGARET, CATHERINE & MABEL WITH THE ENGINEER AND FRIENDS. 1916
CARDINAL STATION, SWITZERLAND TRAIL
The Baker Collection

"Do you know what that tall skinny one says to me, the one that doesn't patch his pants?"

Mabel shook her head "What?"

In a whine Margaret mimicked, "Marg-ar-ite, go wash your feet, the Board of Health is across the street!"

"He doesn't!"

"Oh yes, he does and smiles about it too!" Margaret stopped and put her hands on her hips. "And I won't stand for it any longer."

"I think he's just making a rhyme, Margaret, just like we do in school. He's being friendly."

"Friendly schmendly, I don't see the humor in it."

"I'd say he likes you and he is trying to get you to talk to him."

"Well, I won't." and she stomped on up the hill alone.

Mabel strolled to the top of the hill, where Margaret stood with a big stick.

"I'll tell you a story about when I was six like you. There was a boy my age named Timothy. He gave me trouble just so he could see me. Each day, when I walked to school, I had to go past his house. It was on a sidewalk in the city. He would leap out from behind the hedge and spit on me!"

"Oh, Miss Gurkin, that's terrible!" Margaret whacked the stick on a rock.

"I learned to run before I got to his house, so that by the time I got there, I was practically gone again."

"Well, problem for me that the Post Office is at my house!"

"People are funny, Margaret, they don't know how they make you feel unless you tell them."

"And sometimes they act the opposite of what they really feel. Timothy loved you, Miss Gurkin." added Margaret.

Mabel thought again of Alexander, and why he went away.

As they reached Mess Hall, Margaret stated, "I think I'll write him a jingle that he can say about himself!" and she ran to join the other children who were poking about in the stream.

Mabel stood for a few minutes, letting the children do what they do, while she thought about Christian and the difficult position he was in.

The Marshall came to town, with a deputy riding by his side. His hat was pulled way down as he passed the Cardinal Mill. They didn't slow until they were in front of the office of the mine. Christian, having already supervised the early shift, was waiting for them.

"Thank you for coming." Christian shook the hands of both men.

"Sounds like things are coming to a head here. Words out in Nederland." The Marshall removed his hat, sat down and hung the hat on his knee.

Mabel served the men coffee, and went into the next room to tell Ernestine to take the rest of the day off, and be watching out, just in case there was trouble. Maybe just stay home.

Mabel sat at the desk, just out of sight, keeping an eye down the main street of town toward the Mill. She could hear everything that was said.

"There are certain men, Marshall, that have taken the idea that they run the place; that without them there would be no mine and mill. And Sir, as true as that may be on a day to day basis, it's the owners of the Boulder County Mine and the Cardinal Mill who get to make the rules."

"I'm well aware of that."

"We haven't got a real organized union here. Might be better if we did. At least there would be leadership to negotiate with. But as it is there are a few men who might take things into their own hands, who have the support of others."

"Words out down the hill here that charges may be planted in some strategic places. Seems to me you ought to shut it all down until the talking gets done."

"I hope it comes to talking first, Sir. That's why we called for you."

The Marshall scratched his head, and with a look of impending trouble, he said, "Cripple Creek's mine owners are still holding control. Look at what's happened there. Samuel Lack's cabin blown sky high by dynamite. A woman housing nonunion boarders left town for fear of being arrested. The State declared the County in a state of insurrection and rebellion. Don't think it can't happen here."

"And there was the killing in Ludlow. Things aren't any better with the coal miners." added Christian.

"At least the Pinkerton's aren't publishing rabble-rousing words here yet." the Marshall's deputy spoke.

"You are the Foreman. You know the specific men. We must seek to understand the mindset of opponent." The Marshall was taking a pragmatic approach.

"Yes Sir." Christian knew the anger and irrational thoughts of the most dangerous few very well. "These men have been here long enough to see changes. Unfortunately, changes caused by economics. Changes that don't favor the men."

"You must put yourself in their mindset to properly gauge the trouble here."

"Yes, this is true. I work day in and day out with these men. There are those who understand that without the owners, we don't operate. But it is the men who think operations can proceed independent of the owners who are trouble."

"Do you know what will satisfy these men?" asked the Marshall.

"There must be no conflicting interests between the owners and the miners. That's a daunting order, when you walk the line between the two, as I do." Christian stated, thinking of the financial offices in New York City and the cigar puffing men who saw only numbers. There seemed to be no possible bridge between the owners and the miners.

"These men's desires must be faced without wrath and judgment, which only diminish and consequently anger the opponent." The Marshall had spent many an hour talking to men who had caused trouble.

There was silence among the men for a spell.

"There can be no solution that compromises the dignity or self worth of the miners. I agree with you, Sir."

"For the immediate safety of the mine," the Marshall motioned toward the other room, "I want you to clear innocent people out of harm's way."

Christian nodded and kept listening.

"I don't want to set guards out, but it might come to that. We'll see. We don't want to escalate the situation by bringing the law in right away. We want to get the two parties talking."

"Well Sir, that seems to be the problem. You see the split is within the group of workers—those loyal to the owners, for every kind of reason, personal or moral and those who want to run the operation themselves, which is hardly legal or realistic. How does one find a solution that honors their desires, yet honors what is legal and right."

"If we knew that, I guess we wouldn't be here." The Marshall smiled a resigned sort of smile, and asked, "Who can negotiate for the owners?"

"There is no one." Christian knew, for he himself had to support the needs of his men, or he would have no authority in the workplace. "The men at odds are challenging the wrong enemy. They challenge their very own kind because the men in New York are phantoms. They are not here to fight. I have been called to New York as a liaison of sorts, but my position is working with the men, not representing the owners."

"You, my friend, are in a pickle. Sometimes outcomes are beyond our control." stated the Marshall.

Again, there was an extended silence.

Finally, the Marshall stood.

"I would like for you to assemble this shift of men outside the bottom of the Mill. I will have a word with them."

Christian thanked the Marshall and his deputy and went walking down the road. Mabel watched out the window until he disappeared into the Mill. After listening to the conversation with the Marshall, Mabel worried about Christian's safety. She busied herself with paperwork until the Marshall and his deputy rode down the street.

The following morning, Mabel woke to a loud, frantic knocking on the office door. Next the knock was at her own front door. It was Christian. It was evident that he hadn't slept a wink.

"Mabel, the men won't work today. You must clear out of here. It's not safe for you to be here...in the office of the mine."

"Where shall I go?" Mabel stood in foggy disbelief.

"I've thought it through. The safest place to be is Miss Ruby's house."

"I suppose it's the last place the men would blow up. I will get a few things and go. Thank you, Christian."

Mabel stepped outside and down two steps to where she could extend her arms toward Christian.

As she hugged him she said, "Christian, whatever may come, remember it's only about money. Don't put yourself in danger."

"Mabel" Christian held her tightly, and then released her to look her in the eyes. "It is about money, and without money, there are a lot of people who have nothing. There may be danger, but I'll do my best, I promise. My men are gathering at the top of the Mill, on the road, in front of the Superintendent's House. You must go now, while you can still get through."

Mabel nodded and said "Christian, I love you." Tears of fear began to pool in her morning eyes.

Christian said, "I have come up with a plan. I'll see you soon."

As Mabel approached the Mill from the west, men stood leaning against the building and loitering in the road. There were almost two dozen of them, all with guns and some with metal rods or drill bits. It was unnaturally quiet.

"Mornin' Miss Gurkin." one spoke up.

Mabel, clutching a knapsack, was keeping up a pace that signaled intention. She nodded in greeting and said, "Good morning.", although it felt like a strange choice of words.

As Mabel passed the Post Office on the road she could see a second group of men. They were down the valley gathered near the berm of the tailings pond. There seemed to be twice as many there, and each held a firearm.

Mabel climbed the stone steps to Ruby's house, rapped on the door, and then let herself in.

The women stood looking out the windows as the crowd by the pond began to march up the road toward the Mill.

Up at the Mill, Christian paced back and forth in the dust gathering his words.

When he was ready, he assembled the men and spoke.

"We cannot control what happens here today, but we can control our intentions and our personal behavior. I want your word that no one here will fire the first shot." He looked at the faces of each of the men. Christian hoped he was a model to the men.

A loud sharp whistle went out from the scout who was perched at lookout on the east side of the Superintendent's House. He waved his arm. The group was coming.

The silent men formed a line across the road at the bottleneck between the Mill and the Superintendent's House. They occupied the first section of flat ground at the top of the hill, leaving the approaching mob on the slope with a distinct disadvantage.

Christian felt the minutes tick by like hours as they waited for the group to round the corner and face them.

The first arriving men looked up, surprised to find the way blocked. They worked hard to breathe steadily, having climbed the hill with some anxiety. The men stopped in their tracks and the first one pointed his shotgun at the men by the Mill. Another followed suit, then a third.

Christian watched carefully sizing up the situation. The two groups normally worked man to man, side by side. All knew each other by name. There were no surprises when it came to alliances.

The morning sun had risen high enough to be hot by this hour. Everything and everyone stood still for a long time. There was not as much as a shifting of weight from one foot to another. Attention was riveted on the lack of motion. Christian was afraid to move a muscle.

From the lone pine, which leaned out over the road in front of the Superintendent's House, a resident red tailed hawk broke the silence by screaming as he left his perch and flew away to the east. The men defending the Mill would have watched him go, if they had dared to avert their eyes.

Sweat poured from the faces of the men. None of the men on Christian's side held their guns up, but their reflexes were ready. The standoff crackled with energy.

How long could time stand still? What outcome did these men expect could happen? How could shooting add up to resolution?

Christian wished the world was a wiser, more peaceful place.

Finally, very slowly Christian put one hand out, palm up. He carefully brought it to his head and removed his hat. He tossed it out onto the dirt between the two groups of men. Then he stepped two steps forward and began to speak.

"I may be the Boss," he began "but I am no smarter or better than the rest of you...I just got here earlier or I may have been luckier."

Christian gave that some time to set in. For time was all they had right now anyway.

"I work for all of you." He didn't see a soul move.

"You, who have come to take the Mill, have every right to be treated fairly...and you, who defend keeping the company running, are standing here to defend all we've got. I am with both sides."

Christian stepped forward and kicked his hat to show his frustration.

"I don't believe we will find resolution by breaking the law or dishonoring our own kind here. No one always wins." One of the men lowered his gun and stared hard at the others, who kept their gun sights on the men across from them.

Christian gave them a full minute to make a choice.

Then he began again, speaking loudly and clearly, as Mabel had taught him to do in school.

"I would like to propose a plan." He moved slowly, back to the hill, to face both sides equally. He looked silently at the gunmen. A man beside one gunman gently lowered the barrel by laying the light pressure of a hand. A second gunman sensed the motion, and lowered his also.

Christian couldn't hear the sigh of relief, but he felt it on both sides.

"If all of us, together, would lease the operation from the owners, perhaps we can run this place properly."

It was still quiet. Christian was betting on the relationships he had built over time with each individual standing here.

"We must initially raise the funds to pay the lease. That is our biggest challenge. I, personally, would rather seek investors than shoot each other full of holes."

This time, Christian paused until he heard the first low mumble of speech among the men, then he quickly and loudly began again.

"We need representation from this group." And he pointed an arm to the men who had come up the road.

There was a low rumble amongst them, and then Reinhart stepped forward with the apparent endorsement of all the men.

"We must send our men afar to find the financial backing we will need. We are in this together." Christian paused and looked all around at both sides. The men were silent, but held a look of hope in their eye.

"Now, everybody clear out." he shouted, "We'll get back to work tomorrow."

The peaceful dispersing of men after a standoff feels somewhat anticlimactic. Human nature provides for an uncomfortable mix of emotions in the soul, but it is relief from the specter of the shadow of death that makes a man turn and walk away.

Six men approached Christian to contribute to the plan.

By the next morning, it was announced that Reinhart would be sent to find investors among the Nebraska farmers. A company with a Board of Directors would be formed to lease the Mine and Mill from the owners.

The miner's showed up for the seven o'clock shift with pick axes, carbide lamps, boxes of candles, tin lunch pails and canteens. There was one hundred feet of safety fuse and a blasting machine and several volunteers to jam down the detonator handle.

Christian's crew went back to work, and although a little tentatively at first, the Mill began to rumble again.

❧

The Nebraska farmers had decided to wait until spring before sending John Bergren west to find the Boulder County Mine. It had been spring, thought John, just down the hill in Boulder. As the train crawled up into the mountains, the green prairies, with leafy cottonwood trees and delicate spring flowers, had given way to rocky canyon walls and billowing black storm clouds.

Now the train stopped at Orodell. Here it would turn from Boulder Canyon and follow Four Mile Creek to the town of Sunset. While John waited at Orodell, he put on a sweater.

"It's going to be a mite colder up above today." stated a friendly fellow, who seemed about twenty years John's senior.

"Is that right?" came John's melodic voice.

"Looks like snow for sure to me."

"Snow? Today?" John mused. Why, it was May!

"Where you coming from?" the man looked at John as if he was from overseas.

"Nebraska." John replied with a smile.

"Been here before?"

"First time."

"Oh, you'll love it here. Visiting?"

"Visiting a mine. The Boulder County Mine. It's directly west of Boulder, twenty miles. That's all I know. "He fumbled with the dog eared, hand drawn map in his coat pocket, and decided not to pull it out. This mountain man would laugh if he knew that fifteen gullible farmers had pitched in to invest in a gold mine when they didn't have two cents to rub together. And then to think that they gave up the money to a stranger, who had disappeared leaving only a map and a name. Reinhart.

"Oh, sure! The Boulder County Mine. You'll be getting off in Cardinal."

"Is that right?"

"The Boulder County Mine. Now, there's a good producer." the man said.

John's eyes lit up. Get off at Cardinal. A good producer! Maybe they weren't had after all!

"What brings you out west, Sir?" the mountain man asked.

"Well," John thought he'd still better hold his cards tight. "I've been told the rarified air was good for my lungs. You see, I was gassed in the Great War, and my breathing ain't been so good since then."

"High altitude; it is the best air I've ever had. I came here from St. Louis in eighty-two to train horses, and I've been here ever since. I've gone back a time or two, but these mountains are my home now."

"When they shipped me back from the front lines to Nebraska, I found I wasn't worth a darn around the farm. That hay dust...the hard physical labor. Thought I'd come out and see if what they say is true about the benefits of rarified air. You know, just that one day in Boulder and I'm feelin' pretty good." John sat up a bit straighter and smiled at the horseman. "Why ain't you ridin' a horse?"

"I own stables in Nederland and I train Arabians up here at a ranch near Bluebird. Been down in Denver for a few days. The train sure is the way to go."

"So, might you know a man by the name of Reinhart? A miner."

"Sure. He lives in Nederland. Works up there at the Boulder County all right. Talk to the Superintendent of the mine, up at the top of the hill when you leave the Depot. First house on the right at the top. Right across from the Cardinal Mill. He'll find him for you."

"Pretty small town around here, is it?"

"I know just about everybody after thirty-eight years!" Tyler turned and looked out the window. The years had rolled by just like the slopes outside the train. It had all blended together, but amazingly, the time added up to thirty-eight years. Tyler would have felt old if he'd let himself.

As the train left Sunset, and began to climb the switchbacks toward Glacier Lake, huge wet snowflakes began to fall. By the time the train had gained a thousand more feet of elevation, the snow fell steadily in dry flakes and was already three inches deep. Now the train passed huge drifts left over from the winter. John looked down at his travelling suit and polished boots and laughed a little nervously to himself.

"Don't worry. It won't last through tomorrow." The friendly chap had said before he hopped off the train at the Bluebird Station.

When the train had stopped at Cardinal, John Bergren got off. He was delighted to see the high trestle, and the scatterings of a town assembled about it. Following the directions, he started slowly up the road to find the Superintendent of the Boulder County Mine, and a man he could vaguely picture, Reinhart. The snow was six inches deep. John stepped sideways with each step as he tried to get his boots to hold. It was slow going. As he climbed, the sun came out, and the sky was a brilliant blue, like none he had ever seen before. The sun felt warm.

John Bergren rounded the corner and got his first glimpse of the Cardinal Mill. The building reached from one story above the top of the road, down the hill into the valley. It was six stories high in all; reaching down the valley in four long sections. There was nothing quite so magnificent in Nebraska. The farmers would be impressed.

On his right, sat the Superintendent's House. John found the walkway and came to the front door. For just one moment, he thought he saw a man in a Bowler hat, peering out behind a window, but then there was no one. John knocked several times, but no one answered the door.

John walked further west. He could hear action everywhere; the clanging and banging in the Mill. Compressors working at the mine portal; a rhythmic ringing came from the blacksmith shop. John continued walking west. He arrived at two buildings across from each other. One said "Assay Office" and the other "Office", so he chose the business office of the mine.

A middle aged woman, long graying brown hair piled high on her head, looked up from her work and said, "Can I help you?"

"I'm John Bergren, and I'd like to speak to the Superintendent of the mine. I've come from Nebraska. I'm looking for a man by the name of Reinhart."

Mabel set down her check writing, and came through the wooden gate to the front of the office. She had a pretty good idea who this might be.

"Mr. Reinhart is most likely in the Mill. He is the person who went to Nebraska to seek investors.

"I represent the investors." John clarified.

"Welcome to Cardinal." smiled Mabel. "This is the Fairview Mining and Milling Company. I will have you talk to the two shift supervisors."

"How about the Superintendent?"

Mabel dropped her eyes and acted very uncomfortably.

"Our Superintendent contracted pneumonia. He died three days ago."

"I am sorry for the poor soul." said John, wondering what the man looked like.

"Yes. Thank you." Mabel looked at the clock on the wall, and said, "The second shift starts soon. Let's walk down to the Mill. Christian will be available to meet with you."

As the two approached the Mill, the shift whistle blew loudly, and men began to emerge from the top of the Mill. Mabel waved to one man, and he stepped their way.

"Christian, this is John Bergren. He has come from Nebraska. He represents the investors." She gave Christian a serious stare. "I'll be off to teach the second half of the school day. Maybe you can get some lunch for Mr. Bergren. Nice to meet you, Sir."

"My pleasure to meet you as well." John returned.

Christian shook John's hand.

"We haven't heard a word about gold mining in Colorado, so they sent me to the Boulder County Mine to check up on the investment."

"My apologies for the lack of communication. The Fairview is made up mostly of miners and millers, and maybe not many businessmen. We've recently lost our Superintendent."

"So I've heard." John looked toward the Superintendent's house again.

"The Nebraska investment has kept us operating. The lease has been paid each month. We are a little short handed in the office. Please, join me and the men for some lunch." Christian held out an arm to show the way, and the two men disappeared into the Mill.

The noise had stopped as the second shift was coming in. John was curious as he descended the stairways past each step of the milling process. He found himself immediately fascinated. They ended up in a large mess hall at the east end of the Mill, eating chipped beef on bread for lunch and enjoying the best tasting water that John had ever had.

"I will be here long enough to get a full business report to return to the investors." John stated after the meal.

Christian squirmed a little inside and then said, "Of course. Up in the office, Mabel will sit down with you to review our books. He realized that he had no idea what condition the records were in or why there had never been any word sent to Nebraska.

"I will take you to the Boarding Houses at the west end of town, Mr. Bergren. We'll get you settled in for a few days. I'm sure you are tuckered out from traveling."

The next morning, the sun came up hot and the six inches of snow that had fallen the day before, quickly melted away.

"We'll have a bit of springtime now, at least for a few days." Mabel promised as she opened the door to the office. "I'll set you up with the books, and then I'll be in the next building, over here. It is a school day, you know. I have five students. Come on over if you have any questions at all."

John Bergren opened the door to the Superintendent's house. He looked to the east and saw the kitchen. He looked west to see the bedrooms. John stood in the living room with a few simple chairs and a fireplace. Things were in good order.

"I know you are here, because I saw you." John said aloud.

"You're a burley fellow, probably Irish, I suspect. I want you to know, you are free to go. I am here now. Gonna stay. You can go ahead and leave. Go ahead; your work is done here. You are supposed to move on, right? There's a place you are supposed to go."

John looked around at the quiet house. He didn't expect that he would hear or see anything. He thought he would feel more foolish in front of himself than he did.

"They tell me you were the pit boss and a dam good one too." John decided to leave it at that. He hung his coat on the hook inside the door, and went to light a fire in the kitchen cook stove.

John sat at the table and set himself up to write a letter. When the stove heated up, he made some coffee, and then sat to write.

Dear Gentlemen,

I arrived in Cardinal, Colorado to find that our investment funds are well placed. The Fairview Mining and Milling Company is running two shifts a day. There are fourteen miners and twenty mill workers on the job at a time. The operation appears to be well managed and running smoothly. Apparently, the leasing of the Boulder County Mine and Cardinal Mill has been a good development for Fairview and the workers, as well as the out of state mine owners.

The business office has been sorely unorganized. I spent several days figuring out the books, and then straightening them out. The Fairview Company has paid me for that task. Two lovely women work part time in the office and will manage well enough, now that we have a system.

Unfortunately, just days before my arrival, the Superintendent of the mine passed away due to pneumonia. The excellent management of the shift foremen has kept the operation running smoothly; however, there are some large shoes to be filled.

It will come as a surprise to you all, that I have decided to stay in Cardinal and fill those shoes. My heath has greatly improved upon my arrival in this rarified air, and I find I am able to be productive as ever. The Board of Directors of the Fairview Mining and Milling Company has voted to hire me on as Superintendent. I am quite thrilled with their decision.

Consequently, I shall not be returning as scheduled, but will send for a trunk through my brother, Bill. Rest assured that your investment will be paying off and is in good hands. I shall send quarterly reports hereafter, with dividends paid annually.

In closing, there is work to be had here for any discouraged Nebraska farmers. I send my best to everyone back in Nebraska. Be well and prosper.

Yours truly,

John Bergren

John held the paper up to the light and blew gently on the ink. The letter looked legible enough. He folded it into an envelope.

As John put on his coat and hat, he decided he couldn't feel the presence of a spirit at all, not that he ever had before.

"If you're still here, and you've got to stay, I guess that's okay by me too." he spoke aloud. His words surprised him, but he really meant it. He headed down the hill to the Post Office.

When John opened the Post Office door, he found that the Postmistress was six years old.

"Can I help you, Sir?" The little blonde smiled coyly at John. She squirmed on her tall stool, and flicked her long braids over her shoulders.

"I'd like to mail a letter." he began. "My name is John Bergren. I am the new Superintendent of the mine. What's your name?"

"Margaret Green. Pleased to meet you. I guess we needed a new Superintendent." Margaret looked down with a big sad look on her face.

Then, getting back to business, she said, "Two pennies to mail your letter, Sir. And you will need a Post Office Box as well, so I will have you fill out a card please."

"Thank you, Margaret. You are a big help. How did you get this job so young?" John smiled at her playing along.

"Well, actually, it's my Mother's job." Margaret looked at John as if he was goofy.

"And where is your Mother?" he asked.

"In the kitchen. She didn't hear the bell."

Catherine came through the door as if on cue.

"Excuse me." she said, "I didn't hear you come in."

"I have been well cared for here at the Cardinal Post Office. I am John Bergren."

"Why, the new Superintendent of the mine! Very pleased to meet you, Mr. Bergren! What can I do for you today, Sir?"

"Margaret the Postmistress has sold me a stamp, mailed my letter, and I am filling out my card to obtain a post office box."

"Mother," Margaret smiled. "I've watched you do this a dozen times." And she jumped off the stool, and ran outside.

"I am Catherine Green. Welcome to Cardinal, Sir."

1919

As the motorcar bumped along the United States Forest Service Boulevard, Mabel recalled her trip by four horse Concord Coach back in 1894, when she and John had come along the same route to Central City. She could just picture John debating silver politics. He had seemed so old to her then, certainly too old for her to marry. Twenty-five years ago, she counted. He had been the age she was now. Not old, she thought, just an age with some experience. Mabel sighed.

Now, John lay dying, in his home in Central City. Mabel remembered back to the day when John had first acknowledged her. He had carried her books and escorted her home from the Caribou schoolhouse. He was young then, Mabel decided. She felt the flutter in her heart that she had felt that day and she smiled wistfully. She was young then too. Really young!

The years had gone all too quickly. When a person is young, life seems long as an eternity, full of dreams and hopes. As friends and community meet the challenges life brings, the soul gets glimpses of the other side, but a body keeps going, running some kind of parallel track to the dreams and hopes. A life becomes a story, Mabel thought. Then suddenly, time has run out. The story has a beginning, middle and an end.

Mabel's sadness overwhelmed her, and she turned her head toward the west and let tears pour freely over her cheeks. The automobile turned sharply, bumping Mabel's head against the glass once, as it climbed the steep hill to John's house.

The driver came around and opened Mabel's door with a flourish.

"Ms. Gurkin." he smiled and held his arm out for her.

"It's just amazing, isn't it?" Mabel stated.

"It is Mam." said the driver, wondering just what the woman was referring to.

"I used to come by coach, you know."

Mabel knocked softly, and then let herself in quietly. John's nurse looked forlornly at Mabel as she left John's room. The women nodded politely. No words needed to be said.

When Mabel sat and took John's hand, he opened his eyes and looked at her from some place far away. Mabel squeezed his hand and his being stepped toward this world. When Mabel spoke, John was drawn back to the moment.

"I came by motorcar." she said. "It was a smooth ride; seems that I got here in no time at all."

"I'm glad you are here." John said. "I am very weak."

"So you are." confirmed Mabel, holding back her emotions. "I've come to bring you some good cheer."

"In a bottle?" asked John.

Mabel could see that John could no longer smile, but his sense of humor was still alive.

"That might not be a bad idea." Mabel smiled at him. He was lost in her eyes.

"I brought the fiddle though, and I'll play for you."

"That would be nice." said John, and he closed his eyes.

Mabel sat quietly and watched him. John seemed entirely unaware of time. She sat a long time before he spoke again.

"I never accomplished much. Not really." he said.

"Why John, that's simply not true! You have surveyed more claims than anyone on the Front Range. You have laid out cities!"

"Only one. Old Cardinal. It's gone now." John kept his eyes closed.

"John, think of the years of lobbying you did. You were a voice for the people of Colorado, so involved in politics. Everyone respects you, John. You have an accomplished career."

"I did a lot of things. I always stayed busy."

Mabel moved closer to John. She knelt on the floor beside his bed and took his hand. She ran her fingers through his hair.

"John, the most wonderful of all of the things that you have done is that you took care of me and Christian." She paused, letting these words linger in John's mind. "Do you suppose it was laudanum with Roxy?"

"Or youth." suggested John.

"Well, John, you made Christian who he is today. You should be very proud." Mabel let that sink in. She was getting sucked into John's time warp. Minutes went past.

"John, I am very proud of you. I am proud to be counted amongst your dearest friends. And I am so grateful for all the love and support you have given me all these years."

"My dearest friend." John opened his eyes and squeezed her hand.

Now, they sat quietly for a very long time. John rested.

Finally, when Mabel's legs had fallen asleep, she rose to make some lunch. She ate by John's bedside and tried to get him to eat some stewed apples. He only took a few bites.

Mabel played the fiddle more like a violin. Softly, calming notes floated about the room and out the open summertime windows. She played "You Are My Sunshine", "Sunny Side of the Mountain" and "I'll Fly Away". When she played "Amazing Grace", the nurse appeared in the doorway and sang the words.

The motorcar returned and blew its horn once. A thunderstorm had passed and John was fast asleep. Mabel kissed him on the cheek. He didn't waken. She moved slowly toward the door, knowing this was probably her last goodbye. Mabel was living a moment in time which she had always kept in the future. Now, here it was. Mabel wept silently in the back seat of the auto until there were no more tears to come.

It was when they stopped for gasoline in Nederland, that Mabel heard the news. A massive thunderstorm had hung too long over the foothills sending a roaring flood down Four Mile Creek. The flood took out the railway as it went, all the way to Boulder. Everyone knew this was the end of an era. The Switzerland Trail Railroad had been in receivership again, and could never afford to rebuild.

Mr. Bergren met Mabel in Nederland to drive her the final stretch to Cardinal.

"I will be taking a trip to Nebraska." he said. "My brother, Bill, and his wife, Minnie, are moving to Cardinal. I'm going to marry Minnie's sister, Mary, and bring her back here too!" John Bergren smiled at Mabel.

"Does she know that?" Mabel asked, trying to show enthusiasm on this very sad, strange day.

"Not yet." Mr. Bergren beamed, and his car lurched forward toward Cardinal.

When the bells in the Western Electric phone box rang in the Mine Office, it nearly jumped off the wall. Mabel put one hand on the crank, and slowly brought the horn to her ear. The news could not be good on this day. Mabel braced her heart. And it was that John had never woken from his sleep. It was July 31st, 1919, the day that John died.

DECEMBER 4, 1925

$\mathcal{M}$abel woke early because her nose was cold. The darkest days of the year seemed to block out all memory of the spectacular summertime. Mabel rose to poke the coals in the woodstove. She opened the draft vent and the fire jumped back to life.

"Top of the morning to you, Goodman." She said with a smile.

The inside firewood box would have to be filled this morning and there were numbers to be summed up in the mine office from yesterday before school could get started. Looking out of the mine office window, Mabel could see the seven o'clock shift of the Fairview Mining Company heading into the portal of the mine. Today, Frank Goswich was day foreman, which meant that Mabel would get to see Christian as he walked the twins to school.

The Trammer, Merle Rugg, drove the battery operated train engine as it disappeared into the Boulder County Mine pulling a line of ore cars. Muckers carried picks and shovels. A few men laid air hoses over the section of frozen ground that stretched between the Compressor House and the portal. Mabel saw a puff of smoke as the compressor started to run. Today, she couldn't hear the machine due to the relentless winter wind.

At eight o'clock in the morning, Mabel was just finishing the books, when she saw Mr. Lane reemerge from the mine. He stuck his head into the Compressor House.

"Seen that set of drill bits?" he asked Bill Bryant.

"Could be across the street. Talked to your smithy? He might know."

Lane ducked back out and stood scratching his head in wonder about the lost bits.

In the Compressor House, Bill Bryant turned back around to see huge flames shooting out of the compressor. He immediately dove on the main breaker and cut the electricity off. But the flames that bellowed out of the machinery were already licking the wall behind the compressor. Bill glanced around for the glass globes of water, fire extinguishers, which hung from the walls. He flung two toward the flames. They did pitifully little but break on the floor below the fire. Bill grabbed a heavy blanket which sat on the chair and tried in vain to smother the flames.   As he beat the flames down, the blanket caught fire. Flames jumped to his shirt sleeves and raced to his hair. As he made for the doorway, a falling timber hit his head, dropping burning debris all over him.

Will Lane looked up from the pile of lost drill bits just in time to see Bill lurch from the Compressor House rapidly becoming engulfed in flames. The blacksmith helped Will trip a screaming Bryant into a snow bank. They rolled him about, putting the fire out, but they knew he was badly burned.

Mabel saw the unusual amount of smoke first. She ran to the wall phone and rang up the operator in Nederland to report a fire at the Cardinal Mine. Mabel's call would eventually alert the firefighters of Boulder, Lafayette, Fredrick and Denver. Mabel hoped the tone of her voice showed urgency.

The wind blew Mabel down the street all the way to the Mill, where she met the entire shift of millworkers moving hard and fast as they came out of the top of the mill building.   Men ran with iron bars, shovels, picks and axes. Shouts rose from everywhere, as the smoke billowed from the buildings near the portal. The Blacksmith Shop was downwind. The wind howled out of the west, pushing the fire, which was now reaching the timbers which supported the portal of the mine. The blaze spread in a fury. There was no time to warn the miners.

Inside the mine, most of the miners had followed the tram a good distance in. Lagging behind, was Earl with the two horses. He was taking it slow in case Will needed help with the drill bits. The horse that was second in line had stopped. Earl spoke to him encouragingly, but got no action. He set down his lantern and went back to coax the beast. As he reached for the halter, the horse's eyes bulged and he reared up on his hind legs, bumping his head on the tunnel ceiling. It was then that Earl smelled the smoke. He listened carefully for sound, but heard nothing.

Earl kept his calm for the sake of the animals. He took hand of the lantern and led the first horse steadily but quickly, further into the tunnel to alert the men. The second horse, Buckie, would not follow. By now, the smoke was thickening and Earl shouted ahead.

Christian, clutching his twin sons in each hand, stood outside among the men. Mabel ran up and relieving Christian of the children, she took them to the safety of the business office to the west. As they watched out the east window, men on horseback came at a gallop down the road from Caribou speeding past the office. The smoke would be seen for miles around.

The crowd of men grew steadily.

"We must close the portal to keep the men safe. We must stop the flow of smoke from pouring into the mine!" yelled one of the men.

"Some of you come with me to the powder magazine. We'll blow the tunnel shut." shouted Christian, and he made his way around the fire to the west and up the gulch to where the dynamite was stored in a bunker. Four men trailed behind him.

Within the hour, every able bodied man from all of the neighboring mines and the towns of Nederland and Eldora had arrived.

Mabel was successfully patched through on the telephone line to John Bergren, the President of the Fairview Mining Company, at the Equitable Building in Denver. Just as she let the horn drop from her ear, the telephone line went dead. John Bergren called the Denver Firefighting Chief, John Healy, who promised to ready his crew.

The first of the rescuers had started digging at the old air shaft just behind the portal. Now, they looked through the smoke and they found themselves standing on the burning mountainside. The heat became too much, and choking on smoke, they retreated to the flat open area in front of the Boulder County Tunnel.

While some men rigged pumps to use water from the ponds, others lined up in bucket brigades, heaving water on the burning timbering. The heat was overwhelming, and it felt much like a futile effort.

The first of the professional firefighters arrived from Boulder with trucks and pumpers, just as the dynamite blew. The explosion was deafening, and Mabel felt its impact on her chest. The little boys shrieked and ran to the far side of the office, only to return again, and hide behind Mabel as she watched out the window.

There was a crash as the timbers supporting the portal collapsed and the tunnel caved in a full sixty feet back. When the miners felt the earth shake, they were well back in the tunnel.

Merle jumped from the seat of the tram and wedged the tram's large metal battery cover across the opening in the tunnel.

"Pull some of those old timbers down from over there." ordered the foreman.

Others nodded in agreement. They would have to build an airtight barricade and do it quickly. The men grabbed rocks and iron bars. They filled the space to form a wall, in the end stuffing clothing into the cracks.

John Bergren left Denver by eleven o'clock with a consulting engineer. Two auto loads of electricians, along with two gas mask experts from the Public Service Company of Colorado, brought up the rear.

The Denver Chief sent Captain Cutshall and firefighter, Clarence Jansen, with the former Captain of the Department, Harry Force, at the wheel of the automobile. It was a fast ride; one that none of the men would ever forget. They brought a supply of soda ash and sulfuric acid to douse the fire.

The State Metal Mines Commissioner sent an inspector from Idaho Springs. Thomas Henahan wasn't sure what his role would be, so he put on outdoor work clothes and a helmet, and hitched a ride from the local Police.

Down in Boulder, a young University of Colorado student heard of the mine disaster as he ate at a downtown restaurant. Before long, he had rallied the support of the Head of the University's Physical Education Department. They gathered students from the gymnasium and headed for Cardinal.

By noon, two hundred people had gathered. Fire fighters and volunteers from Boulder, Lafayette, Fredrick and Denver jockeyed for direction from the leaders.

Women and children huddled in small groups on the waste rock pile and to the west upwind of the disaster area. About noon, the Fairview Mining Company Physician stood on a wooden crate and announced that the blaze was dying, but it was still too hot to get close. He believed the fire had been checked by the water soaked timbers in the mine… and that one hundred feet back in the tunnel, a cave in had choked off the smoke preventing it from flowing further inside. He preached to give these helpless ones hope. He pleaded with them to stay vigilant.

The Boulder Fire Chief and Boulder Sherriff had reached the fire quickly by very fast automobile. Now, they organized men from Boulder and Lafayette into crews to save the enormous but vulnerable Cardinal Mill, which sat only two hundred feet downwind of the fire.

John's engineer met with Christian and Captain Cutshall. It was decided to drop a forty-two foot emergency shaft, one hundred and twenty five feet back from the portal. The shaft would have to be four feet by four feet and it would have to pierce between the timbers as it cross cut the tunnel. The men would be winched to the surface in ore buckets. Crews would be kept on the hand pump to get air into the tunnel.

Christian's shift of men went to work on the task. The ringing of steel on rock echoed the valley at a frantic pace as the afternoon wore on. The wind began to still as the weather calmed, the sky darkened and a storm began to threaten from the west.

The State Coal Mining Commission had dispatched a crew, but as their leader spoke to Christian about spelling the Cardinal crew, six large transformers fell from their smoldering timber platform onto tunnel, causing another cave in. The crowd went wild.

Sherriff Blum ran to the Superintendent's House to phone for more po-

lice back up, only to find the telephone lines were all tied up. He comman-
deered a vehicle and drove back down the canyon across the thirty three bridges
over Boulder Creek to Boulder to get his recruits.

Frank Henderson of the Boulder Public Service Company instructed the
coal men digging out the transformers. It took hours to free the debris and haul
it out of the way. All the while, Christian's men kept blasting and digging the
rescue shaft.

In the late afternoon, the heavy smoke finally tapered off, and in the fading daylight, the stunned crowd stood staring at the closed portal. The ringing
of drill bits and picks on rock rose above men giving orders and the hushed
voices of the worried women.

Mr. Henderson rigged new lights focused carefully on the emergency
shaft, as the night crew of more than one hundred men was assembled. The
waning moon would be of no help to the rescuers. The National Guard stood
lined up with fifty men and fifty gas masks.

At six o'clock, an announcement was made. It was estimated the rescue would take between one to three more hours. The announcement was met
with a helpless silence. The temperature dropped with nightfall and the first
snowflakes began to fall. Auto headlights cast eerie beams through the darkness. Mabel could feel the tension heightening. She invited the women to
come inside for coffee and to warm by the stove. There were more than a dozen
wives. The women were quiet. There were no words to speak that wouldn't
make emotions rise and optimism fall. Tears flowed amid wringing hands and
long embraces.

At nine o'clock in the evening, eleven hours into the ordeal, the shaft was
clear into the tunnel. The fan was lowered to the bottom of the shaft and twelve
rescuers were ready to descend. They stood clutching gas masks, in an orderly
line stacked down the steep hillside.

Christian stood ready to operate the winch. He directed Captain Cutshall to step into the tall, narrow cast iron ore bucket. The man was a good size
and fit for the bucket. Christian thought of the many circumstances the Captain must have been in as a fire chief.

"Ever been in a mine?" he asked the Captain.

"This will be a first."

"Then let's go ahead and light that carbide lamp right here."

Christian struck a match upon the flint and handed it to the Captain,
who lit his own lamp. As the light came up, Christian was momentarily haunted
by visions of scenes the Captain and his men might encounter.

Captain Cutshall, Superintendent Bill Bergren, two Denver Firemen and
two local miners were the first to go down, lowered one by one in the ore bucket.

Down in the mine, Captain Cutshall felt himself dizzying. He stood strong against the feeling. Jansen felt it too. His knees buckled. As the last of the six men was lowered in, Jansen turned to Cutshall and said, "I'm not making it, I'll have to go back up." He stepped back into the bucket and gave the signal to pull up. He handed Cutshall his mask and told him to put it on. As Cutshall gave a nod of acknowledgement, the Captain passed out.

To the men above, a signal came back clearly and strong to pull the ore bucket up. The winch strained as it wound the opposite way, and then Fireman Jansen reappeared gasping for air.

"Bring the men up! Cutshall is dying. " Jansen wheezed as he was lifted from the bucket where he dropped to the ground.

Now Christian and his men worked in double time. Cutshall was lifted into the bucket and brought to the surface unconscious. His head was bleeding. The bucket dropped again.

The signal to pull up came again, but the next man, Bill Bergren was unconscious when he reached the top. His body spilled awkwardly from the bucket and it was evident that he had taken quite a beating on the way up.

The bucket was dropped a fourth and fifth time and again each man arrived at the top with masks on, but unconscious and bleeding. The last time the bucket was dropped; there was no signal to rise. Christian did not delay, he reversed the winch.

"I'm going down!" he yelled as the bucket reappeared empty. He stepped into the ore bucket and hitched a gas mask to his face. "Now!"

The men looked at each other and fell into position.

With two men on the winch, Christian disappeared down the hole. For what seemed like eternity, there was no signal. Then it came strong.

The bucket surfaced with the last unconscious masked man tucked neatly into the bucket. His head lashed to the cable with Christian's shirt.

The bucket was lowered again and Christian was brought to the surface unharmed. Christian removed his gas mask and drew several deep breaths before he could speak.

The others had been whisked down the mountainside to a make shift hospital at Superintendent Bergren's house.

"We need a compressor to pump air in there. Keep the men on the hand pump. I'm going looking for a compressor." Christian said, and he took off for the Business Office to use the telephone.

Mabel recognized Christian running up the road. She swept herself out the door as nonchalantly as possible, so as not to raise attention from the ladies.

"I need the phone!" Christian called from a distance.

"It's dead." Mabel replied hopelessly.

"There is no air in the mine. Our rescuers passed out. We've got them all out now, but we need a compressor!"

"Christian, every man for a hundred miles around is already here. There must be a compressor at a mine somewhere!" Mabel ran down the street to the crowd of men with Christian on her heels.

The first person she ran into was a foreman at the Alton Tunnel, just down the valley. She grabbed him at the shoulders.

"Do you have a compressor? Can it be moved?"

The foreman smiled calmly and stated, "It is on its way. The men have it on a wagon and it is half way here."

Mabel hugged him then turned to see Christian standing behind her with his hand extended to the man. Mabel thanked him and headed back to the office.

As she entered the room, all heads turned and eyes were on Mabel. She had to think for a moment. She took the opportunity to draw a few breaths.

"Progress" she gasped, "is slow but steady."

Mabel didn't have the heart to tell them there was no air.

"As a precaution for the rescuers, they are pumping air into the mine. It won't be too long before the men can go in." The waiting would continue.

Christian could not wait more than an hour. By now, the men worked and waited in a blinding snowstorm, but the pumping was going well.

Christian and his two best men donned gas masks. Carrying twenty more masks, the men were lowered into the mine. It was a good sign when their lamps lit and continued to burn. They tugged the cable three times, which meant they were going on in. The miners forged through the darkness along the tracks deeper into the tunnel, calling out as they went.

Just two hundred feet from the emergency shaft, there was a large mass on the tracks ahead. It was Buckie. He lay dead, blocking the way. The three men had to climb over him to continue. It was an ominous sign. They ventured on.

"It has been half a mile..." Rodney mentioned.

"Not a sign of life." Christian didn't mean to sound so negative.

"Keep going, guys. Keep hollerin'" Mike encouraged.

Rodney added, "It's good we're breathing alright."

"So far, so good." And Christian hollered out another hello from behind the mask.

"Listen!" Rodney stopped and the others bumped into him.

There came a knocking noise. It was very faint in the distance.

"It's them! Someone is alive!"

The men held each other's jackets and began to run as best they could through the puddled railroad tracks. The knocking was more definite now.

"It's not a Tommy Knocker!"

Christian yelled, "We're coming!"

"Another five hundred feet, I think … but it is muffled."

At last, Rodney's light flashed upon the makeshift wall. The men yelled and heard voices in response. They began to tear the wall down.

It was a hand and an arm that came through first. A desperate reach. Then the wall seemed to crumble open on its own. All the men were alive! And a horse too!

It was blind with tears that each man came through the hole in the wall. Men hugged men; no one knew who was who. Mike and Rodney worked hard to free the tram's big steel cover from the wall, so the horse could come through.

"Masks everyone! Quickly, it's not good down here! We have lost a few men to the gas."

Before long the men were making their way back along the tunnel, horse in tow. There was not much talk while they walked, as the shocked men processed what was happening. There was the stomping of boots and a horse's feet in the gravel and water. When the first men reached the body of the horse, they fully understood that their own actions had saved their lives. One by one they straddled the beast to cross his body.

Earl set the lead on the other horse's back, knowing she wouldn't take too kindly to this sight. He approached the fallen horse with respect.

"You were a good ol' boy." Earl lamented. He gave the horse a loving pat as he passed across. "I wish you'd a come with me, Buckie."

"Come on, girl." Earl spoke to the second horse.

When the other horse drew near enough to the body to realize what it was, she flared her nostrils, stomped a front foot and screamed, then with a pivot was gone running back into the dark tunnel. The men had to let her go.

When at last, the light was visible from the shaft, cries of joy when up.

The voices and tugging on the cable drew immediate attention above ground. The message reached the Mine Office and the ladies came running. Then word reached the top, "All safe!"

The first man up was Walter Swanson, who promptly collapsed into the arms of his wife and had to be taken to a pulmotor at the Superintendent's House. Each of the men collapsed upon reaching the open air.

Down in the mine, Rodney and Christian stood waiting their turn. The ore bucket had just risen from sight, when the sound of hooves came thundering toward them. The horse had frightened herself again and this time, she had leapt over the fallen horse and was headed straight for the men. Not knowing what to expect, the two men flattened themselves against the tunnel walls. The

ROCKY MOUNTAIN NEWS, DECEMBER 5, 1925

mare came at once and passed them by at a high speed. She returned at a trot blowing and sweating. Rodney grabbed what was left of the leather lead, and turned her several times in a tight circle, speaking softly to tame her again. In time, she was settled enough to be tethered to the timbers.

Christian was last up. Mabel and Christian's wife clung to him immediately. He had worn his mask the whole time and felt he was weak, but alright.

THE ROCKY MOUNTAIN NEWS: DENVER, COLORADO, SATURDAY, DECEMBER 5, 1925

WHERE RESCUE CREWS WON BATTLE TO SAVE MINERS

A BURNED FIREMAN; LADIES HOLD A VIGIL, DECEMBER 5, 1925

He reassured the others that he was fine. Taking a woman in each hand, he walked to the make shift hospital in the Superintendent's house to see how everyone else had fared.

It was Tyler and his stable boy who went down with a backboard to hog tie the mare and have her hoisted up.

Pulmotors ran in every room of the hospital. The first rescuers had suffered the most and were in critical condition. Bill Bryant had been taken to the

Boulder Sanitarium that morning and was still alive. Many miners were being released with a dose of anti-pneumonia serum. All things considered, the rescue had gone well. Outside, men wept gladness and tears of exhaustion.

It had been a fourteen hour ordeal. It was now ten o'clock at night and snowing to beat the band. Mabel gave Christian a last hug squeezing very tightly and said again how proud of him she was, then made her way through the snow back to her home in the west side of the mine office.

"One hundred thousand dollars in damages." Christian read aloud from the newspaper.

The fire in the office stove roared with a heat that had never felt so good to Christian.

"Daddy, were you scared?" asked his son.

"The whole time." admitted Christian.

"Me too." added Mabel.

"I knew he'd save'm." stated the other twin.

Tyler knocked once and entered.

"That horse is eating like always, no worse for the wear." he nodded.

Mabel came forward and hugged him.

"You all saved the day." she said looking at Christian. She was still feeling shaken from the long ordeal.

"And you, Missy, played your part as well." Tyler grinned.

"Now it's time to help clean up a big mess!" said Christian. He looked out the east window, squinting at the sun on the snow, at the men tossing timbers and rocks aside.

"Let's go help."

1930

*B*y the time the snow had melted near the waterfall, the aspen down the valley were already sporting bright spring green leaves. By the time the rocks for Mabel's new cabin foundation had been set, it was the Fourth of July. The building season was short in the steep walled valley where the sun only barely kissed the grass each day. As the men had toiled away the summer, they enjoyed the cool air, knowing the temperatures twenty miles away, down on the prairies, rose well above one hundred degrees. When each day was done, the men stood in the waterfall next to the cabin and washed off the day's work. Work was hard to come by these days.

Mabel looked up from her digging in the garden. She looked over her shoulders in both directions, up the hill through the lodge pole pines and across the valley floor toward the creek. No one was around. When financial institutions had begun to fold around the country, Mabel had seen it coming. She had withdrawn the money John had left her in six different withdrawls. She had decided she would be her own best bank and had buried the funds in glass jars in the potato garden outside her west window.

"Mornin' Mabe" came a voice. Mabel looked toward the livery stable to see Mr. MacIntyre standing at the edge of her garden leaning on a walking stick. The old Caribou miner must have just stepped from around the corner of the building.

"The weeds are taking over, Mac." exclaimed Mabel brightly, "I think I've got most of them now."

"Darn toot'n, they will.' He agreed. "Don't know how we'd make it through without a victory garden."

"Yes, it has been rather tough." Mabel felt a bit guilty saying that when she had a jar of one hundred dollars just twelve inches beneath her fingertips.

The tungsten boom had waned with the ending of the Great War and the price of gold had bottomed out.

"Back when we had the Switzerland Trail Railroad, things were a whole lot better. Then the Colorado and Northwestern went bankrupt. Tore the tracks out in '22, they did. Sold the steel to the Japanese, of all things. Couldn't believe my eyes."

"Yes, Mac, remember… I was here."

"And all misty eyed, I recall."

"I think we all were. We sure loved that train." Mabel stood and brushed her hands on her skirt. "And when the gasoline machines crowded the railroad out of business, the prices didn't stay cheaper for long."

"We're in an economic depression, Mabel," Mac paused, "and everyone's starvin'… but you are building a cabin."

"It looks a bit odd, I must admit. My father, in St Louis, is a very wealthy man."

"Wouldn't know it by lookin' at you."

"I am retiring from the mining company next year, Mac. I'll need a home, and I am providing valuable work for a few men. Christian and his sons are among them."

Each week, Mabel made sure people knew she was waiting for the payroll to arrive in the mail from her father.

"The old man lost his precious pearl to the wild west." Mac grinned a huge toothless grin in Mabel's direction.

"Best thing I ever did, Mac. That's how I got you for a friend." Mabel walked over and gave him a peck on his withered cheek.

"I'd better go check progress." Mabel handed the old miner two potatoes.

"You do that. I'm workin' my way toward Nederland."

Mabel walked in the opposite direction, up the road to the worksite. She could hear the ringing of hammers. This day, the coal shed was under construction. As Mabel watched the last wall rise into position, she wistfully remembered the year that the coal from the western slope couldn't make it through the Moffat Tunnel and the trusty Switzerland Trail Railroad had brought Cardinal its coal from the flats of the Front Range. Now, the coal came by automobile and was frightfully dear. Mabel only used it at night and burned wood by day.

Inside the cabin, baseboards were being laid against wallboard. The days of lathe and plaster were gone. Christian worked in the kitchen, fashioning new bead board cabinets with glass doors on the upper row.

"Christian," sang Mabel, "These are a work of art! I had no idea of your talent with wood."

"Good day, Mabel." Christian stood to admire his own handiwork.

"I enjoy making something that will be around for a while. Nice to see

ORE CARTS AT THE BOULDER COUNTY MINE
Denver Public Library, Western History Collection

the fruits of one's labor, but I hope to be hauling off ore in carts again by the end of the week. Have you seen the boys?"

"Yes, they have worked their way half way around the house with the green paint. Everything is looking gloriously green, even their shoes, I'm afraid!"

"We will have you moved in before the snow flies." promised Christian.

"Then I'd better hire men to put some firewood up for me."

"Yes, you will want that done early in this part of the valley. Everyone thinks you're nuts to spend the winter in here, Mabel. You'll be up to your shoulders in snow."

"Maybe I am nuts, Christian. Have you ever considered that?"

"I knew it the first time I saw you ski down the road at Old Cardinal." Christian admitted with a smile. "Tell the men to come by the mine office for their pay this afternoon. I'm going outside to supervise the green paint."

Mabel walked to the back of the cabin and up onto the berm which held the pond. She sat on the bench by the flume listening to the waterfall. Mabel knew how lucky she was to have this cabin being built ... and in such a special place. She thought of John and how very pleased he would have been. She closed her eyes and conjured up the spirit of him. She held him in her heart for a very long time feeling everything she could to bring him back to her.

When Mabel opened her eyes, she was struck by the beauty of the spot. The cabin was nestled in the only remaining trees in the area. They were good sturdy spruce and pine. She hoped they would stand long after her lifetime. Behind the cabin was a grove of aspens providing the place with greenery. Mabel's cabin was the furthest west in the town and the morning sunrises would be spectacular from here. She felt she had found a piece of paradise.

Mabel stood and walked back to her garden. She resumed digging.

1942

"When Denora Mining Company took over for the Fairview," John Bergren paused remembering the day Christian had retired, "I expected your company would have a long and prosperous lease here at the Cardinal Mill. Now, in just two years, the war has put you right out of business."

War time metals were of priority now. The government cut off supplies to those mining precious metals to redirect their efforts for the war. John stood, signaling the end of what had been an unfortunate business meeting.

"Off the record," he added "any equipment left in the tunnel ... assets gone. Why you could write those off as a loss..."

"Well, I guess it's time to tell the men." the Superintendent rose from his seat and stood silently for a moment before adding, "Perhaps, this will be temporary."

No one felt optimistic. The Board of Directors rose to their feet. Before he headed for the mill, John Bergren shaking his head in disappointment, took Gay Lippincot aside.

"I hope you will consider continuing to live here in the Superintendent's house, in the capacity of a caretaker. It would be a mistake to leave the mine and mill unattended."

"Mary and I would be happy to stay on, Sir."

"Thank you, Gay. We will work out fair compensation for your time and effort."

The Superintendent walked past the grizzly, where men were unloading ore. He walked down the stairs past the giant hopper, the bucket elevator, and the whining motors. He went straight to the master electrical switch and pulled it. The whole mill came to a grinding halt at once.

It seemed the men knew what was coming. Quietly, they all walked to the bottom center of the mill and looked up at the Foreman's desk. The Superintendent stood at this podium and addressed the workers.

"As rumor has had it, the Cardinal Mill is now officially closed … indefinitely. I encourage you men to join the war effort and contribute your skills to the mining of wartime metals. Good luck to you, wherever you may go. On behalf of the Board of Directors of the Denora Mining Company, I want to express our gratitude for your work here. Paychecks, with severance pay, are ready to be picked up at the Business Office. Good luck men. Good providence to all of you. Men, you have fifteen minutes to vacate the premises."

As the Superintendent stepped down, helmets came off. Some men simply tossed them aside. Others tucked them under their arm and bowed their heads as they all watched the man climb the long flight of stairs to the top of the mill. All was quiet except for his footsteps.

At the top of the mill, John Bergren got in his car. He started down the hill toward his home in Denver. The snow will be here soon, he thought, and this place will sure be quiet, except for that howling wind.

John Bergren had told Mabel that morning. Mabel was no stranger to change, but here it was again. This time, she wouldn't be the last resident of Cardinal. Gay and Mary would be staying on and when winter arrived, Christian would be taking Mabel down to Nederland for the season.

Mabel had walked out to the north on the old Switzerland Trail railroad bed and now she sat her blue jeans down on a big rock overlooking the valley. She watched the men streaming away from Cardinal on the road below. How quickly it happened. They were gone.

The mill sat quietly below. The hawk returned to his perch in the tree in front of the Superintendent's House. Mabel sat very still, taking in the silence.

She had watched economics spawn communities and kill them off too. Mabel closed her eyes and her mind went to Old Cardinal in its heyday. She was standing on the platform with the mail stage. She was dressed in a long woolen skirt with a starched white cotton shirt and boots laced up high. Her long hair was still brown then and pinned up in bun. Mabel felt the people around her. Time marked in clothing and a lifestyle now gone by. She smiled when she thought of the Honky Tonk Show. What fun they had. Music and a community of women had embraced her. Mabel's heart felt warm with the company of women. Mabel visualized the place. The small cabins in rows scattering gently up the mountainside. And John's house was one of the few clapboard houses to grace Old Cardinal. She felt John's spirit too. How he had wanted her to come to Golden with him when the town went bust. She remembered that first winter, when a few others had stayed on with her.

Here she was again. A last holdout. Hope and optimism kept those like her hanging on. Hope that the economy would rebound and the mines would thrive again. But with Mabel, she decided, it was more than that. She had simply settled in the hills where she belonged. These mountains were home to her. There was nowhere else she would rather be.

Mabel felt the sun on her face for a while, then, when she was ready, she walked slowly across Cardinal toward her cabin by the waterfall. Cardinal seemed like a ghost town.

1945

*T*he sun had long sunk behind the ridge, but Mabel stayed out on the front porch of her waterfall cottage, rocking the time away. Tomorrow was the day that Christian would come to move her back to Nederland for the winter. Days of leisure had slipped away faster than ever before. Time seemed to accelerate as each year passed. Mabel wished she could freeze this moment. The trees still had a few last golden aspens. It was the witching hour of the evening when the mountain lions were hunting and the elk stood very still. She always loved this time of night.

When it had grown too cold and dark to stretch the dusk any longer, Mabel rose and coaxed her stiff frame indoors. She hated to go inside. She grudgingly lit an oil lamp and put on her nightgown. It did feel good to get into bed and pull the warm blankets around her chilled bones.

Mabel closed her eyes and marveled at how the scenes in her memory had been flashing back so clearly lately. She thought of her studies of India and states of consciousness. She considered how the gypsy woman knew the Tarot. Mabel 's mind rose through what she reckoned were the astral planes, taking her on a ride to places where time and space overlapped in ways she couldn't have imagined. She saw the events of her time, from the horse and buggy to the train. There was clearly the image of the engine's firebox blazing and the steam billowing and drifting off into the darkness of night. Mabel felt the amazement when she saw her first automobile, the phonograph that John had given her! The telephone that first hung on the wall in the office. Oh, how fortunate to have lived these things!

There flashed the horrors too. Death of a child. Sickness sparing only a few. The fires. Hunger before spring. Times the wind blew so hard that the snow stuck in the horses nostrils and they refused to face the wind. And loss. Loss of love and life. The empty feeling of a broken heart. The Great Depression and all of the ugliness it brought. Most recently, the horrific atomic bombs to bring peace. How could that be?

She felt, as if in a dream, an argument with herself. This has been a good life, but you have chosen to live your life alone. Alone? Hardly lonely. She imagined herself stepping out into the forest after a day in the schoolhouse. No fear in the forest. Not alone, but at home.

"I've been so alone." She told a spirit who was to take her concerns. She would do it differently next time, she explained.

"Name the souls who are your brothers and sisters and tell me why you think you were so alone." The spirit leaned so close to her that he was one in her thoughts. She laughed when she saw no loneliness. She felt all who had loved her.

Without words, he took that ride with her in which they relived certain moments. Many scenes flashed past. These were scenes of love. All of Mabel's senses were filled as she sat upon the rock with Ryan, watching John carry Baby Christian on his shoulders toward them. She knew the words...very good care of him. She was absolutely there again. She knew she could return to this moment again and again. The leaves shimmered on the aspen trees. The evening was falling just so, hung for a moment in time, where everything seemed at once very perfect.

Just as she settled into the feeling, she found herself riding Smokey up to the fire at Caribou. Time had quickened and the pace was fast. There was an overwhelming feeling of community and teamwork, of singular purpose. She felt at once what very hard challenges life required. She felt people reaching out to people. She had known this community through fire, birth and death. These people were her and she was these people. Somewhere in this feeling was a sense of relief; a sense that these challenges were over. The spirit soothed her with knowledge. He passed her onto another place.

Here she was, moving along the stream bed of Coon Track Creek. She loved it so much. The bubbling sound. The trees, bushes and rocks were not obstacles. Her movement was smooth. Trout darted as they will. The water followed its course as it does. Light played in the pools. She was at home here. This was her familiar Earth, her Garden of Eden. She was part of this place.

The Bardos, Mabel mused. Tonight I am passing through places and times. I know these things which I am being shown. At once, Mabel was aware of all those who she had ever helped. They sang to her. They rejoiced. They were heaven on high. Some were here still and some had passed, but all were loving her. They filled her with light. She felt her body rising, changing and lightening. She was the vibration of the sound. The sound was her.

What dreams are these?, Mabel questioned. I am not yet asleep. Come now, show me more.

Goodman! Goodman, I see you will show yourself tonight. Mabel giggled.

He seemed delighted to show her his form. I've seen you before. She recalled him clearly as he stood in the schoolhouse window that night in Old Cardinal. You keep yourself, don't you! Goodman, your fire will never go out. It won't ever go out for you, Mabel. Goodman waved an arm, leaving a blue trail. He laughed with delight. Mabel felt the warm fire. She felt all of the times that the heat of a wood fire had warmed her soul. Yes, she always knew it warmed her soul. She stared in a trance at flames and relaxed her mind, lost in hot embers.

But it is not a dream. The mind can go to places that are people and are time. It is freeing up. Mabel felt a sense of curiosity. Her spirit soared in celebration. She was bathed in light. She was bathed in love that was really everything. Of course, it was. And then she saw John.

He held out his hand. He was looking just fine. John's smile drew her toward him. She was moving fast now. She couldn't feel her weight. She didn't need her body to travel this way. She felt her closed eyes, but she could see. She left the tethers, those heavy tethers, those tired old bones behind. Mabel felt her hands in John's.

❧

The people had gone. Christian sat on the rocks alone. He had told his family that he'd be back before dark. The fresh pile of dirt on Mabel's grave smelled of earth. He was comforted that she lay next to John. This was definitely where she belonged. Christian thought for a moment that he should have a little iron fence set just downhill from John and Mabel, for his own family. Silly, he thought. There was hardly a crowd waiting for a place in the Caribou Cemetery in 1945.

Overhead, a night hawk dove with a whirring sound. He looked to the sky and felt the veil was very thin. He knew the feeling would not last. He gazed at the heavens in wonder. Tears fell again from Christian's eyes.

"Why do I cry when her life was so good? Why? Her life was so long. So full and happy."

She was all the mother I ever had, he thought.

"She was all the mother I ever had! She was beautiful. And he was my father. He was the man who raised me… and they are gone." Christian said aloud. Death felt so final.

Now, tears fell in profusion and Christian did not try to stop them. They came in sobs and they made his nose run. When the tears finally stopped, he felt his faith more clearly. He stood , dusted off his suit, and walked down the hill to his car.

1957

CARDINAL, COLORADO

"*E*nough of this damn thing!" LeRoy shouted when the drill bit bound up and jammed.

"Wrong tool for the job." Mike noted, shaking his head. The stoppers drill, normally used for overhead drilling, was all they had for horizontal progress.

"The Donora Mining Company don't have two dimes to rub together. This is down to a second rate operation." lamented LeRoy Busby.

"Yeah, well, we're still underground and I'm glad to have the work."

" I'm out of air. Let's head out for some lunch, Mike."

"Yeah, I've just been sucking air out of this hose. Let's beat it." He disconnected the rubber hose from the metal piping which brought air all the way from the compressor in Cardinal. He rolled the hose up and hung it from a rafter.

LeRoy began picking up the tools. He hoisted the heavy stoppers drill up into the single train car. Mike added two shovels and three picks.

"Nothin' worth a damn in here." LeRoy said as he loaded the empty ore car.

"Glad I'm not paying us." Mike added. "Now, we're backing out of here, so it's your headlamp that's our head light. Keep it pointing out ahead just right."

Mike sat on the wooden driver's bench and started the battery driven motor on the tram. LeRoy loaded himself into the car among the tools and the tram began to push the ore car toward the portal.

Mike found it hard to judge speed as the tram accelerated through the darkness, so he let the throttle set where it felt about right. The air moving past his face felt good and let him breathe a bit easier. Busby looked ahead and Mike could see them approaching the section of the tunnel where years and years of timbering left barely enough room for motor to pass.

It was just when Mike realized he might be going a little bit too fast, that the corner of the battery cover caught a timber and the lid to flew straight back toward his head.

Mike ducked! The cover lid slammed the tram's headlight and crashed to the ground. As it fell, Mike pulled the throttle back and spun the wheel that was the brake. The tram came to a halt.

"Good Lord, Smith! You trying to kill yourself or both of us?" LeRoy stood in the car and his light shone on what had been a very close call.

"I think I'll slow down a bit from here." Mike grinned. A big white toothed smile flashed at Busby in the dark.

They muscled the lid back up onto the tram, then LeRoy Busby climbed back into the car.

When the tram rolled out into the bright daylight, Mike backed off the throttle. Both men closed their eyes and commenced blinking until they could see. They could hear the loud "chunka chunka, chunka chunka" of the compressor as the two huge fly wheels turned pumping two pistons. The little railroad track curved toward the tram house and blacksmith shop, where Gay Lippencott stood next to the gas forge with Mike's wife, Jeanette, looking on.

Gay and Mary lived in the Superintendent's House. He was the foreman and worked the forge. Gay would sharpen up to thirty tungsten carbide drill bits a day with an air driven shaper. He would temper the bits in oil. If he quenched a bit too hard, the bit would shatter, too soft it would dull quickly; but Gay got it right. He was also the master of the compressor, running it from early in the morning, pumping air into the mine, until the tram reappeared in the late afternoon.

The men pulled the car into the shop and shut it down.

"Well, looks like a lady!" Busby greeted Jeanette with smile and a wave of a hand.

"Mike forgot his lunch pail so I brought it up." Jeanette balanced her baby boy on her hip and held out the bucket of sandwiches.

Gay went next door and turned off the compressor. When he returned, he stood quietly in the doorway. The two miners eyed him suspiciously.

"Well, men," he said, although Smith and Busby looked more like boys to him, "We're back out of work here. John Bergren called at the ten o'clock break and he says, "Pull those men. We can't afford to mine the Boulder County Mine any longer.""

"It's just not producing anything commercial grade." Busby stated disappointedly.

Mike looked at his young wife and baby. "Oh well," he said somewhat optimistically, "We'll go looking for work somewhere else."

Jeanette Smith smiled at Mike. Such is the life of a miner, she thought.

Gay said, "Looks like '57 is the year Mary and I might just move to town. She'd like that."

1957

ASHBROOK FARM
MORRIS PLAINS, NEW JERSEY

*M*y family lived on ten acres that came with a history you could feel. You could feel it back to the earliest Indians. You could feel many hundreds and thousands of years of them. I would stare into the water at our pond and think of how many people had done the same thing.

Our house was a cow barn, which my parents had made into a house. Each time a new baby came, and there were six, the carpenter came back to work. If you opened the attic door, you could see the outside of our house inside the barn. It was a very old barn, and the first Morse code had been sent there from Speedwell Lake in Morristown. It was a curiosity to me to be born in 1957 into a family with such a place.

My Uncle John's family lived close by, on the same 10 acres, in a grand old Victorian mansion from the 1840's. On our property were stables, a root cellar covered by a hill, and several buildings for raising consumable animals. My father tended vegetable gardens which grew everything known to man, and flowers that bloomed in profusion. There was also a brook that fed an acre and a half of pond before spilling out in a waterfall and tumbling away in rapids. There were huge pine trees and walnut, hickory and ash. There were pear, apple, and cherry trees.

There were two rows of enormous ash trees that lined a lane from long ago. At the far end of the lane stood a little playhouse. It was miniature, made to match my Uncle John's house, complete with hardwood floors and divided light windows. It was built for Mr. Vail's daughter, one hundred years ago.

All of the kids in our family, and my cousins, had crept and crawled into every eave and secret room on the property. Not one of us believed in ghosts because if we had, we'd have been haunted for sure. We were not afraid of the dark, and we ran faster than the wind.

Outside Ashbrook Farm, the Garden State was being gobbled up quickly by suburbia. Trains whistled by to the east of our property, taking commuters to New York. The older sections of our little town had perfect streets lined with shady trees. The newer developments were clear cuts with modern ranch style homes. I had friends on all of these streets, but all of them were different from me because my family lived on Ashbrook Farm.

I went to the public school through the fifth grade, walking on abandoned railroad tracks that went on past the school up to the State Insane Asylum. About once a month, a train would come on those tracks. It brought food and coal to the asylum. All my friend's mothers said, "You shouldn't walk on those tracks, dear." But my Mum said," Sure you can. No train's going to run you over!"

My Mum was born and raised in Canada. She was different from all of the other mothers. She expected us to play outside, unless we had a damned good reason to be in. So I spent all of my time outside, or in out buildings, talking to myself and living a life of total fantasy. When I strayed far enough to be invited into a friend's house, I went squirrelly pretty quickly and found an excuse to run home to Ashbrook Farm.

Most of my youth was spent waiting for school to be dismissed. As soon as we were out for summer vacation, we packed up our cats and bathing suits, and headed for my Mum's family summer home in Ontario, Canada. My Uncle John said we lived like Indians all summer. I guess he said that because we didn't put clothes on the little ones, and we spent our days fishing and frogging.

Our time at Christie Lake in Ontario made it harder and harder for me to partake in New Jersey society. The small private schools I attended had been steeped in tradition so long that people had forgotten to live their own lives. Choices were whittled down to what was appropriate and expected. I had seen things differently. I had been given the gift of fishing from my Canadian Grandfather. It was my religion. It reduced life to a few basic truths. My value system involved clean water, sunshine and the laws of what the Indians referred to as the "Great Spirit". I struggled to get myself back in the car at the end of each summer.

My Father would wake me early in the morning to fly in his airplane on our way to school. These morning adventures gave me a different perspective on life. From up above, looking down on the morning commuter traffic and large industrial complexes, I had insight as to what I did not want to become a part of. My classmates applied themselves with fervor to do their best. They were driven to become part of a machine I despised.

As the years ticked by, I struggled to accept the people in New Jersey.

Society was getting too far from the basics to be safe or sustainable. The infrastructure made us dangerously dependent on the system. I work to calm those same instincts to this day, but as a teenager, I became obsessed.

My siblings, friends and I joined the counter culture. We had huge parties at Ashbrook Farm welcoming every kind of person we could find. We danced to The New Riders of the Purple Sage. "We live in the Garden of Eden; don't know why they want to burn the whole thing down." My older brother brought music. He played every instrument he could get his hands on. His rock bands shared their music freely with all, using elaborate sound systems to pipe the sounds of the new culture into space.

My parents were also swept into the wave. They were as "right on" as they could be, for parents. My Mum delighted in the excitement of the youth that surrounded her. My Dad gradually transformed from Archie Bunker to Austin Powers, then let the pendulum swing back to somewhere in between. We had fun with them. My folks opened their door to many kids that needed an adult to accept them. I was lucky, and I knew it.

My friends and I were caught up in a psychedelic revolution in a country reeling from Nixon and Vietnam. At seventeen, I went West in search of freedom and enlightenment.

1960

CARDINAL, COLORADO

*T*he Ford station wagon cruised along Caribou Road with dust flying out behind it and the cool mountain air whipping in the open windows. The Baker Family grinned in anticipation as the car drew nearer to the ghost town of Cardinal. As they rounded the big curve, they saw the green valley of willows spread out to the west and the familiar hills come into view. They passed the Caribou Spring. When the bump came as they turned onto the old road into Cardinal, they could see the spot where Great Gramma Catherine 's old Post Office had been. Dad parked the car right there, where the railroad trestle had once been.

When their picnic was eaten, everyone took a huge slice of watermelon and headed up the hill to visit the waterfall. As they passed the tight spot between the old Superintendent's House and the Mill, Gramma Margaret remarked, "Gay Lippencott moved to Denver. Seems real empty here now, doesn't it? Nobody's left."

"Nobody at all." responded Great Gramma Catherine. The long, steep walk up the hill was exhausting. She stopped and put her hands on her hips, drew a few deep breaths of the thin air, and then kept pushing to the top of the hill. Great Gramma Catherine stood just west of the Cardinal Mill resting and paused in thought for a long time.

The kids threw their watermelon rinds and broke into a sprint across the flat ground of the town site. They headed straight for the ponds. They looked for trout as they peeked up over the berm and the trout scattered and hid when they saw the children's shadows. Cousin Lee began throwing rocks into the clear water. Bob lurched up the rocky hillside by the mine portal to get a really big rock. His sister, Becca, threw in a long stick. When Momma and Dad caught up, the kids ran ahead again to hide in the old boarding house to scare Momma when she walked past.

Off came the shirts and shoes when they got to the waterfall. Squeals of delight rang through the steep walled valley. Each child dunked under the

CATHERINE RETURNS TO CARDINAL IN 1960
The Boulder County Mine Portal 1960

crashing water as it poured through the old metal flume from above.

Gramma Margaret sat on Mabel's old picnic table. She watched the kids play in the creek, remembering doing the same thing. She closed her eyes and saw a different day, when three miners sat on a long bench perched above the green cabin on the dam with Mabel. Margaret had slipped on the rocks and cried. Mabel came down to the creek and got her boot wet saving Margaret. Margaret basked in the childhood memory, feeling the warm sun beat down on her face.

"Come on, kids! Gramma and Momma are walking back to the post office. The city beckons. Let's go." Dad called. He peeked one more time into the green cottage.

"Must be twenty years since Bergrens have done a thing to this place." He muttered to himself.

"Don't forget your jacket, Sam." He yelled as he walked away.

On the way back past the business office, the kids stuck their heads over the side of the brick well and peered into the darkness. Bob lugged a rock over and let it fall. They all listened.

"Not much water left." said Sam, "Let's go!"

Dad turned the station wagon around and everyone piled back in. Everyone except Margaret, who stood staring at the spot that had once been her home at the Post Office.

"My jacket!" yelled Sam.

"Well, go on back up and get it." said Dad.

They all piled back out of the car. Becca hung on Great Gramma Catherine's arm. Margaret was remembering the skinny miner's jingle…"Mar-gar-eat go wash your feet, the board of health is across the street." She remembered the Superintendent. He always dressed in a woolen suit. He had said, "I don't believe the girl appreciates that song, Jerome." It wasn't too long after that when he got sick and died. Margaret thought it was sad. He had been a good man.

His jacket tied around his waist, Sam ran back across the townsite. He ran past the mill, and looked toward his left at the closed up Superintendent's House as he went by. On a glance, he saw an apparition of a man in a bowler hat and a suit inside the first door. The man glared hard at Sam and then turned and faded back inside. Suddenly, Sam could not draw a breath, but he kept on running, his eyes frozen open.

"Sam's a freak show!" teased Becca in the car. Bob whacked her arm.

"Stop it you two." bellowed Dad.

"Sam, Sam the Dodo Man."

"Cat's got his tongue." added Becca.

"Leave him alone, he'll be alright." said Dad.

It was two days later, Margaret and Catherine were making pies in the kitchen, when Sam finally spoke.

"I saw a g…g…ghost." he said quietly, and he told them what he had seen.

Catherine set down the rolling pin. She brushed the flour from her hands and pulled out a chair to sit down. She looked hard at Sam. She was sure he was telling the truth.

1973

CARDINAL, COLORADO

*T*he sun came up gradually, glinting through the green aspen leaves and shimmering as it rose through the tall pines. At the green cottage, tucked deep in the steep walled valley, the air stayed cool even in July. The sound of the waterfall was the only sound.

A party had gone on all night around the campfire. There had been the music of guitars, a few rounds of impromptu poetry, and as the night wore on, there was political posturing and a scuffle or two over a couple of gals. The acid laced discussion regarding Communist "super-power" support of North Vietnam's aggression toward anti-Communist South Vietnam and the perception of the Communist threat had digressed into idealistic visions of utopian dreamers.

Now, people were sleeping the morning away. Some were inside the cottage on mattresses on the floor. The two bedrooms were taken by couples, who had the doors shut tightly. Outside, a few hammocks were strung between trees near the creek and on the grass, sleeping figures rolled up in blankets lay scattered everywhere. The fire smoked and had turned to ashes. Beer cans and bottles were strewn hither and yon.

Two fellows sat on logs, staring into the smoldering ashes of the dying fire.

"I'm still high, man." said one of them.

"Yeah, cool." mumbled the other.

"All night, I kept thinking I was a miner here long ago. I just couldn't shake it. I wandered up the road that follows the creek and found this spot...it was really powerful, man. It's like I know this place. I could practically see my cabin. There's a spot. I swear, man. It's crazy. Déjà vu, you know?"

"Yeah, man. I do know." The fellow pulled his hooded sweatshirt up around his neck. "I'm freezing up here, man. Gotta get back to the desert, maybe today."

Unbeknown to the sleeping STP Gang, John Bergren's truck had rumbled up the road into Cardinal. He unloaded five-gallon cans of purple enamel into the top section of the Cardinal Mill. Allied Chemical was leasing the mine for two years. So far, it had yeilded no prospects.

What a bargain, thought John. Rocky Mountain Arsenal had been cleaning out a warehouse to make more room for stockpiling nerve gas. John had only paid a buck fifty a can for this perfectly good paint. Maybe he'd sell it and make a few bucks on the gallon, or who knows, use it up here at the mine someday. Anyway, it was perfectly good and the price was right. He carried can after can into the Mill, stacking them up against the north wall. Sixty five cans, what a bargain.

When the job was done, John drove the truck to the far end of town. As he passed the Compressor House, he saw smoke rising to the west, so he continued on up toward the green cottage. Soon he started seeing cars parked. He passed a Chevy Impala, a couple of VW Bugs, a Dodge Van, an old Ford pick-up truck and a couple of motorcycles.

"Hey Man, do you hear that?"

"Uh, what?"

"Sounds like...uh, listen."

"You're high, man. I don't hear nothin'."

"Oh, shit man."

"Just be cool."

John put the truck in first gear and turned off the engine. He picked up the shotgun from the seat of the truck and hefted it into his right hand as he got out. Damn hippies. They were everywhere. The sleeping forms didn't move. John saw two men sitting by the fire. John made himself feel large and approached them.

"You all are trespassing. You're gonna have to clear out." John stood strong.

The fellows on the log looked up at him blankly.

It is evident these kids are on drugs, thought John.

"Who's the leader around here?" asked John.

"We're all created equal." stated the fellow in the sweatshirt. The other young man had his eyes respectfully on John's gun.

"Can you give us some time, man? Folks aren't awake yet."

"I'd say you better get wakening them up." John shot once into the air and a few people sat up.

"We gotta clear out of here, guys!" said the young man loudly in a wavering voice.

Another man approached the fire. He zipped his jeans and buckled his belt as he walked.

"Hey man, be cool. What's the problem here?"

"The problem" John said, "is that you all are trespassing and you got to clear out of here. I mean clear out right now."

"Whoa, whoa, whoa, Man. We got folks sleeping here. This is gonna take some time..." the guy scratched his head and lit a cigarette. "You gotta mellow out, man. These folks ain't movin' very fast."

John walked toward the house. He walked to the back door and looked around. It smelled terribly of sewage. The hippies had filled the septic tank to overflowing. He was going to need the help of the Boulder County Sherriff.

"I'm going to down to Nederland and I'm coming right back with the Sherriff. You'd better wake your friends up."

"Whoa! Hey man. We don't need no Sherriff to clear out. Come on, man. Be cool. Give me a minute to get everyone awake."

"They gist got to sleep, man." added the fellow in the sweatshirt.

"My name's not 'Man'! Get your friends out of here and tell'm they are not to come back! I'm going for the Sherriff." John made for the truck.

As he drove down the road, he reflected on the times. He decided that his own kids, with their hair curling perilously over their collars, maybe were okay after all.

1975

NEDERLAND, COLORADO

I knew from the start that this small mountain town would be my home. I had heard of Chief Niwot's curse. Some white people come to this area and can never leave. I wondered at the time if I had this curse. It seemed to me to be a very beautiful curse to bear. I remember sitting on a split rail fence, looking west toward Caribou, and feeling as if my soul had come home. It seemed as though a power held me like a magnet to the rock in these mountains. I mused at this, and decided it was indeed a good place to mellow.

I lived with my lover in a tipi. A big potbellied stove kept us warm through the winters, and the moon lit up the canvas like a Chinese lantern at night. In the summer, our inside garden thrived in filtered sunlight. In the winter, deep snow insulated the tipi from the wind. From our mountaintop, we faced the Continental Divide. Our refrigerator was a metal box placed deep in an old mine hole, where the temperature stayed at fifty-five degrees year round. We sat outside by campfires that sparked with spirits of those who had lived here before us.

These were interesting times in the mountains of Boulder County, Colorado. The teachings of Timothy Leary and Baba Ram Dass blew in the wind. Those seeking a sacred life wandered the pine-covered hillsides by day, and danced to live music by night. Life was an experience of expanding consciousness. For me, it was a journey of transformation, from what I had been raised to be, to what I could become.

> We were just hanging out in that place.
> Nobody could predict what was to come.
> - *"Be Here Now"*

"Either you do it like it is a big weight on you or you do it as part of the dance." *-Dr. Richard Alpert*

The reader may ask, "What does this have to do with Cardinal?" It has everything to do with what has happened, for we are the sum of our experiences.

The open space saved around the Cardinal Townsite is saved because of the many nights that my Mum and I walked and talked in New Jersey, confined by the paved streets of suburbia.

The Cardinal Mill stands as a museum, because I lived my youth with ghosts of the past, and an appreciation for the presence of those who had come before me.

The Cardinal buildings are now small homes because I have lived a simple lifestyle recognizing that sometimes less is more.

1982

CARDINAL, COLORADO

*T*he sun rose up over the eastern prairies as a bobcat strode nonchalant-ly down the road behind the old business office of the mine. Dawn breezes blew the aspen leaves with a whirr and a shimmer. The bobcat walked silent-ly through the abandoned townsite keeping a keen eye for a mouse. A rabbit hopped out of sight undetected. Trout flitted about in the stream. A large red tail hawk lit from the tree above the Superintendent's house and flew out over the Cardinal Mill. There was no sound in the ghost town but the wind.

As the sun rose that October morning, a new baby, named Sandi Betters, was born in Boulder.

1994

ASHBROOK FARM, NEW JERSEY

*I*t was just after dawn, when I drove up to the front door of our old house at Ashbrook Farm. My kids and I had a long day ahead of us, as we would drive to Canada. This would be my last visit to New Jersey. I wanted Sandi and Peter to see where I grew up.

Ashbrook Farm is very different now; all kinds of things are gone. The Town of Morris Plains bought our property from my Dad and Uncle. Now, it has become a park with carefully tended flat green lawns that erase a lot of history. Time is an amazing dimension.

We anxiously scanned the property, with me pointing out where various features had been. Someone stood just outside the front door of the house.

I asked this man if the children could have a peek inside. I stated that I hadn't been here in a long time. The fellow was a boarder, renting a room. He said that the Madam hired by the town ran a very tight ship and he would not be permitted to bring us inside. She was still asleep, and he was waiting for his ride to work. I stood blinking in disbelief at all that was gone around me.

The man kept on speaking. He said "There was a family that used to live here...the Armitages. People still talk about them. They have become a legend around here."

At thirty two years old, I felt too young to be a legend. But the dancing and parties that made up that history were part of an era now gone, and times had changed. For the longer range, the history of millennia had been sodded over by the Town of Morris Plains.

1998

*R*andy Leavitt was my real estate customer. He was looking for mountain land; something peaceful, private and quiet that he could meditate on; something with high peak views and enough sunshine. I took him walking west of the New Cardinal Townsite to the Addie M, a single mining claim, which was for sale. He didn't buy that claim, but instead fell in love with a beautiful piece of land looking over the Continental Divide on the west side of the Sleeping Giant.

A month or so after buying his land, Randy called me.

"Lexie, do you remember the Town of New Cardinal?"

"Of course, Randy. It is so amazing."

"If we could purchase it, what could be done with it?"

"I know exactly what I'd do with it." I said, recognizing my passion for history. "The townsite could become a smaller version of the historic mining town of Gold Hill. It could be a healing center and a community of homes. The mill could be saved before it falls in!"

"Well, I've been thinking that you should call the owner, and see if he's interested in selling. You'd have to be the brains and muscle, and I'd put up the money. I'm leaving the country for a while. What do you think?"

"It's certainly worth a try."

That is how my part of the story started. My faith is emerging stronger than ever. I am clear that Cardinal came to me for a reason. I have known from the start that I am just a small part of a bigger story, an ongoing tale. I often ponder though, why it was Randy who brought me into this.

Randy Leavitt is a Buddhist who has made a full time commitment to his practice. Randy is one of the most present people I've ever met. At once, he can be curious and centered. I can only be curious or centered. But Randy and I have something in common. We both seek peace and enlightenment.

We are going about our searches on different paths. I imagine Randy's experience of solitude to be still, inward and peaceful. When I have the opportunity for solitude, it is taken at a physically demanding pace, heading up a couple of thousand vertical feet on a mountain. My heart pounds, my breathing is rhythmic, my eyes feast on forest or tundra, and my mind goes to a place where it sees more clearly.

As Randy goes into retreat, stripping life to its most simple, I am dealt puzzle after puzzle of complexity. The outcome is probably the same for both of us, for the more I am dealt, the simpler it gets.

It was early June of 1999 when Randy and I drove to Arvada, Colorado with an appointment to visit the home of John and Shirley Bergren, the owners of the Cardinal Townsite. I was curious to meet the man who had sounded so young on the phone, but had to be in his seventies.

Randy was a bit nervous about first impressions. But, as we were welcomed into the Bergren's home, it was evident that they were big hearted people, and thrilled to meet us. We were offered a high ball or a glass of wine, which we both politely declined. We wanted to be as credible and professional as possible.

John was young and spry for his seventy three years, his enthusiasm for life boiling over. The twinkle in his eyes made me think he must have been a wild five year old.

John's wife, Shirley, had recently been challenged by breathing problems and stayed in her chair. She was so sweet and cheerful. It seemed to me that she had always made the best of everything.

John told us the history of their family's involvement in Cardinal. Shirley kept adding important details to the conversation. John Bergren and his sister, Ruth, had inherited Cardinal from their father, who had been the last acting Superintendent of the Boulder County Mine. When the mine had closed after World War II, John Senior had invested in the property with two dentists from California. John Senior eventually bought them out.

On the day that John and Ruth buried their father, a letter was delivered to the door stating that the Allied Chemical Co. was pulling out of their lease at the Boulder County Mine. 1974 marked the last commercial use of the mine at Cardinal. John Senior left 200 acres to his children on two deeds. John and Ruth each held a one half undivided interest on each deed.

Both siblings lived in Denver. John had been a firefighter and father. Ruth was a mother and homemaker. They spent many wonderful family summers together in the mountains at Cardinal when their children were young.

As the years wore on, Cardinal increasingly caused problems for John and Ruth's relationship. John spent his leisure time fixing damage caused by

CARDINAL MILL IN 2000; SUPERINTENDENT'S HOUSE, UPPER RIGHT

vandals at the mine. Ruth had little interest in the property. She finally sold an option on one of her half undivided interests to the parent company of the active silver mine up the road in Caribou. This cloud on the title made John livid, as it effectively tied his hands in regard to the property. The two siblings hadn't spoken for twenty years.

Randy and I spent the afternoon absorbing this incredible story. John said he would be interested in selling us his share of Cardinal, if we could give him an offer with no conditions.

As we departed, I thought about the interesting lives that John and Shirley had led. How special it was to have shared the afternoon with them. Making a deal on Cardinal would be a long shot, but at least we had learned that the door was open a crack.

Before Randy left for India and three months of meditation, we formed "New Cardinal LLC". I opened a bank account with ten thousand dollars from Randy, and then Randy left to sit with a Buddhist master. He wished me good luck.

SUPERINTENDENT'S HOUSE IN 2000

As I formulated a business plan for Cardinal, a few things became evident. First, I was motivated to save the surrounding mining claims as forest, as they are appropriate for development. The land is wild, steep, and already doing its job as part of mother earth. I would try to preserve it as County Open Space.

Secondly, I wanted to preserve the history of the Cardinal Townsite by preserving the remaining buildings. The Cardinal Mill still held the original milling equipment, but was badly in need of structural repair. The company buildings would benefit by being held in the private sector, but deed restricted for preservation. I didn't have the amount of money I needed to purchase the Bergren property. Approaching the County to purchase open space would be the only way for me to redevelop the townsite.

My negotiations with Boulder County were to be an ongoing frustration due to the protocols followed by county officials. Having experienced the workings of Boulder County, I knew to start at the top and work my way down. One of the County Commissioners had also been appointed to serve as the Director of Parks and Open Space. Unfortunately, this meant that if he didn't like my plan, there would be no hope for success. I went directly to Mr. Stewart and outlined the project. I knew that in theory, Cardinal was everything the County looked for in terms of historic preservation, open space land, and clustering development rights.

Mr. Stewart was open minded, but tilted his head and gave me a puzzled look as to say, it sounds like a long shot. I had no choice but to take that look as encouragement, and continue to pursue my dream. I knew there could be no promises, but a public process involving many hoops to be jumped.

I took the next step, and called John Bergren's sister, Ruth. She was very sweet, refined and well spoken. Ruth was interested in hearing more about my offer. We agreed that we should meet with everyone who owned an interest in

Cardinal and the surrounding mining claims. We chose a restaurant in Boulder.

The reunion was incredible. It must have been that the time was right. Tight, prolonged hugs and squeezes were passed around, and not an eye was dry. Ruth and Shirley were especially happy to see each other again. It's odd how these things can happen among families. Before they knew it, two decades had passed.

John ordered the first carafe of wine, and the afternoon passed quickly with stories of summers long ago in Cardinal. I canceled my other two meetings between glasses of Chardonnay, relaxed and enjoyed the company.

Ruth was open to selling her interest in Cardinal, but warned that everything would hinge on cooperation from the Mining Company. Even though the mining company had defaulted on their option payment obligations, Ruth would honor the agreement because their president was sincerely a nice man. Okay, I thought, go with the flow.

It was amazing to hear such an intriguing family history. The women beamed at each other with a sisterly love that could be once again. When the day was over, I thought that this wasn't about Cardinal. It was about John, Ruth and Shirley.

❧

A plan to purchase Cardinal had become a reality. I felt it only fair to let the neighbors know that there was the possibility of renovation in the townsite. I telephoned Cardinal's closest neighbor, Tina Isanti, and asked to set up a meeting to share my intentions with her. A hunch warned me of trouble to come.

Tina and her boyfriend, Dennis, greeted me at their door. Dennis looked just like Charles Manson. Tina was poised but stern. The house was typical of our mountain neighborhoods, a combination of wood, stone and windows that had been added on to over the decades. I could sense how much Tina loved her home.

"Thank you for having me over", I said, as I was directed to a seat at the dining room table. "I am grateful for the opportunity to tell you about our potential project at the Cardinal Townsite." My chair was straight backed, and most uncomfortable.

As I looked toward Dennis, he glared back at me. Tina looked as if she would cry. It was evident that neither of them would share my enthusiasm for this project.

"We moved here from California to get away from this very kind of thing." said Tina. "This house is our dream house. Dennis is a hunting guide and I do graphic design. We are here enjoying our peace. This valley is full of wildlife. We protect it. We make sure no one disturbs it. We stop them right here at our gate. We protect the foxes, the deer and hawks."

I had been confronted by Dennis both times that I had passed their house to look at the Addie M Lode. I had been armed with the knowledge that he couldn't deny me access.

"We will do everything within our power to stop your subdivision in Cardinal." promised Dennis. "We know this is all about money for you. You try to put it off as historic and open space, but it's obvious you're trying to make a buck. This will turn into a huge, protracted law suit", he threatened. "We will not give up."

"What would you rather see happen?" I asked incredulously. "It is in the best interest of everyone that the Cardinal Mill be saved. It won't last many more winters. The roof is caving in. The cabins will stay small. There will be one hundred and ninety five acres of land dedicated to open space. I have lived in this area for twenty five years. I am the last person to want its character destroyed."

Dennis reacted strongly to that. He gripped the table and challenged me "Don't you say you live in this neighborhood. You are not part of this neighborhood!"

"Dennis, the Bergrens will sell and something will happen up there. You could have six huge homes with six driveways cut into the mountainside with twelve dogs running loose. What is it that you would rather see?"

After two hours, I had heard all of the reasons that these neighbors felt betrayed. They included everything from saving the wildlife to the fact that this was their dream house, just the way it was. Tina had moved to this valley less than a year before, believing it was stuck in time forever. Never paid mind to the fact that it was someone else's private land.

Little did I know, that Dennis meant to take on the Army Corps of Engineers, Boulder County, the historic groups, the State of Colorado and the EPA.

As I left the house, I pondered how Tina could be so ignorant when it came to property rights. She didn't seem to understand that the law supports a property owner's rights. I believed these rights would be protected by the courts.

Talking to myself, I opened the car door. Why did I come here today? As a courtesy, that's all. Just as a courtesy. I could not expect them to be happy about anything happening to the west of their home. I scoffed at Dennis, and shook my head as I drove away.

Our Town of Nederland is just two miles east of Cardinal. The hub of hustle and bustle here is the United States Post Office. One day, shortly after my meeting at Tina's house, I ran into my friend, Jeanette Smith, as she gathered the mail from her post office box.

"Oh, Lexie, those signs!" she said breathlessly. "I've taken some down for you. What's wrong with those people? People, people...you just can't believe how people behave."

Jeanette had been my teacher's aide for twelve years, when I was the kindergarten teacher in Nederland. Together, we knew all about people's behavior.

I jumped into my car and drove toward Cardinal. As I turned up Caribou Road, I saw the first one, a bright orange sign, reading "Betters is Worse for Caribou".

Nederland is a small town of about twelve hundred people. I was trying to run a real estate business. This was not a good thing.

As I proceeded west, there were many more signs hung on roadside trees. Certainly this would be slander. How could this be legal? The signs grew more plentiful as I drove west. They were everywhere.

I decided there was only one way to deal with this. I would rely on a skill I learned growing up in a big family. I would simply thicken my skin. That and "frontier justice". I stopped to cut the signs down with my pocket knife. In the end, I had taken down two dozen signs.

There are times in life when a person must consider the possibility of a grand plan. Something that melds with the spiritual arrangement you've had in mind. A grand plan that is bigger than you, but somehow you are a key player. As the process unfolds you play a part, but you're not totally in charge. It requires an artful dance of letting go and being open. It forms our faith.

Sometimes, we are aware that we are being asked to step up to the plate. One wonders if there was a point in time and space when he or she consciously joined this plan, or whether it was unwitting.

I was gradually becoming aware of a grand plan as the deal with Cardinal came together. The people skills, patience and perseverance which I had developed as a teacher, were very much essential ingredients to success of the plan. Time and time again, I was conscious of things coming together as if they fit like notes in a melody. But instead of quarter notes, this story unfolded in what felt like geologic time. I have developed a sense not to struggle with the element of time, but to let things play out like a fishing line. When they do, everything makes perfect sense.

Much to my surprise, the project to save Cardinal sustained itself.

On a hot afternoon in August, I drove to the Bergren's house in Denver to get the key to the Cardinal gate. As I pulled into the driveway, I recalled the spring day that Randy and I had met the Bergrens. The spring green tree buds had now turned to late summer leaves.

John is the same age as my father. By now, he had shared much of his life's story with me and we had grown very fond of each other. I knew we would always be friends.

When people are older, their sense of urgency leaves them. Time ticks by at a different rate. My Grandmother told me that as you grow older, time accelerates. Yet, days of leisure stretch on without punctuation. I feel this to be true as I enter the Bergren's home. Again I am offered "a wine", and this time I accept. I am catapulted from my crazy frantic schedule into a time warp where minutes and hours don't count. I bathe in the relaxation, and sit back to enjoy more stories of Cardinal.

John tells me of a fire at the Boulder County Mine. The compressor to the west of the tunnel portal had caught fire. December winds were blowing in a blizzard from the west. The blacksmith shop and the timbers supporting the tunnel caught fire. As the portal collapsed, twenty miners were trapped inside. By the time the raging fire was put out and the miners rescued, six firemen were critically injured. Another tale takes me to long ago. John tells a story his father had told him. There was a time when the men working the Boulder County Mill had to defend the mill from a group who challenged their interest. The miners, well armed with guns and dynamite, blocked the road to Cardinal between the Superintendent's house and the Mill. After a confrontation and a standoff, the aggressors left.

I imagine the men in their filthy work clothes, lined up across the gap where the road still passes. I feel their resolve to not give in. There is power in a group which has set its mind with determination. The men approaching from downhill would have been at a disadvantage. Tension ran high as the men hoped to avoid a gunfight. I can hear the grumbling as the challengers leave the mill to the defenders.

Shirley Bergren tells a delightful account of the honeymoon that she and John shared in the green cabin, furthest to the west. She giggles as she talks about her wedding and the trip to the mountains together.

As I leave the Bergren's house, John hands me a ring full of keys.

"You may as well take them all." he says, "You will need them. Maybe you can figure out what some of them are, but I know this one opens the tramway house, and this is the key to the gate."

I am honored to be the keeper of the keys to Cardinal.

There are all kinds of heroes in the working world. People who get up each day and give their job all they've got. They do it because they're good at it. They do it because the job needs to be done. They do it for a sense of accomplishment, for their reputation, and let's face it, for a buck.

Near Nederland, they do this work no matter what the weather. One very blustery day, I found my surveyors, hard at work. The situation was that part of the road to Cardinal lay on Tina's land.

I had been greeted by the police one day, as I attempted to drive into Cardinal.

"You have no right to pass over Ms. Isanti's road, unless you can show me written documentation of an easement."

"This road was established as a public road long before the turn of the century." I told the officer. "It leads to the Cardinal Townsite."

"Without paperwork, I must ask you to leave." the cop had told me as he turned me away. Steam came from my ears as I vented the anger I felt toward Tina and Dennis. I looked up at their house. They were out of state and the house had been empty for months. I felt some satisfaction knowing I would return to Cardinal within the half hour.

Tina's land wasn't the section of road that passed directly below her house, but was a stretch approximately one hundred and fifty feet long, further up the road to the west. It encompassed the area where the Switzerland Trail of America's narrow gauge train trestle left the north side of the valley to head south to Eldora. In the early 1900's, this had been a population center with a

United States Post Office and a train depot.

In the 1970's, an easement was drafted by Mia Damson, the prior owner of Tina's house. It traded ingress and egress for Cardinal for the right to keep her septic leach field where it lay on Cardinal land. John Bergren had signed the document, but for some reason, it had never been signed by Ms. Damson or recorded with the County.

My attorney had negotiated a temporary right to pass, but Tina insisted that the issue was now to be resolved in court. I wasn't sure where the money to fight would come from, but I was invested enough in the property that I felt I must pursue access. With Tina's septic leach field on Cardinal land, I felt quite sure we'd settle the matter swiftly enough.

I needed the Cardinal mining claims surveyed in order to do the project anyway. So here we were.

"Dave", I yelled into the wind, throwing my voice at the surveyor. "How goes it today?"

Dave came walking all the way over to me and said nothing, but hung his head as if deep in thought.

"There's something interesting going on here." he finally said. "I don't really know yet. It's gonna be a while before I can say for sure... One can't say in this business until the proper points have been located, and one wouldn't want to speak to soon. But...I'm not sure that Tina's house is on her land."

"I think I'll pretend you didn't say that for now."

"I know. I'll be back to work now."

"I'll be up at the townsite."

Late in the day, the survey team had found the points necessary to locate the section line. Dave reported to me that Tina's house just eeked onto her property by inches. We both agreed that this was a good thing. However, her septic leach field and propane tank were on Cardinal land. This too was a good thing, as it would give us some leverage to exchange easements.

In the next few weeks, Dave's survey team produced a map that showed the buildings and the new lots to be formed in the Cardinal Townsite. The map also showed the roads, the creek, the mine tunnel and tracks. This huge task had not been undertaken before, and was very revealing.

If the Cardinal project was to come together, it was as dependent upon the mining company to the west, as much as any of the other entities. I attended a meeting for the board members of the corporation.

I met with five men at the Sundance Cafe. The Sundance is a little restaurant perched high on a hillside facing west toward the Continental Divide. The view of the snow capped peaks is stunning. Bright white snow covered mountains, bathing them in sunshine, crossing the whole western horizon. This is a hippie restaurant serving up great food, if you have time to spare.

I introduced my plans for Cardinal, but the conversation rapidly shifted to sharing good ol' boy geologist stories. Even though I'm not a geologist, I thoroughly enjoyed myself. We discussed the nature of our local rock. I heard of fantastic mines in the Arctic. I was tickled that Bob knew every nook and cranny of the San Rafael Swell, where my family and I had spent many happy camping trips loving the Utah desert.

When we were buzzed on coffee, and it was almost lunch time, it was decided. There were mining claims of geologic interest to the company. If the company could take full clear title to specific claims west of Cardinal, my plan would be of value to them.

I also learned that any decisions to be made for the mining company would have to be voted on by not only its board of directors, but the boards of several parent companies. It seemed that the prices of gold and silver had forced these companies into incestuous relationships, with everyone borrowing money from everywhere to stay afloat. Holding clear title to these claims would enable the mining company to pay some debts and borrow against these properties. I could only hope for a quick vote from the powers that be. It didn't come quickly, nothing has. But in due time, I held a copy of a contract to buy all of Ruth's share of Cardinal minus forty acres which would go to the mining company.

The Nederland Historical Society is very small, but they don't let that stand in the way of their plans. When I phone Dan Martin, who is vice president, I know I'm delivering what will be exciting news. My plan is to get the Cardinal Mill into the public realm, so grant funds can be procured.

I had waited to tell him the news about Cardinal until I was quite sure I had the buy in of the Bergrens, the mining companies, and Boulder County.

Dan jumps with joy! He knows a lot about the Boulder County Tunnel Mill, and his enthusiasm tickles me. Dan is eager to meet me at the mill site, and thrilled about the plan.

I have heard Dan Martin's name for years, as a dependable, local auto mechanic, as well as a historian, but I have never met him. When he arrives at Cardinal in his red jeep with flames painted on it, I am surprised at how young he is. Dan has brought his friend, John, one of the other historic society members. Dan and John would later provide instrumental support, as the project was presented to the County Commissioners for approval.

We introduce ourselves, and walk around the townsite peeking into the various buildings. We cannot walk inside the buildings because they are packed completely with junk from the ages. Everything from long ago, topped with forty years' worth of items brought to Cardinal from Denver by John Bergren, Jr. Every time John got a deal at an auction or a sale, he ferreted it away in the cabins at Cardinal. John is like most of the Depression Era folks I know. Every pie tin, newspaper, tin can, milk carton and scrap of metal was saved for a time that it might be needed. A hunch tells me this behavior is not crazy.

Some examples of these items included a case of tailpipes for a Willys Jeep, thirty two rolls of cork board, every magazine John ever subscribed to (and there were many), chairs, dishes, scrap metal, old clothes, empty whiskey bottles, windows, paint cans, newspapers, plastic bottles, cigarette machines, wooden boards, sixties furniture, quilter's scraps, boxes of shoes, coal, tires, skis, cards and letters, boxes and boxes of rubber sealing rings, batteries, printers ink, car paint, refrigerators, plastic flowers, and boxes of a film made to educate high school students in the Sixties about pregnancy and birth control. Most of these things were wet and moldy, condensing over the decades into a form of junk that you might expect could be pitch forked out. But alas, it would all have to be carefully sorted into recyclable piles of metal, glass, paper, rubber and finally, plain trash.

Underneath these items lay all the old historic goods such as ore buckets, motors, winches, drill bits, mine records, picks, forging tools, woodstoves, benches, assay equipment, ball mills, and more.

In disbelief, we stare into each cabin at history heaped in layers. Everything is rotting and covered in large amounts of pack rat poop. We shake our heads, and wonder about this fellow, John Bergren.

Dan recognizes each integral part of a mining town, the assay office, the blacksmith shop, the tramway house, compressor house, the business office, the shower room and mess hall. He points out pieces of machinery, telling me each by name and purpose. Dan has an incredible mind for details and dates. He's quite a talker too. He's from Jersey, just like me.

By the time we have toured the inside of the mill, I have heard a complete business history of Cardinal, including the names Congor, C.F. Lake, Fairview, and Donora. I have learned about the mining process. Images of what must have been form in my mind, and I am brought back one hundred years to the time when this town bustled with activity around the mill and the train depot. I am convinced that Dan is a reincarnated miner.

Living in the mountains, and walking miles of valleys and hillsides, does a funny thing to the mind. As one watches the seasons change and the sun follow its daily path overhead, the soul attaches to the very land that it dwells upon. I suppose it is human nature to feel protective of the places we love. Our sense of belonging is rooted in the trees and the ground. Because we are here, we are connected.

It is this phenomenon, combined with our love of solitude, which makes it so difficult to share our mountain backyards. As I watched my own neighborhood fill with the homes of a platted subdivision, I struggled with change. I worked hard to squelch fear of overpopulation. I mourned the passing of the Native American culture that had so gracefully lived upon the earth.

The best compromise I can foresee from our capitalistic society is the appointment of public lands. Stewardship for generations to come is our only hope of protecting the earth, both for sustainability and enjoyment. Land is something we must learn to share.

I understand the thought processes of my neighbors as they struggle with the idea that Cardinal be redeveloped. In a perfect world, what would be for this spot? This all depends on one's perspective. From the perspective of the neighbors, who had the abandoned site to themselves, any activity there is unwelcome.

For the year that Tina enjoyed trespassing into Cardinal, she fell into that illusion of false stewardship. Perceptions must be guarded by reason. The reality of Cardinal is that the townsite is privately owned, complete with property rights.

When the County Commissioners gathered in the courthouse for a public hearing on the Cardinal project, they got an ear full. Most of the people who stood outside the courthouse with picket signs were recent transplants from overpopulated states. They had come to Colorado in search of space, wilderness, and that precious solitude. They had found it in the Caribou Valley. Now, they were being called upon by Tina and Dennis to protect it.

County employees made a presentation over viewing the combination of historic preservation, acquisition of open space lands and redevelopment of the Cardinal Townsite. I took my turn at the podium, asking for the support of the County to make the dream come true.

The Nederland Historic Society was well represented. Dan Martin gave a detailed account of the mining history at Cardinal showing reverence for a unique time in Colorado history. The president of the Nederland group explained what an incredible gift the preservation of the Cardinal Mill would be. She promised that the Nederland Historic Society would incorporate the mill into their mining museum.

When the podium was opened to the public, several enthused Nederland residents spoke in support of the project. I was so grateful for the time they took to come and express themselves. All the while, the people on the left side of the courtroom sat like a loaded gun.

The first of Cardinal's opposition to speak was Dennis. He attacked the project with a vengeance that raised the hackles of the County Commissioners. The foxes will have to move, the hawks will take to the skies, and overdevelopment will ruin the Caribou Valley.

Dennis was followed by speakers who were all spouting the same complaints. Few of these people had been in the Nederland area long enough to be recognized as members of the community. They were misinformed and looking for a cause.

A handful of neighbors had met with Tina and Dennis to receive their information about the new "subdivision" and the pollution it would cause to the creek. These neighbors gave testimony about the preservation of their personal lifestyles and the future health of their children.

By the time Tina began to speak, the Commissioners had already heard it all. As the closest neighbor to Cardinal, Tina's concerns were most personal. But her selfish sorrow was lost on the three Commissioners, who hear that "not in my backyard" song regularly.

The date of this public hearing was one month from Election Day. Commissioner Paul Danish, the Champion of Open Space Preservation in Boulder County, was up for reelection. This was no time for controversy. The Cardinal Millsite Subdivision Exemption request was tabled until the Commissioners would be able to make a site visit, and return for a second public hearing.

The protesters left the courtroom ready to rally for another round.

During the month that followed, Paul Danish was re-elected, Tina and Dennis called the local newspaper regularly with more misinformation, and the snow began to fly.

The County Commissioners visited the site, gaining perspective on the situation. They were impressed with the condition of the original equipment in the Mill. They enjoyed the opportunity to spend a couple of hours immersed in the past. The peace of the valley and surrounding mountains gave them a moment to soak up some of what they had worked so hard to preserve in Boulder County.

The Commissioners requested that the Phase 1 Environmental Study be followed up with a Phase Two, and the scientists at Walsh Environmental got right to work. The testing showed nothing scary. The water coming from the mine portal tested slightly high in zinc, but didn't violate stream standards. Zinc is measured and limits set to protect fish, whose oxygen intake can be affected by higher levels. At Cardinal, there is a healthy population of trout in Coon Track Creek and many living in the settling pond as well. People buy zinc tablets at the health food store with thousands more times the amount of zinc found in Cardinal.

The acidity of the water was very well balanced and heavy metals were not an issue. Cardinal's water tested the same as the water one mile down the road at the "Caribou Spring" where people came from miles around to fill their water jugs. The Caribou Spring water flows from what was the Alton Tunnel back in the 1890's.

For a mining town, Cardinal came through with a glowing report. The Commissioners had done their homework for the next public hearing.

The role of a small town newspaper is a powerful one. I have seen character assassinations in feature articles written to stir up controversy, when a simple note in The Police Blotter would have been more considerate. There are many people who have been offended enough by the Editor to swear off reading our local paper entirely, and their lives go on. Somehow though, to be truly involved in the community, one must monitor town politics, the High School sports page, the mountain comics and the want ads.

The reporting done by our "Mountain Ear" about Cardinal in feature articles had been acceptably factual. But, in covering the developments with Boulder County, this newspaper limited its enthusiasm for the project. It focused on the complaints of a few Caribou neighbors. I flinched when I read the words "subdivision" and "development" being used on a townsite that had once been the hub of the Nederland area.

The newspaper's sphere of influence is greatest in Letters to the Editor. By choosing which letters go to print, the editor's personal agenda often replaces objectivity. Does an editor have a responsibility to check opinion letters for misinformation? At what point might a local paper examine the real issues, instead of trying to sell controversy? The fuel thrown on the fire for Cardinal was the ink that The Mountain Ear gave to Tina.

It was my policy not to go to her level and dog fight in the Letters to the Editor. Any response to the letters written by Tina would have to be singular, informational and as concise as possible. I wrote a letter in an attempt to clear the air. I hated to feed controversy for a newspaper which wouldn't support a project that would benefit the community. I was pleased to see the letter published.

It was late November when we gathered again in the Boulder County Commissioner's Courtroom for the final go around. This time, it was too cold outdoors for the picketers. The uninformed volunteers against development were only good for one appearance, and had not bothered to return for the hearing. The only opposition was a small cluster of very angry Caribou Road neighbors. Tina brought her attorney.

Several Caribou residents in favor of the project stood up to speak. Jeanette Smith shared her family's colorful mining history, and gave public thanks for the opportunity to save what was left in Cardinal. Adele and Bob spoke as neighbors who appreciated the bulk of the property not being chopped into trophy home sites.

The Historic Society returned as strong as ever, recapping the value of this treasure, and promising their support. The turning point came when their member, John, dressed as a mountain man of long ago, working his magic through dramatic play to give each of us a sense of the importance of preserving things, such as Cardinal, which feed our souls through imagination and a reverence for people of the past.

The Bergren Family had come up from Denver. Each took a turn at the podium. John talked about his father's job as mine superintendent, and how he had worked so hard to buy the mine when everything went bust. He spoke of the years his family had enjoyed trips to the mountains, but also of his frustration trying to keep vandals off the property. He was clearly happy to support such a sustainable plan.

John's son, Norm, told of summers spent playing in Cardinal with cousins. Norm and I are the same age, and shared similar experiences of growing up with the gift of a special place offering freedom and wilderness.

When Ruth Bergren's daughter, Kris, stood at the podium, she immediately began to weep. Memories of her childhood summers flooded her spirit. She pleaded with the Commissioners to support the plan. Cardinal is a place, but it is also people. The audience became emotionally charged. Commissioner Mendez had to dry her eyes.

The unfounded environmental concerns of the neighbors put Commissioner Danish to sleep. As each droned on beyond their allotted ten minutes, I began to have hope that Cardinal would be saved. When the vote came in, it was unanimously in favor of the project. Five development rights would be transferred to the existing buildings. Modest additions would be negotiated to allow plumbing and mudrooms. One hundred and ninety-five acres would be sold to Boulder County Parks and Open Space, and the Cardinal Mill would be transferred to County ownership to be preserved. Faith had carried it the project this far, but it wasn't over yet.

Dan Martin was convinced that Murphy's Law would have this Mill fall down before we could shore it up. He wasn't taking any risks. Dan wrangled "in kind" services for the historic society, and brought in a back hoe to figure out where the water was coming from which flooded the bottom of the Mill.

The appearance of this backhoe got phone lines buzzing. Tina called up her recruits. They presented themselves as an angry mob, walking up the public easement which I so graciously provided them. They arrived shaking their fists and yelling down the hundred feet to where the back hoe unknowingly worked away.

I was working on the west end of town, measuring cabins, when I heard the ruckus. When I saw Dan, I knew what his intentions were. He was trying to save the mill.

These overzealous objectors didn't understand that the back hoe wouldn't move enough dirt to merit a grading permit if we asked for one. But the objectors shouted and stomped. I approached the group in disbelief. I was amused to think, all this for what? Immediately, they began hurling insults at me.

"What are you doing for this community?"

"How can you destroy the wetlands?"

"You are an irresponsible property owner!"

"Evil developer!"

They'd bring justice in the end!

It amazed me that they couldn't find a better cause.

"Welcome to Cardinal." I said and walked away. I wondered if the County would be willing to close the public easement until all work was completed.

This event prompted the County to assign Cardinal its own cop. He was happy to explain to Tina that if she abused the right to pass on the easement in the future, she would lose the privilege. The angry mob seemed comically absurd to me.

Living in a small town and knowing most of the people can be bittersweet. When our son was born stillborn on his due date, it was the people in our community that held us, fed us, and helped us to heal. At the same time, a walk through the grocery market was more than I could bear. Folks would see me, not know what to say, then turn their cart quickly, and high tail it in the other direction. I didn't go to the post office for over a month. People in a small town share your life whether you like it or not.

As the word got out about my plans for Cardinal, I experienced some of the same behaviors. Anyone who has lived in our mountain area for a

while has experienced a genuine sense of loss as their once lonely mountaintop has had to accommodate new neighbors. Emotions run high when
it comes to development. In Boulder County, any and all development is
considered a negative. Seems to me, only my father's generation or those
in economically depressed areas see development as progress. Redevelopment is considered development.

Here I was again, watching those shopping carts turn in a hurry. People
struggled with the idea that their kindergarten teacher had turned into an evil
developer. Even my friends didn't really want to know the details. So what, I'd
say to myself. It just doesn't matter. This thing called Cardinal is bigger than
me. I am simply a catalyst.

Each time someone acknowledged the new Open Space, or appreciated the effort toward historic preservation, I was recharged anew, good for
another hundred thousand miles. My skin is thick, and I chose to dwell only
on the positive.

An essential early step in the evil real estate development process is to dig
profile holes, so that the septic engineer can do her soil percolation testing. I use
the Grapes Boys for digging jobs. These brothers have competed nationally in
digging contests, and they can dig you the fastest, neatest hole you'd ever see. Not
only that, they are from Gilpin County, where unlike Boulder County, it is still
America. People have property rights and they value that ideal. In Gilpin County,
people use common sense and their self-esteem is born of hard work.

The only thing is, if you hire the Grapes Boys, you want to be standing
right there when they fire up machinery because these aren't your tree hugging guys.

In the spring, I had the Grapes come up to dig those septic profile
holes. They had arrived at the Cardinal gate one half hour early and were
brumming the back hoe outside Tina's house with grins on their faces. They
had heard the stories.

I was just leaving the Boulder County Building Department when the
phones there started ringing off the hook.

"Lexie, it seems you've got some oversized machinery digging up at Cardinal without a permit!" hollered the Land Use Director. "Do you know anything about this?"

"Yes, sir, those Gilpin County boys are up there to dig my profile holes,
and I guess that makes me running late."

"Tell your neighbors to get a life!" yelled someone from behind the counter.

I darted out the door chuckling, and decided I'd best take it nice and slow up the canyon. I'd be willing to pay a little more on the hourly rate to have Tina twitching.

Sure enough, if it needs to be done and can be done without a permit, my guys will do it while they wait. They groomed the driveway with the back hoe so it would drain properly.

Steve Grapes laughs heartily at Boulder folks with their self righteous green ways.

"I gunned the engine for a few minutes outside the gate, just for you, Lexie."

I thanked him for his support.

When the holes were dug, I asked Steve to move the old brick well ring for me. Steve could change the diaper on a baby with that machine. He gingerly picked the ring up with the back hoe and set it aside.

I told Steve that we were clearing the way for the well rig, and he immediately wanted to pulverize the fallen down shed that also stood in the way. I explained that the historians would want me to save this wood. The men looked so disappointed. They said, "Shucks, you spoil all the fun."

Within a week of the County accepting the Cardinal proposal, Dan Martin called me to say that the townsite had been vandalized. Buildings were broken into, windows and doors smashed. We called the cops and went up to file a report. As everyone, when they first see this time capsule, the cop couldn't believe his eyes. Damage aside, he was fascinated to see all the junk stuffed in each of the cabins; newspapers from the '60's, benches from the turn of the century, Nike running shoes to cartons of unused soap labels.

We toured the property, and as we approached the last cabin, I told him of the 70's cult and the really bad smell. I wondered aloud if we might find bodies buried there one day. The cop said he didn't think so. This was a smell he smelled every day on his beat. The smell of low life drunks, "park pukes". The ones that wake up plastered in the night and pee on the wall next to themselves. Well, good to have that confirmed. Did we have any idea who might have been our vandal? Just a hint from the newspaper this week where Dennis said, "We got screwed."

It was interesting that this should happen right after the Commissioners approved Cardinal's plan.

Dan Martin said "We have no idea who has done this violence to the property and we're not accusing anybody." The neighbors seemed to be out of town for the holidays and that was a good thing.

December 6, 2000 was the day scheduled for closing the Cardinal deal. The County Attorneys and Open Space employees had worked many hours to verify the legal descriptions of over forty mining claims. The Bergrens and Ruth Eagan hired attorneys to be present. Tim Ronson would be signing for the mining companies. His attorney, Mr. Henderson, had reviewed their documents. In the weeks before the closing, Walsh Environmental had finalized a Phase Two report, and the County was satisfied with the results. We were finally ready to close the deal.

I had no attorney because when there are already five attorneys involved in a real estate deal, that's too many. They leave no stone unturned. The Bergrens were not accepting any conditions on their contracts anyway, and the County had very straight forward guidelines. In retrospect, the deal never would have come down if I had hired an attorney for myself. No attorney would have been flexible and optimistic enough to endorse to the terms I accepted from the County.

In the morning, all parties and their attorneys gathered at the title company to review and sign documents. At ten o'clock, Tim stood and said he must to go to his attorney's office for a moment and would be right back. I assumed one of the many documents that the mining companies were to produce for the title company was still at the attorney's office. The rest of us continued to work.

I was called out into the hallway by the County Attorney. The County had a sudden concern that the Boulder County Mine up at Old Cardinal might need grading and seeding in the spring before it would be acceptable for public open space use. They wanted me to escrow enough money to cover this cost. This sent me into a panic. All I was working with for money was a hundred thousand dollar line of credit from the bank. I had extremely high surveying bills, and not much left after the purchase of the property.

Who was to make this last minute determination? To properly find a dollar figure for the reclamation job involved hiring engineers, and getting bids from excavators and reseeding companies. It was absurd to be starting this process at the closing table!

I suggested we ask Walsh Environmental to give us a number. It was a desperate idea, but the attorney agreed to it. I made it clear to the attorney that all I had left was ten thousand dollars. Any more than that and this deal would die!

My heart raced and head pounded. I called Jim Walsh. Luckily, he was available. He agreed that this was a crazy way to come up with a dollar figure. After much back and forth on the phone with Jim Walsh, the County Attorney announced that the magic number was ten thousand dollars.

I had just enough credit left to cover this surprise expense. I agreed to escrow the money. The number seemed so arbitrary, but I had to be relieved they hadn't killed the deal on the table after all we'd been through. I returned to the closing table emotionally drained, but relieved that we could proceed.

Soon, we were all wondering about Tim. Where had he disappeared to? I explained to the group that he should be back soon. The attorney's office was only minutes away. We waited. We waited a long time. It was very uncomfortable watching attorneys sitting idle, being paid by senior citizens living on a fixed income. I decided to call Tim's cell phone.

Tim answered, and I asked where he was. He replied, "At the grocery store. We won't have the documents we need to close with today."

I returned to the closing table at a loss to explain what was happening. Tim would not be returning today. Everyone was stunned. This deal was a team effort. We all knew that from the beginning. For the second time that day, it appeared that the deal would die on the table.

We had all put so much effort into this that we decided to take the optimistic approach. We would close in escrow, with everyone's signatures ready, using our closing date as planned. When the documents from the mining companies arrived, the funds would be released and the documents would be recorded.

By this time, we were all starving. I ordered pizza and I paid with a credit card knowing I had no money left. We finished the task of signing. As we were wrapping it up, Ruth's lawyer managed to extract an additional three thousand dollars from me to cover the costs they had incurred negotiating the defaulted option with the mining company. At this point, he knew he had me. Why didn't I say "No."? I was out of steam. I wrote a check not knowing excatly where the money would come from.

Having spent the last four months under an enormous amount of pressure, my husband and I had tickets to leave at dawn the next morning for a week in Mexico. We would go no matter what, or I expected I'd lose my mind.

The next morning, as we switched flights in Phoenix, I called the mining company's attorney. Because I had no attorney, I was able to speak directly with the mining company's attorney. I had to have a better understanding of what went wrong before I could relax on the beach. This attorney had always been approachable and candid with me. This time he was also, true to his character, he told me that the mining companies hadn't been able to pay him for his work in quite some time. He regrettably had not followed through locating the various documents required by the title company because he needed to be paid. Very simple.

I thanked him for that information, and called the local Nederland bank. The bank was to be paid money owed by the mining companies from proceeds of this closing. I asked the banker to reduce the amount owed by the mining company by the amount of the attorney's bill. It would save the deal, and they would at least see some money as a result. The banker agreed. The airline was making the final call for passengers as I hung up. My husband stood frantically waving the tickets at me.

Feeling much better after a week on the beach to put life back in perspective, I checked my messages on the return trip through Phoenix. Our closer explained that they were almost ready to release funds. The mining company's attorney would be paid from closing proceeds. He had gone back to work the next day and all the documents were on file at the title company... except one.

The missing document was most important. It was a promissory note for two and a half million dollars, executed from one mining company to the other. The original was lost. To insure over it would cost one thousand dollars for every hundred thousand on the note. I knew first hand that the mining companies had no more resources. The whole reason this deal worked for them was that they would now be able to borrow more money against their newly acquired titles. This promissory note would have to be found before the other parties' attorneys pulled the plug on the deal. The Bergrens had lost their faith in Tim, and were feeling snubbed by the lack of communication. Ruth felt slighted. I was furious.

I called Tim. He didn't know where the promissory note was, but he suspected British Colombia. I tried hard to keep my cool. I had seen nervous, cold feet make people pull out of real estate deals before, and I knew that time was of essence. Tim had never displayed a sense of urgency in past months, so I decided to find the document myself.

I had the name and number of a member of the Board of Directors of the mining company in Chilliwack, B.C. I reached his secretary on the phone. She was fantastically helpful, her musical voice sounding like an angel to me. She listened to my story, and called her boss at home. He phoned me back and promised to drive into Vancouver the next day, despite the fact that it was a Sunday. He believed he could find it in an attorney's file downtown.

I now had one last thread of hope for Cardinal. The Canadians were helpful and polite. They were communicative and they cared. They were positive. They gave me hope.

On Sunday, I tried to pretend that it was a normal day. For a little while, my practiced denial was working. When the phone rang from British Colombia, I could hardly believe my ears. The document had been found in the file downtown, and would be overnight mailed in the morning. If the others were still on board, Cardinal had been saved.

The closing of the Cardinal land deal created one hundred ninety five acres of County Open Space. The Mill was now on its own lot so that its ownership could be transferred to the County. Lots had been created to preserve the five clusters of cabins that are the Cardinal Townsite. I was very happy.

I picked up my skis and headed out into the hills, knowing I had plenty of time before spring to think about the remaining access issue, financing, and the work that would be required by the Historic Advisory Board.

Once more, I called Tina; this time, to make an offer to resolve our remaining differences, the road situation.

I could tell as I entered the house that this would not be a long meeting. We sat in the straight backed chairs in her dining room, looking out the windows over what was now all open space.

Bluffing slightly about New Cardinal LLC, I stated that our Board of Directors (me, myself and I) was willing to offer fifteen thousand dollars, deed her an acre and a half of the land that held her septic, and offer a first right of refusal to purchase one of the finished cabins. I let her know that this offer was very generous, a stretch on the part of the Board. If she didn't accept it quickly the offer would not stand.

Dennis sat at the table grinding his jaw. He was very obviously under strict orders not to speak. His eyes bulged from his head. He gripped the table top. I sensed my instincts to retreat.

Tina took a moment to consider the offer. She closed her eyes and pursed her lips. She turned her head away from me, and concentrated on breathing deeply. Finally, Tina politely stated that she was absolutely insulted by the offer. How could I expect material compensation to take her pain away? Her life would never be the same.

Dennis rose to his feet, shaking his finger at me. He vowed to fight this in a court of law.

"If that is your choice," I retorted, "no one will be the winner."

They escorted me to the door. That was the end of that meeting. Nestled in among the Christmas cards in the mail, I found a letter from Ted Fern,

P.C. As Tina's attorney, he was writing to inform me that I was not to contact his client again for any reason, but should make all correspondences through him.

After the holidays passed, I began to communicate with Mr. Fern regarding the fact that Tina's septic leach field and propane tank were on my property. I needed paperwork for one hundred feet of road where an easement by right obviously existed. Now that New Cardinal, LLC had taken title, perhaps we could get some resolution on these issues.

Just as Dennis had threatened, it became immediately evident that there would be no negotiating with these folks. Fern put up smokescreen after smokescreen, not responding to specific questions and confusing the issues with irrelevant points. His dialogue showed that he was still fighting the development plan which had already been granted by the County.

I contacted an attorney in Boulder to advise me on the access issue. He felt that the cost of having my easement adjudicated in court would be higher than the cost of moving the road. This attorney was not able to cut to the quick, and apply the law to my situation specifically. He couldn't be sure that I would win access.

I concentrated instead on moving the road from its historic road bed to the south about 20 feet. Using money that I had earned by selling residential real estate, I hired an engineer to work up a design for the new road. The process of satisfying Boulder County's Land Use Department took the better part of the winter. In between, there was lots of skiing to be had.

In March, a few things happened that changed my life. A friend, who I had taught with for years and whose daughter grew up with my daughter, became very sick overnight. Within a few days, the doctors said she couldn't be saved. Gail hovered between life and death, reminding us all that each day is a gift. In the long run, thankfully, Gail was fine.

About the same time, I was skiing in a steep gulley at Arapahoe Basin, when a rock the size of my torso came down the mountain at a high speed. People yelled to me from the ski lift. I stopped in time to see it flash past me only inches away. That day, I decided to do the things in life that I'd always wanted to do, and not wait for the time to be "right".

I decided to learn to fly airplanes. As a child, my father had flown me all over in an Aronca Sedan, and later a Cessna 205. My brother, Matt, who lives in nearby Boulder, has been a pilot since he was sixteen. This was something I had always wanted to do.

I met a flight instructor who helped with some carpentry in Cardinal. He agreed to teach me to fly. As it turned out, Martin and his family would become precious friends.

Learning to fly helped me keep the trouble yet to come in perspective. It occupied me intellectually and minimized the amount of time that I was willing to think about what creeps these people were. To sprout wings and fly, free of the bounds of earth, is exhilarating. Imagine being able to see the world from the sky, and Colorado's landscape of contrasts is most incredible. I am intrigued by the distances that can be covered in a short amount of time, and the places that are suddenly within reach. Floating above the mountain peaks in a small plane buffeted by drafts is a gift I treasure. Nothing compares to the freedom one finds flying.

Flying helped keep me from becoming a bitter person as things progressed toward unbelievable regarding Cardinal. To make up for the time stolen from me, which amounted to hours each day, I slept less and squeezed in my lessons. Often, I was wheels up at dawn flying east into the morning with a grin on my face. As long as Tina couldn't steal my personal freedom and my mind, I could remain the happy soul I had always been.

One beautiful day, I stepped out of the car in front of the Mine Office, and took a deep breath of quiet. I found myself momentarily stunned by the forces of nature that washed the city from my senses.

I hadn't had time to choose my thoughts in so long, to let the mind wander for even a second. I flashed on old age, and savored the thought that there would be a time when my mind could exist in a stream of consciousness not obligated to be anywhere.

The conditioning of a mind to keep moving relentlessly forward is something like a four stroke engine. With the just a spark, my mind was running again.

Suddenly, I was acutely aware that the collapsing shed in front of me would have to be removed. The well drilling rig would pull into this spot one day, and sink the new well against the hillside. This shed had served for many years and many uses. The evidence inside confirmed that the donkeys for the mine had lived there and it had been a tool shop, a garage, and a private saloon.

Without fighting the impulse, I approached the shed and pulled at a board. It came right off into my hands. I tore off three more and started a pile. It felt so good to do a physical job. My efforts were rewarded each time

I pulled a board from its moorings, and pitched it into the pile. The wood was so old that the shed was coming apart in my hands. The sun brought an amazing energy into my body, and I was tantalizingly aware of my pale skin soaking up the warmth.

As I worked, I knew full well that the day would come when Tina would have her digs about me removing the shed. I didn't care. I laughed out loud, thinking of the pragmatic nature of those who built it. How they had lived so accustomed to boom and bust. These men hadn't even bothered with a foundation. This shed needed to last only until the job ran out. But at the turn of this century, overzealous historians would cling protectively to it, holding the shed sacred. How amazed the old timer's would be to see me pulling it apart by hand over a hundred years later. I felt them chuckle with me over the irony.

I went to the car, opened the doors and turned on The Rolling Stones. I went back to work on the demolition. It was no time at all before I felt a sort of hunch...or was it a request? "Turn up the music" came the message. I cranked up the volume and went back to work. Those guys from one hundred years ago would have dug this music.

Not five minutes later, there was the nudging again, "turn the music up!" I looked around, and saw only the beautiful day, with the glorious aspens quaking in the breeze. Hummingbirds flittered about their business at the creek. But, from somewhere I was being told, "Turn the music up. Louder!" I returned to the dashboard and gave it a crank. Right on, boys! Rock out! For a short while, I sang as I stacked the old boards.

EMILY LADD'S "TURN UP THE MUSIC"

The third time I turned the music up, I thought I might blow my speakers. But I turned the music up despite myself. An overwhelming dancing joy had swept up my spirit. "Louder! Louder!" came this message from the souls of the past. Rock and roll filled the valley breathing new life into this place. I shook my head and laughed and danced back to work.

One job that kept me occupied that spring was working with the Historic Advisory Group for Boulder County to determine exactly how the cabins would be remodeled. One day, the group had come to Cardinal for a site visit. As I showed them around the townsite, we made a visit to the mine's business office. The office building had housed a caretaker, as well as the business. There were three separate rooms. We all stood talking in the west room.

One of the historic advisors, Jane, took me gently by the arm, and led me back to the main office.

"Do you feel them?" she asked me.

Right away, I knew she was talking about spirits. I am a skeptic, but I had to admit that I was aware of "somebodys" in this particular spot. These were the ones who loved my music. They were the feeling I had often had. They welcomed my perky energy and the new life in Cardinal.

"There are two here, sitting on stools" she pointed out, "and one over there in the corner by the window."

"Yes" I said, "I know these guys. They watch me work, and they have asked me to turn up my rock and roll more than once!"

I was shaking my head at my own response. I am a skeptic. What was I talking about? But it was true. The presence of these men could be felt. It is a subtle thing, but there, all the same. I'm not sure I caught Jane's reaction. I was so shocked that she knew they were there. I was struggling with the fact that I knew they were there all along, but the 'here and now' me wouldn't normally acknowledge them.

I know that my skepticism is a healthy thing. A mortal must be able to live in the here and now. That's what life is about. But, sometimes the veil thins, like when someone we love dies. It can thin when we are very sick, or when memories of the past slip into our present. Sometimes our dreams are too lucid to be dreams, and the spirits that visit in them stay long past the waking hour. But mostly, we are settled to think of earthly things.

Jane explained that these fellows were concerned about the move of the office trimmings down to the museum in town. She asked me to clear up a dilemma for them. Were they to stay in Cardinal or move to town with the office goods?

"It's okay." I said. "They are welcome to stay here when the office moves. On the other hand, they may have fun in town, if they'd like..."

Who would these spirits be? Did they live in Cardinal? Did they die here?

I'm not afraid of these ghosts. Some days, I talk to them as if they are good company, and interested in what I think. Other days, I am the skeptic, with my strong earthly shield up. I'm sure if they are here, we get along alright.

Tina complained that I would harm the environment by moving the road off her property. This time she was right. She wrote the Mountain Ear editor again, never pointing out that the road wouldn't have to be moved if she would trade easements. There was no mention of the fact that Tina's septic field was on Cardinal land. Tina's letter to the editor helped inflame another round of activism among the self righteous.

The week before the public hearing regarding the road, slanderous fliers were hung all over the Town of Nederland. Lead and Arsenic at the Cardinal Townsite; information had been taken out of context from the Walsh Environmental reports. The flier explained that the newly formed "Citizen's Alliance to Save Caribou" would bring justice.

A financial lender with First National Bank in Boulder, bicycling in Nederland that weekend, was interested to see the flier on a property they were about to lend on. He took a copy to my man at the bank, who called to say the flier had been rather damaging in the eyes of the bank. I mobilized an effort to have Walsh explain their reports in layman's language, and put the bankers at ease.

The morning of the public hearing about the road, my husband and I had lunch with our banker. I was looking forward to signing construction loan closing documents the next day to secure funds to begin an infrastructure of septic, power and water for Cardinal. At lunch, we talked baseball, and joked about the hassles with our neighbors at Cardinal. Anticipating that moving the road would win approval from the County Commissioners, we invited the banker to come to the hearing.

The Boulder County Land Use process allows opportunities for public input. Sure enough, the citizens turned up in droves at the public hearing to speak for the protection of the Community Garden plot located a mile and a half downstream from Cardinal. The road, they claimed would disturb the wetlands, and bring toxic runoff to their vegetables. They had read the flier and were armed with misinformation regarding lead and arsenic.

The Commissioners were hip to this rap. They knew that the results of the environmental studies showed the situation to be safe. They approved the request to move the road, but for public relations and historic preservation, asked that the waste rock pile not be used as road fill. It was a victory for the project, but our banker went away rattled by the public testimony. He called later that day to say that the bank was pulling the infrastructure loan.

It was prime time to start construction jobs at our elevation, and now I was left with no funds to begin. I believe this is the first time that I felt these people had pushed me too far.

I gathered together a loan application package that outlined the nature of the Cardinal project. It was the most paper copies I had ever made in my life. I personally peddled my proposal all over Denver that summer, but in the face of a struggling economy, the answer "No, thanks." came back from each lender. The project was too far "out of the box" for them. They couldn't fit my project on a form. These city lenders couldn't figure who would ever want to live in a one thousand square foot house. With a recession looming, they weren't about to do anything risky. It became evident that once I had an infrastructure in place, anyone would lend on the place, but until then, I was Simply Out of Luck.

With everything hung in limbo as far as construction was concerned, I occupied myself with the task of cleaning out the Cardinal Townsite. I had earned enough spare cash to hire "Squirrelly Jim" to help haul this wide variety of junk to the land fill. We started in early spring and finished at the end of August. It was a huge job. Every cabin was filled toward the ceiling. One had to climb across the pile to get to the next room. Many rooms were just plain full, and you couldn't get across.

When Jim and I first met in Cardinal for the tour, he realized he'd be spending the better part of the summer there. Jim is a hard working, self made man. He started his own company from scratch, working mostly by himself. He's a small wiry guy but he's strong enough to lift almost anything. Jim has expressive eyes that pop when he's amazed, and he's got enough unruly hair to have found the name "Squirrelly" in our town of eccentric characters.

Jim and I decided we might as well start at the east end of town and work our way west. The Superintendent's house was full to the ceilings in every room. The roof had been leaking into the mess and the bottom layer of junk was frozen to the floor. We removed truck load after truck load of everything one would find in a household, and fifty years of bargains pack ratted in as well. We had to leave a bunch of stuff that was frozen to the floor until summer.

We would sort the entire town into categories of metal, glass and newspaper for recycling, and landfill junk. Jim and I started the process with masks to filter our breathing. About ten minutes into the process, we both agreed, it would be too long a summer if we were to wear masks. Tossing caution to the wind, we dove back into the job, strategically holding our breath when dust billowed, or running outside when it got too bad.

The hype about Hanta Virus had me concerned enough to call the University of Northern Colorado for information. The advice was to spritz the area with bleach water. This townsite was beyond spritzing, the mess too large. I decided to go with my karmic protection, and Jim determined to kill the virus with beer.

As we worked we laughed. We were the people to do this job. We were really good at throwing things away. Most of the junk was too old to be useful, but not old enough to be valuable.

Visitors would see an interesting item and say "Hey, you're gonna save that aren't ya?"

We'd say, "Go ahead, it's yours!"

They'd say "Well, no thanks." and up into the truck it would go.

One day, I had hired two teenage friends to heave a room full of rotten clothing out the window of one of the boarding houses. The girls giggled and shrieked as they made their way down through the pile. At the bottom, laid out on the old mossy sleigh bed, was a wedding dress. Katie carefully peeled it from its resting place, holding it up for the camera.

Back in Atlanta, at the end of the summer, Cecily developed the pictures to find that there was a ghostly image behind Katie as she held the dress. Cecily's first two attempts to mail me the picture never made it through the mail. Her third try was to bring it to her Mom, who was flying out to see me, but Cecily was in a car accident on her way, broke her arm and never made it. Years later, living alone in the townsite, I examined the picture and chose to not see a ghost.

It's a clean town now. You would have had to see it to believe it.

Did I mention the amount of rat shit? When Martin pulled the ceilings out of the green cabin, eight inches of packrat feces dumped down on him. I can assure you there are not many people who would have done the jobs that Squirrelly Jim and Martin did. They are more of those working heroes.

Whenever I see Squirrelly Jim driving around town in this white Dodge truck, I smile, wave and think of the tons of junk we took out of Cardinal.

I delivered a loan request package to the bank president of our local mountain bank, hoping he would have the vision to see what this project offered our community. Until this point, I had not thought to approach him. Ten years earlier, at a loan closing table, he had surprised us by asking for two points to be paid out of pocket on a refinance. We were very hand to mouth, being a ski patroller and a kindergarten teacher. We were feeling desperate at the time, with Steve's Dad dying, a teenager gone punk rock, and a new baby on the way. We paid the extra two points to get it over with, but I held a grudge for ten years.

Time and again Cardinal taught me lessons. This time, it was clear that I had an opportunity to let go of the past. Maybe Steve and I had missed something way back when. Maybe communication from the bank had been poor. Who knows? But here it was, time to try again.

The banker accepted my paperwork graciously. Trying not to appear totally desperate, I explained what I had learned about financing my project, and what my hope was for the community. I outlined the structure of the loan I was requesting. He seemed open minded and said he would take my package to his loan committee. I left the bank wondering about human nature, with its ability to nurse a grudge. I should have come here first, before meeting every banker on the Colorado prairie. Within a week, the banker called to say the bank would give me a construction loan.

By now, it was August. The building season was two months from over and I had no sub contractors lined up to work. Our family headed out to Idaho, with a dozen friends and trucks full of boats to raft the Salmon River.

Driving across the Wyoming prairie completely cleans a person's mind. It is a wonderful thing to see so much nothing. The vast expanse of grass and sky take me away from my reality and bathe me in awe. We listen to music that has carried us through the last thirty years, tunes so familiar that you hear the first notes of the next song before it has even started.

These are songs that come with memories that are the stories of our lives.

We pass hundreds of miles of sage brush, and prairie grass, until we finally turn north into the Idaho mountains.

We also listen to the new music of our teenagers. Each time we hear one of these songs again, we keep the beat a bit better. We catch ourselves singing. Is this music? Yes, it is the music of these times, somehow fitting. Our kids are sent to us to broaden our horizons.

As we drive along the west side of the Bitterroot Mountains, I check in by cell phone one last time. There is a message waiting for me. It is John Bergren and he says, in a thin shaky voice, that he has been served a "60 Day Notice of Intent to Sue in Federal Court". This has to do with The Clean Water Act, and the newly formed Citizen's Alliance To Protect Caribou.

I immediately realize the impact this has had on John. I also realize that he has been served these papers by mistake. It is me they are after. I am aware that John's name and address are still on tax records due to a mistake in the Assessor's Office of Boulder County. I cannot disappear for two weeks leaving John to sweat this out. At the very least, his attorney will need to understand the tax record mistake.

I call John at home, and thank goodness, he answers. I explain how he ended up on the hit list. John understands their motivations, for he has seen them in action in the Commissioner's Court. Neither of us is too surprised.

John reads me the first page, so I can gather the gist of the charges. They are challenging us for not having State Water Discharge Permits.

I have already spoken with the State, and off the record, was said that the state does not generally give permits to inactive mine sites. The State and mine owners do not have the resources to test and permit the thousands of inactive mine sites in Colorado. Lady, Lady, they had said, don't call us, we call you.

I think back to our Phase Two Environmental Tests. There is no pollution in Cardinal. I encourage John to explain to his attorney about the mistake in the tax records, apologize for the hassle and tell him, I'll see him in two weeks.

My next call is to Brad Bartlett, the Nederland attorney who has been hired by the Citizens Alliance to Protect Caribou to file suit. By now, there are mountain ranges closing in on both sides of the truck. My family listens in disbelief. Can there possibly be more trouble with Cardinal? The cell phone connection is sketchy but I have Mr. Bartlett. Just as I identify myself, the line goes dead. At the same time, I realize I shouldn't be talking to him anyway. I will need my own attorney.

The truck winds into the mountains, as Steve and I consider what this news might mean to us. We both fight an ill feeling, and brace ourselves for what is to come.

By the time we drop into the Salmon River Valley, we are determined to put this on the back burner, and enjoy our family summer vacation. A combination of optimism and denial are the best way to accomplish this.

Living on the river with a group of twenty friends, we are entirely removed from the outside world. As a floating commune, we share the rhythm of each day. When we wake in the morning, we scan the sky to assess the weather, and then stumble from our tents for coffee. First one up has put on water to boil.

Our river family has been organized into cook crews; no siblings, spouses or parents and children on the same crew. Today's breakfast crew starts rummaging coolers on the boats to find ingredients for a four star meal. The crew pulls out lunch too, and restocks the lunch cooler. Our kitchen is deluxe. We have tables and chairs, a four burner stove, pots, pans, dishes and a dish washing set up.

Those who are not on the cook crew this morning enjoy a leisurely social hour around the kitchen and the camp. We pack the tents, recycle yesterday's cans and pick up last night's party. We share jokes and stories. There is a call "Breakfast!" and everyone lines up with a plate to be graciously served by today's crew.

After breakfast, the group works together to pack the camp back onto the boats to run the river. It is an amazing thing to watch it come together. The kitchen is folded up, our chairs pack into little bags; the tent community is rolled up and stowed in dry bags. Sunscreen makes the rounds as the sun peeks over the top of the canyon rim. Clothes come off as the morning warms. There's a "Last call for the Groover" before the toilet is packed. Then we are ready to launch.

We are all smiles as each boat starts moving down river. We delight in the current as it tumbles us through the rapids, and pools into eddies. On the rubber rafts, passengers and captains have an opportunity to visit at a pace rarely afforded in today's society. By the end of the trip, we will have developed a very special bond. Rafts link up with each other on the flat water, and the flotillas party their way along.

Our kayaks and small "rubber duckie" boats have freedom to surf the waves which form on the downstream side of rocks. They also link up with the big boats for a snack or a bite of conversation. These "Yakkers" are a subfamily bonded by their boat type which is essentially part of their body.

When we come to a big rapid, we park and scout. We stand high on the rocks above the river to watch how the water makes its way down through the obstacle course. Each person has an opinion, and each is respectfully considered. Usually, some crusty old boater has the prevailing good idea of how to run the rapid. All things having been considered, the boatmen gather their crews to have a go at it. The first boat to run gives the others insight on what to do, or not to do. Each boat watches the others carefully. We have a symbiotic relationship. We are one. If a rescue is needed, teamwork does it. The safety protocols are common to all. We pull the floaters from the river, dry them out and warm them back up.

By lunchtime, we are saturated with fresh air, wind, sunshine and water. We choose a beach with sun and shade to picnic, nap and recharge. Lunch is a feast. River lunch is my favorite lunch. Many hands make light work, and before you know it, we are floating again.

Many miles of paddling, great adventure, and curving river bring us to the next camp. The kitchen is set up as the cocktails are poured. The new cook crew serves h'orderves with a flair. The boaters lounge in chairs or on beached boats, taking relaxation to an art form. Some play a ball game or swim. The party heats up, sometimes going long into the night. Boaters fall asleep in their chairs around the fire, and eventually stumble off to their tents for bed. The night is passed with a symphony of snoring. In the morning, we will do it all again.

This life is heaven to me. It fills my soul with harmony and recharges my spirit. River life puts everything in perspective. Living day after day in the wilderness of the canyon, the cycle of days and nights, with moon and sun, make me feel at peace. Living in the company of friends is soothing, never lonely.

As we pull our boats up to the boat ramp at the end of the trip, reality comes as a sudden shock. We tear down the boats that have been home to us for a week. We reverently wash, dry and fold the boats, then load them into the trucks. We kiss our river family goodbye, squeezing extra tight, for we will miss them. As our truck winds out of the canyon, I remember where things were when I left. We were headed to Federal Court. I am recharged, and ready to face it head on.

Upon our return from the Salmon River, I phoned one of my favorite people, my friend, Geoff. Geoff comes with a unique history. His great grandfather was a surveyor for the USGS in the 1800's, mapping the mountains of Gilpin and Boulder Counties. He homesteaded a ranch which would be home to his family for generations to come. Geoff graduated from the Colorado School of Mines in Golden, and became involved with mining worldwide. Geoff answers the phone the same way every time, and I love it..."This is Geoff.", his voice matter of fact, while floating on a breeze.

"Geoff, I need your advice up in Cardinal." I give him the Reader's Digest condensed version of my problem.

"Why don't I come on up there to see you?" he says just like the western gentleman that he is.

After a full tour of the mine and townsite, Geoff proclaims my neighbors "bastards". He knows who I need to speak with. He gives me the name and number of an environmental attorney in Denver. "He is the big gun." promises Geoff. "He is also a dear friend. I think he can help you."

A few days later, I sat at lunch with the big gun attorney, Paul Phillips. The only sign of big guns was the office of Holland and Hart on the 37th floor of a building in downtown Denver. Paul himself is a small man with a very big heart. Immediately, I was dazzled by the twinkle in his eyes. His enthusiasm is genuine. He loves life.

Over lunch, we talked about our families, our passions, and the situation at Cardinal. Paul is the kind of very smart that you would want on your side. It was only fair to warn him that my pockets weren't very deep. I hoped like crazy that he would be interested in taking on a small case like mine.

I believe the reason Holland & Hart took on Cardinal was Paul's keen sense of fairness. My project was a good one for the community, and it was threatened by this law suit. Paul probably knew the mess some attorneys could make of this. I believe he took the case for the satisfaction of seeing justice done. Paul and his team of associates were thoroughly focused on that goal throughout the lawsuit. I can't express the relief I felt as I drove back to the mountains that day. Cardinal was in good hands.

From that point on, I worked with Paul and his team almost every day for over three years. Little did I know I was enrolling in the equivalent of the following college courses: Clean Water Act 101, Protocols in Water Testing 201, Recycling 301, State Environmental Regulation 406, Federal Water Regulation 205, Anger Management 502, Finance and Lenders 202, Characteristics of the Insomniac 201, Philosophy 201, Ingress and Egress Law 202, Colorado Mining History 506, Family Crisis 501, Maps and Cartography with an Emphasis on the History of Boulder's Historic Roads 201, Surveying 201, Introduction to the Court System 101, Case Law 101, Writing 201, Environmental Reports 301, Field and Laboratory Water Testing 301, Psychology of the Deviant Plaintiff 501, Toxology 201, Stream Biology 101, Theology 201, all the "Ologies" and Patience 501.

And I had no scholarship.

Right away, Paul Phillips mobilized his troops. They included Mike Sawyer, a younger, greener attorney to compile all information pertinent to Cardinal; a litigator, Steve Black, and a support crew. Also, there were scientific experts and engineers in the field to analyze data, write applications and reports.

The charges that would be filed in Federal Court were specifically that New Cardinal, LLC had no valid Water Discharge and Stormwater Permits with the State of Colorado. Paul enlisted the services of Katie Fendel to write permit applications. He arranged meetings with the Colorado Department of Health and Environment to explain our situation. He too was told that normally, the Department wouldn't issue Water Discharge Permits to inactive mine sites because the State of Colorado doesn't have the resources to hold thousands of abandoned mine sites accountable. But, the Federal Clean Water Act has the provisions to enforce permitting at the State level. The State Department immediately realized that they would have to issue permits and that these permits would be scrutinized in Federal Court.

We sent Bjorn, from Leonard Rice Engineers, out to Cardinal to test the water on an ongoing basis. Bjorn sampled water and shared the test results with Katie Fendel.

The tests reflected what Walsh Environmental had found. They consistently showed that our water was slightly high in zinc, but when it mixed with Coon Track Creek, it was undetectable. The PH level was fine. Where was the beef these people were looking for? It was obvious that they were grabbing for straws. Looking for anything they could do to slow the project.

Katie worked closely with the State to perfect permits that would cover the water which originates in the Boulder County Tunnel, and the water seeps that come out of the ground just downstream of the Cardinal Mill. For my birthday present that year, I got two water discharge permits. I was very happy!

Valid permits were issued before the sixty day deadline that had been given by the "Intent to Sue" notice. I was so pleased that I was hooked up with Paul Phillips. There was no way I would have, as a private citizen, known how to accomplish this task, let alone in that amount of time. Somehow though, we could sense that the harassment wasn't over. Tina and Dennis had vowed to never give up, and so far they had a nasty track record. Sure enough, The Citizen's Alliance to Protect Caribou filed their Federal Lawsuit even though Cardinal had no pollution and was in compliance with the State.

There are certain dates that define the world as we know it. 1066 AD, the Battle of Hastings; December 7, 1941, Pearl Harbor; and now, September 11, 2001. To experience America coming to a standstill was an incredible thing. As the Pentagon was hit, I wondered if this wasn't the end. We had been brought to our knees. I watched my son, listening to the radio with me, as he ate his breakfast. What kind of world would he live in?

The weeks that followed showed us all that our country would never be the same. It was indeed a brave new world. I remembered the sixteen years that I taught Kindergarten. When I retired from that job, one thing I took away with me was a feeling that generally human nature is good. I had rarely encountered evil. Teaching eight hundred souls at such a transparent age gave me this insight. Had this evil been spawned from George Bush's irreverent swaggering?

September 11 brought me the recognition that our very community is the reason why my view of human nature was so positive. When people have their basic needs met, when they have freedom in a functioning democratic society, and have the identity and support of a small mountain community, people raise children that are of healthy mind.

As I ponder evil, I decide that the people who have done this atrocious act are certainly evil. They have come to a mindset that is selfish and not based in reality. I question the line between sick and evil. Evil is sick, but sick is not necessarily evil. Our court system allows for that distinction. We put people in mental hospitals when their minds are so sick that their behavior is not based in reality. We extend them a different label, a qualifier. But then, we have our limit. We measure premeditation, passion, and remorse. We have the death penalty. We use it for those who are just too scary for us. It is for the truly evil. These suicide bombers took care of that for us.

I walk the hills pondering these things. Again and again, I come back to how lucky I am. I wonder about people's lot in life and the different cards each are dealt. I compare the life of a street person in downtown Denver to the life of a woman under the Taliban regime. I compare the life of a miner in the 1870s at Caribou, Colorado, to life of a dairy farmer in North Dakota, to an African herdsman. I think about the relativity of it all.

Are the members of the "Citizen's Alliance to Protect Caribou" evil? It sure feels that way when I consider the damages they have inflicted on my professional and personal life. When the facts are that Cardinal is not a "Superfund" site, these people seem to meet my definition of evil... selfish, hurtful and not based in reality. I look it up in the dictionary.

> Evil adj. 1.a) morally bad or wrong, wicked, depraved b) resulting from conduct regarded as immoral 2. harmful; injurious 3. offensive 4. unlucky, disastrous.

Yes, they are all of these things to me. My problem is a microcosm of evil. The events of September 11 made my problem so small that it went away altogether for a while. But as time goes on, this problem grows back to its relative size.

Eventually, I admit to myself that the words of Jesus as he was dying on the cross, "Forgive them Lord, for they know not what they've done." would be a healthier outlook for me to focus on.

One sunny day in the fall, I loaded the last of John Bergren's five gallon cans of Rocky Mountain Arsenal purple enamel into my husband's truck. As I lugged the twenty eighth can out and heaved it up into the truck bed, Dennis and Tina stood watching. Regular folks always give a "howdy' or something to let you know they are there, but not these two. They had materialized on the periphery, standing carefully on the public easement I had granted, supervising my work with stern faces and a video camera.

"Hey!" I said, "It's great of you to come by to help. Yes, siree, these things are a lot heavier than they appear, so many buckets too. Sure, just pitch right in!"

They stood there looking blankly. I guess they thought I was joking!

When the truck was almost full, I drove down to the gate in front of Tina's house. Just south of the driveway was a fifty five gallon drum of motor oil mixed with rainwater. There was a three inch opening in the top. I had borrowed an oil hand pump and today I emptied the drum into plastic five gallon jugs with screw on tops. These were old empty fire fighting foam containers which had been left at the mine by John. As I carried the last one toward the truck, I was aware of the video camera humming away up on Tina's deck. Good, show the world that I'm cleaning up.

I set the can down hard on the driveway. Much to my surprise, a rock punched right through the bottom of the old plastic container. Motor oil began to spread like a miniature environmental disaster. I quickly flipped the jug over, stopping the spill. I had lost about half a quart.

Any red blooded American would have kicked sand over it and left, but

I was being videoed. I transferred the remaining oil to another container. As I worked, three friends came walking along. They were out for a hike. Great! I had three witnesses. They looked up at Tina and laughed and waved for the camera.

I drove to town and bought kitty litter and garbage bags. I collected every last speck of my oil spill. But now, I had exactly one hour to get to the Hazardous Waste Center in Boulder. I arrived there with fifteen minutes to spare. I knew the intake worker would not be happy to see me so close to closing time with a big load. He was never happy to see me anytime.

"You can't leave this here." he said. "The drums say 'Rocky Mountain Arsenal' on them."

"They are the same thing I brought down yesterday, purple enamel. Go ahead, open them." I snipped.

"You will have to speak with my boss!"

"Who is your boss?" I asked.

"Ron Stewart."

"Ah, the County Commissioner! I have his number right here in the speed dial of my phone...Ron knows me."

"Never mind" the waste man said "I'll take them."

He had told me on another day, that he was friends with Tina and he knew "all about what I was doing up there". It was this young man's opinion that mine was a commercial venture and I had no right to bring waste to this collection center. But when I had asked him where else I could go, he responded, "Right here. This is the place." Whatever, dude.

"Also", he puffed his chest out, "You brought me eight drums of an unidentifiable substance yesterday, "Monile Liquid", and you will have to take them back. I spent all afternoon of the County's time searching the Internet for identification. Unidentifiable. You can't expect me to take them."

"Monile Liquid." I dialed my Dad on my cell phone. He graduated from Princeton in '48 with a degree in Chemistry and worked all his life in the industrial paint business.

My good Ol'Daddio had the information in a jiffy, complete with web address. Moline Liquid was a floor sealant. The humbled young man unloaded my drums and sulked off.

The next time I saw him was in passing, at the Boulder County Courthouse. He yelled to me and waved. I was puzzled, not recognizing him out of context, and waved back.

"Ha!" he said, "You don't recognize me without my white suit on!"

I smiled graciously and nodded. 'Yeah, that's right!" Even though that was my last load, you never know when you may need a friend at the Hazardous Waste Facility.

❧

Unfortunately, there is no check on the system early on in the legal proceedings of a Clean Water Act suit. It would be almost a year before we would be heard by the Federal Judge. In the meantime, we would have to prepare for the eventuality of a trial.

The costs of the attorneys, state application writing, environmental reports and testing were occasionally making me nauseous. Steve and I had always managed our finances responsibly and for the first time ever, we were totally strapped. We didn't have much choice in the matter. With a Clean Water Act lawsuit filed, you are guilty until you prove yourself innocent. And no lender would lend against New Cardinal, LLC's property.

For the first year of New Cardinal's existence, I had not borrowed money from the pockets of my family. I had taken profit from my real estate company and lent it to New Cardinal LLC in anticipation of seeing it come back as soon as the construction loans began. Now, I couldn't recoup a dime of that. I had to pilfer the kid's college money. The astronomical debt we were incurring had to be borrowed against our own home and our Gold Hill cabin. We had always had a policy not to borrow against our home. At the same time, the economy had slowed to a halt, and the real estate business went dead.

When you owe that much money, you have two choices. The obvious one is suicide. This didn't seem like a good choice for many reasons. First, it screws up too many other people, family and friends. Second, it doesn't pay the bills. The other choice involves acknowledging that life is great, and money isn't everything.

I put the second choice into practice by skiing cheaply on a season pass. At the same time, I found every opportunity to learn to fly airplanes. When the bills range into the hundreds of thousands, learning to fly looks like a bargain. I stayed focused on my real estate business to keep food on the table.

I counted every blessing I had; my husband, who cooks dinner most nights, my daughter with her optimism and energy, my son who always gives me hugs and encouragement. Among those blessings, I also counted numerous incredible friends and my parents, who mean everything to me. I counted the spectacular sunshine, the highest mountains and the rivers. Money is nothing when you simply don't have it.

The bottom line was that my husband supported me in our family financial decisions. Our local banker lent me money for legal fees, which was risky. And, the attorneys at Holland and Hart, who stopped receiving payments two thirds of the way along, assured me that they would not abandon Cardinal.

The truth is, I struggled more with the financial problems, than the moral issues. I had to believe that the people doing this to us had rotten, miserable lives. They lived rotten, miserable lives every day. In the end, they would still have rotten, miserable lives. My life is incredible every day. I could keep the faith. But when I thought of the amount of money I owed, I felt nauseous and overwhelmed.

Once a week or so, I would go to Cardinal to remind myself what all this trouble was really about. As I would open the gate below Tina's, I would blare my music as loudly as possible without blowing the speakers. It was the only thing I could do to bother the enemy. Taking the higher road isn't much fun, but it is the right thing to do.

Driving into the townsite, all negativity would drain away. The valley is a peaceful place. Interestingly enough, I would become recharged by my visits. An overwhelming message saying "It's going to be okay." always engulfed me as I got out of the car. As I walked through town, I felt as if others went along beside me. I felt comforted. Very quickly, I would forget my troubles and bathe in the beauty of Cardinal.

I wished my family could feel the same satisfaction. But they each had their own perceptions of this place. To Steve, Cardinal had caused too much trouble to be ever be a place he would visit, let alone be fond of. My son, Peter, felt spooked by Cardinal. Even before the trouble had begun, he said it was too creepy for him. My daughter, Sandi, was intrigued by Cardinal. She left for college in the fall and stayed curious about the progress of the lawsuit. The following summer, Sandi and her boyfriend, Harlan, would become the first people to live in Cardinal in sixty years.

I always wonder about the people who lived and worked in this town. I feel spirits dancing and following me around, like a mountain lion elusively tracking me at a distance. I purposely let down my natural guard of skepticism in hopes of being proven wrong. What a tease the past can be, when it is so gone.

I walk to the green cottage, the furthest west in town. It is peaceful and quiet in its little grove of woods near the waterfall. It is here that I feel a special familiarity. My mind escapes onto dreams of times gone by.

I go inside and imagine what it will take to fix the place up. I will knock out a wall to make a dining room by the creek. There will be bunk beds for kids to sleep in. I can't wait to light a fire in a woodstove and spend the night.

These visits remind me that this project is good. It is fun. It is fascinating. It is right. The problems from the neighbors will pass, and all will be well.

With the Federal Suit holding up progress, I abandon the idea of moving the road. On credit, I hire Holland & Hart's Mike Sawyer to get road access through the court system. Mike knew the situation and "forewarned is forearmed".

The April snows are very deep on the north facing hillsides in the Colorado mountains. One sunny day, Mike asked me to take photographs of the road from the hill facing north above Cardinal. Our intent would be to show the configuration of the old road bed in relation to Tina's house.

I put on full snow gear and climbed the mountain. Walking straight up was the way to go in this deep snow. I searched for a spot where a photographer had taken a picture one hundred years ago. That picture showed the Mill in its heyday, complete with three other sections that no longer exist. It showed the road into Cardinal, the train station, the Switzerland Trail train trestle, the Superintendent's house, and westward into town.

I had hopes of snapping some shots for the Judge that would show this same area in relation to Tina's house. Surely, he would recognize how absurd a fight this was.

I climbed and climbed above the Switzerland Trail until I was high enough on the hillside to see it all. The old photo showed the mountainside stripped of every last tree. But the past hundred years had grown an entirely new forest. In fact, I could not get the photos I'd hoped for because the forest was too thick. Instead, I found myself peeking through trees, spying directly down on Tina's deck where the great white hunter, Dennis Masters, was puttering around outside.

Twigs snapped as I made my way across the mountainside, and I suddenly remembered Dan Martin telling me he saw Dennis shopping for a semi automatic rifle at the gun show in Denver. I became totally paranoid thinking of him hearing what he thought was an elk and finding me in his scope. I got the heck out of there.

One complication prevented us from filing a Motion for Summary Judgment sooner. Without this complication, the Judge would have had a look at my situation earlier.

Our water permits dictated that we use two species of water fleas in our monthly testing, as well as flathead minnows. As it turned out, the Ceria Daphnia Dubia fleas had an unacceptably high mortality rate. This was confusing, as the water met stream standards in all areas.

Bjorn, Katie and the lab folks worked hard to find that when there are certain levels of zinc and cadmium, combined with a specific PH level, this particular species dies in profusion. Thus, Ceria Daphnia Dubia are not considered a reliable indicator in this situation. Unfortunately, these little buggers had caused "violations" on the permit which called for this species. This discovery turned out cost much time and money.

The fine for WET test violations is $250,000 per day of violation. I had long ago hit the wall on worrying about Federal fines. It seemed like a crap shoot anyway. If I was going to lose, I was going to lose big. I had to have faith that this wouldn't happen. When people would ask how my lawsuit was progressing, I could only answer "Fine, thanks" and chuckle to myself at the pun.

When the State was notified of our situation with these particular water fleas, they suggested a change in the permitting configuration that would be more appropriate for Cardinal. We would combine our two permits into one "Individual Permit" and the Ceria Daphnia Dubia would not be part of it.

This new permit would be better protection in court as well. When the Individual Permit was issued, we would then file our Motion for Summary Judgment to request the case be dismissed. A Summary Judgment is made based on undisputed material facts and we felt strongly that ours were undisputable.

As we prepared our application for the new permit, the "Citizen's Alliance for the Protection of Caribou" made what appeared to be a strategic blunder. The Alliance filed three Motions for Summary Judgment in two weeks time. The judge had requested that any motions be presented together at once. These motions all involved statements that our side was not disputing. They were clearly wasting the Judge's time.

This move by the plaintiffs caused Judge Kane to call for all information from both sides to be on his desk by May 6, 2002. Paul's team had us so well prepared that our brief and affidavits were polished and in place on the sixth. Reading the affidavits from the other side made me optimistic. They were all bun, but no beef. It would still be at least two months before the Judge would look at the case, as both sides would have opportunities to respond to each other.

I had to accept the fact that a second summer would roll by without construction. The most I could hope for was to prevail and have a future shot at recouping litigation fees.

The Clean Water Act is a law meant to protect the common citizen. It is to protect us from big polluting corporations. It empowers the citizen. Typically, suits are filed when there has been a breach of some significance. Case law does not support defendants getting damages in Clean Water Act cases. The very least I could hope for was for the law suit to finally be over.

2002

*I*n early June, the kids started driving from Albertson College in Idaho to live in Cardinal, Colorado. It would be twelve hours on the road with Sandi and Harlan each driving their own cars. But, it was only three hours into the trip, when Harlan's engine seized, and they found themselves staring under the hood in the heat of a summer day.

Luckily, Harlan's Aunt was lived in nearby Pocatello. The kids shuttled all of Harlan's goods to her house, and had the car towed. It was decided that Sandi would take "Lizzie", Harlan's little yellow dog, and continue on to Colorado. Harlan would go to his family home in Portland, buy another car, and then make his way down as soon as possible.

At ten o'clock that night, Sandi called home from Green River, Wyoming to say she was late, but on her way. It had been a long day, so I offered to pay for a motel room. She'd sleep and start fresh in the morning. I hung up the phone, comforted to know my daughter would be safe.

The next morning, I woke at five o'clock to go flying. I love the dawn in the summertime, when the world is asleep and it is cool and quiet. At our mountain home, the wild animals are just finishing up business, the aspen trees shimmer softly, and the sun comes up big and red over the prairie.

I was just getting out of the shower, when Sandi came through the back door. It seemed that every motel between Green River and home was full, so Sandi drank four "Red Bulls" and drove all night. She came through the door cranked up, and so excited, shouting "I'm home!"

Steve was sleep walking his way to the bathroom, and was jolted into reality by her energy. We were so surprised, and so happy to see her. It had been a long year, and our baby was home! Sandi always lives in a whirlwind of energy, and we had missed her. Within seconds, Peter, who normally would sleep through an earthquake, was standing in the living room freezing, blinking and smiling. Sandi was back.

After hugs and more hugs, we heard the story of the drive, while Sandi braided my hair. When she finished, she leapt up and ran to the car to fetch a surprise. She returned with little "Lizzie", the dog. I was intrigued to meet her, especially because my husband has little patience for dogs. Lizzie looked like a golden retriever puppy, but she was really a thirteen-year-old house dog who was embarking on the adventure of her life.

Later that day, Sandi and I took our goat fencing to Cardinal and set up a place for Lizzie, where she could go in and out of the old livery stable. We set up the beginnings of the house for the kids in what had been the mine's business office. Then we left to do errands in town. While we were gone, the biggest thunderstorm of the season rolled in. As it pelted hail and rained torrents, we drove back up Caribou Road to check on Lizzie.

The plaintiffs in the lawsuit had been delaying for months, yapping that they really needed to experience a "storm event" to test the reliability of the water system from the mine before any judgment could be made. If there was ever a storm event, this was it! Water cascaded down the road through Cardinal. Hail piled two inches deep on the west side of the buildings. Rain poured and ran off in cataracts. I grabbed my camera and recorded the water flowing out of the offending pipe, which was subject of the suit. It ran clear, despite the storm runoff. Pictures could not do this storm justice. The irony of the clear water coming from the pipe was not lost on me.

Sandi and I called into the livery stable for Lizzie, but she was nowhere to be found. We searched the townsite several times, calling and calling her name. We knew the little dog could not have escaped on her own. I fought my suspicions as I imagined our neighbors kidnapping Lizzie. How would we tell Harlan that we had lost his dog? Sure enough, a few days later, Lizzie turned up at the pound in Boulder, reportedly "found" by the neighbors.

When Harlan arrived a few days later, the kids decorated their new summer home. They set up a kitchen in the office, the living room in the middle room, and their bed in the green "bedroom". They got summer jobs, and settled in as Cardinal's first residents in over sixty years. I imagined that the ghosts were happy to have live company, and out of respect for that they kept a low profile. The only sounds to be heard in the quiet night were the pack rat who ran about in the ceiling.

One night, the packrat happened into the bedroom. While Sandi squealed from the safety of the bed, Harlan caught the beast with his ski gloves. He held it up for examination. Colorado's wood rats are fuzzy creatures with a furry mane and a tuft on their fuzzy tail, like a miniature lion. They have a black bulbous nose and a teddy bear face. Sandi asked, "Can we keep it? It's so cute."

Harlan, half naked and freezing, carried the packrat across Coon Track Creek and let it go. It was back by morning.

Within the month, a letter arrived at our attorney's office from Isanti's attorney. Complaining of strangers living in unsanitary conditions, it was a thinly veiled attempt to keep residents out of Cardinal. We ignored it.

In the dog days of the hot Colorado summer, it is breezy, cool and perfect in Cardinal. I go to the townsite often to walk around and enjoy it. I take people of all kinds on tours, loving every opportunity to share the history and beauty of this place, which I am appointed interim caretaker. The daisies grow in profusion. Trout jump in Coon Track Creek. Baby birds have hatched as they do every year in a nest in a wooden box nailed to the wall inside the Assay Office.

Now, I wake each morning wondering if this will be the day that we finally hear from the Judge. He has had all the information from both sides for two weeks. He might call anytime to ask to hear oral arguments by the litigators. He could simply call with a judgment or he could decide this whole mess must continue on to be decided by a jury at trial. Each hour that goes by, these thoughts occur to me for a few moments.

On one hand, I just want this chapter of the Cardinal story to be over. On the other hand, I want the Judge to take all the time he needs to understand the truth. I worry that the plaintiff's agenda will be hidden by the reams of water test results and the smoke screen of tangents their attorneys have offered. But again and again, I remind myself that Cardinal is not a superfund site. There is no crime.

I resent having my life be put on hold. I have been compensating by exercising the choices I do have. I survive by filling my days with marvelous things to keep the lawsuit in perspective.

I climb to the Continental Divide several times each week. I practice flying in my friend's little Cessna 150 every chance I get. I indulge in conversations with friends. I am thankful for any real estate work I get. These are the keys to my staying power as I patiently wait out the Judge's decision.

In mid-July, my car speeds across the sweltering prairie toward Coal Creek Canyon, my quickest escape route to the cool mountains on this particular day. Paul Phillips rings me on the cell phone. I must pull the car over to keep our phone connection or I will lose him in the steep walled canyon. The temperature immediately soars past one hundred degrees.

These days, each time I hear Paul's wonderfully calming voice, my heart stops until I can discern whether he is calling with news of a judgment. Today,

Paul informs me that we are obligated to offer one last try at an "out of court" settlement.

After two years of offering more than generous proposals, I know there is no hope for such a settlement. Paul tells me this is an opportunity to show the court that we are willing and eager to put this nonsense to an end.

Paul reads me a statement that his team has drafted. The statement offers to end it right now, and rescind any rights to further claims against the plaintiffs. As I consider this offer, the heat of the prairie becomes unbearable. My patience with the whole situation grows thinner by the second.

"Paul" I say, "This has gone too far for that. I have lost everything Steve and I have ever worked for. I have borrowed against the little that remains. I cannot let them devastate us, and walk away. I don't think I could ever forgive them. I am not that good a Christian. I cannot agree to this."

"Okay, Lexie. I understand. We are here to represent you." Paul is patient and gives me time.

"I want to go with your professional judgment, Paul." I offer. "I don't want to tie your hands. But it isn't right that they can simply get away with ruining us."

Paul tried to help me see the way.

"If we were in a British Commonwealth, they'd be held responsible." he reminds me. "It's just not the way the law is written here. Our hope is to show the Magistrate that we are the reasonable ones."

My mind has had free run for too long. I think we have been the reasonable ones all along. I have not committed any crime. These people have attacked from every angle they could think of threatening not only the Cardinal project, but also my family's well being. I can't afford new shoes for my children. We haven't had our teeth cleaned in ages. Our credit cards are maxed out. We have paid all we could and still owe more than two hundred thousand dollars to the attorneys and it's not over yet. It has certainly all gone too far to simply let them off the hook.

Paul went back to the drawing board with the litigators. This time, we would offer to settle only if litigation fees were paid, but we would forgo expert witness fees, which were in excess of fifty thousand dollars. I agree to this not realizing the limitations of "litigation fees".

The next day, word came that the plaintiffs were insisting on us paying their attorney fees, as well as asking that concessions be made in the permitting requirements with the State of Colorado.

The attorneys from both sides requested that the settlement conference be cancelled. There was no hope of resolution. It would be up to the Judge to decide the fate of the federal suit.

❧

Two summers had now gone by with no work being done in Cardinal. The buildings were deteriorating before my very eyes. The townsite's patience, like my own, was wearing thin.

I fight cynicism every day. I think back to the time that I lived in a happy idealistic bubble. I cannot say I am a better person with my bubble burst. People always admired me for my optimism and positive attitude. They drew strength and encouragement from the energy I exuded. Now, those people forget what it was they saw in me.

I am a different person. I find condolence in songs that sing the blues. I no longer have much to say, for I have been losing for so long. I gather with friends only to find that I can no longer delight in silliness and frolic. As they drink and play flirtatiously, I find myself mired in broken illusions, hopes and dreams dashed. No one seems to notice, which comes as a relief to me, but it also tightens my waning spirit.

As I walk endlessly through the mountain paths, I find solace in the forest. My mind plays like a recording, repeating the same course of reasoning over and over again. I am hanging onto threads of faith. Pearls of wisdom fall from my fingertips.

My vision has turned from one that believed human nature is basically good, to a discernment of distrust and suspicion. I struggle not to perceive everyone as self-serving. The moral fabric of society seems to have rotted away, threatening to take my beliefs with it. Disappointment eats at my soul.

Just as I feel I am hitting bottom, we get word that the Federal Judge will not have an opportunity to consider New Cardinal's case until after the New Year. I am sinking into an abyss.

In early August, just before the Cardinal road issue would have gone in front of a judge, my neighbor's attorney, Ted Byrd, called Mike Sawyer to say that he had misunderstood the Ingress/Egress Federal Statute R.S. 2477. Now, he suggested we go to mediation with Tina and Dennis. Mike assured me that this was the least expensive way of bringing this issue to a close.

He is very impressed with the brief which Mike has produced. The brief outlines the fact that the road to Cardinal is indeed a public road. Ted Byrd, Tina's road attorney, admits that for two years, he has struggled to interpret the law, which clearly states that if a road was used as a public road prior to the patent of the specific mining claim, it is indeed a public road. His feigned ignorance has cost me tens of thousands of dollars. Given this, he is asking that we attend mediation to resolve the road/septic issues. A date is set almost two months away. Delay has been a constant tactic.

Mike outlines for me the benefits of settling out of court, and the reasons why we need the extra time to prepare for mediation. Pragmatically, I know Mike is right, but I struggle with principal. The brief is complete; the work is done and ready to go to summary judgment. Why would we settle now? For money only. I am afraid that for me, money is not the only thing involved here.

I am now hundreds of thousands of dollars in debt thanks to these people. Realistically, money should be what this is about. If I settle out of court, I can gain something back. I can hope to recoup about twenty thousand dollars and I will exchange easements that could have been exchanged two years ago. Mediation could bring a quick end to the suffering. My sense of fairness, so well developed teaching years of kindergarten, begins to scream at me. My heart resolves to not give in.

Mike pleads with me to not be stubborn. This is not the time to be principled. Take what money we can from these people, it is the only bite they will feel.

Anyone who has had to wrangle in the court system of the United States knows the system is not working. If this were England, Canada or New Zealand, people would pay damages to the party that prevails in a lawsuit. These people never would have filed the Federal Suit in the first place. We would have exchanged easements in a heartbeat and become neighbors.

Here in the United States, there is much to be gained by simply filing suit against another. The law forces the defendant to prove innocence. One must go to all lengths to build a defense for it is not enough to trust that the truth will prevail.

I relentlessly discuss the injustice done in damages from the Cardinal case with my attorneys. They must wonder why I cannot accept that the system cannot help me. I am a hopeless idealist. I keep coming back to the story of the lady who wins millions for spilling hot coffee on herself at McDonalds. I wrestle with the costs I have incurred to prove that Cardinal is environmentally sound. These lawsuits threaten to leave me financially and emotionally bankrupt.

As the weeks roll by, I only strengthen my resolve to have the road case decided in court. If we settle for a private easement, we will have bastardized an already toothless law. What honor will I have upheld for the people who lived in Cardinal City when I deny the history that went on there? How will I have helped others needing case law to fight similar battles? How will I sleep at night? Is extracting money from these people the only justice our system can attain? And is that justice at all?

By now, my attorneys are beginning to worry about me, and rightfully so. They take turns trying to talk some sense into me. Litigators are particularly pessimistic when it comes to the prospect of utilizing the legal system. In their experience, the chances of truth and right prevailing are clearly not worth gambling on. My tears of frustration bring me no closer to resignation on this matter. I will go to mediation, but I cannot imagine that there will be terms offered that I can live with.

One night, I awaken to the sound of rain. It is a real rain that pours incessantly and drips noisily off the trees and roof outside my open window. Could this be the end of the drought that has plagued the West for a year? It could mean that things might turn around. I listen to the rain as hours tick away in the darkness of night. I count and discount all that has happened. Sleep does not come.

On the morning of the mediation for the Road/Septic Trespass case, Mike and I drive to the far west end of Boulder. Tucked into the green jungle next to the Anderson Ditch, right up against the foot of the Rocky Mountains, is the office of Steven Meyers, PC. It is a fabulous hidden, understated location. It feels good to me and gives me power.

Mike and I are as prepared for this day as any two students of life can be. We come fortified by an All-American breakfast of pancakes and eggs. Our homework is done and triple checked. We have a smug feeling from knowing we have the facts on our side, yet neither of us is naive enough to think that we can have expectations.

Outside, I shake Tina's attorney's hand, at once feeling furious and glad he has finally brought us to the table. Tina and Dennis are already seated in the conference room. I have successfully fought off an anxiety over sitting in a room with them, as I have been told, it will only be while the mediator introduces himself and his technique.

No one says hello as we enter the room. I take a quick glance at Dennis, who is seated across the table from me. He looks years older than he is. Being miserable and negative has worn nasty lines on his face. He wears a permanent grimace. My face is deadpan as I avert my eyes. I do not make eye contact with Tina.

Steven Meyers, mediator and attorney, resembles a Muppet. I say that with all due respect. From his personal history, we learn that Steven came to the Boulder mountains in 1976, just one year after I did. Now I understand the mop top curly hair and the subtlety disheveled look. He is a soft edged, sensitive new age kind of guy. Exactly what one would expect from a Boulder mediator. This combination of Muppet and attorney strikes me as incongruous.

Mr. Meyers finishes his introduction by telling us that he is usually the biggest optimist in the room. I like that! Most people rarely state that claim. I am usually the biggest optimist in the room! Today, I think he might be right and this encourages me.

Mr. Meyers escorts the enemy to a separate conference room and returns immediately to start with us. For quite a while, we talk about the history of the past two years. Mike deftly inserts information of the sideshow known as the "Federal Suit" which technically has no bearing on this lawsuit, but has everything to do with my attitude. Meyers sizes me up correctly as entrenched. The cryptic notes on Meyers's notepad bear our position when he leaves the room to speak with the other side.

We have adamantly requested that Tina concede Bergren Road is a public road. We also expect her septic tank to be moved off Cardinal land. This, after all, is the goal of a trespass case. We also want a monetary figure for compensation for legal fees. Mr. Meyers tries not to scoff at this last request.

When our mediator returns over an hour later, he has a look about him. I recognize the effects of listening to Tina's sing song whining about the great loss of her dream. Mr. Meyers has, for the moment, forgotten what he left in this room. When he states that Tina wants to trade easements across the board, he elicits a reaction from Mike and me that brings him back to reality. He realizes we might very well fall into the five percent of the people who end up in court.

Two years ago, I offered Tina fifteen thousand dollars, a deed to an acre and a half of land including her septic field and a right of first refusal on the purchase of a cabin. Two years ago! Now, fifty thousand dollars later, she could kiss my stern. Refreshed on this train of thought, Mr. Meyers smiled pleasantly, and departed again.

Mike and I kept ourselves entertained in various ways until, two and one half hours later, Mr. Meyers returned. This time, he looked as if he had been pummeled. Mr. Meyers appeared harried. For an instant, I felt sorry for him, until I remembered that he was making two hundred dollars an hour. But Steven Meyers had worked his Muppet magic.

He reported to us that Tina had agreed to the fact that this was indeed a public road. She also agreed to remove her septic leach field from Cardinal land.

Mike and I looked at each other in disbelief. You might have expected a hoot, or a "high-five", but we were truly shocked. After a quiet pause, Mr. Meyers spoke. He said, "I would declare this a victory."

It was indeed victory. It had been such a long time coming.

The rest of the day was spent negotiating the specific protections in the plan. The challenges of installing a new leach field were lost on Tina, despite the evidence, which I had obtained from the engineers at a hefty price. Meyers suggested that they take seven days to explore the feasibility of installing a septic system on the hillside. At that time, they would commit to the plan, or we would find ourselves back at the table.

As Mike and I drove away, we knew this news would take a little while to sink into our heads. We had both spent countless hours, day and night, pondering the facts and possible outcomes of this bizarre situation. Now, we had a settlement.

I was in the Whole Foods Market when it hit me. We have a settlement! When I sat down at an outside table with Mike, my face blossomed into an enormous grin. "It finally just hit me, Mike, and it feels really good!"

Mike shot back a very proud and equally huge grin.

At the Denver History Library, I find an article published by the Rocky Mountain News on December 5, 1925. I have found the story, which John had told me so long ago. My eyes bulge with excitement as the article shows up on the microfiche screen. Here is our town and its people captured in drama by the camera. The past comes to life for me.

The morning shift of miners had gone to work when a fire broke out in the compressor house at the portal of the tunnel. The fire spread quickly in the early morning wind, burning the timber frame that supported the portal and collapsing the mouth of the tunnel. Smoke and dust filled the air. Twenty miners were trapped inside the mine.

As the call for help went out, electricians and firemen hurried up the canyon from the prairie towns of Boulder, Lafayette and Denver. Women and children bundled in layers of clothing and came to the mine to await the fate of their loved ones. Every available able-bodied man helped the rescue. A forty-foot deep rescue shaft was dropped behind the cave in to access the tunnel. As they worked, power poles burned and six huge electrical transformers fell to the ground causing the Boulder County Tunnel to further collapse.

Tapping every man's resources, the rescuers managed to set up lights, fans, and a come along. All the while, the fire fighting and digging proceeded. By late afternoon, the fire was under control and by dusk a mighty blizzard began to rage. Undaunted, the rescuers continued and the crowd persisted. By ten thirty that night, the new shaft reached the tunnel, and shouts of encouragement were passed around.

Six firemen were lowered in ore buckets into the main tunnel. It wasn't long before the rescuers were overcome by gas, and had to be rescued themselves.

A makeshift hospital was set up in the Bergren home, the Superintendent's House. The six firemen were in critical condition.

I can feel the initial panic and horror. My imagination runs with the commotion of spreading the news, searching for help, organizing a rescue plan. I know the weather at that time of year at nine thousand feet and I can feel the impending snowstorm in the air. Who were the people? They feel very real to me, people with families and lives of hard work.

In the end, they found the miners alive, but suffering greatly.

Despite the price, I order museum grade copies of the newspaper pages, so I can learn every detail. The history of Cardinal has become an obsession for me.

One would expect that the Federal Judge would have looked by now at the stack of papers that was gathering dust somewhere in his office. The flaw in our system surely is that there is no preliminary check to overview the situations involved in these cases. Perhaps if the Judge had recognized that New Cardinal, LLC was not Exxon, this might not have gone anywhere. What if someone could have given him enough information to realize that this actually wasn't much of a Clean Water Act case, but instead, a case of NIMBIES making a self righteous attack?

We filed the Motion for Summary Judgment in May. My spirits soared and my expectation was that there would be an end in sight. I patiently waited two months, believing we would soon have an answer. When August came with still not a word, I was becoming exhausted by thinking each day might be the one. I would squelch urges to get working in Cardinal.

Now, it was evident that I had to change my focus or lose my mind. The saving grace was my insatiable appetite for flying the little Cessna 150, Delta Poppa. I was very close to taking my final check ride to get my "private ticket", so I relentlessly called on Martin to help me polish my skills. Martin shared my excitement and as a teacher was happy to bring fifteen months of training together toward a check ride. He met me to practice night flying in the dark hours of summer mornings. He rode around and around as I botched short, soft field landings and went around again. In the end, Martin tried to increase the pressure on me, but the supportive teaching style he had used for over a year stood solid in my mind. He upped the ante with emergency situations and multitasking. He heightened the pace of my tasks and doggedly tired me out. Each time I'd look over at him in the right seat, he tried to wipe that proud teacher look off his face and we would both grin at each other.

"Martin," I spoke emphatically, "As a kindergarten teacher, I once had a principal who sent me home to practice stern faces in the mirror. I believe you need to do the same. You are not intimidating me."

Martin affected a wounded look. He had mastered that! We laughed.

Martin instructed me to set up my check ride with '"Doc" Calendar for Monday. It would be the day before I was to leave for Idaho and the Salmon River. I could hardly contain my excitement. Martin reminded me not to forget the donuts for Doc. Doc's reputation had preceded him and I knew the donuts were a prerequisite to a passing check ride.

I flew and flew in the days preceding the test. I felt ready and prayed hard for good weather. I was anxious to pass so that I could take my daughter up for a flight before she left for her school year in Idaho, which would be the following day.

On the morning of my check ride, I woke to unsettled weather, but knowing our weather patterns on the Front Range from years of living here, I knew that the low lying clouds would burn off midmorning and then be followed by increasing winds. I jumped out of bed early; my mission included getting donuts for Doc.

When I arrived at the airport, Martin had already been up in Delta Poppa, flying with his nephew. They had cleaned, oiled and fueled the airplane. There was no sign of Doc yet, so Martin and I had a donut. They were terrible! The donut store had recently changed hands and these donuts were dry and tasteless. Now I was nervous!

Doc Calendar was late. When he arrived, I was relieved to find him to be a cheerful, light-hearted human being. Not what I expected of an FAA Examiner. We reviewed the test process. Then we chatted a while. Doc asked me questions for the oral portion of the exam with a style that left me wondering about the question being asked, let alone the answer. In between questions, we chatted some more. He was sizing me up to measure my judgment and self-confidence. I felt a sense of urgency as the wind appeared to be picking up. I nervously drew a blank on the airspace questions as the trees outside were blowing hard in a stiff wind. Finally, Doc said, "Let's go fly".

Doc is a large man and a Cessna 150 is a very small plane, but he good-naturedly crammed himself in beside me. By now, the wind was wailing. Doc watched every move I made and questioned me with his indirect way. It was hard to read him, but he hadn't made me head back yet, so I assumed the check ride was going well.

By the time Doc told me to park Delta Poppa, I was starving and the day was late. I cut the engine and Doc said, "Let's go in and I'll sign you off."

I looked at him blankly, until he restated himself..."You've passed. You are a fully fledged pilot now."

The next morning, Sandi and I were leaving in her old Toyota to drive her to Idaho. Before we hit the road, there was one thing we had to do. I couldn't wait to take Sandi for a flight in Delta Poppa.

As the airplane lifted from the runway, I looked at her face and she was beaming. I felt like the coolest Mom in the world. We flew over the areas that she had worked all summer installing pumps into water systems. She excitedly pointed out the miniature farms below, telling me to look for each important feature. We flew along the front of Boulder's Flatirons, the huge vertical rocks bathed in early morning light. A hawk peeked in our windows trying to make eye contact. "This is the greatest." she said.

FLYING OVER CARDINAL

My trip to Idaho lasted two weeks. We installed Sandi in her new home. We prepared for the arrival of her horse from Colorado. We scoured second-hand stores buying furniture and a bed.

Sharing an unlikely and bizarre story about a ghost town, I negotiated a payment plan for Sandi's tuition at the college. That was one tale of hardship they'd never heard before. I felt like I was telling the teacher that the dog ate my homework.

With our jobs finished, we drove to meet twenty-four of our dear family friends for a boating trip down the Main Fork of the Salmon River. I couldn't help but reflect that it had been exactly one year ago that we were headed into the same river canyon, when I received the call from John Bergren alerting us to the Federal Lawsuit. How our lives had changed.

The river puts me in a state of suspended animation. I think of my situation endlessly, but from my boat, nothing will change until I come to shore seven days later. So, I float with the current. My boat takes the path of least resistance. We weave around obstacles, seeking the smoothest course, knowing all the while we will reach our destination.

Reentry to the lives we have left for a week is always a shock. My cell phone reconnects me at the first city. It deprives me of the two days travel time that, not too many years ago, used to ease me back into civilization. I am jolted back to my reality. Real estate clients are screaming from neglect and still not a word from the Federal Judge.

When Paul Phillips and I talk, we agree that it is time to inquire at Judge Kane's office as to the status of our file. Kane's secretary tells us that the Federal Courthouse is moving across town, justifiable reason for delay. Also, there are criminal cases, which take precedence over civil cases. Be patient. It will be after the New Year that the judge looks at our case.

Again, my moral crashes hard. This spells certain financial disaster for Cardinal and our family personally. Again, Paul bolsters me with hope, telling me that as soon as the Individual Water Permit is issued, we will file a motion for expediency with the Judge. That seems like it might happen in my lifetime.

We have been told the issuance of the Individual Water Permit is imminent, yet it is six more weeks of active frustration, for Paul, Katie and me, before we get resolution. Even with constant vigilance on our part, the State of Colorado Water Quality Control Board's cogs turn slowly.

As we waited for the Individual Permit to be issued by the State, the season has turned to winter. With the cold, a mountain packrat moved into our house one evening. He investigated every square inch of the house, awakening me several times in the night. The sounds, magnified by the contrasting silence, were busy and full of intention. I decided this was not one of our cats, but a packrat.

By morning, he had left a path of destruction, and then crawled into a hidden nest to sleep. I drove to Cardinal to retrieve my Have a Heart Trap. I set the trap and went cross-country skiing, leaving the house quiet. Upon my return, I heard the scuttle in the cage. I had successfully captured the beast using cat food.

The packrat froze when he saw me. He looked guilty and begged for mercy. I assured him that he had simply arrived at the wrong house and I would straighten that out. He looked up at me with big black eyes. He had a bulbous black nose like a circus clown. His fur was thick with a winter coat, complete with a ruff around his neck. Beige ears stood up from all that fur.

I knew exactly where to let him go. He rode in the trap on the front floor of the car. Tina's deck is only twenty-four inches from my property line. I didn't have to trespass. I thought of all the times I had exercised self-control and not flipped them off, not mooned them, not turned off their propane tank that sat on my property. I gave this rat all that energy and bid him a fond farewell. It felt good. He ran straight up the hill to the house.

Little did I know, Tina and Dennis had just left for their Moab, Utah home for four months. Each time I visited Cardinal in the weeks that followed, I snickered in disbelief as I saw that no one had been home. Hopefully, that little bugger had made himself at home.

Getting mail is a timeless thing. I imagine the mail being brought to Cardinal by stagecoach. The stage would have been placarded with an official sign reading "U.S. Mail", possibly written in gold leaf and trimmed in black.

Opening the mail can bring a full range of emotions, news of every sort. People send word of babies born, of travel, love, change and the passing of souls.

I can picture the Cardinal miners getting news from Texas or the East; opening a letter with the same trepidation or joy that we might. Upon reading the handwritten script, the letter would undoubtedly have been clutched momentarily to the chest. The recipient would have looked skyward, closed their eyes and pictured the sender in a mental image that would be stored in the mind as part of this individual's reality.

Each day, when I checked my mail in Nederland, there was another envelope from Holland & Hart, Attorneys. Sometimes, the contents would be a brief, a response, a motion, a draft or an official notice of our position on a point. But usually, it was an invoice.

When one owes as much money as I did, and there is no immediate hope of paying, one develops a systematic approach for dealing with such paperwork. My ritual was always performed at the trash bin of the Post Office. It is there that one sorts the immense amount of junk mail from the good stuff, jettisoning these misused resources at the cost of the taxpayer and the environment.

First, upon recognition of an envelope from Holland & Hart, I would wince and cringe. This reaction would be followed by a look over each shoulder, the Post Office being such a public place. Next, I would suck in a big breath, hold it, then open the envelope. There were always several pages of way too expensive paper folded into a business envelope by a professional envelope crammer.

I would identify the introduction page, signed by Paul, in blue ink. The damage pages would follow. I would glance at the total amount and groan. Next, the papers would separate and curl into an unmanageable display of scary, unpayable nuisance. By weighting them flat with my pile of other mail, I could then proceed to flip through my other bills to look for any personal correspondences. Thanks to email, personal correspondences, of course, are a vanishing breed. Even a small handwritten note can bring a large smile to the face of the beholder.

One particular day in October, I tugged the mass of mail from my box and saw that the Holland & Hart envelopes were accompanied by a bounced check notice from the New Cardinal, LLC account. Yes, indeed, my loan interest payment to the bank had been returned. New Cardinal, LLC had paid one too many water laboratory bills, and consequently, the money had run out.

I had been waiting on a five thousand dollar check from Boulder County as payment for a purchase option on the Cardinal Mill. The County had agreed to purchase the Mill from me for twenty five thousand dollars, the balance payable when the Federal Lawsuit was gone. I regarded this offer as a sympathy payment, but was not too proud to take it. It is customary for some consideration to change hands with property and given the inherent liability of this structure, I was willing to take whatever I could get.

My gal, Emmy, at the County understood my financial predicament and was working on getting me the option payment to help me out. Unfortunately, this check had not come through yet. A check from the County must never be counted on until it is hand. Hence, my depression set in.

Cardinal's resources were depleted. There was no relief in sight. Paul was waiting on a call from me to firm up a meeting time at the State Water Control Division. This meeting would require me paying Paul and Katie for many more hours of work. Where was this money to come from? How long could

I go on incurring bills that couldn't be paid? The damages had passed the five hundred thousand mark, and there was only that much equity in the property. It was time to pull the plug.

Big crocodile tears poured from my cheeks. I cursed the hormones in my body that made these tears so prolific. There were too many tears to wipe away. I lowered my head and made for the Post Office door. As I departed, three people greeted me with a "Howsit goin' Lexie?" This made me cry even harder. Why couldn't I just be normal?

Why is there no shut off valve for tears? I cried all the way home and called Paul Phillips. He was quite used to this type of call from me.

"Paul", I whimpered, "I've got to pull the plug on this whole thing. I'm all the way out of money. There's no more money to borrow, and I am in default on the interest payments to the bank."

There was a patient silence on the other end, as Paul searched for the words that would bring me back to reality. Reality was that there was no "pulling the plug" possible.

"This is not the time to quit." came the words. "The meeting tomorrow should produce the water permit that the State has promised for a year. Katie and I will be there at no charge to you. We need you there too to remind them they are dealing with a human being. We are getting close, Lexie. Hang in there."

Tears of frustration burned from my eyes. There is no quitting allowed. There is no escaping this thing that is bigger than me. Why was I subjected to this? Why was Paul? What did he do to deserve this client from hell and her falling down town? And how about Katie? How could she justify going to work for Cardinal again? How could they not? We had all been sucked into this thing. I thanked Paul and humbly hung up the phone. There is no quitting. There has been no quitting. And there will be no quitting.

The afternoon of our meeting with the State Water Control Division was the first day of winter in the mountains. Clouds hung grey and low, and there were inches of snow from the night before. I went to Denver in warm clothes that I guessed would look ridiculous down on the prairies. I found it was cold there too. I was dressed for it and everyone else shivered. Street people on the road medians were freezing. I gave a Jamaican man some banana bread.

Paul, Katie and I met at the hotel next door to the State Health Complex. I brought my copies of the newspaper article about the fire in 1925. I wanted to share a bit of history to help remind Paul and Katie what this was all about. It was the history of the townsite that continued to sustain me. Intrigued, they took a moment to read.

The machine that is the State of Colorado pales in comparison to the Federal Machine, but it still stands firmly mired in itself. Like a rat in a maze, my directionality disappears quickly as we wind through the institutional hallways. This unsettles my very being, as it is designed to.

In a conference room, we meet with the State's Attorney and three Water Quality Control employees. There are permitting issues, which have been, and will be, scrutinized again by the EPA. The State and the EPA have an ongoing power struggle. It is a dance danced carefully, so as to step on no toes. These dancers are excruciatingly careful to step on no toes among themselves as well. Our Katie understands this and is a good dancer. Her style is comprehensive erudition presented at pace that stays one step ahead of these bureaucrats. As Paul points out, she runs on an energy not common to anyone else. Katie knows the science at Cardinal like no other person.

There is present among us today, the man who can give the official nod. Katie dances information out across the table to him. He is quiet and smiling pleasantly. He gives the nod when there is no more that Katie can add. Even then she does not stop talking though, he nods and she confirms, checking for understanding. Under the table, I tally the nods on my fingers, which are the only thing I can move.

As each issue is discussed, my future is defined. We are fashioning the terms of the water quality permit that I will have to live with into perpetuity. Katie is doing very well. Paul, despite his diminutive stature, is bigger than the biggest bodyguard in the world. He sits quietly, ready to speak if need be. I am in extremely good hands.

We discussed the situation of the Ceria Daphnia Dubia flea's mortality rate, again and at length. Then we got the nod. We discussed the location and numbering of the water seeps, again. We got the nod. It was when we were discussing the low flow of Coon Track Creek, again, that I began to lose my mind.

The inability of the State employees to think outside the box frustrated me beyond all reason. Here we were, in the fall of the worst drought in one hundred and fifty years and Coon Track Creek was running merrily along full of trout. This theatre of the absurd had pushed Paul beyond his limits too. Finally, he spoke. He reminded everyone that the expert witness reports had decided this issue. Then, changing the subject, he began a monologue that commanded the attention of everyone on a more rational and human level. He reminded the group that the agenda of the plaintiffs had little or nothing to do with water quality. He tactfully described the financial hardship caused to New Cardinal, exasperated by the State through a series of delays, adding that Holland & Hart had not been paid in six months.

Paul's perspective combined with Katie's dogged persistence on the unresolved issues brought the state employees through the final steps of a permitting process that had taken over a year and several hundred thousand dollars. My two discharge permits were now called one "Individual Permit". I was perplexed to think how an ordinary landowner, such as myself, could have ever accomplished this feat without professional help. I was even more perplexed by the overall situation...how a person could need a permit to discharge perfectly clean water when nothing on the site was being changed or had been changed in the last sixty five years or more. What is this really about?

I would be testing the water at Cardinal monthly for many years to come, at great expense, just to prove to the State that this healthy stream was healthy indeed. But the outcome of this meeting pleased us. Every last detail outlined test standards that were tailored to our situation. Now, it was time to take a final step toward resolution of the Federal Lawsuit. We would file a Motion for Expediency with the Judge.

'The first day of December, as it turns out, was the day I had been waiting for. Steve Black, Cardinal's litigator, left me a message at the end of the business day. The Federal Judge had responded to our request. He was asking the parties to choose a date for a hearing. The eighteenth of December was selected. It would be upon us quickly.

For the first time in so long, I felt that there could actually be an end in sight. I called Mike and peppered him with questions about the process ahead. I was so excited I could hardly stand it. Even the fact that the Judge had acknowledged the existence of our file was progress. My spirit lifted to a place it had not dared go in over a year. It seemed at last there might be an end to this trouble.

By the seventeenth of December, Sandi had come home from Albertson College for Christmas. Steve wanted no part in anything relating to Cardinal. It had caused enough trouble for him. He kept himself immersed in his reading and radio.

My emotions and financial difficulties had reached critical mass. It reminded me of the feeling a woman has in labor, when the circumstances must become all the way unbearable to make the transition. Sandi's presence tethered me to the earth, and her spirit gave me hope. She promised to be by my side for the hearing. Sandi, with all the faith in the world in her mother, bolstered me. She prepared me for battle, insisting on my wearing her flecked short gray gabardine dress suit and a long French braid.

"You look great!" she said, "This is my Mom. My Mom is gonna kick ass."

On the morning of the hearing, Sandi and I drove to Denver. As we waited a few minutes for Steve Black, Sandi looked out the thirty-seventh floor window over the city to the mountain peaks.

SANDI & LEXIE READY FOR FEDERAL COURT, DECEMBER 17TH, 2003

"I've definitely never been in a building this high before!" she delighted. "This is incredible. I need this office. I could be an attorney. I like to argue."

Steve Black gave us a brief overview of what he expected to happen in the hearing. The Judge would hear oral arguments from both sides then there would be rebuttals. The plaintiffs would attack the State of Colorado's water permitting process and question the timing of New Cardinal's permits. Our strategy was to stay focused on the fact that we were in compliance with the State and that Coon Track Creek was completely clean and in excellent condition.

Steve Black spoke the legalese which I had been immersed in during the past two years. Sandi listened carefully, grasping each concept. She was clearly impressed by the caliber of the help I had enlisted. When Steve Black stepped out to find Paul Phillips, Sandi said so, adding, "I guess I'd need to polish my act to work here."

As we walked the few blocks to the Federal Courthouse, I expressed my concern over the State requiring an average citizen, like myself, to bear the costs of professional permit writers, engineers, scientists, field and lab testers, to be in compliance with their regulations. Most landowners do not have these resources. Steve commented that most people don't buy properties involving a mining mill and a waste rock pile.

As we graciously chuckled at his comment, I reminded myself that I had gone through the Phase Two Environmental Study before purchasing the property and knew the site was healthy. I counted several properties in my mind, which friends had purchased, that qualified as unpermitted tainted mine sites. These places would never receive the clean bill of health that Cardinal had. How could justice be served in my case, while all of those other sites existed unpermitted? The State did not enforce its own law. Yet, I would never wish this on anyone.

I cringed through the formality of greeting and shaking hands with the opposing counsel. John Barth represented the scum of all attorneys to me. He had been a weasel throughout this process, wasting everyone's time as he filed motion after motion on uncontested issues. I wanted to spit on his feet. Sandi was appalled that we would acknowledge the other side. It was a lesson on taking the higher road and I was glad to have my attorney's model professional behavior for her. Offer a genuine handshake, and then clean their clocks.

Paul Phillips and the State Attorney, Annette Quill, sat in the first row, while Sandi and I were invited to sit at our counsel's table before the Judge. I was not surprised to see that "The Citizens Alliance for the Protection of Caribou" had not appeared at the hearing. What were they doing that was more important than appearing in Federal Court for a suit they had filed? At the other table, their attorneys, Barth and Bartlett, nervously shuffled papers.

Steve Black methodically arranged several documents in front of him, concentrating with great intent on the words that would be our defense. Just like a surgeon, he lined up his tools, as he mentally prepared for the task at hand. I watched with fascination. I thought of all the different people in this world who have learned their vocations well, practicing a carefully honed art, and contributing finely polished expertise.

We all rose for Judge Kane as he entered the courtroom. He smiled and nodded once, then told us to be seated. The Judge sat barely visible above his court. He was an elderly man, just short of retirement. He looked as if it was most inconvenient for him to have come.

He called on Steve Black to begin and settled into an uncomfortable slump. Judge Kane took off his glasses and began to rub his eyes. He rested his head in his hands and appeared to be falling asleep. He rubbed his head and eyes some more, and arranged his jowls in his hands with his head resting to one side then another. Occasionally, he would peek out of one eye and spy Sandi, who happened to be a twenty-year-old knockout. His eyebrow would rise for an instant, then he would remind himself he was in court and settle back into his slump. All the while, he took in every word Steve Black spoke. Despite the sleepy bulldog mien, his mind was working.

When John Barth stood to speak, the Judge peeked out at him just once, silently making a statement regarding Barth's appearance. Barth was clearly from another league and perhaps another time. He wore a cheap suit, which bound him a bit tight. It seemed to be the one his mother gave him when he graduated from law school. His hair was long and thin. It was cut in a seventies style shag and was squeaky clean for this special occasion.

John Barth began his argument by explaining that the Citizen's Alliance was made up of all of the downstream neighbors on Coon Track Creek. They were extremely and simply concerned about water quality impacts, as they used the creek for fishing and wading. Never mind that they couldn't make it to court this particular day.

Fishing, wading and trespassing, I thought to myself. Where are these cowards? At least they wouldn't have to trespass anymore, now that New Cardinal and the County had provided them with public open space. I checked my attitude, reminding myself that those types of thoughts served no one and only fed the devil in my soul. I smiled pleasantly and looked attentive.

Paul Phillips and Steve Black took notes as they listened. Annette Quill stared in utter disbelief as the aimless whining spilled out on the courtroom. The Judge appeared to have shut down entirely and gone to sleep. As Barth wrapped it up, Paul Phillips shot over to Steve Black, delivering a pad of yellow paper. I could read it from my vantage point. The note outlined the points of our intent. It served to refocus Steve Black on our objective. However, Steve had not been the least sucked in by Barth's whining and rose to make a succinct final plea to the Judge.

At the moment Steve Black finished his last word, and before Barth could rise for his rebuttal, Judge Kane banged his gavel. He spoke as rapidly as an auctioneer. He ruled from the bench.

"The charges against New Cardinal, LLC filed under the Clean Water Act of 1968, amended 1974, regarding any present violations with the permitting by the State of Colorado are deemed by this court to be moot. The charges against New Cardinal, LLC filed under the Clean Water Act of 1968, amended 1974, regarding any future concerns of violations in Coon Track Creek are deemed by this court to be moot."

Then the Judge did a most unusual thing. In a state of full alert, he put on his glasses, sat up tall, leaned forward and addressed Sandi and me directly.

"I must apologize." he said. "I have over three hundred and fifty cases pending at this time. Many of them have also asked for expediency, and all with good reason. Regarding the matter of past violations, I will try to finalize your case in the next month. I will try to get to it by the end of January."

I'm sure I was beaming at him. I was certainly nodding my head with great appreciation. It was one of those moments which a person lives fully. A moment forever recorded in the memory banks. Sandi looked at me for confirmation and I nodded at her. Steve Black wore a proud, satisfied, controlled smile. Paul Phillips looked as if his team had just won a championship game, and it had.

Judge Kane stood up, dismissed the court and promptly disappeared into his chambers. I glanced at the opposition. They were busying themselves with gathering papers, most likely they were stunned.

As Paul, Steve, Annette, Sandi and I left the courtroom together, Paul clarified for Sandi and me that for a federal judge to rule from the bench was a very rare occurrence. It had been a decisive victory for our side. Steve chimed in, "And for a federal judge to apologize to a defendant? Unheard of!"

We were giddy, all of us. Sixteen months of work, strategy and anxiety were almost over. Judge Kane would still have to rule on whether or not there were past violations, but he had addressed the issue of timing to me personally, so I had faith in him. What a Christmas present!

On February 3rd, I woke with the knowledge that to save my spirit, I must leave my troubled marriage. I was exhausted. Through tears that hadn't stopped in months, I told Steve that I would be gone a week, as a trial separation. We both knew something had to give. A week felt like a stepping-stone. It softened the truth, for all of us. I filled the back of my Subaru with firewood and left my home of twenty-two years.

At a time like this, I needed to be alone. I would stay in Cardinal.

Within hours, my cell phone rang. It was Sandi calling from a ski patrol room in Idaho. Her crying voice had the tone of escalating pain. This is something a mother recognizes immediately.

"I've hurt my knee. I'm out for the rest of the ski season." Her disappointment was as great as the physical pain.

We would find out that it was more than a knee. The femur had come crushing into the top of the fibula, compressing it three inches down and splitting the bone vertically. I couldn't jump on an airplane for Idaho, because I was penniless. I couldn't tell Sandi that I had left home. She would find out later, when she was drugged on Vicodin. Steve and I wouldn't get a real separation with such a crisis. We kept in touch, talking daily, because of Sandi's leg.

I drove to the office of the mine, where Sandi and Harlan had lived the summer before. I felt numb with all that had happened in this day. I moved Peter's old bed from the caretaker's room to the east facing business office, where the woodstove was. The temperature dropped to fifteen below zero that night.

With no insulation, no electricity, no water, a broken daughter and a life in ruins, I kept my wool hat on and sunk deep into my down bag. Every two hours, I woke to stoke the woodstove and I remembered the day before.

I stayed in Cardinal for the week. During that time, I decided to use my business credit card to live and the cash I had in my real estate account to gut the mine office and begin renovation on my new home.

During the course of the Federal suit, the State of Colorado was tried in court, by the Federal Government on my family's dime. The charges were that allegedly, I was not in compliance with the State with Water Discharge Permits. The State Water Quality Control Department had to show that I indeed was in compliance, or it would have reflected poorly upon them. So I found myself allied with the State. I got to know many employees of the Water Quality Control Department on a first name basis.

When Coors Beer was fined for a fish kill over in Clear Creek, the State was required to put the money back in the system. The powers that be recognized an opportunity to right a wrong.

The original wall to the west of the Cardinal Mill had been sixty feet high and forty feet wide. It was built before 1920, and had crumbled in recent years. This had allowed water, which had previously run along a wooden aqueduct across the wall, to enter the Mill, supporting a healthy trout population living inside the Mill.

The State offered to rebuild the wall, rerouting the water with French drains, so that the water would miss the Mill entirely, thereby protecting the citizens downstream from whatever it was that they feared.

An engineer named David Stromm was sent to Cardinal by the State Water Quality Control Department. He would visit the site to determine if his engineering company would be interested in the job of redesigning a wall that the miners had built almost a century ago.

The temperature was below zero and the snowpack was considerably deep. I had managed to keep the road open with the help of Mike Smith's plowing, but it was touch and go. I offered to meet this man in town and drive him to Cardinal.

The first time I met David, it was just three days after the "day from hell", and I was reeling. I put on my tour guide hat, and gave David Stromm and his girlfriend an abbreviated tour. I was hoping no one would notice my distress as I showed them the freezing cold Cardinal Mill. When I drove them back to David's car in Nederland, David left his coat in my back seat.

The next day, I called the phone number for the engineering company and told David that I would bring his coat to Boulder when I was down the hill the next day. He said to be sure to call him out if he was in a meeting. He wanted to say "hi".

One of a dozen errands, I dropped David's coat with his receptionist. Feeling too shy to call him from a meeting to give him his coat, I just left.

Later that day, I had a voice mail saying, "You were supposed to call me out of my meeting!" The message warmed my heart and made me smile. Later, I would reflect on the timing of my meeting David Stromm.

The months of February and March crawled by like a time warp. I left the mine office at night to stay in a house which Steve and I had built to sell on speculation. The house was "under contract", which seemed like a miracle, as the economy had gone totally flat after 9/11 and stayed that way. A gay Hollywood hairdresser would move in by April, so I would take advantage of a place with heat, light and running water while the mine office was being torn apart to become my new home.

A house freshly-built has no heart until someone makes it a home. I had only a futon, a guitar and some books. The contrast between my days in Cardinal and nights in the huge fancy, empty, unfurnished house contributed to the effect of a time warp.

We had still not heard from Judge Kane. As we waited for closure, my family's financial picture went all the rest of the way down the drain. Our credit cards were maxed out, savings gone, and income spotty. As I struggled to refinance debt, our credit report went to hell. Everything Steve and I had ever worked for was gone.

I had four hundred dollars left in my real estate bank account. I decided that since all was now lost, while I was waiting for the final stage of financial crisis to set in, that I had nothing to lose by going to Mexico. If I stayed in Colorado for the week, I would blow through four hundred dollars just staying alive. If I went to Mexico, I'd spend it on perspective. A ticket to Cancun was two hundred and sixty dollars. Hostels could be found in Cancun, Isla Mujeres and Tulum. I took the last of my money from the bank and packed my backpack.

The night before I was to leave, it started to snow. The weatherman promised a big one, so last thing before bed, I shoveled the area in front of the garage using a scrap of plywood as a shovel. I woke in the night and found the snowfall was dumping hard. I woke again at five to shovel. No snowstorm was going to keep me from going to Mexico.

By now, the snow was three feet deep. It took everything I had in me to get that car out. I shoveled for hours using a ski and that piece of plywood. When the neighbors woke up, I borrowed a shovel. Finally, I busted the last drift and made it to the state highway.

My plane ticket was for late afternoon, so I called "Skypilot", my main ski buddy.

"I'm stuck!" he reported. This is a man that has never been stuck in his life. He is a very determined soul.

"I'm out!" I had worked twelve hours to be able to say that! "I started digging last night. I have a ticket to Mexico leaving at four o'clock. I'll come get you and we'll go to the ski area and ski this powder for a bit!"

"It's a plan. I'll walk out to the main road and meet you."

Getting through the state park was touch and go the whole way.

By now, there was four feet of snow. If the car had slowed its steady pace, it would have been stuck for days. I was so glad to get out of the backwoods of Gilpin County. My mental state could not have handled being snowed in at that house with a ticket to Mexico.

By the time I arrived in Lower Coal Creek Canyon, everyone everywhere was stuck. This would become known as the Blizzard of 2003. Skypilot was well past his waist in snow trying to winch his Land Cruiser out using a small tree. But there was nowhere to winch it to. The roads were now blocked and the snow was five and a half feet deep.

We attached the winch to my car and pulled with everything it had. We finally got the Land Cruiser out of the driveway, but all the roads in all directions were closed. It kept on snowing.

We shoveled the roof. We shoveled out the hot tub and the woodpile. We shoveled the front steps. The snow kept coming down. In twenty-eight years of living in these mountains, I had never seen anything like this. It was obvious that I wouldn't be in Mexico that night, so we sat in the hot tub with snow piled higher than we could have imagined all around us.

I was glad to be in Colorado for this storm. It was a once in a lifetime experience, maybe. By the time the snow stopped, it was seven feet deep. In Cardinal, this fell on top of the existing six-foot snowpack already accumulated over the winter.

I was also happy to be with my friend, instead of with cabin fever, alone and hungry in the big empty new house. Skypilot had enough food and wine to keep us. The snow continued for three days. When it finally stopped, I caught the first plane to Cancun, Isla and Tulum.

It was ten days after the big snow that I finally made it back to Cardinal. It skied up the road to find that the southwest corner of the Mill had fallen in and the ridge beam on the west boarding house had collapsed. The amazing part was what was still standing. The steep roof pitches and tin roofs had saved most of the town. I guessed Cardinal would probably last another hundred years.

One thing for sure, when you spend your last four hundred dollars on a trip to Mexico, you don't come home and borrow money. In fact, it was best to bluff to the world that I was fine. Residential real estate deals that I had been incubating looked promising, so feeling like a gambler with nothing else to lose, I holed up in my half finished Mine Office and minded my own business in a very minimalist and solitary way. A payday came along just in time to float me for another brief spell.

APRIL 1, 2003

*I*t was April Fools Day. I was cross-country skiing to a mountain top with my friend, "Skypilot". He had spent the last few months picking me up and dusting me off each time the trauma of life had become more than I could bear. It felt right that we were together when my cell phone rang this time.

It was Paul Phillips saying he had good news. I knew it was no April Fool's joke! The Judge had handed down an Opinion and Order that supported our case entirely. Paul was thrilled. I was stunned. We had won the case at Summary Judgment. The Federal lawsuit was over! This phase of the disaster had finally ended.

It was time to celebrate, at least for a night. The damages chapter was yet to come and a hunch told me it might prove to be the most tedious time. Somehow, I found it hard to believe it would be worse than waiting for the Judge to rule.

One night in mid-April, I share Cardinal's victory with my friends. As I breathe in the scent of two dozen red roses from Paul, my faith in gentlemen and good smells is reaffirmed.

It was a fine dinner celebration. Katie and Bjorn, my water scientists and engineers and my attorney, Paul Phillips, gathered to toast our success. Tales, cheers and roasts over West Denver's best. Paul asked about our lowest low point in this ordeal. As we each told our story, I manifested a high that is higher than the highest high. I can do that, having sung the blues so many times.

This was my idea of a celebration. It's not often in life that one gets to gloat in this manner. Our wine glasses tinkled in tune. By the end of the night, when we all stood, Katie's little boy, Andy, was limp on his Mom's shoulder, three quarters asleep.

"We are headed for the fireworks competition at the School of Mines", sang Rick and Katie, as if Andy might have another round in him.

Our kisses cascade around us and we part. I drive toward Golden and

DC Bot6
FILED
United States District Court
Denver, Colorado

IN THE UNITED STATES DISTRICT COURT
FOR THE DISTRICT OF COLORADO
Judge John L. Kane

APR 0 1 2003

JAMES R. MANSPEAKER, CLERK

By_____
Deputy Clerk

Civil Action No. 01-K-2182

CITIZENS ALLIANCE FOR THE PROTECTION OF CARIBOU,

Plaintiff,

v.

NEW CARDINAL, LLC,

Defendant.

MEMORANDUM OPINION AND ORDER

Kane, J.

This citizen suit under the Clean Water Act ("CWA"), 33 U.S.C. §§ 1251-1387, is

before me on the parties' cross-motions for summary judgment. For the reasons stated

below, I grant Defendant's motion for summary judgment and deny Plaintiff's motions.

I.

The following facts are undisputed by the parties unless otherwise stated:[1]

---

[1]   These undisputed facts include statements of fact asserted by Defendant,
with supporting citations to the record, to which Plaintiff claimed ignorance or which it
evaded or otherwise failed to admit or deny with supporting evidence as required by Fed.
R. Civ. P. 56 and Section V of this court's memorandum regarding pretrial and trial
procedures. *See, e.g.,* Fed. R. Civ. P. 56(d) (once moving party carries burden,
nonmovant must respond and set forth specific facts showing there is a genuine issue of
fact for trial); *Conway v. Smith,* 853 F.2d 789, 794 (10th Cir. 1988) (party cannot rest on
ignorance of facts in response to motion for summary judgment); *Stegall v. Great
American Ins. Co.,* 996 F. Supp. 1060, 1063 n.1 (D. Kan. 1998) ("when plaintiff claims
that she cannot admit or deny, the facts set forth by defendants are deemed admitted for

COURT ORDER

the School of Mines. I see nothing but glory all around me. As I pull up to the
stoplight, where the canyon meets the prairie, a flash of light explodes, followed
by three big booms. I look at the girl driving the car next to mine, and we smile
at each other, thumbs up.

I park on the hill nearby to watch the fireworks. It is with amazement
that I study this hybrid of miners and engineers.

AUTHOR'S MOTHER AT CARDINAL IN MAY, 2004

This year's pyrotechnic engineers could be declared legally insane. A thousand feet up, rockets burst into sunbursts over the college. A crowd is centered around a spot which emanates repeating booms. A fury of spermazoa lights dance up toward the exploding heavens. Roaring lawn lights have bred into turbo blasters. Intense sparkling twinkles float below. The firepower is well beyond most Fourth of Julys.

There blazes an "M" for the School of Mines on the mountainside above the town. The miners I have come to know have an especially rich heritage and this school is out to prove it tonight.

I dance to music outside my car, cradling my flowers in my arms. I am breathing the bouquet of gunsmoke and roses. Powerful explosions continue for ages. My mind is blown by the pure experience of celebration. I have been in good hands and for that I am humbled and grateful.

When it is over, my car heads north toward Coal Creek Canyon. Lightning is flashing and electric bolts splinter to the ground. Nature takes over where the fireworks left off. It begins to snow harder than I have ever seen, and I've been to Wyoming. Cosmic action is at hand. The snow in the headlights resembles fireworks as the visuals intensify. Yes, this is the kind of storm I will never fly into. This is when you chant Su-ba-ru and rely on a driving method carefully honed on mountain roads. Driving in this snowstorm is a warp of space and time.

The mesas in blizzard crown wide-reaching valleys. I know this area. It is where the Utes once camped among the giant cottonwoods which line the creek. In my mind's eye, I drink in an image of that pastoral scene, then I picture it in the snow with teepees closed tightly.

The snowstorm has a distinct edge, and my senses are shocked as my car emerges out the other side into clear skies and starlight. The mountains are illuminated in soft moonlight. My excitement is slowly and sweetly turning into peace as I reach the dirt road that takes me home.

The next time David Stromm came to Cardinal, it had turned to early spring. He brought several engineers and geologists with him. We spent the afternoon touring Cardinal, with me sharing both past and recent history. At the end of the day, we were discussing the only existing photograph of the old wall and the men mentioned that they had not received a copy of the photo. I believed that I had a copy in the mine office, my half finished home.

By this time, Ed's workers had gutted the office and begun to reframe the interior. All of the demolition trash was lying in the snow out front. I had moved everything I owned into the back bedroom, which was newly framed and sheet rocked. That room was my entire home.

The original stone wall at the Cardinal Mill
Carnegie Branch Library for Local History, Boulder Historical Society Collection

I walked toward the Office at a brisk pace, full of intention. I would find these men a copy of the picture so that they could imagine what they would be designing. Suddenly, I was aware that someone was following along with me. It was David Stromm. We began to chat. David asked me if I was going to rent the mine office out when it was done. I was embarrassed enough to crawl in a hole.

As we stepped into the building, I volunteered, "No, I have recently left my marriage and I am living here." I cringed at the idea of him seeing my meager possessions crammed in the room with a crummy old bed in the middle. I blundered around lifting stacks of file folders, knowing that normally I'd have found the picture in an instant. I couldn't find it. David put me at ease by saying "When I moved out of my house, I lived out of my car for weeks.'" So he was divorced.

When the men were ready to leave, I mentioned to all of them that should they need to come through the gate for further work, there was a lock box with the combination 1957, the year I was born.

A voice came from the crowd, "That was a good year."

"For what?" I asked, confused.

"That was the year I was born." David Stromm smiled at me.

So he was my age and divorced. My clouds were beginning to thin enough that I actually took notice of this handsome man, and smiled back.

Each month, I must test the water at Cardinal and report the results to the State. During the course of the lawsuit, it was necessary to pay professional water engineers to take the samples, keeping a chain of custody as the samples made their way between Cardinal and the lab. Over time, the engineers trained me to do the job, so that the cost would only be lab fees when the suit was over. Now, it was my job to test. The lab fees amounted to over a thousand dollars each month.

I crack the ice from around what I refer to as the "offending pipe", an old ceramic pipe delivering my drinking water from the Boulder County Tunnel. I stick a bucket underneath and using a stop watch, I time the rate of flow three times and take an average of the numbers. I test the temperature. I test the PH, which is always perfect. I fill several little plastic bottles that have come to me shipped from the lab, blessed as clean and viable.

After testing the pipe, now named 001A, I test 002C, at a site down below the Mill in Coon Track Creek. I park my car near Tina's house. I cuss and swear at the house as I pull gallon bottles from the cooler, which is iced and ready for the run to the labs in Denver.

To get to the site 002C, I have put on my full snow gear, including skis. I bush whack through tight pines in snow that is easily six feet deep. When I have tread a path through the willows and pines to the creek, I look for my mark on a tree to be sure I've got the spot. Side stepping my skis carefully downward, I cascade with a ton of snow about fifteen feet vertically until I am standing in the creek on a platform of snow that I have brought with me. One by one I fill the bottles.

Climbing back out is always an adventure. Even where I have descended, the snow avalanches down on me as I try to climb up. I hold the gallon jugs, two in each hand, and thump them above me into the snow, using their weight as leverage to pull my weight upward. This test of endurance, balance and experience uses a unique set of skills, which I have managed to acquire in my lifetime. It makes me wonder, what if it wasn't me? How would this be getting done? What if I couldn't get out of the hole? If I never came back, would anyone miss me before the samples were overdue?

I claw my way back up the hill to my car, swearing up at Tina's deck the whole way. I allow myself this indulgence of verbal diarrhea once a month, whether it's Buddhist of me or not. I put the water samples in the cooler and skis in the back of the car, shed six layers of clothing, and crank the defrost on high. Off I go to the labs in Denver.

To get to the first lab, I drive down Coal Creek Canyon and skirt the foothills into Golden. I can smell hops where they are making Coors Beer. I head east into the fray.

At the lab, I hope the right hand doesn't know what the left is doing. As I sign the chain of custody form for the receiver, I watch him anxiously, expecting him to say, "I don't believe your invoice was paid last month. We can't accept these samples, mam."

I'm prepared to tell him of the fines I face from the state if my report isn't in on time. In my apoplexy, I fumble with two credit cards in my pocket, wondering if either of them might work. But he cheerfully takes my samples, signs the receipt and wishes me a fabulous day. What kind of look must he see on my face? That crazed woman that comes in once a month, looking for heavy metals in perfectly clean water. Next, I run the gauntlet across the city to the far-east side, to the second lab, where they will put several live species of minnows and water fleas in Coon Track Creek water for 72 hours. Not only will they thrive beautifully, at the cost of three hundred and fifty dollars, but they will be fruitful and multiply. I go through the same nervous meltdown over credit here too. Paul has stressed that I should always pay the labs before anyone else. Without the reports, our case is lost. I'm doing my best.

By now, it's lunchtime. I eat my peanut butter and jelly sandwich, refill the gas tank and head back to the hills.

This is an exercise in futility. There must be something I am learning; some gain which is too subtle for me to glean. I search for purpose, but come up completely stumped each time; patience. That is as close as I can come.

The lab results will come in the mail. I will transpose the numbers from mg/l to ug/l, compile them on the reporting sheets, and then make multiple copies so they can take up file space at Holland & Hart, the Water Quality Control Department of the State and in my ever growing pile of white banker's boxes in Cardinal. When I'm done mailing them out, another whole day has passed. I give two days a month for more than five years to this strange meditation.

When the task is completed each time, I surrender bitterness toward Tina and Dennis with a grand symbolic exhale, and thank the powers that be for delivering me safely from the bowels of Denver to my beautiful mountain home.

Following the ruling by the Honorable Judge Kane, there was to be a settlement conference. Both sides would offer to settle the damages out of court. The Magistrate Judge had warned the Plaintiffs not to schedule the Federal Court's time if they were not bringing six figures or better to the table.

For New Cardinal's part, we had to show good will. At the same time, having prevailed, we were in the position to expect damages. New Cardinal had to hire an independent attorney, for many more thousands of dollars, to ratify that our request of litigation and expert witness fees was legitimate.

As the day of the settlement conference approached, I was fearful that the Citizen's Alliance would offer one hundred thousand dollars and that the Judge would see that as a sufficient amount. An underpayment would leave me owing Holland & Hart and the engineers so much money that I doubted I could repay it in my lifetime.

If the Cardinal project had been allowed to proceed without the lawsuit, I would have paid six hundred thousand dollars to develop a property that would have been worth a million and a quarter. Instead, Steve and I were now three quarters of a million dollars in the hole.

I had continually reassessed my moves throughout the course of events. Many times I had considered what I might have done differently. I have never been able to figure that out.

If I had not hired attorneys, would the corporate shield have protected me from the State's fines for an old mine without permits? Not likely. I knew I was too principled to simply give Tina and Dennis the property, although then I might have been able to walk away. With the pending lawsuit, the County would never have taken the land.

Had there been no suit filed, this would have been a successful project. The fact that there was no pollution in Cardinal when the Citizen's Alliance filed the suit had long been disclosed.

On the day of the settlement conference, Steve Black and I walked to the Federal Court House. I repeated my mantra to myself... the Cardinal Mill and Open Space are saved.

We were ushered into a small conference room. The settlement conference would be a mediation session. The Plaintiffs were in one room and the Defendants in another. On a side table were little toys. They were of the stress reducing variety, a spongy squeeze ball, a foot-massaging roller, worry stones, a Mickey Mouse.

As we sat for what seemed like ages. We chatted about Steve's upcoming wedding plans, but all the while, Cardinal loomed in front of my thoughts, I tried to remember the excitement and anticipation of a new relationship. Hope is always a good thing. It is the seed for manifestation.

Magistrate Judge Boland entered the room without fanfare or flourish. We rose to acknowledge him and he put us at ease. He was a gentle soul. He would be approachable. Boland quickly got to the point.

"The plaintiff's attorney has not graced us with his presence today." he said.

Steve Black looked at Boland in complete disbelief.

"I beg your pardon, Your Honor?"

Steve doesn't miss a thing. The Magistrate knows this.

"That would be professional suicide!" Steve blurted.

The Magistrate heartily agreed. "And he never called to tell us his mother died, or something of that nature. He has simply decided this wasn't important, I gather."

"Furthermore," Boland offered, "The plaintiffs have offered six thousand dollars for a settlement." He gave that a moment to sink in.

"Your Honor, there is a lot of history to this case," began Steve.

"I am very aware of that, Mr. Black. I have had the opportunity to read the material."

"I don't suppose that sounds like a settlement to you!" Boland added.

All three of us sat in disbelief.

"This makes my job rather simple today, doesn't it?" the Magistrate began. "Can you shed some light on who these individuals are? Obviously, some of them have played a more active role than others."

It was my turn to talk. I described the first meetings with Tina and Dennis. I explained how the local newspaper fanned the flames with misinformation, reinforcing fear of environmental concerns among Caribou Road residents. These people jumped in righteously to save their beloved valley. They were guilty of ignorance. They took Tina's bait; hook, line and sinker. And the extras, the dreadlocked twenty-somethings, who had been involved in the community garden, were drifters who didn't even have post office boxes.

As the morning wore on, the story unfolded once again, until the conversation strayed into sports, families and Denver politics. There was no lunch. In the afternoon, Magistrate Judge Boland said, "I guess I could let the other side go now. This matter will be referred back to Judge Kane to consider an award of damages."

He encouraged us to rise and follow him out. Across the hall, Boland opened the door and six members of the Citizen's Alliance entered the hallway. I looked at Dennis and Tina if they were objects, not people, to insulate me from emotion. The others looked vaguely familiar to me. I could guess which of these neighbors fit the names of the Alliance members.

Steve and I walked back to Holland & Hart. It was so amazing that John Barth had not graced the conference with his presence. And just as incredible, the plaintiffs had the nerve to offer only six thousand dollars.

With Judge Kane's track record, I never expected a decision on damages to be swift. It was several weeks later that word traveled through the legal community of Denver. Judge Kane had been diagnosed with breast cancer. He would be taking a year off to get well. No one else would be assigned to take his cases. We would have to wait.

Susan and I were doing aerobics together, therapy for the body and mind. I answered a cell phone call. It was David Stromm. It had been two months since he'd been to visit the mine. David was mumbling something about locating the old picture of the wall, but it seemed he wasn't making much sense to me. I interrupted his thoughts, trying to clarify his question. He said he forgot what he wanted to ask. I chatted on about the beautiful day, and springtime and such, and then said, "Now do you remember what you wanted to ask me?"

David said, "I wanted to ask you out to lunch."

When I hung up the phone, my eyes were bugging out of my head. My mouth was wide with a smile.

"What?" asked Susan, laughing at my excitement. "What?"

"He asked me out to lunch! What will I wear?" I was forty-five years old, and I had never been asked on a true date in my life.

Minutes before our first date, I rented a fiddle. I was thinking that if I was going to live all by myself in the middle of nowhere, I might as well squeak and squawk on a fiddle. It was something I had always wanted to do. Twenty bucks a month, which I could hardly justify, except that it was an opportunity of a lifetime to me. As I signed up for the fiddle, my brother's old friend took his sweet time getting the paper work together. He flirted and flitted, barely taking his eyes off me. I decided at that moment that I must be emitting a strong pheromone. And it was going to make me late for my date!

I threw the fiddle in the car and raced to the Masa Grill. There was David, a sweet smile, with a remarkable calm about him. He was waiting patiently. I was blushing before we even spoke.

The first thing he asked me was "Did I play a musical instrument?" Being a three-chord guitar player, I said, "No." It was only extremely awkward that I had to say, "but I have a fiddle roasting in the car. Excuse me while I bring it in!"

He tilted his head to one side amused, and smiled. David has a gentle manner about him. That was the quality, which stole my heart.

I felt my heart go sliding down a tube, straight into a deep ocean of love. I had no intention of hooking up with a man. I reminded myself, pay no mind, you dispense love freely. He's just a guy. But in the months to follow, when I was with David, time warped. It slowed and stood perfectly still in fantastic moments of sensuality. Time disappeared in a dream essence when we spent nights together. David's tender, considerate nature cast a magic spell on me.

Life always offers me a balance. And the tribulations of the lawsuit would exact something magnificent. It seemed that my moments with David sparkled with a clarity that was bright light, reassuring me that all is divine and perfect. This new relationship gave me the opportunity to be the spirit I had fought so hard to save; an opportunity to manifest love and grace.

On one of our first dates, David came to Cardinal for a walk. He warned me that his knee was a bit fussy. He had to mind it, but I walked him up the hill to Old Cardinal anyway. When I realized my mistake, I panicked and sat us in a most unlikely spot in the forest to eat our picnic. David looked at me as if I was a wild animal and remarked that I seemed so comfortable in nature.

I agreed, knowing that nature is part of me and I could never leave it. David would not be able to imagine the places I'd been and the number of days of wilderness that I had so fortunately passed over the course of my half spent life.

It took many careful steps to get David off the mountain that day. When he drove away, despite his enduring good nature, I thought he'd never be back.

David did come back. And I in my turn visited his home in Boulder, a place where water and electricity ran effortlessly.

Once or twice a week, we began to share our respective lives. It tasted like candy to me. We giggled, and talked and shared long luxurious silences. It had been a very long time since I had been able to relax and enjoy myself. Like a bath in heaven must feel, my troubles were washed away when I was with David.

One morning at the end of June, just after the summer solstice, I stayed in bed until eight. I was enjoying my new home and my solitude. I had awakened at dawn and propped myself up with many pillows to read. It had been decades since I had stayed in bed this way. I thought of all the work I've had to do, work that was now done. I thought of my kids off in Idaho, grown enough to need distance between themselves and their mother. I thought of the many mornings that I left my bed early to squeeze in a long run before working all day, knowing it wouldn't happen otherwise. I remember the times I rose in the dark to fly Delta Poppa at daybreak, heading east over the high prairie before the sun would come up and heat the summer day.

I sat in my bed savoring this feeling of work done and wondered if this would be the satisfaction when one is truly old. I looked out of the tall Victorian windows with their wavy glass. They frame a green jungle of growth that can only exist four months of the year at this elevation. The light and colors danced as the aspens blew in the morning breeze. I was sitting in an impressionistic painting; a mountain Monet which has magically come to life, a study done in yellow, white and green.

I was enjoying the whole cabin from the bed. I love my little yellow kitchen which sits in the morning sun on the east side of the house. I think of the old window glass with air bubbles in my son's bedroom. I enjoy the image of my living room, the flames dancing in the woodstove offering year round coziness at 9000 feet. And as I sat propped up in my big spindle bed, I wondered who lived here for the forty years that this house was occupied. Wouldn't they be tickled to see me here now, the walls reframed from the original office, the old floors sanded and refinished. Everything is freshly painted, windows washed, wildflowers in vases. New life breathed in. And all paid for on credit cards. I'm thinking a woman can love a cabin more than a man.

People look at me in amazement when they hear that I am living in Cardinal with no electricity or running water. It's not something that makes me proud. I can do it. I had to do it for years on end when I was in my twenties. It takes a lot of time and effort is all. I am lucky to have wonderful water flowing from the pipe from the mine year round. In the summer, I have an old bathtub beside the creek. In the winter, there is a basin and pitcher. My trusty wood-stove burns so well you think there was someone else tending it for me. A spicket pot on the woodstove keeps hot water ready at all times. I cook on my propane camp stove. Mostly, I miss having an oven to bake breads and cookies.

In the evening, I light the lamps and candles. I am careful to never leave them unattended. The soft mellow glow calms my spirit. I play my fiddle in the dim light, and read by headlamp before falling asleep. What I really love is how brightly the stars shine at night, when the eyes have not been spoiled by electric light.

My little mine office is a perfect home for me. Perhaps I was meant to have this time, living in the style of the 1800's, to make me slow down, reflect and consider all the changes I have experienced in the past few years. Determined to love life, I won't waste a day in sorrow. When pain comes to me, I see it through, allowing myself to feel it fully, knowing this too shall pass. The shimmering aspen trees outside my bedroom window are enough of a miracle for me.

With the Clean Water Suit closed, I began anew the search for financing Cardinal. I spent my time working with loan companies, in vain. My credit was slipping, due to bills unpaid as I had awaited a ruling from the Judge. The local real estate economy had gone flat. Banks were not lending for construction.

Our local banker had pulled out in April, siting environmental complications, combined with a poor economy. His promise of a loan when the lawsuit was over had carried me through the winter. Now I struggled to not take this decision personally. Where was the support for a vision, which was good for our community?

The next most likely candidate was a private lending firm, who touted its self on lending "out of the box". For weeks, I had pumped information to Amir Singh. He seemed increasingly satisfied. By the fourth week, he made the trip to Cardinal from south Denver. He had been working full time on this project, and I was encouraged.

When he stepped out of his car in thin Italian loafers, I was glad it was a warm day in May. Amir had always been very proper and polite. I had appreciated this as we had spent endless hours on the phone. Now, he toured Cardinal with his hands clasped together, looking like he was afraid that the dust and time would soil him. History was lost on him. The buildings appeared to be shacks. In his wildest dreams, Amir could not imagine living in Cardinal.

In the end, it was the stack of paper that held the legal wrangling which was cited as the reason that Amir's company could not make the loan. That, and I'm sure, the mining shacks and my outhouse were a far cry from Amir's idea of a good investment. I felt the summer building season slipping away, as it had just begun.

I left for the mighty Yampa River to gather my forces and try again. I was basking in love and the companionship of my river family. The river soothed my soul from the moment my boat pushed off the bank.

As I floated through the Yampa's sandstone canyon, I reflected that each attempt at a loan had taught me something. The experience with Amir made me aware that I must focus on the environmental suit with potential lenders more heavily from the start. But now, I was out of leads for money. On the river, a person can have the perspective that money doesn't matter, and only love is real.

The Yampa River carried my rubber raft downstream. It took me on a path of least resistance. Sometimes my boat hung on obstacles. Sometimes I worked too hard, in vain, to make my way. The biggest water flushed me along nicely. The flat water gave me a choice, to persistently row forward or to float. I watched Jeff, whose nature it is to push. He rowed his days away in his sixteen-foot bucket boat. In contrast, there was Craig, who had refined the art of floating with nary a stroke. I decided I was somewhere in between. The river was an analogy. The struggles in Cardinal seemed more manageable when I could go with the flow.

The river days past blissfully, resetting my life with perspective. My eyes feasted on the spring green foliage that grows along this desert river. Features of rock and river occupy our interest. Time becomes irrelevant when one lives each day in the moment. Nights are precious under the stars, with the river singing a lullaby to sooth my soul. The laughing and smiles of my friends are the greatest gift of all. I return to Cardinal, with a renewed focus and recharged energy.

The Calvary Chapel in Nederland posts messages from our Higher Power on the light up message board out front. Sometimes I drive by and shake my head, but often the advice happens to ring so true that I can't help but wonder. This time, it reads "Extraordinary challenges are accompanied by extraordinary gifts." I marvel at this truth in my life every day. I imagine that the person working at Mac Donald's scoffs as he drives past this particular light up aphorism, but this balance of gifts in my life sustains me.

SPRING 2003

I have a new plan. I am willing to sell the compressor house to raise capital for the infrastructure. When the infrastructure is in, conventional lenders would consider me for construction loans. In the meantime, I continue to pray for the real estate market to make a come back. But it doesn't. After years of making money hand over fist, contracts are now hard to come by. All of the local realtors whisper the same news to me. We have plenty of listings, but no one is buying.

All the while, I pursue private financing, through old family friends and new connections offering hope. But the interested parties drag their feet too slowly to be serious. Every bit of cash I could conjure through real estate went to floating the loans on Cardinal. I had stopped telling my kids that they'd get new shoes or their teeth cleaned when the Cardinal loan came through. Another month blew by.

By June of '03, I am unable to pay bills or buy food again. I learn that I am proud to a fault. My dear friend Susie has been in my shoes. I confide in her, and she brings me a care package; a box of food that gets carefully rationed. Never having been in this position before, I am greatly humbled and thankful.

When I date David, I am too shy to tell him how badly things have deteriorated. I look forward to our time together to escape this reality. Our relationship is too new to burden it with such issues. I want him to get to know me for who I am, without the Cardinal disaster defining me.

I only see my son once a week, when he will meet me for pizza in Nederland. I haven't a dime to buy pizza, but I have saved my last bit of credit on my Visa card for our visits. He wants no part of my new life in Cardinal. He is angry with me for my leaving home and I can't blame him. His newly done bedroom in my home goes empty except for guests. I can hardly call it Peter's room. I am feeling very alone.

As if by extra-sensory perception, my dear friend Larry comes to Cardinal when I have reached my lowest point. We ride our bikes up to the top of Caribou, boosting my seratonin levels out of the suicide range. As we pedal up the steep climb, he sings me our favorite Neil Young songs. I marvel at his energy and light. He saves my psyche. When Larry leaves at the end of the day, I feel my heart has been rescued. Larry takes a copy of my manuscript so far. My writing has been my therapy.

My friends and their love are holding me together at the seams. Andy and Wendy loan me two thousand dollars so I can keep my car and buy gas. Roy and Rosa bolster me with encouragement, wine and cheese in their magic rock outcrop. Susan listens patiently and endlessly. Skypilot feeds me dinner with a movie. Bob's faith in me is beyond my wildest imagination, and he makes sure I don't go hungry. Sandy Cook's consistent love reminds me it will all be okay.

I find fifty dollars in the lock box at the gate. Another fifty mysteriously slips through my kitchen window onto the floor. I know who is helping me, and I thank them with love and appreciation.

But the changes in my life are overwhelming. I miss my children, and I worry that I can no longer provide for them. At the same time that I feel greatly relieved, I am devastated by my failed marriage. Everything I touch seems to fall apart. Again I reach bottom. My spirit is feeling thin and exhausted. I drag myself through the motions that might or might not save my business.

Music always soothes my soul, so I go to the Folk Festival in Lyons to dance. Among the crowd, I find David Stromm, accompanied by his old girl-friend. As if this is not enough of a blow, he walks right by me without as much as a hello. This pain in my heart hurts more than I could have imagined. I try my best to be strong, to understand, but it doesn't add up. Later, when we talk, he excuses himself saying she is very depressed over their break up. I find out there's more. In the weeks to come, I see her car parked at his house as I fly the downwind leg of the airport pattern. I must abandon hope for a relationship with this man who had brought me such joy. My heart can risk no more pain. From now on I will protect it more carefully.

Larry calls from his home in Breckenridge.

"I had no idea what you have been through until I read your writing!" he cries. He sputters magnificent words of amazement as only my friend Larry can do.

I realize this is true, for my communication with others has had to be limited. It has been all I could do for several years now, just to keep moving forward. There has been no extra energy to explain. There has been no place to begin, and no end in sight.

When I venture out, I try to act normally. I can no longer be honest in my relationships. I must represent myself as all right in order to keep an image which will not scare others.

"I'm coming over. We will ride...and I'm bringing lunch." He promises.

How does he sense when I am as low as I can go? With his relentless optimism, Larry saves my spirit again.

On Thursdays, I walk to the Continental Divide with my lady friends. I have little to contribute to the conversations about family and travel, and they can't conceive of my situation. But I am grateful for the company of these women who have shared so much of my life. We hike up to the snow to picnic where the rocks meet the sky.

On one hike, an old teaching partner asks me about real estate investments. We discover that the Compressor House suits the needs of her family. They are looking for a garage to use as a workshop and the sale of the Compressor House would mean an infrastructure for the town.

A visit to Cardinal confirms this. I am elated. They share my vision of historic preservation. They love the property and its location. Their enthusiasm bubbles over and brings my hope along. I keep moving forward, racing the clock of shortening days. Legal documents are drafted and reviewed at great expense to both parties. We progress through inspection, title work and disclosures.

Feeling encouraged, I using airline miles acquired from too many dollars spent on credit cards to visit my family at the lake in Ontario, Canada. My parents relax as they see that my spirits are up. I am able to be positive. I am pleased that I am not adding worries to their lives, as they meet their biggest challenge yet, aging together. With the lawsuit won, and a financial prospect on the table, they share my hope and excitement. Together, we enjoy two weeks of love and laughter. My family's cottage at the lake has been a respite from the world for four generations. From my little sleeping cabin on the lakeshore, I am lulled to sleep by the gentle tingeing of the rigging of our sailboat at anchor. Loons call to each other in the night. I am rested and renewed.

But, upon my return, my illusion of relief is shattered. I receive news that the Compressor House deal has died. In the eleventh hour, an attorney advised my friends that the risk of a potential water quality violation fines from the State of Colorado was too high. Uncertainty and potential fines kept these buyers awake at night. Heartbroken, they cancelled their plan. I understand fear of water violations all too well. I had danced that dance until that particular fear was dismissed in court.

In reality, everything environmental that could happen in Cardinal, already had.

It would not be wise to have people in Cardinal who would be anxious. But, there went the cash that would have built the infrastructure and turned the townsite around. Five more weeks of building season had slipped me by. My soul went another level deeper learning acceptance.

My next creative idea was to find someone willing to cosign a loan, independent of Cardinal. I pretty quickly realize that no one but family might be willing. The only family who would be able is my Boulder brother, Matt. He has always tried to help me in this endeavor by offering counsel. Matt also shares my fascination for history. For Matt, the Switzerland Trail Railroad has been a personal passion.

We sit outside the business office of the mine, watching Matt's children play, drinking a beer, and discussing the possibility of cosigning a loan. In the end, I remind myself of the pitfalls of mixing business and family. It would be too much to ask Matt's wife, Susie, to be involved in something as uncertain as Cardinal. It is not a risk that Matt and I can take.

Suddenly, as if a light bulb has gone on in his head, Matt remembered a private lender, Chuck Miller, whom he had encountered in a railroad restoration project. Matt produced a dog eared business card from his wallet. I have another lead to pursue. It is now mid August, and I have already noticed my first yellow aspen leaf. Another building season has slipped me by.

The day Chuck Miller first came to Cardinal was a sunny fall day. The aspens were bright yellow and the sky was azure. It was absolutely the last possible chance for building this year. Quite possibly, it was too late.

As Chuck stepped out of his little Audi, I thought of Amir Singh with his fine leather loafers on the rocks. Another shot at another lender. What the heck, I had everything to lose and nothing better to do. I tried hard to stay positive.

This man wore a pleasant little smile on his face. He appeared intrigued. It was his ethereal nature that struck me immediately. His spirit seemed to be marked by an unusual delicacy and refinement.

As we shook hands, I silently said a prayer, asking that Chuck Miller could possibly be the man to save Cardinal from financial doom. So far, there had been a team of very special people. I flashed on Paul Phillips, Mike Sawyer, Katie Fendel, the Canadian in Chilliwack, Steve Black and John Bergren. Could

Mr. Miller be part of this chain of significant people?

I started the tour that I had given so many times before. This time, I consciously included the details of the siege of the "environmentalists". Beginning with the history of the area, a profile of the Bergren family, and the acquisition of the property, I unfolded the tale that had brought Cardinal this far. Chuck Miller looked amused. But he didn't say anything.

As we walked around the townsite, I sensed that Mr. Miller had an appetite for the natural beauty of the valley. He seemed to relax into the experience. Every once in a while he gave a little chuckle, almost a giggle. This charmed me.

Our visit lasted four hours. As Chuck Miller drove away, I realized I really didn't have a sense for what might happen. There are moments when one totally lets go of the outcome. Surrender and release. It wasn't long before a phone call came.

"I think I'd like to help you out up there." he said.

My building permits were already in place. My subcontractor's were hungry enough due to the slow economy. We went to work, racing the winter, as fast as we could. You have never seen anyone as excited as I was. Chuck Miller saved me personally as well, with his loan providing a contractor's fee for my pay. For the first time in ages, I was able to temporarily relax about daily living expenses.

Each day, the workers fired up gas powered compressors, as the Public Service Company would need a few months of lead time. We dug up the townsite, poured concrete, laid in septic pipes, drilled wells. And true winter held off, as if it was just waiting for Cardinal to be done. By the time the first serious snowfall blanketed the townsite, Chris had finished framing the additions, windows were set, and the roofs on the Office and Assay Office were dried in. I was well on my way to having running water and a real bathroom.

I continued to date David Stromm while the work proceeded in Cardinal. But it was different. I was so guarded. It is my nature to forgive, and I figured he was out there learning with the rest of us. He promised he was on a search now for himself, and I gave him a wide berth, being sure to keep my own personal and spiritual growth a priority. Don't gamble more than you are willing to lose. I didn't consider him fit to meet my Mother when she arrived on December.

The first Christmas in Cardinal in sixty two years was a vision I had held in my mind's eye from the very beginning of my discovering the Townsite. My imagination had conjured an image with cabin windows lit up by electricity. Each house in the cluster would shine with colored Christmas tree lights, standing as a sign of peace and the return of life to Cardinal. Interestingly, Christmas 2003 was to be much like it would have been one hundred years ago.

From the street at night, only one cabin showed signs of life. A flickering low warm light glowed from the within. The light of lamps and candles is a mellow light, not bright enough to detract from the starlight in the night sky. The only sound to be heard was the winter wind when it would blow off the Continental Divide, whisk overhead the Mine Office, and hit full force at the Cardinal Mill.

My Christmas tree was a narrow fir, chosen to reach to the ceiling but not take up the room. It had been removed from a spot in the forest where I intended to cross-country ski. It would have stood in the path. On the day that I cut it, I was feeling the slight touch of a flu that was ravaging the Front Range. I had decided that if I was going to get full-blown sick, I would like to be resting by my Christmas tree. As I trudged slowly up the old wagon trail toward Caribou, bow saw in hand, I thought of the influenza epidemics that took so many people from these mountains years ago. Now, people recover because their bodies are fortified by nutrition, the modern conveniences of daily life allow for rest and antibiotics. I willed that germ away,

I decorated this tall thin tree with gold beads and tinsel garlands to give it sparkle. It was dressed with ornaments from my years of being a kindergarten teacher. Two small strings of lights ran on four "C" batteries that could be turned on for a little while in the evening. Candy canes hung from the branches waiting for children to visit. My kittens watched with curiosity as I decorated. A pale sadness hung on me as I was aware that this was my first Christmas without my own little family. I was sad for my husband Steve, who had lost his Mother the Christmas before.

When the tree was complete, I laid on the couch, visualizing the love that the Christmas season celebrates. My mother was coming to Colorado to see my brother's new baby and stay for Christmas. The frenzy of work in the townsite would slow, and I would have a chance to appreciate the progress. I looked forward to skiing and being with friends, so many reasons to stay well. I closed my eyes and focused on my lovely home, my strong healthy body, and all of the love in my life.

Cardinal was dusted with fresh snow regularly and the Switzerland Trail on the north facing side of the valley held a snowpack for cross-country skiing. With the length of the days being so short in December and full of work, I often skied at sunset, arriving back at the cabin after dark. Rosy cheeked, I would light each lamp. I would make a wish, or say a prayer for Judge Kane, as I lit each candle. The house would glow in soft light as I poked the fire and stoked it up. Outside, winter would play wildly through the night.

On the twenty third of December, I left my mother painting the new bathroom, and headed to Denver to refinance the cabin in Gold Hill. Legal debt from Cardinal saddled the Gold Hill property so that it wouldn't cash flow, and the predicament gave me waves of nausea when I thought about it. To compound my discomfort, my ruined credit had made it very difficult to get the loan, so I had been struggling for four months to get to this closing.

I expected to sign the documents and be back to Cardinal directly, but the lender wasn't prepared. It took three and a half hours to close the deal. As I jumped the last remaining hoops for the lender, I received a phone call from my insurance company. They were cancelling the insurance on Cardinal because there had been an excavation machine in the digital house picture emailed by the insurance surveyor. I frantically made calls to understand this situation and remedy it. In between phone calls, Steve and I jockeyed over divorce obligations and paperwork. By the time I had beaten my way through Christmas traffic and escaped the city, I was fit to be tied. There seemed to be no end to the trouble Tina and Dennis had caused. Refinancing lawsuit debt against the Gold Hill cabin had me frosted.

As I drove into Cardinal my troubles came back into perspective. It always amazes me that when I enter the townsite a peace and calm returns to my soul. When I approached the cabin, I was greeted by rows of newly cut wood stacked neatly on the deck. My buddy, River Randy, had come up from the city and brought me this gift. Inside the house, my mother stood proudly showing me her handiwork. The new bathroom gleamed with beige paint. Once again, I was struck by the constant balance I am given in my life. Light poured into my heart and I felt so loved and cared for.

My Mom told me all about the day, the comings and goings of the different workers, progress reports, details. The terrific visit she'd had with Randy, and how they had stacked the wood together and shared a beer. Then she said, "And Lex, there's been a new development. I didn't want to tell you when you've had such a day, but I think you need to know... the water pipe ran dry when the Public Service Company sunk the power pole to the east of the Mill. The water is gone." She cringed.

I stared at my mother in disbelief. The pipe that was subject of the Federal Clean Water Act Suit had virtually no flow. This pipe had run from the mine consistently for the four years that I had owned the property, just as it had run for decades. It had run through subzero temperatures and the one hundred year drought.

This seemed highly unlikely, impossible! A Christmas miracle had happened in Cardinal. For an instant, I felt the presence of a higher power laughing hysterically, and then I joined in. My Mom, who had been hauling our household water to the cabin from the pipe all week, looked confused. But the look on my face explained it all. This was not bad news, but good. Beyond good, incredible. If the water never flowed again, there would be no perpetual water quality control testing of the offending pipe 001A. The subject of the Clean Water Act Suit had dried up.

I had spent hundreds of thousands of dollars and too many hours to keep this fantastically clean drinking water tested for the State of Colorado. Now, I would report by simply checking a box on the state form marked "No discharge".

Christmas brought singing, feasting and skiing with family and friends. I cooked a turkey in the new propane fired oven. Lamp and candlelight offered a taste of Christmases past. Slowly but surely, Cardinal was coming back to life.

In January, I started seeing more and more of David Stromm. It seemed he had worked through his stuff with Julie. He seemed stronger about it, with a definite resolve. I was delighted while still guarding my heart.

The Public Service workers trenched the townsite in early January. Winter held off like it never had before. By the thirteenth, they were ready to power up my house with electricity. Having lived for a year without power, I felt as if I was skipping the twentieth century and entering straight on into the twenty-first. Ed took my picture as I threw the main breaker and lit up Cardinal. Running water, music and lights! I was elated. At the same time that I threw that electric switch, my beloved Grandmother, Patsy, passed away in the city of Toronto at 96 years old. It was a bittersweet time, and the wheel of life keeps turning.

2004

I cross-country ski away the months of January, February and March. It is a time of year for me to take my soul to the forest and seek my peace in the trees. The snow conditions vary with the weather, and I have adapted over the years to meet the challenges of nature. I am as happy in a raging blizzard as on the bright clear days. The wind at timberline can howl, and it only makes me feel more alive.

My soul is coming to center for the first time in so many years. The lawsuit is won. My spirit is free to be myself. The town site is coming along nicely. My children are adjusting to this different life. I have just enough real estate work to eek by. I'm feeling pretty good, considering my life has been turned upside down. As I lean into long strides that move me quickly along the trail, it seems that the worst is over. There is a glimmer of hope that I am approaching normal. I ponder the chain of events that has brought me here.

I ponder this man, David, who my heart is focused on. The connection feels as if it comes from the past, another lifetime perhaps. We are incredibly compatible; sharing peace with each other.

On the nights when David Stromm is home with his kids, he talks endlessly on the phone with me, warming my heart and tucking me in from afar. When we're together, we take walks, share meals and stories. He is a quiet fellow, quite solitary and pensive. But I feel close to him and appreciate his calm. I actually bask in it. I wonder if he would ever have any fight in him. This relationship feels safe and a charming relief. David seems content with simple pleasures. I curiously watch how his engineering mind works. His processing is different than mine, and I am intrigued.

It is the end of March. I am standing alone on my skis on the spine above Yankee Doodle Lake at 12,000 feet. This is a commanding spot, with the Divide to the west, and the slope dropping off over a thousand vertical feet to the lake on the south and Middle Boulder Creek on the north. I am very happy. I am feeling incredibly good. It feels like it's been a long time. I consciously choose to let go of negativity. I consciously choose to trust life again. It feels like time to lean into my love for David Stromm, to stop holding back.

I began to give this man my whole heart. Can a man tell when a woman surrenders herself to him? It was not soon after that we sat down for a late dinner at David's house. I noticed he was particularly quiet.

"Are you very tired?" I asked.

"No." he said.

"What's up?"

David looked down through his plate past the dinner to somewhere far away.

"Is there something you want to tell me?"

"I guess there is." he said.

I looked at David, confused. There was too long a silence. Then it came.

"You're not the one." he said blankly, with no emotion. "You are not the love of my life."

I sat momentarily stunned.

All this time, I had just been enjoying him. Living the moment. I didn't know there had to be more. I was just getting to know him. But I was loving him.

He didn't say another word.

He didn't offer a touch to soften the blow.

My heart was laid wide open.

When I finally spoke, I stumbled, "I won't be spending the night then."

He just shook his head, and let me leave. He didn't even get up from the table.

I guess there aren't many other words when a person has decided you are not the one. I guess it's pretty simple. You are not the one.

I couldn't breathe as I drove my car back to Cardinal. I didn't sleep that night. I just cried.

The next morning I rose early, as I had planned, because I didn't know what else to do. I flew Delta Poppa to Pine Bluff, Wyoming. It was a little airplane flying along, buffeted by light winds, carrying a broken heart. A broken heart is a thing. The physical pain hurts so much that the heart is actually felt in isolation from the rest of the body.

It was harsh, the delivery of this news. I consider myself a realist. When I get used to the truth, I can accept it. Better to get hurt by the truth, than comforted with a lie. And why would I want to be "the one" to one who didn't love me. But, as much as I could rationalize, it couldn't touch the pain in my heart.

Each morning I woke to sadness. I was so confused. My Buddhist soul knows that nobody does things to us. It is mind. It is attachment. There is learning to be had. But why does it have to hurt so much? A physical pain present in the heart.

Why did this hurt more than the end of a twenty-one year marriage? David set a grieving wheel in motion for me. I am one with so much grief and loss that the pain it is causing is severe. I mustn't displace this pain as all caused by David. I must ride it like a wave, feel it fully, and know that one day it will be diminished. But ouch.

When a person has just lost her marriage, family, money, possessions, business, and reputation, she is perhaps as vulnerable as one can be. I had told David this about my vulnerability. I had asked him to be careful. Was he so self-centered? Or was he being merciful to let me go.

I attended the Conference Of World Affairs the week after David dumped me. My heart was broken and the conference helped staunch the bleeding. For hours at a time, I was able to get him off my mind. The state of the world seemed to be suffering from the same things I was. People are human beings with hopes and dreams for peace and love. We are challenged to face the fears which cause behaviors resulting in bad communication, prejudice and war. More often than not, it seemed to me, testosterone is at the heart of the matter.

I went to David's office and asked him the question I had been too stunned to ask that night. Was there someone else? He said no.

I ran into David's teenage daughter a couple of weeks after we had split.

"He didn't tell me." she shared, biting her lip. "I wish he'd talk to me. He's so bloody narcissistic."

Maybe that was it. It might explain a lot.

I reminded myself, that he told me the truth and I must be grateful for that. There's nothing wrong with David. I'm just simply not the one.

Mostly though, I spent the next few months torturing my mind with these thoughts. In the end, I must look at myself. Why didn't I see it coming? Wouldn't I want to be with a man who shares his thoughts more freely? Why did I care so much? Why did I feel like I'd do it all again with David, in a heart-beat? Because, as Rumi wrote...gamble all for love.

One must shape an explanation to be stored in the mind as "the way it went". Experiences are encoded as the stories of our lives. I decide the closest I can come is that grace had given me a little reprieve from the saga of Cardinal. I had experienced delight. I found I had a capacity to love. In the end, I was not the one for David Stromm.

Within the month, I received an email from David. He had become reacquainted with a woman at the Star House on his personal quest for selflessness. Turns out, she is the love of his life.

Note to self: Do not deliver news of the heart by email.

Eventually, I have clarity. Love is not about what we get, it's about what we give.

I am flying Delta Poppa on credit, and faith that somehow I will pay the bill. I've never lived like this. But flying makes my heart soar at a time that my spirit needs it desperately. So I keep on doing it.

Scooter and Heather danced at the prom breathing fresh mountain air and watching the light fade over the mountains to the west of Boulder. As if it wasn't coincidence enough that they shared the same airplane hanger, but their fathers owned twin Luskom airplanes. Heather and Scooter would fly the light planes side by side together to the east coast then down to Florida and back to Colorado.

The sun was about to go down when Scooter talked to the guys in the FBO. He bragged with sparkle to his friends about the prom the night before. He was operating on a sleep deficit.

Scooter scooted out the door and untied Dave Elliot's Delta Poppa. He exercised this plane regularly enough to be very familiar with it. He did a pre-flight check and took off on Runway Eight. Scooter did a couple of touch and go landings. He was up for the third time, at six hundred feet, when the engine began to sputter. He adjusted the mixture and the engine died.

Scooter nosed the plane over into a glide as an automatic reflex. He started looking around for a place to land. It would have to be straight ahead, so he scoped each side of the windshield. Ahead lay a lake. He had so little time to choose a spot. There was grass out there to the south but there were other obstructions to consider. And the plane descended quickly into the lake.

It landed like a tail heavy goose breaking the water then the windshield. Scooter swam for his life. He was free of the plane.

A pilot's biggest fear in a case like this is the press, but Scooter handled it well. He smiled for the cameras and was genuinely happy to be alive. He told the reporter, "Any landing you walk away...or swim away from is a good landing."

I was completely relieved to hear that Scooter had survived the crash landing.

Delta Poppa was photographed and mourned by all who had soloed her.

I buried my first airplane with some candles and tears. Martin buried his beloved mother-in-law and his oldest flame, Delta Poppa, in the same week. It was amazing to me, but I knew, that this airplane had a life of its own because it had given pleasure and been loved by so many people.

As I share my weekly pizza with my son, I sense that his social life is becoming increasingly important to him. He is a junior in high school and more interested in people than academics or team sports. His friends are old kindergarten students of mine. They have been hired by me over the last few years to do various jobs around the townsite. They have brought light and hope to me as I have watched them grow over the years. They are good kids.

"You can have a party in Cardinal anytime you'd like." I tell Peter.

"I might." he answers, showing a bit of enthusiasm.

When Chuck lent me the money to renovate my house, I made room in the budget for the remodel of the old livery stable just west of my house. These same kids pitched in to insulate and paint, turning the room into my new pottery lab and the "teenage hangout". I knew, as my own parents did in my day, that if you create a space, and open it with respect and acceptance, the kids will come.

One Friday night in May, just as I was closing my book and turning out my lights, I heard car rumblings and voices. Coming to the door in my nightie, to investigate, I was surprised to see three vehicles arriving and kids already walking by to the playroom.

"Hi Lexie!' a cheerful voice rang out.

"Thanks for letting us come!" sang another.

"No problem." I said with my eyes bulging in disbelief. "Where's Peter?"

"He's coming." they said. "He's with Jake."

Cars continued to arrive. Clusters of high school kids passed the house, all waving to me and thanking me. The townsite resembled a parking lot. I ran inside and got dressed again.

"Mom!" it's Peter. "I'm having some friends over!"

As I throw on a jacket, I say "Fine. I see that. Its fine, it's great. I'm glad."

By the time I enter the playroom, it is packed with partiers. As I search the faces, I experience a strange and wonderful time warp as I recognize so many. They have turned into young adults. Some look like dead ringers for their parents and siblings, others I recognize by those same characteristic features that I knew so well at age five.

Slipping back into my role as the kindergarten teacher, I command a presence, and find myself a loud voice.

"Welcome to Cardinal everyone." I can see the wine coolers and beer. "I want you to spend the night if you're drinking. We have blankets and room for everyone. I'm happy to call your parents and tell them that you are invited. If you're not staying, you need to leave by one o'clock when I'm locking the gate for the night. And I want to talk to each driver before you go."

Everyone listened. Peter shot me a "that'll do" look. Then Smiley stood up. All the kids were quiet and watching.

"We promise you, Lexie, we won't screw this up. We really appreciate you letting us be here. I'll personally make sure no one leaves here that shouldn't."

"This place is really cool.' came another voice.

"Really cool." said another.

"Yeah, thanks!" said Jake.

'We'll be cool, don't worry." added a cute gal.

Everyone went back to their business and a crowd surrounded me, asking if I remembered them and asking questions about the mine.

I slipped out and went back to my bed. Now, it was eleven thirty. The music blared a loud, steady bass beat resembling the night streets of Mexico. I could peek out my bedroom window and see the party through the window next door. Scenes from my youth flashed back to me, visions of dozens of kids hanging out in the cabana by our pool and my Dad making regular appearances to check on the scene. A wonderful family tradition was to continue.

At one o'clock, the party was warmed up and happening. At the risk of being the pooper, I entered and called that the gate would soon be closing. I could tell some were tipsy. As they filed out, saying their goodbyes, I spoke to each driver. They were in better shape than my crowd in our day. Or was I being naive? I knew I was taking a risk, but I credit my own parents for opening their home with respect and trust to many a teenager over the years. In my parent's sixties and seventies, those kids, now with families of their own, returned to tell my folks how they had changed their lives.

And Peter would learn the subtle art of being a host. The resident kid knows the effects of alcohol better than most. You learn to swoop in and relieve certain people of their drinks when they are past knowing. You track the movements of the group unconsciously. Responsibility becomes a real word. Sometimes you stand up to trouble with an authority you don't have on the school grounds. Judgment becomes honed. And in the morning you clean up the mess.

The parties in Cardinal went on for a year, until Peter tired of the responsibility. Everyone was respectful and had a grand time. The only close call was when some crashers left a drunken friend, who luckily stumbled into my kitchen, passed out, and almost barfed into my shoes. Peter drove him to the other party, mumbling under his breath, that these guys weren't welcome and would never be back.

Each time there was a party; kids would stay the night. Peter would tuck in his buddies in the playroom, and then crawl off to his own bed. In the morning, I'd make pancakes and talk with everyone. Gradually, Peter began to claim the bedroom as his. It made me so happy that Cardinal was becoming his home.

The Cardinal Mill had been stuck in the Federal Lawsuit time warp since 2001. The original plan was for the County to take title to the Mill. A collaborative effort with the Nederland Historical Society, Historic Boulder, and the State Historic Fund would restore it. At first, I had paid two thousand dollars a month in liability insurance on the Mill, as I waited for the suit to be dropped. As the lawsuit rooted itself firmly in our lives, and Steve's and my lifesavings disappeared, there was no money to pay insurance and nothing left to protect in the way of personal assets.

With a Federal lawsuit in full swing, the County had changed its mind about taking title. The plan would have to be reconsidered after the suit was over. For three years, the Mill hung in limbo and I wondered if it might be mine forever. What a strange but fantastic albatross. Every opportunity I had to share the mill with others, I happily did.

One day, as I puttered about the north side of the Mill cleaning up the perpetual supply of junk, a young man in bare feet came walking down the old wagon road behind my house. In its day, this was the main road that ran from Boulder to Caribou. I never see people in bare feet walking in the Rocky Mountains. Having spent my Ontario summers completely barefoot, I was intrigued.

"Fine day." I said in greeting. "What brings you here?"

"I was sent by God into the mountains. I come from North Carolina. I've been living in the woods for forty days. You see, I have a stick with notches on it, one for each day."

He looked like he'd been out for forty days. I refrained from asking how he lost his shoes.

"The Lord wanted me to be without temptation. You see I've had too much temptation in my life. I needed to come here to the Rocky Mountains. This is where he sent me. I've been living up there in a cave. I started to build a lean-to, but it is time for me to come out and face the world again."

"Would you like a tour of the Cardinal Mill?" I asked.

He was one of many people who got to see the Mill before it was restored.

When the Federal suit was won, the County agreed to buy the Mill from me for a nominal amount of consideration. Enough to pay some bills, but I was relieved to let go of the potential liability. Finally, Historic Boulder was able to submit the grant application to the State Historic Fund.

As I waited for the Judge's decision on damages, we waited for the State to process the grant.

I obtained mortgages for my house and the Assay Office. I had guarded my credit as best as possible. Considering my situation, I was stunned that I had pulled this off. It was only possible because my creditors had agreed to not file liens against me.

My mortgages would carry the burden of the entire town's infrastructure for the next thirty years. There was no other way. Chuck's attorney helped us with language for the release of Chuck's loan. As we came to agreement on the terms of this second phase of payment of the construction loan, the attorney's voice came over the conference phone.

"So I guess this means I'll be turning in my Sheriff's badge," he said.

Chuck was the Mayor, his attorney was the Sheriff and I was the Treasurer of Cardinal.

"Not so fast, Quick Draw." I shot back. "We want to negotiate a loan for the renovation of the Superintendent's House. As long as Chuck holds title to the rest of town, you are still Sherriff."

As work began on the Superintendent's house, I knew this particular property would be either the success or failure of Cardinal. Everything rode on the national economy. If the house could be sold, the loan to Chuck paid and the profit used to repay my creditors, all might be well.

The costs of repairing the deteriorating building were busting the budget from the day we broke ground. The house had to be jacked up and the foundation dug out by hand. Temporary walls were built to hold the remaining structure in place. The pouring of concrete marked the beginning of the resurrection. Demolition of the old floor and half of the roof took place before the new framing could begin.

I was banking on the attractive location of this house to sell it. Everyone said it was the best house in Cardinal. Time would tell. The pressure to find a buyer was especially intense as the summer was slipping away with a depressed real estate market. We had listed Sandi's Idaho house and Steve's and my last asset, another rental house, all summer at rock bottom prices with no luck. Financially, I was sinking like a ship.

Peter, Sandi and I were just about to make our annual pilgrimage to the lake in Ontario, when I got word that my Gold Hill renter couldn't make rent. Now I would be carrying three mortgages on empty houses. Luckily, I had bought our airline tickets months before and they were non-refundable. Emotionally, I was counting on the trip to Canada to spend time with my children, neither of whom I had been with for way too long.

I was all the way broke again, but hesitating to take pay from the construction loan when the house was already over budget. I cleaned out my bank account, turned my head on my problems and left for the lake. I was painfully aware of what a master of denial I had become.

Upon my arrival at the cottage, I ran upstairs to see my Dad. The last few years had been very difficult for my father. He had battled depression unsuccessfully with no positive results from oral medications. In the spring, he had received a series of electro shock therapies which only drove him deeper into his depressed slumber, totally frustrating my Mother. Mom had finally given up on the doctors, thrown Dad in the car and headed north for the summer. It was the best medicine for everyone. Dad's long days in bed were punctuated by loud abusive rants and outbursts. My brother had warned me that he wasn't well, but no one could have prepared me for what I found.

My father lay on his side, his eyes glazed, staring into space. When he realized it was me, he tried to blink. I couldn't get a satisfying response, so I pulled back the covers and rolled him onto his back. He had wet his bed. His body stayed in a curled position, flattened, as if he was a dead roadside squirrel. He moaned in pain as I straightened him out.

Downstairs, it was a loud free for all of people. Doors were slamming, kids shouting, high excitement of newly arrived cousins. Complete chaos. I focused hard on my father. He was dehydrated. Something was very wrong.

Sister Libby popped into the room, delivering a fresh load of laundry.

"He's not okay." I pointed out.

"I wondered", she said, "It seemed he didn't eat a bite last night...but he doesn't do anything anyway, so he's not really hungry. He was up in the night last night. I heard him make his way to the bathroom." She peered closer.

"He's wet the bed." I pointed out.

"I was concerned enough to buy these diapers when I went to town yesterday. And a plastic for under the sheets ", she said, pulling the bag from the dresser. These turned out to be a saving grace.

I knew that Libby had very little time to be watching my Dad. Her four children, nine and under, kept her attention full time. Dad roared at the children so they all tried to keep a distance. My Mom too was focused on her grand kids. My father had cried wolf too many times to have any remaining sympathy from my mother. Dad had made a series of choices over the past decade which increasingly limited his experiences. He had been verbally abusive of Mom and taken her love for granted. Dad had been diagnosed with spinal cancer, which was in remission. My entire family knew he chose to sleep the rest of his life away, but there was a profound change here. He couldn't move.

Here lay a man who had been a successful businessman, chemical engineer, international traveler, skeet-shooting champion, African hunter, private pilot, sailor, party host, husband and father of six children. My father. My life seemed to be accelerating as I stood there.

Muscling his body, I pulled Dad into a sitting position on the edge of the bed. Holding a glass of juice to his parched lips, I tipped the glass up. He was so thirsty. He took it in one try.

The next morning, our Kiwi friend, Tuie, came across the lake by boat. She is a nurse and a darn good one too.

"Jim'", she said in a loud clear voice, "How are you doing? Can you move? Roll on your back and take a look at me." Her New Zealand accent delighted us all. I knew that if he could move, he would for Tuie, but he couldn't.

"It's unbelievable. He was just drinking wine on the deck with me the other night. Up and down the steps. Jim, we're going to get you up, friend, you've got to have a bite to eat."

I showed Tuie how I had been moving him. Getting him up to sitting, then standing, and with me supporting his full weight, he slowly, shaking, managed to shuffle to a chair to be spoon-fed a meal.

"Good on ya!" Tuie encouraged us both.

"We've phoned for a doctor," my Mom said, "but they all say they aren't taking new patients. Truth is they won't have anything to do with Americans. Their malpractice doesn't protect them from Yankee lawsuits.'

"Well, there's always the Emergency Room," offered Tuie, "but they won't do a darn thing there that you aren't doing here."

Tuie was right.

It was evident that Dad had had a stroke. His speech was gone and his motor skills were severely damaged, but I could tell his mind was still good. He would need a lot of loving care for both his heart and his mind. I would take my Dad back to Colorado with me. With three of his kids out west, we would take him. My Mom needed relief desperately. I felt I was saving her as well.

I nursed my Dad constantly for the ten days I was at the lake. In Boulder, my brother, Matt, found him a nursing home. Finally, he was strong enough to make the trip.

Dad didn't struggle or object. He knew he needed help. The day we flew through Detroit to Colorado was certainly one of the toughest of my life. Physically, it was a terrible challenge for Dad. And his heart was breaking so wide open as he left the cottage that he had gone catatonic to cope.

By the time I made it home to Cardinal that night, I was more exhausted than I've ever been. Again, Cardinal soothed my soul. The next day and the next day, and each day afterward from July into August and then September, I went to Boulder to help Dad relearn to eat, walk and talk.

It seems that fall is the time of year that milestones happen for me, both good and bad. It had been a year since I met Chuck Miller. On October third, we had signed our loan agreement, and Cardinal's renovations had begun. Now, a year later, living without electricity and running water still seemed like yesterday. I will always sing Chuck's praises as I sink into a hot bath. The flick of a light switch, as we headed into the darkest days of the year, brought a leap in my heart. The townsite was halfway finished, all cleaned up and replanted. My dream had come true.

Larry's bright blue truck appeared at the east end of town as I tied my mountain bike shoes. He popped out, bringing his energy and unsurpressable joy. The warm autumn sun sparkled his long blonde hair as he gathered it up into a ponytail. My friend is a hippie in the purest sense. He's the real thing. He has brought the message along for so many years. He is love. Larry smiles at me as if he hasn't seen me in years.

As we start riding up the steep road toward Caribou, I muse. I am remembering two summers before, when it was Larry singing Neil Young to me, on this same ride. He brought my spirit up from the depths of depression. And here we go again. This time, luminous yellow leaves quake on the aspen trees. Larry tells me of his most recent hockey game, his goal in the final seconds, a sweet coup after a painful blunder in the previous game. There is no end to this man's energy and enthusiasm, and he makes me smile. Next, he sings me some Grateful Dead, interspersed with some nostalgic remembering of specific songs played at specific concerts twenty-five years ago. He wasn't as high as I was, I gather, but I know better. Then Larry takes off on the Federal Judge, a subject he is quite passionate about.

"Yes", I remind him, "Justice is overdue." Each day, I am more aware that my life has been on hold for five years.

The bicycle ride takes us up to the field that once was a city of six thousand people. All that is left of Caribou now is a couple of stone ruins which once housed the bank and a mercantile. I huff and puff my way up to Caribou Flats. Now, we are two miles above sea level. Larry and I barely notice this as we have lived in the mountains for thirty years, but we do notice the brilliant fresh new snow on the mountain peaks just to the west of us.

We share the experience.

Coming down off the Caribou Flats into Hick's Gulch is a fantastic ride. I think of my friend, Randy, saying "celebrate your capabilities". I point the bike straight down the fall line on this steep single-track mountain trail, easing the brakes to control my speed as I encounter logs, bogs, and rubble of rock. Conversations with Larry disappear as we both live the moment to stay moving and upright on our bikes. A thrill comes with honing a skill which you have worked on since you were three years old. I can speed and stop time with the squeeze of my brakes. We meet the Switzerland Trail railroad bed. The old narrow gauge tracks are long gone, pulled out for scrap iron in 1922. I imagine what it would have been like to ride the train into Cardinal.

As we approach my humble cabin, I am happy as I can be. I thank Larry for getting me out for a ride and reminding me to count my blessings. It is time for me to drive to Boulder for a fiddle lesson and to visit Dad.

At the bottom of Boulder Canyon, my cell phone comes back to life. I have a message. It is from Paul Phillips. I immediately discern from his tone that the news from the Judge is in, and it is not good. I remember what Mona Lisa had told me last spring. She said "a settlement is made, it works, but it's not what you expected". My heart sinks, but hovers half way with hope. I autodial Paul.

As Paul tells me of the Judge's decision denying any award of damages to Cardinal, I pull the car over at the top of Mapleton Hill. I can't drive. I can't breathe. I begin to cry. Paul is very disappointed himself, but I can't see beyond my own predicament. At least, he has a roof over his head and a secure lifestyle. For once, I don't worry about anyone but myself. And I feel very alone.

The same sensations a person feels upon learning of the sudden death of a loved one overtake me. I know it should feel differently than that, but it doesn't. Paul listens patiently to me as I completely emotionally fall apart. He is used to this. This time, he shares my disappointment. But what he cannot understand is how much nothing I have had to live on, and how much less than nothing, it seems, I will have now. The loss of my marriage, my home, my family, our money, my children's college education, my time... all of the losses that I have experienced in the last five years, come crashing down on me. I know that life is not fair.

I finally realize that I should not be doing this to Paul. He has always been my advocate. He feels badly enough. We say goodbye with his advice to me being, "Don't despair. Holland & Hart will not abandon you now."

How could I not despair? There is a point with tears of frustration and loss when one cannot turn off the faucet until it runs dry. It was evident to me that I had fallen into an emotional abyss. I stepped out of my car and made my way through the red fallen maple leaves to the sidewalk. This neighborhood was built in Cardinal's heyday with money generated from the mines. The opulence and grandeur of these homes seemed a cruel reminder that this is a world of have and have nots. It was injustice that made me cry so hard.

My body buckled bringing me to the sidewalk with great heaving sobs. No one was around to see, or they probably drew the drapes, not considering this ugliness to be part of their business. Time rose up in the air like a twister. It left me altogether and I knew that I would not make it to my fiddle lesson.

I cried first with frustration with the legal system. How could it be so wrong? I cried for my children and all I could not provide for them. I cried for Cardinal, that its honor had been slapped in the face.

When I could control the sobbing enough to drive, I turned my car around and drove back down Mapleton Hill toward Bob's office. I needed someone desperately. I called Larry and in disbelief at the news, he turned his car around at Georgetown, making the hour back track to be with me. Parking in Bob's lot, I crept through the vines to his office window. He was on the phone and smiled and waved, not realizing something was very wrong. I couldn't breathe. The craziness was returning. I stepped to the sidewalk and dropped to my knees sobbing again.

This time, a stretch limousine pulled up directly beside me. It seemed longer than any I'd ever seen. My mind took note of this, while at the same time, being overwhelmed with my situation. Three people bounced out of the limo laughing. Irony made me cry even harder. What cruel joke would this be? I've never seen a stretch limo here before! My faith told me that someday, I would look back and laugh at the limousine.

The people stood on the sidewalk and stared at me for the longest time. I did not pay them attention. I did not stop my grieving. When they finally asked if something was wrong, I blundered an answer, pointing to Bob's office.

"You know him?'", they asked, in disbelief. But then I read their minds... yes, that would be our Bob, he helps everyone. Someone had the good grace to get Bob for me.

In Bob's office, he set aside his obligations and listened to the news. No attorney would be surprised to hear it. When possibility exists, probability flourishes in the mind of an attorney. But Bob understood the repercussions for Cardinal and me personally. He had bought me many a beer as we had waited nearly two years for this verdict.

"You don't have the luxury of falling apart now.'" Bob reminded me with a clear firmness. "You have kept it together for so long. You'll have time to be emotional later. You have to stay focused. You are not done yet, there are things you'll have to do right away."

I looked up at him through pouring tears. I honestly could not think of anything I would have to do. The wolves were circling and they would simply take me. How difficult could it be?

"First, we need the best bankruptcy lawyer. Who do you want in your trenches? At a time like this, who do you want in your trenches?" He phoned Nancy Miller, while I mouthed the words, "I have no money."

"How much is owed? You'll need exact figures and a list of your creditors."

I thought of my folder, labeled "The Damage". The total was three quarters of a million dollars in damages. I thought of the thousands of times that I had done the math in my head, awake and sleeping. If the Judge had awarded the damages we had asked for, and if I had sold the remainder of the properties renovated, the math problem broke close to even. But with this decision from the judge, the situation was hopeless.

Tears continued to flow in profusion. Bob didn't pay them any mind. Not even a Kleenex.

"Then there is the matter of the Title to the property being held in Mr. Miller's name. He's in first position." Thank goodness Bob knew the whole story. He reveled in the complexity of the situation. Bob's wheels were turning.

"How will he react to this development? Yes, indeed, this will be a fascinating peek into Chuck Miller's soul!" Bob Stone can find adventure in anything!

"Bankruptcy could be good for you." he went on. "Your work is done. It doesn't rest on your shoulders anymore. If you make the decision swiftly, there is no reason for you to have to work for these people any longer. A bankruptcy trustee will be hired to handle everything. The assets will be sold and your creditors will take what is left. You will be able to keep some equity in your house and car."

It was these words that caught my attention. I felt the extreme exhaustion accumulated over the five years since I had met Tina and Dennis. Dennis's threat came back to me, the words complete with their evil intonation. "There will be a huge legal battle." he had promised.

I suddenly realized it was over. It had been a draw. Cardinal won the lawsuit, but they had won the war. I was extremely tired.

In pilot training, the flyer is taught that it is very rarely mechanical failure that brings an airplane to an unfortunate fate. Rather, it is a series of mistakes in judgment on the part of the pilot. This is a simple and haunting metaphor for what has happened to my life. Perhaps, I have made a series of poor choices. Bob went on. "Essentially, your bankruptcy will make little difference. As a result of the damages incurred, the properties would have had to be sold anyway, would they not? At this point, you can stop working so hard. You can be done. The payment of debts will happen and the assets will be what you have built. Your perseverance and hard work will not be lost on your creditors. The assets are what they are today because of your diligence."

I had heard him say that in bankruptcy, I could keep my house. Now, I knew that I would be okay. I tried to breathe a yogic breath.

Bob continued. "You must gather your wits one more time. You've got to make them understand that you are not the same person you were when you started this project. You are stronger, wiser, more educated. Your dream has largely been realized. The land is saved, the Mill is protected. You have an appointment on Monday with Nancy. You still have a lot of work to do, but this can be good for you, Lexie."

I smiled at Bob, a pathetic little smile, to show my appreciation for his amazing blend of counsel, understanding and friendship. This person had been sent to me by divine timing, several years ago, to remind me of my spirit. To remind me that all there is, is love, because Bob knows that, and he lives it. All of the poems he had sent me over these years, some by email, some by snail mail and many hand delivered, softened his focused intention today, and made me know...I was seeing the light at the end of the tunnel.

Bob was grateful for Larry's arrival, I'm sure. I introduced my two moral supporters to each other. Larry had called Andy and Wendy. We were invited for dinner. It wasn't the first time my friends had held me together at the seams. I sat at the Cookler's table in a state of shock, floating in a protective bubble of friendship. I was in a state of suspended animation. I knew that when the dust settled, I would be alright, somehow, if I could make it through the night.

Before bed, I called my brother in law, Vancouver attorney, Brian Samuels. Brian's consistent, gentle counsel had been indispensible to me from the beginning of the lawsuit. I knew I must tell him the disappointing news first hand. He took it hard, knowing that British law would never have allowed this to happen. My sister, Lacey, reminded me that my work in Cardinal is done and accomplished. She acknowledged me, pointing out that the Mill and the open space were safe.

I climbed into bed, astonished about the order of things. Brian would be attending his friend Buck's memorial service in Colorado this weekend, and he would be staying with me in Cardinal. And Lacey, my one sibling who had never even seen Cardinal until a week ago, now offered me support because she had just been here and seen what Cardinal was all about.

I held a Tarot deck of Angel Cards and asking for anything, I pulled three cards. They came up Healing, Truth & Integrity and a representation of the Archangel Michael. Michael is the archangel known for courage and his ability to release one from a sense of fear. He is an angel with a sense of humor. I should have recognized his presence when I saw the stretch limo.

I wake in the night. It's three o'clock. I'm suddenly aware that my sleeping habits had returned to normal in the past year. But here I am again, wide awake. I am familiar with this routine. My mind begins to churn. It's only money, everyone says to console me. But it's not true. It's not only money anymore. It's my home.

In the morning, I wake to the phone ringing and cry aloud, "How can a person keep on keeping on, how?"

Injustice has emptied my soul. But Faith struggles hard in my heart, arguing that too many things had lined up for me yesterday. My strength had been bolstered by love on the ride with Larry. I had driven to Boulder to receive the news from Paul, then I had made my way to Bob's office and he was there. Brian was coming to stay with me. The judge's decision would bring long needed closure. It would be wrong to abandon faith.

Just a week ago, the Colorado River through the Grand Canyon, had returned me safely, restored of perspective and vision. My family had gathered for my parent's fiftieth anniversary and enjoyed the fruits of my labor in Cardinal. They reminded me of the strength of our love and their incredible support. And there were the cradling arms of my friends when I needed them most. I decided that Paul was right, I shouldn't despair. I rose from my bed to get dressed and brush my hair, realizing the story was not over.

While I had been rafting down the Grand Canyon, my brothers were towing the line for Dad. The nursing home doctor had drugged my father to subdue him. She had sent him on a really bad trip. From what my brother Matt said, it had sent him on a bad trip as well. Such an experience is very hard on everyone. We made it very clear that Dad's medications were not to be changed without our permission.

I told Dad that I was preparing to move him to Cardinal. It would take some organizing on my part. It would take a bit of time, but he would be able to be the boss of his own medicine there. He would have helpers 'round the clock. His care would be better and I could see him many times each day.

On Thursday night, I helped a completely drugged out father try to guide a spoon to his mouth. It had happened again. He held onto his wheelchair and cursed the bastards who had drugged him. I investigated at the nursing station and found no one could be accountable for what drugs he'd had, or not. I told the nurse that he would be spending the weekend with me, as he often did. She would prepare his medicine packs for me.

I decided then and there that he would not be coming back to the nursing home. I didn't have the energy to fight the system, so I planned to bust him out. I would call by telephone to say he wouldn't be returning.

As I kissed Dad goodbye that night, I whispered in his ear that tomorrow would be the day that he would come to stay. Cardinal would be his new home. He was happy. I knew that if he told anyone he was moving, no one would believe him anyway.

The next day, I made three trips to the car, removing Dad's few possessions from the room. On the fourth trip, I loaded Dad into the wheel chair and stacked the last of the stuff in his arms. No one noticed as we wheeled by the nursing station looking like a forklift. They just went about their shift work. There was no fan fare or big goodbye.

I felt exhilaration as I broke Dad out of there. I hoped like hell my plan in Cardinal would work because there was no turning back.

My life changed completely and for the better, the day my Dad moved to Cardinal. By chance and circumstance, my son, Peter, came to live with me in Cardinal too. Counting the caretaker for Dad, the population of the townsite quadrupled in a day.

The nesting feeling that one can only have with family made everything feel alright. Suddenly, I was returning from my work day to find that I wasn't a divorced single middle aged woman with estranged children, but a loving daughter and a mother again.

My father's caretakers loved him like I loved him, by watching me. They cared for him with a devoted passion that elevated them, in my perception, to angels. And the caretakers wrapped me in their soothing care as well.

Mohammed taught my father about his own religion, Islam, demonstrating his compassion in practice and prayer. Tony, who Dad called "Bob", was a dead ringer for Dad's old friend from a time gone by. We called him "Tone-Bob". The ladies, Naomi, Red and Lisa, worked the weekdays and flirted him up. Jason took some night shifts and was on a learning curve taught by bizarre behavior.

Each night, I gratefully sat down with them to a dinner served with a flourish. Dad would share his day, with as much strength as he had, while his caretaker eagerly filled in the details. My father was being escorted sweetly from this world.

The experiences Cardinal has brought to my life have taught me that how I react has everything to do with the outcome of the situation, my mind and free will being my strength.

I have seen people who, long after a tragic incident has past, can never make a come back to normal. Myself, I have struggled for years with the loss of my baby son. I was more determined than ever to not become damaged goods by what had happened in Cardinal.

All along, I had chosen to not focus on the people who had put this fiasco into motion. Anger toward individuals would only make me an angry person. Now, it was the judge who challenged my soul. I decided that if I was this judge, I should be worried about my personal safety. I was feeling angry as a hornet.

It was a struggle to not take Judge Kane's decision to deny damages personally. Reason dictated that his bout with breast cancer had plunged him into focus on his own personal survival. His diligence toward work was set on the back burner for over a year and when it returned, if it ever did, his already overloaded case load had only grown in magnitude.

There were more than a few days when I walked out into the hills to dissipate the anger which threatened to take root in my soul. Arguing with myself, I became the queen of rationalization. I could talk myself into and out of anything. I remembered well my Psychology 101 class at the University of Colorado. It was my first introduction to the concept of the defense mechanisms in the human mind. Our quiver of tools for self defense is fashioned by our free will. Gift or a nemesis, state of mind is up to the individual.

Another thing to be considered was my sanity, or at least the appearance of it. As an adolescent, I had been obsessed with psychology and its implications on society. If only I could teach the "down and out" bum on the street the importance of presenting himself with credibility. A person could save them self a lot of trouble and find a life of relative comfort. Sanity can be a bluff. Whether or not the person philosophically shares the value system of society, doesn't matter. It is how one presents himself that puts others at ease.

People had been watching me carefully for a long time now. Asking me, with that sideways tilt of the head and knitted eyebrows, "How are you?"

"Are you keeping it together?" is what they really wanted to know.

Our social norms protect us beautifully.

"I'm fine, thanks." delivered with a reassuring, gracious smile was all they really wanted to hear. Keep your craziness for yourself. Don't scare people.

I would have to make a preemptive strike to assure the attorneys and other creditors that I was still functional, despite the gaping hole that had been blown in my ship's side. Bob was right, it was not time to lose it yet. The appearance of sanity was important.

One might wonder why we form corporations expecting a corporate shield to protect our personal assets. It was very early on in this game that I had been told by Paul that the corporate veil would be easy to pierce. It was basically non-existent. If I wanted attorneys to go to work, I had to personally guarantee my debts to them because New Cardinal, LLC's assets were not able to be liquidated. From a practical stand point, no one would have purchased Cardinal's land until the lawsuit was resolved.

More than once, I have reflected on Paul Phillip's amazement and genuine disappointment that Judge Kane had denied the damages. If an attorney had ever gambled on anything, Paul had gambled with my family's relatively meager financial well being and lost. His gamble had also compromised himself and his partners by running up more legal bills than I could ever pay.

Now, he was not in a position to finalize a settlement.It is unusual to find an attorney who will make such a gamble. I realize what a stretch this whole situation was for Paul, so very against the nature of an attorney to defend someone who had limited resources. I am very fortunate that Paul represented me. In the end, we both lost financially. I can only hope that the moral victory of winning the suit at summary judgment was as satisfying for him as it was for me.

Larry came from Breckenridge to help me again. This time, using his experience of running a retail business, he dove into organizing the numbers that defined my assets and liabilities. Together, we took stock of a mess that previously couldn't have been tallied due to being hung in limbo waiting for the judge's decision.

I had to show the creditors that if they allowed me to finish my renovation work in Cardinal, I could pay them more on the dollar than if I declared bankruptcy.

This was a challenge because property values were very speculative until buyers materialized. It would be to my benefit if I could settle with the creditors out of bankruptcy.

I had worked so hard over the last five years to keep my cabin in Gold Hill. I had managed to hold on to it by keeping it rented and leveraging the mortgage to the hilt to pay the attorneys cash. I had held on through economic recession, a soft rental market, unsavory tenants, a federal lawsuit and a divorce. Now, the fact that there was no equity left in the cabin was the reason I might be able to keep it. I hoped to retain title to Gold Hill.

Value is relative worth. In the case of creditors, circling like vultures, value is a numerical quantity assigned or computed to describe what is essentially determined to be fair return or the equivalent in marketable goods. I would build a proposal assuming that the cabins in Cardinal would be desirable to home buyers. The values I would assign were based on comparable properties sold on the market. It wasn't the first time that I was painfully aware that Cardinal was "outside the box".

Even before I had moved my Dad to Cardinal, I had been gutting and remodeling the Compressor House for him to live in. I had a verbal agreement with Chuck Miller that he would "quit claim" the building from New Cardinal Construction LLC to my mother. Chuck had more than enough equity left in the rest of the townsite as collateral against the Superintendent's House construction loan. Mom had been dumping cash into the renovation. I was walking on thin ice to protect her investment from going to the creditors. My mother would be paying my creditors a settlement for the property. It was up to me to make sure it would be a rock bottom price.

Chuck graciously deeded the Compressor House straight to my Mom. Honoring the situation, the creditors settled on fifty thousand dollars for Mom to keep the title to the Compressor House. It was my relationships with people that made this possible and I know that Paul had a hand in it too.

When one considered that the Assay Office and the Office, my home, were mortgaged to their maximum, it was obvious that there was no value to be had from either building being sold. When I borrowed from Chuck on my original loan, I had borrowed, not only for the improvements on these two buildings, but the entire infrastructure for the townsite as well. This made the equity in my home less than what I would be allowed to keep in a bankruptcy. Ironically, it was lack of equity that would save the titles in my name.

The twin boarding houses would have to be sold unrenovated. The Superintendent's House would be finished on the loan from Chuck Miller, using the property as collateral and then be sold to pay creditors.

The greatest irony of all was that the "green cabin", up at the west end of town, with its privacy, large lot and waterfall, was of no value in the eyes of the creditors, because it carried no residential building status in the eyes of Boulder County. The same went for the Mess Hall and Shower Room which sat half on National Forest land. I would propose to keep these structures in my name.

The proposal that went to the attorneys, water engineers and laboratories promised to pay them forty cents on the dollar, as opposed to fourteen cents on the dollar, if I was to declare bankruptcy. I hoped my creditors would accept my proposal.

Reaching a settlement took many months. By now, I had accepted that nothing goes smoothly or quickly in this business. The single greatest cause for delay was that Holland & Hart now transferred my case to their credit collection department. I was no longer dealing with anyone who knew any history of the lawsuit, the property or the unique circumstances that had brought me into debt.

Holland & Hart had assigned a woman attorney to the task of extracting the maximum possible amount of money from me. Her focus was single minded. She had a high need to exercise her power and control in our interactions. What she couldn't grasp was that she was arguing over money that didn't exist yet. She was arguing about potential dollars. What would have brought her comfort was something which I could not promise. Until I could finish my renovation work and sell the properties, the value in Cardinal was purely speculative.

As it turned out, it would be a full six months of negotiating to get all parties to agree to my proposal. During that time, as I teetered on the brink of bankruptcy, Holland & Hart's gal was forced to learn the story of Cardinal. It was the only way to make sense of the uncertain value.

In mid November, I explained to Dad and his caretaker, that I would be leaving them for two days and a night to attend a bluegrass camp in Denver. I had begged for a scholarship and received it. I would be leaving them, three feet deep in snow, without a car and only a telephone to connect them to the world. The caretaker said, "Go Lexie, and have a good time."

That same weekend, a group of local divorced female friends had planned to attend a black tie singles ball which was being held in south Denver for the Harvest Moon. My reservations at the Centennial Airport hotel were just two blocks away and I had no dinner plans, so I agreed to attend. The last thing I needed to add to my life was a guy, but I always need food.

Whatever the statistics represent, one might wonder if my generation is a failure or success at relationships. On one hand, the large number of failed marriages means we are quitters. Or it might mean we are holding our spirits to a standard of truth.

The party was a far cry from my mountain life. I flirted with the Channel Nine weatherman, the only man at the party without grey hair. He found me interesting because, never having had television, I had no idea who he was. I excused myself when he said he would never fly in a Cessna 150. The music was horrid for dancing and the deejay didn't take requests. The men seemed to be twenty years older than I.

More focused on fiddling at eight thirty the next morning, than men, I was sipping a scotch when I was introduced to a tall man named Curt. He was standing next to a large potted tree, minding his own business, also sipping a scotch.

For a few months, I had been writing back and forth on the internet to a man named "Tall Ed" in Wyoming. Tall Ed was six foot five. I couldn't imagine quite how tall that was. So I asked this man how tall he was.

"Six seven." he replied.

It wouldn't have been polite to just walk away. And he was the most interesting looking man in the place. He had a laid back western sort of air about him. We began to chat. He seemed preoccupied, but sweet and polite. I was uncomfortable with the whole idea of a meat market. I was about to let this fellow go back to his daydreaming, when his answer to the standard question, "What do you do?" got my attention.

"Real estate." he answered. "More along the lines of land acquisitions... development projects."

"Me too." I smiled.

"It's a long time between paychecks. You've got to have a lot of stick to it." he shifted on his feet and yawned.

"Yes, you do." and I added, "I have just spent three years in Federal Court for a ghost town."

Curt's eyes opened wide and he looked down at me in disbelief.

"I have been in Federal Court over a ghost town too! The Town of Gilman."

So maybe I wouldn't leave just now after all.

We talked about this long enough for my girlfriend to lose interest and leave us alone. Curt's court wrangling had lasted eleven years, and his marriage had not made it through year two either.

Curt was starting to look at me, all of me, right down to the floor. He said we should dance and led me by the hand through the crowd. I giggled as we walked to the dance floor. This really wasn't part of my plan. But when we started to move to the music, I realized, this guy fits me just right. When we danced, it was sexy and I couldn't get the smile off my face.

"Come downtown with me. I'll take you to a place with real dancing music." he said.

My girlfriends were scattered and didn't expect me to check back anyway, so Curt walked me to my car. I would take my own car, as I would be driving south again at the end of the night. But when I looked at the clock on the dashboard, it was already the end of the night. It had flown by!

"I can't go." I leaned out my window and told him. "It's two o'clock, and I have to play the fiddle in the morning with a group. I'm the only fiddle player and I really suck at it on a good day."

My good common sense came up with a plan.

"I have a hotel room just two blocks away. Maybe you'll come there and we can talk for a while, but I will have to get some sleep."

While we drove the two blocks, I thought, I don't even know this man. Yes, I do. I've just talked to him for five hours. No, I don't. Not really. But he's sure got all of my attention. Lexie, you've just invited him to your room! He's going to kiss you.

Then it occurred to me that for the first time in my life, I could have a one-night stand. I wasn't married. I didn't have to be accountable to anyone but myself. No girlfriend or sister to judge me and enough maturity to not set myself up for heartbreak or delusion.

As we walked through the elegant lobby, we passed a grand piano. Curt's fingers started dancing and he said that he wanted to play for me, but it was two in the morning and we were in a hotel. So instead, I took his hand and led him away. We never did go to sleep that night.

I was an hour and a half late for bluegrass camp in the morning. I hadn't eaten a thing, and my head was in the clouds. I felt dangerously charmed, completely swept off my feet, and I wasn't the least bit tired.

Our teacher, Dr. Banjo, poked some fun at me for being late.

"A good night, was it?"

I smiled smugly, and then when no one was looking, I grinned ear to ear.

When I returned to Cardinal that evening, I went straight in to kiss Dad. He'd been waiting up for me.

It took an enormous amount of energy for him to speak, so he had saved his words all afternoon. He took one look at me and said boldly, "You got laid, didn't you!"

I blushed in front of the caretaker.

"Daaad, I don't have to answer that question!"

"No, you don't!" he grinned.

Curt did call me, and I was so pleased. A few weeks later, he met my father.

It was getting very difficult for Dad to talk. He looked up at Curt from his wheelchair.

"You're a big bastard, aren't you?" Dad found the words with a smile. He knew how much I liked Curt. I was happy that he had shown Curt his true colors.

Christmas of 2004 was the first Christmas in Cardinal with electricity. My dream of cabins in the snow, lit with Christmas trees from the inside, had finally come true. Mom and I cross-country skied each day. My brothers and their families came up on Christmas Day to sled, feast and visit with Dad.

Tone-Bob stayed in Cardinal to care for Dad. Tone-Bob didn't believe in Christmas. He didn't want to explain why, hinting a bit at the commercialism surrounding the holiday. It was such a gift for me to have him helping, and I think that my family showed him that Christmas can be about love and fun, not just presents.

It was on New Year's Eve Day that Curt's stepfather died of a sudden heart attack. While my friends came to Cardinal to cross-country ski and bring in the New Year, Curt and his son headed out to Nebraska to be with his family.

At midnight, my friends and I woke Dad up to play him "Old Lang's Ayne". Dad had always thrown grand New Year's parties on Ashbrook Farm, so I could not let his last New Year's Eve slip away unacknowledged. With the electricity of my friends reveling, I wondered if he might not be launched by psychic energy to his next plane, but the next morning he awakened and stated simply, "Don't ever wake me to play music again."

2005

*M*y Father passed away on January 8th, 2005. The week before he died, I sent an email to update my siblings on his deteriorating condition. Without speaking amongst themselves, each called me that week and said, "I'm coming this weekend." Libby came from Toronto, Lacey came from Vancouver, Doug from Florida, and Matt and Cliff from Boulder and Estes Park, Colorado. Our adopted sister, Ellen, came from California.

My Mom had been in Cardinal with Dad and me for over a month. My parents had spent enough time together to find peace with each other. It was peace that had been destroyed by dementia, helplessness and depression in his last months at the lake.

As the kids all gathered by Dad's bedside, he must have had a sense that his time had come. He had little strength to visit, but each held his hand and gave him love. I knew his time was near, but it is a hard thing to judge until the last breaths come. When we tucked him in that night, we told him we'd see him in the morning.

I awoke to the wonderful sounds of my family in my kitchen. Doug and Lib were up making coffee. I needed them so badly. I needed emotional support, more opinions and some relief. My heart was so grateful as I greeted them that morning.

"Has anyone checked on Dad?" I asked. "I always go over first thing each morning. He expects me first thing." I flew out the door and Doug came with me.

Tony met us at the door.

"I've been trying to call you, but the call won't go through. Your Dad is unresponsive this morning. We had a great time in the night. He was awake, laughing and joking. Really happy."

I realized at that moment, Dad and I had already said our goodbyes. I have read many times of the last surge of energy, the moments of clarity and presence before death. I ran to the bedroom and spoke to him.

"Dad, I'm here, and so is Doug. Doug is here." He peeked from his eyes and took a good look at Doug, then silently closed them forever. He was barely there. He was going away. When he closed his eyes, his breathing changed. It felt for a second like a struggle, but very soon, his breath slowed and gentled.

Doug and I looked at each other. We didn't need to speak. Tony nodded as we took off the oxygen. I knelt beside the bed and put him in my arms. He felt light as a feather. It was just minutes before he left. The father I had all my life was gone.

Mom and Lib came in at the moment Dad passed away.

"He's gone." I cried.

"He just died." Doug told them. "Just now."

I held my Dad all the while that he was still warm. I felt peace and sadness. I could tell his spirit had gone far away.

THE AUTHOR AND HER DAD IN BETTER DAYS.

❧

The winter solstice marks the New Year in Cardinal, because the length of the day is so important in a place of so much winter. The solstice is a turning point that the soul experiences profoundly.

The holidays had come and gone with all of the constant social action and playing outside that comes with my family. Cardinal had been the center of it all.

The steadfast activity so characteristic of the caring for the infirm had disappeared with a delicate and serene finality with the passing of my father. I was left with a sensation which felt like sitting in a pool of calm. Each time my instinct to check on Dad and his helpers came to conscience, I reminded myself, it was over. My Dad had gone on to that place without time. My part was done.

The town had quieted back down. Now, my son, Peter, and I were alone together. It was finally Peter's turn to have my attention. Peter's presence in this home was a gift I had not expected I might ever have just a six months before.

Our lives took on a rhythm of normalization that I had not had the luxury of sustaining in longer than I could remember. I basked in this rhythm. The rituals of motherhood, blueberry pancakes and sorting socks, settled me into an old, familiar place I had missed so much.

The ordeal of Cardinal had certainly taken a tragic toll on Peter. My heart knew this pain well. I had been carrying it around since the first days that I had added the Cardinal project to our already busy lives. I had watched him get lost in the drama that consumed our home life and ultimately, our marriage. Peter had paid dearly, and now I finally had the chance to begin to make it up to him.

It is a fine tiptoe of a dance one does to tame a wild cat. Rebuilding shattered trust doesn't happen overnight. I listened carefully to Peter and honored his passions with support, and a calculated amount of enthusiasm. There was no "choosing battles", as most parents of teenagers do. There could be no battles for Peter and me. We were both two bruised and battered souls. Pete's dyed shoe polish black, long hair in the eyes was simply a developmental stage to me. Nothing I would try to change. My job was clearly to create a loving home for my son.

A balance of all things is necessary for a healthy life. While Peter struggled to recommit himself to school work, I focused on rebuilding my waning real estate business. As Peter carried in armload after armload of firewood, I baked him his favorite cranberry cake. When Pete's friends came to Cardinal, I welcomed them and gave them a place to be together. I listened to their issues and concerns. I fed them at every opportunity. And when Peter went off with them looking for action on the weekends, I was fortunate to have the great company of my friend, Curt.

One day, a car drove up to my house with a family inquiring about land for sale. Hunter and Jan immediately fell in love with Cardinal. They purchased the twin boarding houses to the west of me within the year. They would renovate the cabins and I would be relieved of the task. The family lives on a horse ranch north of Boulder, Jan running the stables and being Mom to three young children, while Hunter is a pulmonologist in Boulder. I liked their energy right away. It felt as if they had been part of the plan all along.

Jack and Ari, a young couple from Maine, became tenants in my Mom's Compressor House. They loved Cardinal with a passion and spent many hours roaming the hills surrounding the townsite.

As the Superintendent's house was finished, Eric and his little daughter, Maya, moved in, to occupy the house until it sold.

Cardinal had blossomed into a town again. The summer passed blissfully green, with a calm vibe humming. Each day, I waited in anticipation of a buyer for the Superintendent's house.

By mid August, I returned to the cottage in Canada to spend time with Peter and my Mom. It was my first time back at the cottage since I had taken my Dad away the year before and I missed him terribly.

When I returned to Cardinal, the State of Colorado began rebuilding the historic stone wall to the west of the Cardinal Mill. The first of one hundred and ten gravel trucks roared up the road to Cardinal just as Tina and Dennis arrived for their two weeks a year of peace and quiet. I had nothing to do with the timing of this, so I just chuckled quietly at the karmic justice. Yenter Companies had been hired to do the work and they proved to be exemplary in performance, communication and follow through.

The digging machinery had to be operated with utmost care as the workers could not touch the almighty historically landmarked Mill, yet they had to dig right up to within an inch of where it stood. Starting at the bottom, the French drain and base of the wall were laid. As the machine approached from the top, it teetered on the brink of disaster. I said more than one prayer as the operator carefully balanced as he built himself a road off the edge of the precipice.

An engineer was sent from Zen Engineering, Inc. to oversee the process, but there would be no sign of David Stromm, even when the wall was completed. As I gave my own personal inspection each day, I reflected on David and the temporary lift he had given me as I went through one of the hardest times of my life. That, I decided, must have been all our relationship was about. A temporary lift and a permanent wall! Gifts from a higher power.

The wall grew upward tier by tier, as the workers would carefully place each stone by hand to form the face of the wall. A few men stood shovels in hand, receiving load after load of gravel backfill. They installed soil nails and laid a structural fabric every so often, the magic tricks from Stromm' design. In five weeks time, the new stone wall was finished.

With the water rerouted out of the Mill, the State Historic Fund grant work could begin. Now, contractors came to the Cardinal Mill to inspect and bid on the project of stabilizing the Mill structure. About half of the six contenders shook their heads, said thanks anyway, and bowed out. It was indeed overwhelming to look at the magnitude of the project. One wondered how men built it back in 1904. The huge monoliths of concrete and massive wooden timbers, where did they come from, and how did they get here? Not to mention the gigantic motors, fly wheels, compressors and the crushing mill itself! Who were the people, names lost in the past, who built this incredible mill?

The right man was chosen for the restoration job. Pat Minear, twentieth century Mill Boss, a man with a "can do" attitude. Pat's crew descended upon the Mill at just the time of year that they should have been heading to Mexico. They roped themselves off and dangled above the two story hopper to replace a fourteen inch square beam. They shored up the bottom of the mill allowing them to sister each roof rafter double with "two by twelves". The old busted out windows were replaced with new ones, and the entire roof was retinned with corrugated metal. It was a brave fellow, who I photographed standing six stories high in twenty mile an hour winds, roofing the very top section of the mill. The sides of the mill were patched and the construction trash was cleaned up and hauled off.

When the big March and April snows came, I was able to relax, knowing that the Cardinal Mill would stand another hundred years.

REBUILDING THE WALL

MILL & WALL REPAIRED 2005

🌿

For a couple of weeks in the winter, the temperature in Cardinal drops well below zero, reminding me of my first nights living here in the Mine Office. Now, my house is insulated and has electric heat in the mudroom, bedrooms and bathroom. A cheery little propane stove in the kitchen looks like a miniature woodstove with fake logs and real flames. The airtight woodstove in the living room warms the whole house, never going out for weeks at a time, burning as if it is tended by a Good Samaritan.

This week was a cold one, featuring fifteen-below-zero. Our cars grimaced as we started them, the old wavy glass windows in the house frosted on the inside and the snow crunched loudly under our feet.

Chuck Miller's New Cardinal Construction, LLC still held the title to the Superintendent's House. The joint bank account that Chuck and I used for the construction loan had one hundred and six dollars left in it. I had been marketing the house for almost a year and still, no buyer. On January first, the title would belong to Chuck and my creditors would be out of luck. So would I. I was staring bankruptcy in the face again.

The collections attorney at Holland & Hart could not believe that I had signed the title over to Chuck to get the construction loan. I explained to her that no one makes a loan to someone tied up in Federal Court. Come hell or high water, I would pay Chuck's kindness and the balance remaining on the loan. I would save the title, liquidate the building and pay my creditors. I intended to honor my settlement agreement and end this thing called the Federal Lawsuit forever.

The price on the Superintendent's House had been high all summer. Holland & Hart were setting the terms and they wanted as much as the market could bear. By September, it was obvious that it was too high. I convinced them to drop the price by forty-thousand dollars. After that, I came close to selling it three times, but people's circumstances had not lined up. One couple needed to sell a house in Virginia. A man fell in love with the house but needed a job transfer from the east. Another had a true passion for Cardinal, but had to divorce a wife and three teenagers in Minnesota. In the meantime, I was paying the bills to float the house, and beginning to lose too much sleep over the fact that the January first deadline was rapidly approaching.

As I faced imminent bankruptcy, I considered every option. I had just deposited a ten thousand dollar paycheck in the bank, and knew that the money would be the first to go, right off the top, never mind that I would need it for living expenses. I had been flying a Cessna 150 for my friend, Joel, who

JOEL AND THE AUTHOR WITH N7766E

had been temporarily out of his FAA Medical for a year. I asked Joel if he'd sell me half of his airplane. I was ecstatic when he agreed. We figured the creditors would have a hard time liquidating half of a 1959 Cessna 150. This would keep me flying and Joel was the best partner a person could ask for! Buying into N7766E was a decision I will never regret.

It was December 6, 2005, when I called Holland & Hart to remind Collections of our deadline. I suggested an extension from Chuck and a "fire-sale" price on the house.

The Holland & Hart attorney had called Chuck and he had asked for ten thousand dollars, paid up front, to extend the loan agreement for six more months. She balked at this. How greedy of him! But I reminded her that Chuck had lent me money at a time that no one in his right mind should have. He had believed in me and he was the only reason the assets were redeveloped and bearing fruit. She backed off.

If Holland & Hart would pay the ten thousand dollars, they could have their six more months to get top dollar. Holland & Hart decided this would be a breach of ethics. I saw it as good business practice. Why not put in ten grand to save one hundred and fifty? Funny to me that lawyers would deem this unscrupulous behavior.

The law firm would have written off the loss from Cardinal several years ago anyway. They are a huge firm, which gives away millions to charity each year. If I hadn't been a paying client, maybe Cardinal would have qualified as charity.

Without the sale of the Superintendent's House, I would not be able to honor the settlement agreement with the creditors and stood to lose everything. This shouldn't happen in the very end. It was time to take action.

"Take out a loan for the ten thousand." The attorney told me. This was not an option, as I could never have serviced the debt.

"Drop the price way down." I pleaded.

"I'll get an extension from Chuck." she stated confidently. "He won't want you to declare bankruptcy!"

I went out on my cross-country skis to vent my frustration. The cold bit into my lungs. Clouds blew out my nose from my mind. The fresh snow fell like a fine dust off the branches as I blazed by. I went south on the Switzerland Trail, steaming along like an engine. I went up through Hick's Gulch, across the land that I had worked hard to save as County Open Space. My mind raced with thoughts of disbelief. How could this fantastic, newly rebuilt house not sell? Why did Holland & Hart care so much about money, yet they'd risk losing it all, and take me down with them? My legs and lungs pumped the negativity away. I had to trust that it would all work out. I had to play the game carefully.

By the time I came back to my house, I had completely surrendered. I was ready for bankruptcy, if it was to be.

Sleep escapes me. I am lucky to get four hours a night before waking to the familiar problem of circular despair. I visualize my furniture and white banker boxes of files being stored away in the drafty old useless buildings in Cardinal, which are so valueless that I will always own them. Packrats will nest in the paper files and poop on top of the furniture. Eventually, the roofs will fall in. Even my old standbys, a banana and Sleepytime tea, no longer lull me back to sleep. I am being sucked into a vortex, which leaves me increasingly less effective and capable during the day.

In the months to come, I will lose everything. I expect I will be out on the street. What will I have in my shopping cart? Bundles of clothes which are well-worn remnants of my former life, a computer, a fiddle and a copy of Cardinal Sin.

I could change my lifestyle. Get a regular job in town. The cabin in Gold Hill and the Assay Office would go to others. I would work in a relatively stress-free environment to pay my mortgage each month. I wouldn't be supporting Peter much longer. He was about to graduate from high school and his college money had already gone to fighting the lawsuit. I'm low-maintenance. I would live simply and accept all that had happened. Most importantly, I would count my many blessings– my children, my family, my health and my beautiful home.

By now, Peter and I were getting used to the temperatures being below zero. When Pete went off to school, I got to work sending an email to all my friends and relatives. I explained the predicament with the Superintendent's House. The email outlined what the rock bottom sale price should be and what the investment could be expected to bear.

My experience selling residential real estate had taught me the finer points of human nature. I knew what it would take to satisfy Holland & Hart. They would succumb to the right offer because they were rapidly losing options. I hoped someone would know someone who would be interested in buying the house. It was time for another Christmas Miracle.

It was only minutes before my computer screen showed a response from our adopted sister, Ellen.

"We've been thinking of a real estate investment! Your timing is good. I asked Paul, and he said 'Huummm!', so what do you think? We've got the cash."

'I think this unbelievable, Ellen." and it really was. "I have felt all along that the house must be waiting for someone special."

Mona Lisa, a psychic, had told me that there was a spirit in the Superintendent's House and that he had been the "Pit Boss". She said this spirit was holding up the sale of the house until I found the "right" person. The new owner was to be a handy fellow, resourceful, pragmatic and he was to have a passion for the history of the townsite. This was tall order for someone as desperate as I was. She described this spirit as strong and burley. She saw him kicking up dirt in agitation, to make his point.

"What does the pit boss think of me?" I had asked hesitantly, remembering a story told to me about a apparition being sighted by a teenage boy in the '70s.

"Oh, he likes you, and he likes what you have done to the mill."

This information came from a person who didn't know anything about Cardinal.

Now, here was Paul and he is all of those things.

My call to Holland & Hart caught the attorney off guard. She had been tracking down Chuck's attorney, the Sherriff of Cardinal, to threaten him with my bankruptcy. I had fought off the urge to call Chuck and tell him that the last thing that I would do is declare bankruptcy if I could afford to, after all this time on the edge. I trusted that Chuck knew me well enough and he did.

I presented Ellen and Paul's offer. It was attractive. I felt her circle around the bait. A cash offer. A quick close. No conditions. Only Ellen, I knew her so well, had the rare combination of impulsivity and good business sense to pull this off.

But the collections attorney had been on a mission. She wanted that extension from Chuck. She wanted it now and not at Holland & Hart's expense. She was determined to get the extension, and get top dollar for the house.

"We'll lower the price for two weeks." she said firmly. "Maybe we'll get it sold."

"Maybe.", I countered. "But we won't get it closed before the deadline."

I pointed out that there was no time left for appraisals, inspections and financing a buyer. She circled around again, this time, she sniffed.

"Okay then," she relented, "We'll counter, if your sister will do it right away."

I didn't say she's not my sister, although, I knew she had said it to make me feel that there may be a conflict of interest here which she was willing to overlook. Well, she is my seester and she has the cash you need.

Ellen shrewdly countered back with a lower offer, offering to pay all of the closing costs. And it was done.

I flashed on all the people and all of the days I had spent working to get a buyer. A whole year! I flashed on all of the times that I had hoped and prayed that certain individuals would not become my neighbor, and times that I had hoped and prayed that certain others would. I must have been putting time in the Karma Bank. Ellen and her delightful family would become homeowners in Cardinal. I looked to the sky and thought I felt my Dad's spirit smiling a big, broad "I told you so" kind of smile. The message for me was Trust in the Grand Plan, baby. It is at work.

When Ellen and her family were dancing with excitement at the news of acceptance, I called my Mom.

"It has come full circle!" she exclaimed. "Way back when, we helped Ellen. I'll never forget when I had to tell your father that she was living with us, because he hadn't figured it out...and I was so afraid he'd say she'd have to go. But he didn't. We all loved El. And now, it has come full circle! She has saved us!"

I felt a surge of love and support when Mom said "us". She had been sharing my anxiety for every day of the seven years that Cardinal had been a drama. The drama had finally come to an end.

❧

It was only two days later, when Chuck and I met at the title company to close the deal on the Superintendent's House.

Ellen had wired the funds the day before, and emailed documents had been notarized and sent to Colorado by Federal Express. This was the fastest closing on a house that I had ever done. Forty one hours from signing the contract to the closing table.

The proceeds from the sale would pay my construction loan to Chuck, as well as the remainder of the settlement fees to six creditors, including Holland

& Hart. I had promised Holland & Hart that I would hand deliver the check.

Chuck signed the quit claim deed putting the house back in New Cardinal, LLC's name, then I signed the warranty deed over to Paul and Ellen. I was one step closer to freedom. Chuck and I rejoiced for me, for both of us. Once again, I impressed upon Chuck my appreciation for his willingness to lend to me in the midst of the Federal Suit. He had truly been an angel. We decided to go to the bank together to close out our joint account. I would have insisted on a celebratory cocktail with Chuck, except that I had promised delivery of the check to Denver.

As I rode up the elevator to Holland & Hart's office on the thirty-second floor, I smiled at the thought of Curt in my life. I giggled that I was spending so much time at his place on the twenty second floor of a high rise only blocks away.

The delivery of the check turned out to be completely anticlimactic, as neither Paul nor the collections attorney was there to receive it. But as I handed the check to the woman from Accounts Receivable, the cell phone in my pocket began to ring. I resisted the urge to answer it. Anti-climactic as it was, I wanted to honor the moment I had only dreamt of, by being present in it.

It wasn't until I was back down on 17th Street, that I checked my message. The message was from a man who was quite interested in a plan which would save another ghost town. I wondered if this might be the end of the Cardinal story.

2006

*I*t had been a great relief, to say the least, when I had settled with the creditors in December of 2005. I was left with a mountain personal debt. I might get by, if my real estate business could provide. As the residential market remained flat, I spent my time representing Sellers who were interested in selling their land to the County as Open Space. I had managed to preserve most of Hick's Gulch, on the other side of the ridge to the south of Cardinal, as well as mining claims north along the Peak to Peak Highway. Each month, when I balanced the check books, it was uncanny how every last penny was spent to pay the bills, but I was actually making the grade.

I had been feeling like the mother bird, tempted from time to time to give the baby bird a good push over the edge, when Peter told me he was leaving home. He would go to Idaho to work the harvest season with his sister and her boyfriend. This was a fantastic choice. Sandi and Trevor were hard working, successful commercial farmers. They managed to make payments on tractors and combines, owned snowmobiles and dirt bikes and kept Sandi's horse in good shape. I knew Peter was in good hands, which eased my empty nest syndrome. It was time for this bird to fly.

The final chapter of the Cardinal's ordeal began when I applied for the dismissal of Cardinal's water permit from the State. I had consistently proven for six years that there was virtually no toxicity in Cardinal's water.

An inspection by the State's water engineer took place in June of '06. He came to Cardinal to witness the changes to the water flow with the new wall and French drains in place. After much conversation and careful deliberation, the engineer decided, after studying the engineered plans, that the County should take ownership of the water permits from New Cardinal, LLC.

I paid my seventeen-hundred-dollar annual water permit fee with re-assurance from the State that it would be refunded when the permit was dismissed. The year came and went without a change or a refund.

It seemed illogical to me that the State could consider dismissing the permit after all I had been required to do, but who would argue with such a possibility?

It was with guarded skepticism that I relished this new development. Nothing moves quickly in these circumstances, I knew from experience. The County was not thrilled to hear that the State had identified this as their responsibility. They began the educational process that led them to request that my "Individual" Permit, which represented a higher level of concern, be reduced to lower level "General Permits" before the transfer could take place.

Ironically, the attorneys had taken my past "General Permits" and at great time and expense, had turned them into an "Individual Permit" to provide better protection for me in court.

When the '07 annual fee invoice arrived, I was still the unlucky permit owner and I was as penniless as ever. In a flat market, I had no real estate under contract, no paychecks on the horizon and not a dime to pay the State. The fee invoices would be sent to Collections, and again my mailbox would be filled with bills from the State which couldn't be paid.

Each week in '06 and '07, I called the same people at the State and County trying to get action on the permit transfer. It was at the top of no one's list. Each month invoices arrived and were put in a stack where I wouldn't forget to continue to deal with the ongoing drama. All the while, I continued my water reporting to stay legal. The County kept promising to pay the fees when the permit would transfer.

Finally, both entities recognized that we had a "Catch 22.". The County couldn't pay the fees until the State put the permit in the County's name; the State couldn't put the permit in the County's name until the County paid the fee. It took sixteen months for these bureaucracies to acknowledge this conundrum. By that time, my carefully repaired credit had taken another mean hit.

In January of '08, the County stepped up to the plate, writing the check for what were now back fees for the water permit, in exchange for an easement from me to park their vehicles near the Cardinal Mill during the construction of the east wall. Problem solved.

The transfer of the water permits to Boulder County marked the end of Cardinal's water issues and the end of what had been an eight-year ordeal for me personally. My neighbors, Tina and Dennis, rarely stay in their Colorado house. As I walk by their place, I reflect that they don't know that Cardinal's troubles have come to an end.

In a faltering economy, I am finally free to reinvent myself financially. I dream of the day that what I still own in Cardinal is no longer on the chopping block. Foreclosure looms presently. Again, I prepare to let it all go. I work the real estate market hoping for a break that will bring me some security. Remembering Randy Leavitt and his Buddhist ways, I am reminded that security is but an illusion anyway. I have become Buddhist by default.

No one has read about what happened here, as the local Mountain Ear Newspaper never showed interest beyond the initial hoopla which fed the fire which fueled the Federal Clean Water Act Suit. Few people in the Town of Nederland ever knew about the Federal Suit or who filed it, and why. So now the tale has been told and the story is put to rest. Cardinal's struggles are over.

Where do the ghosts of Cardinal reside? Perhaps just in my mind. Mabel, John, Tyler, Miss Ruby, Alexander and Christian still dance across these pages. John Bergren's family history and the stories about Margaret and Cardinal's post office tie the past with the present, but the past is long gone. Mike and Jeanette Smith still walk the streets of Nederland representing the last of a mining culture which is fading into history.

Visitors are intrigued by the words "ghost town" and some claim to feel the presence of spirits, but for me the experience is different. Whatever happened here, in the century gone by, seems quietly put to rest with the writing of this story. The wind blows the snow sideways some days. The snow falls silently and deeply other days. In the summer, I watch a lone bobcat hunt for mice. But the spiritual energy of Cardinal seems to me to be open to the next century.

Everyone wants to read a happy ending. My life has returned to normal. It is different now. Significantly changed, but change is the one thing in this world we can count on. My reward is great. It is peace and quiet, and a fine home in Cardinal.

I close the rickety wooden door between the old business office and the new mudroom addition to my home. Inside, the fire burns very nicely in the woodstove, thanks to Goodman. I light a candle to the spirits of the past with a smile and curl up next to Curt on my saggy old couch.

⚘

THE INDIAN PEAKS FROM THE SWITZERLAND TRAIL
Carnegie Branch Library for Local history, Boulder Historical Society Collection

THE CARDINAL MILL CIRCA 1920
Denver Public Library, Western History Collection

Made in United States
Troutdale, OR
11/12/2024